Shock and Awe on America
Bad Politics, Bad Religion, Bad Consequences

Teeluck Sooknarine

Copyright © 2010 by Teeluck Sooknarine

This work has been copyrighted: any duplication, printing, copying, or forwarding which results in a copy or duplication to occur, without written permission by the author, is prohibited and may be punishable by law.

DEDICATION

This book is dedicated to the brave soldiers who have lost their lives in the pursuit of duty to their country.

This book is also dedicated to the innocent bystanders who became victims of war and collateral damage.

This book is especially dedicated to the children who were made orphans by wars, were mortally wounded by wars and forgotten by humanity.

This book is dedicated to generations lost and misled by religious misdirection.

This book is dedicated to those who are victims of unfettered capitalistic greed by predatory lenders and corrupt politicians.

This book is dedicated to the teachers in our schools and elsewhere, who try to help us become the best that we can be. This includes the people who follow in the traditions of Mother Teresa and Princess Diana, by helping those in need.

There are many celebrities stepping up to the podium to do this honorable job of helping the needy, and I thank and commend them for doing something for others. They are also teachers, for teaching us to do the same, no matter how small that contribution may be.

Music is the food of love, and I pay tribute to our dearly departed musicians, including some of my favorites: John Lennon, Michael Jackson, Bob Marley, John Denver, Marvin Gaye, Barry White, Luther Vandross and so many more. Remember their music, and use it to cure the world. I also applaud those alive today who voice our desire for peace and love.

ACKNOWLEDGMENTS

This book is a testimony to what unselfish love can produce. The unselfish love of my wife, Allyson, my son, Nik, and my daughter, Sammi, has made this book possible. With their love, they created a free man...me.

I would like to thank my mom, Margaret, who has always been my lifeline. I am so proud of her and Richard, my second dad. He is a truly great man in every respect; no one could have asked for a better father. I am very grateful to be his son. To my brother and sisters, thank you for being you. You are beautiful people.

My friends are very special and I would like them to know that they are truly irreplaceable.

This book is the product of years of research, and an equal amount of time spent listening to radio and TV hosts, and their guests, who furnished me with the information and direction I needed to have, in order to complete this book.

Many thanks to the hosts, some of whom I humbly salute, as they try to make the world a better place with their work. I have followed them for the past few years and have drawn inspiration from these folks, including Ed Schultz, Montel Williams, Errol Louis, Ron Kuby and team, Sam Seder, the radical Janeane Garofalo, Thom Hartmann, Chris Matthews, Keith Olbermann, Alan Colmes, Randi Rhodes, Mark Green, Katrina vanden Heuvel, Arianna Huffington, Robert F. Kennedy Jr., Mike Papantonio, Reverend Al Sharpton, David Bender, FFRF (The Freedom from Religion Foundation), Senator Al Franken, Jerry Springer, Richard Belzer, Whoopi Goldberg,

Joy Behar, Stephanie Miller and Ron Prescott Reagan.

Special thanks to Rachel Maddow and Lizz Winstead, whose radio show, Unfiltered, was instrumental in my introduction to the world of American politics. I have followed Rachel and her programs religiously ever since.

Special thanks also to Marc Maron and Mark Riley, who with their radio show, Morning Sedition, helped initiate me into the world of American politics many years ago, with majestic assistance by the irreplaceable Thomas Kenton "Kent" Jones.

I thank you all for the inspiration you planted that created this book.

Lastly, I would like to thank Sigrid Macdonald, for editing my manuscript with the professionalism and dedication needed to bring the true message of this book to you, the reader. This spiritual message is unblemished by time and she made sure that it stayed that way. She is truly worth her salt.

FOREWORD

The word "American" is a special word and more; it indicates where you were born or where you reside, but it is also a term, an ideal, a one-word phrase, which embodies the principles of all that is good and hopeful in a country and a people. It says to others that we are the defenders of freedom. It says that we are patriotic and are always willing to help our fellow man. In any crisis around the world, when people say the Americans are coming, or have arrived, they breathe a sigh of relief, and are instantly overcome with joy and renewed purpose. They feel and say that the light has pierced the darkness. We must not let that light fail.

The crisis diminishes when the Americans arrive. People immediately see a more successful outcome. "American" means something to every person on this Earth; it embodies honor, strength, honesty and the common good. The enemy cringes in fear and hatred at the thought or sound of the word. It is an instrument of hope and relief to many in the world, and we are the flag bearers: the ones who have to protect that ideal, and help it to endure abroad and at home. America turns to help even countries who harbor ill will and cold relationships with us, in their hour of need when disaster strikes.

Why is this book named *Shock and Awe*? I started writing it during George W. Bush's presidency. When President Bush initiated the invasion of Iraq under the disguise of retaliation for 9/11, rescuing the Iraqi people and liberating them, bringing freedom to a troubled land

and the hunt for WMDs, he called the action "Operation Shock and Awe." I think we were the true intended recipients and not in a positive way. He was, and still is, an undisciplined capitalist, and undisciplined capitalism always translates into fleecing people and making them victims of greedy practices. This book is a critique of his presidency and deceptive practices, some of which he inherited and enhanced, creating a much larger culture of corruption than had previously existed, which gave us the real Shock and Awe. It is also a critique of the harmful religious practices that have in the past and now also cause Shock and Awe to us. America has been attacked and undermined from within, in many different ways in the past, and most recently during the Bush era of 2001 to 2009, using religion as a tool, to validate his horrendous policies.

George W. Bush, after eight years as America's president, cannot blame any negative results he has had on past administrations, be they Republican or Democrat, as he had more than enough time to change any ineffective policies. He let down his party and the good people in it, and he let down the country in the end: we who were all counting on him as president, regardless of party. All the old policies that he chose to keep were his responsibility, as he had to make a purposeful and conscious effort to maintain these policies, good or bad, and keep them functioning.

We can see that we, the people, Republicans, Democrats, and those in between, have all been made the victims of the real Shock and Awe caused by the Bush administration and its policies. Each bad policy kept or started was a weak link in our economic and social chain; each good policy was useless as the chain broke at the weakest links. History recorded the horrible results Bush achieved, and his legacy is reflected by the wars and recession he left.

It is wise to see which policies were purposely kept by the Bush administration to see their true intentions, and what results they wanted, as all the results they received were easily planned, allowed to come to fruition, and were a predictable and purposely achieved outcome. The reasons and people behind these outcomes are things that we may never know, but one can be sure that we did not have eight years of unplanned mistakes, and we are certain that people profited. We had a culture of corruption, and rule by fear and hatred resulting in a multitude of problems. Fear and hatred worked well together to give the population a one-two punch — fear of terrorism and hatred of gays, and others, were just one of the many combinations used upon us.

Remember that who you are character-wise determines what you are, and vice-versa, so we must judge all of our leaders harshly as our lives depend on their actions. That's our job and our children's futures depend on it. We are usually victims of our circumstances and our leaders, and we must let our inner strengths, goodness and courage determine how we bring our families through the crises caused by our various administrations, as the crises ripple around the globe long after they leave office. Some actions and policies make us more unsafe in the world day by day, while the greedy profit.

I am not affiliated with any political party. I am just a human, alive on this Earth, with kids who I must teach to be fair to others and defend themselves. I try not to lean left or right, as America has been done wrong by both

Democrats and Republicans in the past; I may be critical of President Obama after he is done, as I am of President George W. Bush now, because he was the last; the 43rd president. I don't think the constant well-being of this country is such a little thing that it can be efficiently defended by people who can willingly place themselves into a cage of rules and prejudices, espoused by one political party or the other, or one religion or another, and be expected to do a good job of taking care of the country without letting petty prejudices get in the way.

I think all people are inherently good, and can work together for the betterment of this country and the world, if they try. We, the people, are under constant attack by prejudiced politicians. Many from both parties have been jailed in the past; it is sad. However you look at it, prejudiced people help bring about the undermining and demise of this great country in some way from within, with their opposition to peace between the parties. We should stay united as there are worse threats to America and the world. Divided we fall and are attacked — again.

The Constitution states that we, the people, as one group, must defend the country against attacks from outside and within. The framers of the Constitution knew that we must give limited power to the executive branch of government, and they wrote the document to reflect that. Bush tried his best to dismantle that part of the Constitution. We must follow the framers and keep executive powers to an accountable minimum.

The executive branch must always be responsible for any decisions they make, so they can't blindside us into another unnecessary war, as happened with Iraq. The term bandied about is "disaster capitalism," meaning making or using disaster for profiteering and profitable enterprise, as we saw abundantly in Iraq during President George W. Bush's war. This is your introduction to the Military Industrial Complex, and yes, unknown to many of you, it is real.

It is said that absolute power corrupts absolutely. We saw that the past Bush administration accrued enormous power and they waged war, made untold profits and encouraged torture with it. I would like both political parties to ask themselves, when enormous powers are given to any administration, how will you defend yourselves when the other side is in power and wields this absolute ax of power against you?

We have seen it in the past administrations — those with absolute power doing wrong things and the list is long. When either party is in office, the other will be at the mercy of the executive. This will prevent both parties from uniting and doing what is best for the country, as it takes both sides' cooperation to bring the right policies to fruition, for the benefit of their employers, who are the people and the country as a whole.

Religious misunderstanding and misdirection are another instance of the Shock and Awe we face, and are just as, or possibly more, important than bad politics, as religion has no boundaries or time limits around the world. Religion has always been here. It is nobody's fault that it is; we just have to see it now for what it was and is, and mold a brighter future for our children in spite of it. I do not want or need my children to kneel in submission and be slaves to any religious ideology, or anyone — including myself. We have seen the extremists in all religions wreak havoc using religion as a tool. September 11th was only one instance. I will discuss and give my opinion on the subject of religion, as it can be an instrument of destruction and distraction, for modern man and our journey into the future. When we take, or are directed to, path A, we miss or destroy the results of path B. I will discuss the ancient religious path A that is failing our children and society, and the alternative path B, which can help them.

The backbone of this world is thought to be its strength in religious belief. But what if that belief is misinterpreted, confused by different cultures and weak in its application of goodness, as most religions support killing and victimization of others for various reasons? Ancient, ignorant man was haunted by his imagination. Knowing nothing about science, he naturally accepted everything as evil or mystical, and heaven sent.

Because I am religiously eclectic, having grown up in the three major religions, and studied them and others, I have come to see their potential for goodness and also indiscreet destruction. I think our focus should be to seek a higher purpose than religious servitude, and we each could and should change this world for the better by using our inner goodness, and by having faith in our own capabilities, not in any outer religious hope and blind faith in gods. There can be a more effective way spiritually than we see in our religions now, to make our world a better place for our children to inherit. Therein lies the higher ground to which we human beings must aspire.

The truth is a seed — when it gets buried in the dirt of evil, sadness and despair, and is watered with the blood, sweat and tears of the victims, it germinates, grows out, and blooms for all to see, so it never stays buried forever. The truth that I will discuss is the true meaning of Jesus' words and actions, as I see it.

Speaking in tongues is neither religious nor evil. It is

just an ability to tap into an unseen and largely unknown force to regular humans, but it is well known and common in spiritual circles. People tapping into that force do things unfamiliar to us, but quite normal to them and their community, in different cultures around the world. It is a part of their culture and a spiritual state of communication, and not something magical, as we have come to learn. Many nonreligious people do it as well.

Eastern cultures all have these things and I remind you, Christianity started in the East and was morphed, altered, modified, evolved and reinvented in the West. We still change it constantly, allowing its evolution, as we invent thousands of new denominations and churches of Christianity globally. It is interesting that the religious do not support, or in some cases do not believe in, evolution, when the very religious denomination they are members of is an evolution of the original religion from thousands of years ago. They do not see the forest for the trees.

One such reinvention was the cult of Jim Jones, who massacred his faithful at gunpoint in Guyana in 1978, according to the locals who lived around the area and interacted with them. Another group was the Millerites in the time around 1830. They said Jesus would return in the 1840s. When this did not happen, they splintered into the Seventh Day Adventist Church, also morphed into the Jehovah's Witnesses in the 1900s, and another group, the Branch Davidians in Waco, Texas. Globally, there are thousands of Christian denominations harboring disagreements with ancient Christianity. These folks have lived and worshiped within this ancient religion mostly all their lives, and they have found the faults and discrepancies that they denounce, so I believe that they and their religions are faulty. How many denominations do we have right now in America? More than 40,000, according to some authorities.

A wise man not only sees what is said, but he hears what is not. Information concealed from you is sometimes more valuable than what is not concealed; hence, the tight cover-up and attempt to conceal information, under the guise of national security and executive privilege during President Bush's tenure is suspect. The refusal to allow his subordinates to testify under oath in hearings, after being subpoenaed by The House Judiciary Committee, is evidence of deception, for all who can understand and see the truth of concealment.

The Shock and Awe we are struggling with from President Bush's various policies (economic, foreign, domestic), and also from religion, are rotten fruit. I critique not with the intention to blame, as history will do that job, but to help people to see that their families are being torn apart, their children's future stymied and there are ways to help themselves, their countries and their families. If this book changes your understanding then it will have served a useful purpose.

Robert Kennedy said, "There are those who look at things the way they are, and ask why…I dream of things that never were, and ask why not?" That is truly an inspirational statement. A great person is one who elevates the world as a result of his or her existence, making the world a better place than he found it, as everything you do affects the world in some way. Having fun and not trying to attain a higher direction or level in your spiritual existence is okay, but ask yourself, do you just want to be plain and unspectacular?

Seek and ye shall find. It is not at the end of the

journey that you find the answers to what you seek, but rather in the discoveries made during the journey itself. Your physical and spiritual journeys on Earth will always have an end; you just have to make it both peaceful and fulfilling. Likewise, this book is itself a journey of great rewards and just one gem in your journey.

Honor is a very important element in human interaction. It takes a higher precedence than pride as pride, like beauty, is in the eye of the beholder and honor reflects something noble of you to your peers, many times, through your actions. There is as much destruction caused by false pride as is caused in the name of beauty or honor. It is not a big deal to lose your pride, as it is a feeling that is easily regained, and beauty can never be lost as it is really internal; but if you lose your honor, it is harder to regain and that can make it more difficult for you to interact with others and complete your life's journey. We, as a country, have lost our honor in the world because of our invasion of Iraq, torturing our prisoners and weakening the world economy. Now when we look to others for help to get things done, we have a more difficult time receiving that assistance. When countries attack each other, this action also affects us and we may not get the help we need to stop the invaders, as we are also looked down upon as an invader.

Honesty is next to honor as a necessity in communication with others: a tool we have sadly lost in the wilderness of deception and the preemptive act of war in Iraq. There are those who misunderstand, and think that doing nothing and accepting the status quo is being a great American, but I hasten to disagree. Wanting the same old bad politics, and ill-conceived dogmatic religions, to be the frontline in determining America's policies and future is being unpatriotic and Anti-American. That's what our enemies do themselves and want us to do also. Wanting the same as America's enemies do is not being patriotic, and history sometimes puts you on the side of your enemies. When we removed Saddam without consideration of the results, we did a lot for Iran and others, making Iran the powerhouse in the region. Wanting to bring change to these old and unthoughtful ways is being a real American. Raising the standard to what America was meant to be is being a true American and a true patriot. Let's bring change.

Teeluck Sooknarine
January 2010

TABLE OF CONTENTS

PART ONE — *19*
- ADMINISTRATION/NEW ECONOMY — 21
- AMBITION — 27
- BROKEN EXAMPLES — 30
- CREATION OF TERRORISTS — 33
- CONSTITUTION — 35
- COLUMBINE — LOSING YOUR CHILDREN — 38
- DECEPTION — 50
- DRUG COMPANIES — 57
- ECONOMICS — 62
- EDUCATION — 66
- EVOLUTION — 73
- EVOLUTION OR EXTINCTION? — 80
- FEAR — 85
- FINANCIAL HOSTAGE — 88
- FOOD — 92
- GANGS — 103
- GREED — 109

PART TWO — *111*
- GOD — 113
- IN THE BEGINNING — 129
- WHO OR WHAT IS GOD? — 133
- CONFUSION, CHRISTIANIZATION — 144
- PROTECT YOUR FAMILY. DON'T WAIT FOR GOD. — 197
- CHRISTIANITY AND JESUS — 208
- GOD CONSCIOUSNESS AND AWARENESS — 221
- GOD AND RELIGIOUS ILLUSION — 277
- JESUS REVEALED — 301
- GOVERNMENT MEGALOMANIACS /MORE SHOCK & AWE — 317
- HATE — 325
- IMMIGRATION — 329

IMMIGRANT ECONOMICS	336
MASS MEDIA	341
PREDATORY LENDERS AND PERSONAL LOSS	346

PART THREE — *359*

PRIVATIZATION	361
FOREIGN PROBLEMS, LOCAL IMPACT	364
PERSONAL PEACE OF MIND	368
RIPPLE EFFECT	373
THE MONEY TREE	384
TORTURE	386
WAR	389
WAR PROFITEERING	410
WATER — THE NEW OIL AND POISON	415
9/11	422
WOMEN	441
YOU AND THEM	444
YOU AND YOUR CHILDREN	475
YOUR GRADUATION	485
YOUR POWER OVER ADDICTION	498
Luke 17:20-21 (King James Version)	507
RECOMMENDED READING	509
REFERENCES	511
ABOUT THE AUTHOR	517
Index	***519***

PART ONE

ADMINISTRATION/NEW ECONOMY

I ask people not to think like a politician but rather as a concerned parent. Were we deceived by President George W. Bush? Were we economically and socially attacked from within by his team? The Constitution addresses this. It says we must defend ourselves. I say we can, though not by the sword but by the pen and with ideas, inspiration and awareness. Your concern and your votes count, and can be tools used in your struggle for survival and freedom from corrupt politicians. This was evident in the election of 2008. Be aware of what goes on in government and make leaders accountable by constant communication with them, by phone, regular mail, e-mail and your votes.

It is wise to see what is said, and hear what is not, by any administration. When the Bush administration said it was best if they did this or that, they apparently meant it was best for them, and their friends, not us or the country. It worked out best for a select group of people who made absurd amounts of money in contracts and profits, all from our taxpayer's money. "It is what we do that defines who we are." This reveals a lot about the past Bush team.

Government policies are introduced time and again to solve the problems of that particular time, and possibly future ones as well. Any new administration is charged with the task of housecleaning, and it is their responsibility to change policies that old administrations used and left in place, which have become ineffective. This is why we should credit the problems we have been burdened with through the Bush years to the Bush administration and none prior. All administrations make errors, some through incompetence or inexperience, and some through greed. The Bush administration said they did not change the old regulations in time to deal with a 21st century economy and that caused the present recession. I believe them.

An alert Obama administration attempts to stop the adverse consequences of Bush's bad policies. Sadly though, there is much opposition by Bush's supporters who have lost sight of a possible united America succeeding, or a divided America failing. America is suffering from the Chinese technique of a death of a thousand cuts, not just one large disaster. President Obama has the monumental task of economic recovery from all these cuts, and we should do everything in our power as concerned citizens to help him, as his success means our success.

All new administrations must recognize when a good policy becomes ineffective because of changing conditions, and then should do what is necessary and best for the country by changing or eliminating these policies. The American economy is an unfortunate example of how serious conditions can become, if policy changes are not made in a timely fashion, as happened with President Bush. With his nonchalance, he tarnished the office he once held, and put the country in dangerous and unpredictable waters.

We now have a wounded economy. It is not yet down and out, but it is staggering and still being pounded, to the mat of submission. Submission possibly to a final collapse and disappearance into the ether, never to be seen again, if the Obama team is unsuccessful in turning the tide. Many banks have closed their doors, reeling from the trauma of

Bush's blind-eye policies. If we, the country, ever needed we, the people, to serve it, it is now.

The enemies of the American economy reside within our borders, our banks and our financial sector, and we have seen that while we gave them money from the Troubled Asset Relief Program (TARP) and other help, they continued to squander millions in executive bonuses and lavish unnecessary expenses, while they carried on predatory business practices as usual without a care.

If the economy dies, totally crashes, or even becomes too weak to survive on its own, we can rebuild a new vibrant economy, but it will be different, having more strings and masters attached to it, as they will be the ones to assist in rebuilding this new economy. Specifically, it means the foreign investments and loans that were made to us in the past by China and others, though assisting in the stabilization or creation of a new economy for us, leave the lenders holding substantial decision-making power, enabling them to influence the making of policies which would be more to their country's and companies' advantage than if we were to rebuild our own economy.

Bush had well-educated people in place at the helm of the economic ship, so this leads me to believe that this economic crisis in America was allowed or manipulated into existence and not just mismanaged, for the obvious reward of someone: people or companies who we may never fully come to know, though I have heard the conspiracy theories. All this planning and execution, done to destroy or weaken our economy was not to rebuild it with the same old rules and rulers. No, there will be a new plan, a new economy with a new set of victors and masters, added to the same old rulers who are the rich families and companies of the world, and the same set of victims — us — the middle and lower class.

What the established higher-class society of the past has come to realize is, there is a new set of captains who now steer the economic ships around the world and they are multinational companies, who will eat everyone up and spit them out with no effort or compassion. To survive, they can't beat the companies, so they must join them and become multinational conglomerates as well. This may be why the old economy was allowed to crumble and burn, so the new economy could rise like a phoenix from its ashes, with the old powers being reinvented at the helms of new multinational companies themselves, and in new partnerships with foreign companies.

People want to keep some kind of lofty position on the ladder of the affluent so naturally, they get in line because as we have seen all through history, mankind will sell their souls and country for the right price. Some folks don't care who their masters are — foreign funds and foreign governments, or sovereign foreign interests — as long as they think they occupy the economic rung above the rest of us.

Everyone must change with the tide or be washed away. That has always been the human dilemma and no one has a choice. We, the little people, must also fall in line, as we have to feed our families and can't survive on our own fighting the tide of change. So we have to pay the higher prices for goods and services, which is the lifeblood of the companies — the economic vampires sucking our blood, sweat and tears, for their very survival.

Many in the Bush team thought the Iraqi occupation

went well and should be kept up indefinitely. They were wrong. They spent between eight and 12 billion dollars per month, on Iraq, while our infrastructure crumbled at home. They fabricated information to have an invasion and occupation in Iraq that was totally unnecessary. On 9/12, oil was $22 per barrel. By 2008 the price rocketed above $140 per barrel and in 2009 has only dropped to about half that amount, much to the pleasure of some. Are you Shocked and in Awe at the cost of living?

President George W. Bush's drug-and-alcohol tarnished history proves he had the uncanny ability to amplify or multiply disaster. His failed business ventures are testament to this. When he took the helm at the White House in 2001, unfortunately he did not prove his history wrong. Some of the disastrous policies he inherited were indeed there before him, but instead of correcting them, he simply did what he did best and let them spiral out of control. One thing Bush succeeded in doing, intentionally or not, was raising the price of oil. This made the oil that was already bought and owned in long-term contracts with foreign countries reap more profits and cause more pain at the pump. I ask, who was really meant to be in Shock and Awe: the Iraqis or us?

The other edge of the sword involves the oil-rich nations who dislike America and also made six times the profit on the elevated prices. This made them love our war much more and they rejoiced at our insanity. We took out Saddam, Iran's biggest enemy, so we made them, Venezuela, and others happy and rich; they really love us now.

The Bush administration came into power with a

strong economy. While there, the Bush team caused a loss of trillions of dollars in our economy and around the world, and is responsible for the loss of lives that will result. How are lives being lost here, and around the world, due to our recession, you ask?

Well, the countries, states, towns, companies, charities and investors who put finances into our Wall Street products and unchecked Ponzi schemes, and lost them, were misled to believe that the investments were safe. Around the world, the return on those investments was to be used to supply medications, health facilities and health programs, building schools and hospitals, helping to finance medical students, supplying means of transportation for the public and the hospitals, supplying the food transport lines and roads in remote villages, and up-keeping the infrastructure of the municipalities, cities, and towns that were depending on that return of profits.

We all remember the Minnesota bridge collapse in 2007. The loss of that transport route or roadway forced ambulances and other essential services to use different routes, which could have caused lives to be lost just by the extra time lost to get to accidents and hospitals. Think of what happens in Third World economies when that occurs. Some of those communities can't even afford to rebuild a bridge. They were actively being helped by the charities that also invested. Unfortunately, many charities have closed down due to Bush's tenure. President Bush allowed this economic problem to fester in every corner, hence his responsibility for the debacle and the consequences it returned. Are you Shocked and in Awe yet?

AMBITION

Don't aim for 50% of something; you might get 49%. Aim for 100%. You will surely end up higher than 49%. Have confidence and pride in yourself, and what you can accomplish. Don't discourage yourself because life and the world are there to do that — some may envy you when you shine. Just ignore them and do a good job. Make the world a better place for your descendants and your brethren. Let us not have reasons to run and hide from the daylight of truth when we have to look in the mirror of our deeds.

There are some dishonest politicians and businessmen who can't stand the light of scrutiny. They have to hide in the shadows of secrecy and that's their cross to bear. Help your community, your country, your world, your children, your family, your sick and dying, your elderly, your uneducated, your homeless, our veterans, and your brothers who have lost their way. Don't let the children live in despair and in fear of a bleak future.

If you had an invitation to visit your God's home for dinner (or after death), you would want to take a shower, put on nice clothes and a new pair of shoes, but what about a bloody hand and a greedy mind? Can you clean those? Blood on your hands can't come off. Can you leave your prejudices and hatred at the door? So save yourself the grief of these ways. Sometimes "I'm sorry" can't fix things. Do good deeds and have fewer reasons to say, "I'm sorry." "You're welcome" is a better reply to give someone.

When a person fools you, shame on him or her; if you fool yourself, shame on you. Are you being fooled by a religion? Possibly. If you let them fool you, then who are you fooling? Only yourself. If your God sees you willingly being fooled, will He have mercy on someone too carefree or superstitious to think for and help himself? He will think you aren't worth the effort.

Is there real forgiveness of yourself by yourself? Not really, not in the end of your life, but you can have acceptance. You'll know you could have done better, when no one else knows, so you will be your own harsh critic. Other people's forgiveness can't make you clean, can't change you, can't erase your history. The church's forgiveness can't save you from your deeds, no matter how much you donate. Holy water can't cleanse your character. You can't bring back the lives of any who have died by your hand. More than 4,000 Americans and more than one million Iraqis have died needlessly by Bush's decisions in Iraq, according to the Iraq Casualty Coalition, so who will forgive Bush and his team? Obviously, the warmongers wage war because they think there is no Satan or God waiting to judge them, and that's true, but they don't know a far worse fate awaits. They get to experience for themselves what they have done. They haven't just let themselves down but all of humanity. That's a heavier cross to bear than anything else.

We must have the courage and common sense to fight any force that can prevent us from protecting our families. That's not always foreign terrorists but rather the ones who weaken us by not doing what we elected them to do, time and again. That is the real threat to our families, America in the 21st century and thus the world: domestic terrorism, politicians and religious fanatics who perpetuate wars — with the terrorists. The practice called disaster capitalism, a proven system that has been used throughout history, to encourage and then profit from disaster.

The Bush team conveniently used these terrorists by not eliminating or neutralizing them, in order to create a distraction, and they kept us distracted for years, so we would not see them misappropriate our money under the guise of contracts in Iraq and other deceptions. The common belief is that if it had not been Iraq, they would have found some other disaster to accomplish the theft. To some, politics is a game, the results of which, to us, mean life and death. We are the ones being Shocked and Awed

BROKEN EXAMPLES

If a tribal leader is strong and magnificent, the young warriors will all aspire to be that way. The tribe eventually ends up with magnificent warriors and better stock to carry on the breeding. In this age of billion dollar Ponzi schemes where our leaders are liars, murderers and con men, what will America as a single tribe turn out to be? It's monkey see, monkey do. Our youth will do what their leaders do and turn into con men themselves.

Don't they all know that they can't take their ill-gotten gains with them when they die? They will take only their shame, guilt and the pain they caused others. They will carry their regret of the destruction they caused, and the lives they changed or wasted. Their ill-gotten gains will stay here only to change hands eventually. They kill innocents in wars and rob people to leave their money to their pets, and their decedents who spend it all or are themselves swindled out of it by another con man, or the spouse donates it.

When the recession started in America, it unintentionally went out to the rest of the world. Did the Bush people really not think about that, or did they plan it to transfer their wealth into foreign companies and foreign accounts, as disaster is profitable to a capitalistic system because it generates new businesses and opportunities from the old and crumbling ones? The truth may surface eventually.

Some greedy politicians and businessmen, because of

their personal riches, are so detached from reality that they don't realize the destruction and suffering they cause, and the real price they and we eventually pay from their decisions. Because of their greed, they can't face their conscience in the mirror of life, so they look away: away from their loved ones, away from themselves. They are rich but they are seldom happy. They even look away from their past and do not learn from the lessons it provides. Theirs is truly a lonely life. They bury themselves in their work out of greed, shame and guilt, and some even commit suicide for financial reasons, when their empires come crashing down. They allow their greed to be their only friend in life and their only companion in death.

This has to change. We are allowing criminal elements within our leadership, in government and business, banks, and among predatory lenders and credit card companies, to steal our families' futures by poisoning our communities with the crooked deals they think up, while we are distracted and don't see it happening.

People must do more. Join groups that support the community. You will interact with others, and be able to learn from and support each other. When the crooks and politicians see that the community is united, it will be a deterrent to them. A united community will be strong and able to stand up to the criminal elements and the bankers. We must teach the children to avoid criminal activity and encourage them to educate themselves, so they can be productive in their community. Education is their best friend. We must get them interested in their own future through the benefits of voting and involvement, which empower them.

I have seen how much pride these children have in themselves when they are participating in a community group. They feel proud to be helping others and that strengthens the community. They help paint the schools, clean the parks and beaches, and spend time with others in the neighborhood. They make new friends, and learn to socialize, and respect other people and other people's property. The community as a whole reaps the rewards and security of this bonding, as it discourages gang-styled groups with destructive tendencies. When the children learn the power of voting, this makes them appreciate their community even more, as they have an active hand in shaping it for their children. Why don't we give a small tax break as an incentive to vote? Ten, fifty, or a hundred dollars? Even this will encourage the children, and their parents and friends, to become active and to vote.

CREATION OF TERRORISTS

Bin Laden and other outraged people didn't just happen or fall out of a tree; they were created by external forces over a long period of time. For example, look at that tray of water in your refrigerator. After a while the water freezes and you have a tray of ice cubes. The organisms in the water die and the water turns to ice, just like the man whose hopes and compassion die. Then he turns stone cold and merciless. That inner death is what creates angry killers and terrorists like Bin Laden. If the water melts, organisms in the water may live again, but can a man's love and hope be rekindled after all the hate and death he's been subjected to and caused?

Man could destroy himself long before global warming tickles his toes. After all, we are destroying the global tribe from within with greed, vanity and jealousy. Mostly greed, from which deadly things emerge: ideas to kill and steal from others, just for money, fame and power. Those actions do create repercussions by others.

What happened after Katrina was terrible. There are a lot of people who hate the Bush administration because of how the whole affair was mishandled. Their families, their parents, their children died. Americans died in America — not Republicans and Democrats, but *Americans* — by the incompetent and prejudiced hands of other unpatriotic Americans. Won't these people's surviving relatives and friends become hostile to the leaders and the country? Can't they become homegrown terrorists?

Was the Katrina mismanagement an accident? Evidence of video conferences between Bush and others at the time suggests otherwise. It suggests that the tragedy could have been avoided by one group of authorities or another, and it was surely purposeful inaction and a lack of human compassion. Those people are still pointing fingers at each other, while others mourn the loss of family and friends tragically left to die by these incompetent authorities' inaction. They were allowed to lose all that they owned. Their pride in their country and even their right to life were stolen. They were deceived, swept aside, and left to drown, as if they were not human. Remember Timothy McVeigh — he was a homegrown terrorist. I fear we have created more of that hatred in the Katrina affair.

Our children are born into the burdensome shackles of a debt- ridden country. During Bush's eight years, people who were supposed to protect the country's interest were instead taking care of their own interests, and are still profiting from America's economic demise. Our children may find this debt too much to bear and simply resort to an "eat or be eaten" attitude — as the gangs do, having no regard for the rule of law and taking their survival into their own hands, essentially becoming homegrown terrorists performing their crimes on us, as they are taught, and indeed encouraged to do by our corrupt leaders.

CONSTITUTION

The Constitution is constantly at risk and so are our rights. It has been dismantled, stripped bare and whittled away quietly by Bush's signing statements, and the USA Patriot Act, which negated the rights guaranteed by habeas corpus, among others. The Constitution was written by wealthy and elite landowners for the benefit of the elite, but with some basic protections included for the poor. These protections have all but disappeared.

The Bush people had no place for God or compassion, even though they boasted of being good Christians. On their watch, the price of oil passed $100 per barrel and climbed to the heavens, heaping impoverishment on an unsuspecting people. Allowing predatory lending and Wall Street investment products to go unchecked caused the sub-prime mortgage fiasco. Companies continued to receive tax breaks in the billions while this debacle unfolded.

They called the tax breaks "trickle down economics," which had been referred to in the past as voodoo economics by Bush Sr. I believe him. We have seen that the tax breaks don't trickle down as touted. Why should they? Giving back to us just means less for the businessmen. No one can make them give back. These companies are now multinational; they will continue to, as some of them already have, move their operations to different countries, along with our jobs and wealth, instead of giving back.

The population has been cowering in fear for so long, many have lost the will to stand together to right the wrongs that have been done to them. Many people now suffer from the "Stockholm Syndrome." They have all but embraced the constant beating inflicted upon them by the powers that be: the banks, the previous governments, credit card companies, oil companies, and too many other big businesses to mention, and some folks now support these entities against their own interests and that of their families.

What's the Magna Carta and who signed it? The Magna Carta was an English Charter that the king of that time, in 1215 AD, was made to sign. This document gave special rights to the king's subjects including the right of habeas corpus, which is your right to be brought before the court, for the court to decide if you are being detained unlawfully. The king did not believe in rights for peasants but was forced to sign it. The Bush administration has removed those rights with the Patriot Act.

The Stockholm Syndrome worked well for the Bush team. They herded and corralled us by shouting "terror" in a crowded arena, with the color codes they invented and used. Those color levels almost had me fooled and scared, and they did fool some. Sadly, if you were fooled, they weren't the only ones who fooled you; you were! As Bush said, "Fool me once, shame on you; fool me twice, I ain't gonna be fooled again." When they lie to you and you convince yourself that they are right, you fool yourself. You become a problem to yourself, your family and the country. You start to deceive yourself, and begin to fool others into believing them, as some in the media do, with their crooked schemes of voodoo economics and preemptive war. They fool themselves and their fans every day, on the TV, radio, the newspaper and now online.

America has been terrorized by Bush's team, who only pillaged and plundered the country's resources and economy, while ignoring the Constitution and what it stands for. They lied to send America's bravest to fight and die in the Iraq war. They enriched themselves at our expense and that of our children, who sacrificed themselves in their wars. These men see themselves as politicians and businessmen. I see them only as they are: traitors, guilty of treason against this great country.

They did to us what the terrorists are not wicked enough to do. They severely damaged our economy and our means of survival, and left us to suffer, and slowly die of hunger and thirst. Even our enemies will strike swiftly, not torture and let their enemy suffer and beg to die. These are not Christians. Bush's team tortured prisoners, so I'm not surprised they did this to the country. Worst of all, they squandered our good name. They did everything against the Constitution upon which this great country was founded, was fought for and died for. America had been hijacked. In 2008, we, the people, started a revolution and elected a new leader. That's one up for us. I hasten to caution, though, that this is just the first step in reclaiming our country from the clutches of corruption and recession. We must now become intricately involved in every aspect of our country's politics so we can never be hijacked again. Accountability was in short supply during the Bush years, while we slept, so we must be alert from now on or be condemned to repeat the past, as we have done so many times before.

COLUMBINE — LOSING YOUR CHILDREN

The greatest asset of a country is its young people: the young adults who will lead tomorrow by what they learn today. I would like to address the increasing incidence of school shootings like Columbine, Virginia Tech, and others in America and overseas. While my theory may not apply to all shooters, I do think it applies to some. In every community there are groups of dominant people, bullies in the schools, who take advantage of a smaller group that has traditionally been referred to as the geeks or squares.

In this dominant group you find the countless wannabes, who try to fit into the general populace and adopt a follower mentality of not thinking for themselves but following the crowd, or the directives of the louder, usually more destructive, individuals who lead these packs.

In the disadvantaged group you will find geniuses and slower-thinking individuals — people who are overly shy, or have been taught to have a low opinion of themselves. Also those who may be scared of their own shadow, to exaggerate a bit, but nonetheless do still think for themselves, and are not really mindless followers and bullies.

Many people with different social or medical problems are grouped together in the geek crowd, and society wrongly teaches us that these people are not deserving of good treatment or concern befitting a human being, by the more dominant and aggressive folks. When the quiet ones are pummeled repeatedly with negativity, they will sooner or later reach their full storage capacity of stressful pressure — they reach their breaking point. When this pressure is not dealt with and reduced, the proverbial balloon bursts, and the person takes the route of switching to survival mode, trying to destroy or remove the source of the stress or danger to them.

Unfortunately, some of these people become the shooters. In better days, these children, courageous champions of fairness and common sense, would grow up to become our generals, inventors, teachers, doctors, legislators and presidents. They are normal, well-meaning people who are prodded by our actions of ridiculing, isolating or worse, to become the individuals who we eventually encounter behind the trigger of a gun on the campus and in the mall.

By isolating them, subjecting them to all sorts of detrimental and demeaning treatment over and over, we create what we eventually call monster shooters. We force them to retreat within themselves or to seek out similarly-affected individuals, who then take the place of the teaching, comforting parent, and who go on to guide them in the wrong direction. This could be avoided and be less costly in terms of expense and lives, if our citizens are educated to be more sensible and tolerant of all people who we perceive as different.

It is believed that the shooter may sometimes kill at random. He fantasizes about becoming a hunter standing in the middle of a group of sheep. All these sheep are of equal importance: that is, they become insignificant. There is no need to be selective. They are all the same; it's just the hunter and his prey. Each kill sends the same message of vengeance, revenge and opposition to the system of isolating and ridiculing the weak, teaching the world a lesson, like a bad child being punished by the teacher or, in this case, the master hunter.

The lesson is, don't pick on the weak because their hands aren't tied. There will be revenge. We learn the hard way, albeit too late, that there is strength in the weakest of us…strength to pull a trigger in a crowded place; strength to savor murder and vengeance, and think it is right; strength to take revenge. A pound of flesh to be collected, and probably friends and followers to avenge them as well. There is a great urgency in solving this problem but how? Well, the pen is mightier than the sword. So parents should use words — the right words, not from a book as much as from the soul. Also whenever the time comes, vote for a better country — for them.

By neglecting your kids, they lose your support, after which you lose them. It starts with you. You have to stay close to your children, by talking, loving, supporting and listening. Every opportunity that you get, just be the parent: the strong parent, the understanding parent, the brave scared parent, the passive aggressive parent, the split personality parent, the obsessive, loving, caring, concerned parent, the ridiculous, weird, funny, happy parent, and definitely the proud parent. Keep telling them that you are proud of them. Make them tired of hearing it. They never do and it works. It gives them comfort and confidence to do the right thing, and keeps their minds at ease.

No matter how old you think your kids are, they are still learning from you. What they learn when they are adolescents will be different than what they picked up from you when they were five or eight, but they are still picking up information and patterns to follow. It's easier for a child to start smoking or drinking excessively if the parent does it. You can help them to solve each different problem they encounter in real life, if you are there for them, without you even knowing you are helping them. Your presence in the home — in their space, not their face — is sometimes all that is needed.

Some of us work long hours and this reduces the amount of quality time we have with them. Ask yourself if it is worth it to be away so much. You gain money but lose your child, and sometimes your soul, because that's what they are to you. The answer is clear. Lose the extra job and the extras it helps you afford. If one job can't cut it, don't get a second job but move to a cheaper home. I did. We moved to an apartment and sold the house. Believe me, we are as happy and close to each other as we ever were.

Your kids are as mature as you give them credit for. You have to explain properly why you moved, why you did this or that — they will understand. Don't be afraid to tell them you could not afford the big house or apartment. They will see that you respect them enough to tell them the truth and they will feel proud of you. They will hear you when you tell them they are more important to you than a new car or living in a nicer neighborhood than the Joneses do. If you live as you can afford, you will also be teaching them a valuable lesson to do the same by living within their means. They will learn not to be greedy but to be as wise as you are, and to recognize that they are the truly important piece of the pie, and worth more to you than anything you can buy or gain in life.

Money, wealth or fame is no replacement for their reciprocal love. You must not leave them alone to fend for themselves against the wolves of the world. With the love you instill in them, they may sometimes be lonely, but never alone, because your love comforts and sustains them in your absence. All these shooters seem to be left wanting some kind of attention or comfort that they might not have gotten at home. It started there. Remember, a house is not a home — you have to *make* it a home.

Parents can't see or solve everything. In fact, two years ago, I had a particular argument with my son. I did not get my way because of my wife intervening — fairly and gallantly, of course. Predictably, we argued afterwards because I should have left well enough alone, but I'm not perfect and that's cool. Something was taught and learned: that love is there between everything in our lives together.

Whether he realized it now or then, my love for my son was reinforced. He saw that I will fight for him, and with him, because I love him. I care enough for him to fight with him, about what I want for him, and from him, and I love him enough to treat him as a normal person when we're done. Of course, that goes double for my daughter. Twice the stress but equally fitting rewards. My son was 16 at the time, a junior in high school, and he did not think he needed preparation classes for his upcoming SAT/ACT exams offered in his school by Princeton University. What an opportunity to pass up, huh?

But it's okay because he thought, and his grades reflected, that he could do it without the extra lessons. I just didn't want to take unnecessary chances, or pass up good opportunities like that, but I trusted that he would keep up the pace in his studies. His mom thought that he could too. I much prefer an argument about education than some sort of gun or gang thing. We can save dozens of potential shooters from taking that fateful, frightful, terrible step, if we fight for them, with them and about them. They will understand and appreciate that. They gauge your love for them by how much you are willing to fight with them and about them. Some kids will listen to you and that cuts down on the amount of disgruntled kids, looking for a friend with a gun or a gang to enlist in. That leaves just one shooter out there instead of ten. That makes it a dozen victims instead of a hundred.

I may be far from the truth or closer than I thought. You decide. The results are worth it. Understanding the adolescent teen takes a lot of thought and intuition. We grew up playing in the sand with a dump truck and a doll which was highly advanced enough to say, "Mommy" when you pulled the string. No large amount of thinking needed from the child. Now their computer and video games require the brains and coordination of an astronaut just to get to level five, and this high level of thinking and understanding comes naturally to them. They understand and are capable of more than you think, so help them and challenge them to grow. I write from experience with my own kids.

When he was 14 years old, my son started to learn computer programming. At the same age, my daughter began learning Chinese (Mandarin), one of the most difficult languages I've encountered. This is normal for kids their age if the parent can find ways to inspire their kids to pursue education and improve themselves. This also gives them increased pride and ambition to propel themselves down the road of self development, self challenge and ultimately, self achievement. Talking to them and supporting them constantly is hard work, but easier than bailing them out of jail or burying them, so it's worth it, and there is a fine line between one and the other. Being there for them is a choice of giving up your lifestyle for theirs, or them losing their lives in different ways, for your lifestyle. It is your choice, and a shooter's life and future depends on it. If you choose to spend your time in a bar or extra jobs instead of at home with them, we all lose.

All children who can play a video game demonstrate their ability to learn higher forms of education, if you, the parent, do not slow the children down by letting them even suspect they are incapable of realizing their true potential. Think of it this way: if you let the children think they can reach the highest level of anything they try, at least they may reach more than halfway, which is more of an accomplishment than if they didn't try or didn't have confidence that they could do better.

What is important is for you to encourage them to believe in themselves — as you must also. Make them aware that they deserve the best, and they can achieve the best for themselves and others just by making an effort and not accepting failure, because failure is only an opportunity to do better, in disguise. After your children start to believe in themselves, and are confident that you feel proud of them, they will start to learn and understand at a faster speed, which naturally makes them think that you are stuck in the Dark Ages, even with religion. This is normal. Don't be scared to let them take the lead in certain things; they need to see that you have the confidence in them to achieve, so show them that you think they won't hurt themselves and others. They need to learn this so they can learn how to lead.

Why don't these shooters turn to religion? That is the obvious avenue that a well-meaning parent or guardian will make available to them. The answer is that kids see past our blind misconceptions about religion. Some of us follow religion like hypocrites, saying one thing and doing another, and some of us blindly follow religion like fanatics. The kids see these examples as proof that submission to religion is not the way. If we do as Jesus said in the Gospel of Thomas and go through the doorway of religion — go past the dogma — to find the real truth, instead of what we do now, then more children will follow.

You have to realize they are young leaders, but they trust you and only you to tell them what is right or wrong. So you cannot appear to be hypocritical by following a faulty and failing ancient religion devoid of reason. They don't have the time or patience for prehistoric religious beliefs. You can't teach your child that killing is bad except if it is done in the name of a god, as was done all through mankind's history of invasions and occupations since before Jesus' time until now. Killing is never the way, except maybe for shooters in a mall, so does that mean that the shooters followed their parents' mistaken lead to kill in the name of something? Maybe for justice, religion or revenge?

Any religion that spreads murder to reinforce its beliefs is suspect, as was done during the later part of the "Time of Antiquity" — 8th century BC to 6th century AD — by the practice called Christianization, which started after

Christ's death. Since his death Christians conveniently forgot their commandments condemning murder and continue to do so up to this day. Thou shall not kill. Jesus taught this, that we should not kill for any reason. War was not condoned or sanctioned by Jesus. That is proof that what we are now taught is not Jesus' religion, but something invented after his crucifixion by the Pharisees and other cults of that time. You should read up on Christianization, which was an exercise carried out in some instances by force and death.

Our children see this hypocritical thinking plainly and they think, okay, if that is your false religion that kills, then I will make my own religion that kills, and when I shoot up the mall or join a gang then everyone will respect me and I will share my own justice, with bullets. Do you want your kids thinking this way or hanging around with other kids who do, like shooters and gang members?

Compare numbers in the last 100 years between gang membership and church membership. Gang numbers are rising worldwide by the millions and church numbers are falling — there's your proof that religion is failing. Soon there will be overwhelming odds that your child will be pressured to join a gang. Gangs are in their schools right now, on every street corner, and all around the world, so how much can they resist? You have to strengthen them from within.

When you show the children that you are weak by following any misguided religious beliefs, they will move on. They will lose respect for you as you lose your credibility with them. They will find someone else to walk with them along their path or journey in life. This may not be someone you approve of. Don't let that happen.

Do the good things that they can learn from and follow. They learn to respect themselves by first learning to respect you, by you teaching them what self respect is. Walk with them — teach them; don't force or imprison them with your understanding of your religion or your politics. Don't teach them to use common sense and then tell them they should not apply that intelligent way of thinking when it comes to killing or blindly accepting any form of religion or political party. I am not telling you to tell them religion is wrong, but show them that the real truth of finding love is within them, not outside, not in any TV ministry, church or political group. If they don't find it, they can become shooters, in a mall or in a gang. It's the same thing.

We sometimes teach them helplessness and hopelessness when they see us accept or willingly submit to a perceived superior person, religion or company, like your boss or the bank. The kids think that no one or thing is superior to you or them because they are fearless. We teach them to have fear and defeat themselves, through our weak actions of following others with their questionable practice of ancient religions. You don't want them to follow their irresponsible friends, do you?

They see your fallibility and that is why we have teens going astray or rebelling. It is to show their power and resistance to the system of control they are subjected to — by us or society. They show courage, that they will not accept defeat, and that they are willing to fight insurmountable odds for themselves and their family. You have to show them that you are that way, too. In fact, you must teach them to be that way or they will be taken advantage of, by the banks, credit card companies and so many more people — even some of their priests.

We cannot treat them like fodder to fight wars and be discarded after use, as we do right now with some of our veterans. Children see the poor care we give our veterans and even the enlisted troops. They are tomorrow's leaders; we must teach them to be proud of themselves, so they can lead. Help them to understand honor and character. Instill that in them. Show them that the road is bright, not bleak. Let them become hopeful that their future will be better and you will be there for them. They will not be alone…with a gun…in the mall.

Teach them that love does not have to come from others. It can come from themselves, to themselves, for themselves. When they love themselves first, only then can they love others. Tell them, "Show me your friends and I'll show you who you are." Let them understand this phrase and have friends who can enhance their well being, and will not encourage them to take drugs and join a gang. Motivate them to want to make a difference in their community.

Let them know that you trust them, love them and believe in them. Let them know that they deserve the best, and that they can achieve just that, and they do not need a gang or prison to make them whole. Give them good role models to look up to, people who are helping the community, especially you. They want to feel proud of you, so give them reason to do just that; it shows them that they can grow up to be like you, and kids always are most easily impressed by their parents. Let them create their destiny, not accept it. Tell them to use the brain or lose the brain.

Their young minds will be nurtured by you, or the

local gangs and drug pushers, so take your pick as to who will be the most important person in your child's life. The alternatives are not pleasant. Unfortunately, we have become so busy that we put our children second, not by the things we can't afford to buy them, but by how little quality time we spend with them: time which enables them to do other things to fill the empty space our absence leaves, often resulting in their downfall, and ours.

DECEPTION

"Every society gets the kind of criminal it deserves." (Robert Kennedy) Is the current state of our affairs because someone elected George Bush and they got what they were voting for? Twice? That answer is yes. He was incapable of running the country, as his prior history of dismal failures proves and we should have seen that. Although we did not wish for a recession, the country was deceived and let down by Bush's actions of lax oversight and not ensuring *disciplined* capitalism.

It was easy to predict. Notice how many people George W. Bush allowed to be executed when he was the governor of Texas and you can see that he's comfortable with death. Look at his past jobs and the failures he had in management of those entities. Look at his past lifestyle of abusing substances, legal and illegal, which numbed down his feelings and detached him from his compassion and accountability to others. See how little he did to help save your family from his greedy corporate friends or to save the victims of Katrina.

He gave us a death sentence, here at home and in Iraq, albeit a slow, painful, suffering death, laced with the poison of poverty. His first four years in office should have been the red flag of warning for people to learn from and not elect him for a second term. Unfortunately, it didn't deter some people who were consumed with fear and hatred for others who are different from them. As a result, hundreds of thousands of us now have children who fought in an unjust war and are broken with PTSD (post-traumatic stress disorder), or are injured or deceased.

Did you ever notice in a cartoon the bad guy always confesses at some point? If he did not confess, then all his diabolical planning and deeds would have been for nothing, because no one would know how brilliant he and his plans were, and he would not receive his deserved credit. It is a boost for his ego. I think George W. Bush suffers from the same need to be recognized for his diabolical brilliance. He is not as foolish as some think. A smart man could act as a dummy quite well, so as not to be blamed for things, when he planned them all along. I noticed that he played the game of dropping subtle hints for those who can recognize them.

Bush called others the axis of evil, and then he did what he said they do. He's the one who invaded another country with "Operation Shock and Awe." He has brought about mass destruction of an entire nation, and in mid 2008, the rising price of oil was six times what it was during the week of 9/11, which made the cost of living and medicine more expensive for us. He blessed us with a tumbling American economy and a tumbling world economy, as a ripple from our own recession.

The Iraq Casualty Coalition (icasualties.org) estimates that he caused upwards of 1,284,105 Iraqis to die as of the fall of 2008; more than 4,000 of our own proud, honorable soldiers to be sacrificed; at least 30,000 of our proud, hard-working soldiers to be seriously wounded; and more than 300,000 honorable troops to be afflicted with some level of PTSD. More than 180,000 women have seen active duty and many will be afflicted with varying degrees of PTSD from the war.[1] Countless millions more have been displaced from their homes in Iraq. That is real Shock and Awe.

He is indeed quite diabolical. He kept changing his story quite cleverly to distract us, about why he invaded Iraq, from weapons of mass destruction, to Iraqi involvement in 9/11, to Saddam trying to acquire yellow cake, and last but not least, to spreading democracy to the people. Why did they invade Iraq when other countries were more of a threat? North Korea has nuclear weapons and constantly threatens to use them. President Bush said they were trying to help the Iraqi people to escape from tyranny. If they had such noble thoughts, they should have gone to Darfur instead, right?

An intelligent businessman does not spend large sums of money without larger returns — by coincidence, Iraq has a little oil and a lot of reconstruction projects. Also many opportunities for people to steal billions in cash without anyone knowing, being able to track or even to prove it, if they had suspicions. We've lost billions in cold, hard cash, which inexplicably disappeared in Iraq. It is wise to follow the money.

In their pursuit of wealth, power, deception and happiness, were murder and the destruction of two countries acceptable? Iraq is beyond any reasonable swift point of return and easy repair. It will take years of immense reconstruction. So, too, America's economy is

---

[1] Iraq Casualty Coalition, "Operation Iraqi Freedom," www.icasualties.org, and "PTSD Statistics, World War II to Iraq," PTSD Combat Blog, http://ptsdcombat.blogspot.com/2006/04/ptsd-statistics-wwii-to-iraq.html, website accessed November 17, 2009.

suffering severely and the natives of both are restless.

While the brave American soldiers were doing their best in Iraq, their homes were being foreclosed on. Their families faced untold horrors at the hands of Bush's friends — the banks — and he refused to even give the soldiers a pay raise. The families suffered and received little or no help from Bush's government, as they financially spiraled into the abyss. The soldiers who did return home received terrible medical care, if any at all. They came home with PTSD and were told that they had a pre-existing condition, not PTSD. That means they were not qualified to receive care. We still have thousands of veterans not being cared for. A sad follow-up to the treatment we gave our returning veterans from the Vietnam War. One third of the homeless on our streets are Vietnam veterans who are not receiving proper care. Bush just added to it. They were not being helped to put their lives back together.

Our female soldiers' cries in Iraq were swept under the rug while they were being raped and assaulted there, and then hidden and trivialized when they complained. They were treated with a standard less than they deserved. If you mistreat an animal in America, you can hear the objections miles away. Under Bush's rule, I saw these female soldiers and vets being deceived and mistreated constantly, and I heard no shouts of anger or disgust at their shabby treatment. Are you in Shock and Awe, and as bitterly angered as I am?

The boogieman that you can see is always worse than the boogieman you can't see. I saw Bush and didn't see Bin Laden. What if the unseen boogieman was allowed to hide out in the hills, and the story about him was used by the real boogieman to distract and scare you, to paralyze you with fear, while he and his friends emptied the treasury? The question is, would you consider it a heist or just defense spending with no bid contracts? How gullible are we? Bush supporters were quick to say, "No, that'll never happen. That's just conspiracy theories. We can trust these people — God sent them — and Bush talks to God." These are the people who are fooled by all kinds of con men, including the religious kind, and always end up supporting and voting for the con men, against their family's own interest and safety, time and again (Remember the Stockholm Syndrome?). It is sometimes hard to accept the truth, or even see it, but when you do, it is better than living a lie or letting your family die in the wrong war.

They say Saddam was a bad man but he kept that region in check. You need an ax to cut the trees; a feather won't do. When we removed Saddam, we opened that whole region to the likes of Bin Laden and his followers, which makes the world less safe.

It is easier for them — the Bush supporters — to say nice words and to trust the wolves than to get off the couch and call their representative…today…every week…to write their congressman…today…every week…every month. E-mail takes two minutes… to save the country? That's an easy price to pay, isn't it? We, the people, should not let the greedy and misguided amongst us divide and deceive us, and sell the lives and well-being of our families to other countries or sovereign funds, for their profit. Big business is already running the world. We are now just the consumers: the expendable sheep, for the greater good…of the bottom line.

You and your family have to become active. Read and educate yourself to see what is going on. Read the newspapers. Read books that grab you by the scruff of your neck, and shake you and make you think, like this one. Watch The History Channel, National Geographic and The Discovery Channel on TV to learn new things. You don't have to believe me; just prove me wrong. As you try to do that, you will be learning the truth, and that may set you free from your lack of knowledge and help you to save your own family, yourself and your children. Aren't they worth it? Turn off the game shows and soap operas on the TV. Your kids are dying, taking drugs, getting AIDS and other STDs, joining gangs, selling drugs, going to prison. Watch them instead of the TV. Also watch the news instead of the other unimaginative reality shows that litter the tube. Do your duty as a parent. The TV companies can only lose money if you stop watching, while you can lose your family and their future if you don't.

The Bush government pulled the wool over our eyes with their brand of deception. They gave a weak stimulus package of $150 billion in 2008. That gave a person who was broke and foreclosed on enough money to buy food and gas for a short while — days or weeks, depending on how large the family was, instead of giving us a solution to the housing crisis, which started the recession. The $150 billion could not restart a recession that firmly planted its roots a whole year before. They had programs that helped 3% of the people facing foreclosures, and they were happy to do just that and not much more, so President Bush could say they did something to help the public. That's like giving you a thimble full of water to go through the desert.

It was too little, too late, purposely. The top financial people refused to admit we were in a recession, in February, 2008, a whole year after it started, purposely.

Seventy percent of the American economy, seventy percent of our gross domestic product, is consumer spending. We are not financially able now to spend money as we were before, and this issue needs to be addressed. If we can't spend, the economy starves to death. We have lost all our equity in our properties, so we have no money to spend. We really didn't have money before but we were able to borrow against our homes' equity.

The people who let the recession happen think they are followers of Jesus. What would Jesus think about them? He would be hurt and ashamed that they use His name, and not His ideals. Liking the tree but not the fruits. They are fake Christians. You have heard of the drug cartel but what about the oil cartel, loan cartel, and soon, Bush's South American water cartel?

DRUG COMPANIES

Drug companies go hand in hand with food companies. Since we started eating mass-produced food, we have been increasingly poisoned by dangerous additives. We never had so many cancers and exotic diseases 50 or 100 years ago. We had real diseases, not manufactured ones. The drug companies are making billions treating these medical problems arising from unsafe food.

Unfortunately for us, medicine is now a business and that takes precedence over the doctors' oath or good sense to cure people. The drug companies have realized that they make more money treating the symptoms rather than finding a cure. The company is also required by law to try its best to make the most reasonably profitable decisions for its stockholders, who expect the highest return without killing patients — quickly, but they are allowed to suffer a long time and take lots of medications. If the drug companies cure everybody, they will be out of business, so they do not.

The drug companies know that the mass-produced food will make us slightly ill in various ways, depending on how our body functions and reacts to foods and additives over long periods of use and abuse, what allergies we have, and how healthy we are at the time the symptoms take hold. The food and drug companies try to produce fairly safe food and medications, but will not go further to make them better than that, so that they are absolutely safe, and cause no problems from long-term use, as that means more expense to produce safer foods and medications: lots more money to do testing and less profits from a more healthy population.

They conveniently ride in on their white horse, and manage our predictable and pre-determined illnesses. We are the money fields, the crops that they rear and pick from daily. They harvest us. They live off of us. They suck us dry, like vampires at a feast. They grow us like livestock, much like we do cattle and hogs, so we can all feast on the dumb animals. In this case, we are the dumb sheep.

There are medical cures that the companies have stopped producing because not enough people develop that illness, so it becomes unprofitable for them to produce the medicine. It also costs many millions to produce, test and market the drugs, as much as $800,000,000 per drug in some cases. If there is not a market for it, the company cannot continue making it and losing money. The investors can probably sue them if they do; remember, the law states that they have to try their best to be profitable. Of course, there are more problems that we unknowingly fall prey to when using whatever medications they do choose to produce. There are certain pills that have really terrible side effects, like diabetic medication.

In 2008 I saw a feature story on CNN which showed a drug company that had to stop the manufacture of a medicine because of the cost (there was not a large demand for it), so the few patients who had that disease would eventually die from it. This is a case where the government should have a program to subsidize the cost. It will not be only one life they save, but even the few lives that are saved are enough to validate the cost.

When I took my first set of diabetic medication, I was warned that there would be certain side effects. Diarrhea, organ damage and sexual problems were just some of the potential problems. After a while, I was told that I would have to add an ACE inhibitor to my other pills to protect my kidneys from the damage the pills will cause over time. Then the doctors decided that although my cholesterol was normal, they wanted it 100 points lower, so I was given a cholesterol-reducing pill. Keep in mind that each new pill comes with its own set of side effects. It certainly looked as if I had become a human guinea pig, waiting for the promised sexual side effects. There are so many exotic-sounding names for ED (erectile dysfunction) medications on the market now. I can't wait for them to put me on those; should I be worried or excited by the promise of four-hour power?

So far I think I only have diabetes but as I get older, I'm sure more complications will show up with all these drugs they give me. Because drug companies are usually inventing their own drugs, I have to wonder if they engineer them to have specific, treatable side effects, so they can sell more drugs and make more money. Who knows? My head hurts just thinking about it. Isn't selling drugs illegal? Or is the government the really big drug pusher, the big importer, and the drug companies are its smaller drug pusher on every corner, in a pharmacy, with us as the crop of junkies shooting it all up?

Diabetic men like me experience the side effects that I described. Unfortunately, women have so many hormonal problems due to menstruation and menopause, physically and emotionally even before they start taking medications, the medicines' side effects can really make their lives a living hell. You see it in the movies all the time; the actress has to make a choice to take the medication and suffer through life, or stop the treatment and vibrantly live a little, while waiting for death. If you speak to people who take chemotherapy treatments they will tell you, it is not the easiest thing to go through but hopefully, it has a happy ending if you do decide to try it.

Ask yourself, why do they allow cigarettes to be legal, when there are smokes that are less harmful that are illegal? There are hundreds of toxic and harmful additives approved by the U.S. Government for use in a cigarette. If they weren't approved they would not be found in a cigarette. Why? The answer is money. You can't grow enough tobacco to satisfy your needs, so there is a profitable market to supply cigarettes, tax the sales and keep them addictive. Right now they make a fortune selling you cigarettes and there is a whole industry built around supplying your fix. Check how many people die from alcohol related issues daily, yet it is not made illegal.

I think some of the diseases that we are afflicted with are allowed to exist. Why don't they give us a larger dose of medications to cure us instead of harvesting us with smaller doses? If larger doses are dangerous, then long-term use of regular doses may also be dangerous. So why not develop safe, non-toxic medications? Profits are the answer.

Mike Papantonio, co-host of "Ring of Fire," with Bobby Kennedy, a program on the radio station Air America, claimed on his show that Bayer, one of the largest and most well-known chemical companies, knowingly sold medication tainted with the AIDS virus to children all over the world, including the U.S. The name of the product was Factor 8, a blood medication for hemophiliacs. Thousands of kids died and they also infected their families, causing more to die. A search for Factor 8 on the Internet brings up a video of an interview of Mr. Papantonio, who is also a lawyer who worked on the case. The show was "Scarborough Country," on MSNBC, and Joe Scarborough was the host.[2]

There is a lot of fraud done by drug companies. This was further highlighted when the Justice Department, in September 2009, announced the largest settlement for charges of fraud paid by a drug company, in a combined amount of more than $2 billion. This story was carried by many sources, including *USA Today*, CNN and the VOA (Voice of America) news agency. Are you Shocked and in Awe yet?

---

[2] "Bayer Exposed (HIV Contaminated Vaccine)," YouTube.com, http://www.youtube.com/watch?v=wg-52mHIjhs, website accessed November 17, 2009.

ECONOMICS

The American economy in 2009 is in the worst condition it could be, in this always turbulent world economy. That can only put us at a sharp and severe disadvantage. This does not mean it has never been worse, but then we didn't have thousands of militant terrorists led or inspired by Bin Laden trying to kill us, at home and anywhere else in the world at the same time. In 2008, people were pulling their money out of the country in droves: $20 to $40 billion per month, it was sometimes reported.

We were spending more money in Iraq than we had, so we begged and borrowed from our abrasive communist foreign lenders. The dollar was falling in value compared to foreign currency. Some foreign businesses stopped accepting the American dollar as early as November 2007.[3] The world economy is heavily dependent on the American economy, thus as it fell into a deep hole, so too the world economy became battered. It is estimated that America accounts for 25% of the world GDP.

The people who said we were not in a full blown recession in 2008 are in the minority and they are rich. These people are usually so far above the poverty line that they don't feel the pain and reality of the economic plunge.

---

[3] Singh, Jyotsna, "Dollars no good for the Taj Mahal." BBC.com (BBC News, Delhi), http://news.bbc.co.uk/2/hi/7098370.stm, November 16, 2007.

For the first time since 1945, more than 50% of homeowners in 2008 had less than 50% equity in their homes (Story cited by CNBC.com,).[4] Was this a part of the plan by the Bush folks all along to create the recession so that among their other heists, they could get their hands on the $350 billion they fleeced from us in the TARP funds? Very few of us could work for a lifetime and make $10 million, much less $1,000 million (1 billion dollars), so these folks must be really happy with $350 billion, and I am sure the planners all will get their cut somehow — they always do.

Businesses are just looking for profits; it does not matter where they come from, and they are not required by law to be humane, or loving and responsible to their customers or the different countries they do business in. They may leave these countries at any time with all of their profits. We already see this happening with companies that are reaping the rewards from this war and recession.

There is a genuine concern that smaller banks will continue to falter and close; many have in 2008 and continue to do so in 2009. The price of gas and food go up with the price of oil, as it costs more to transport products around the country and the world. If China pumps billions of dollars and products into Mexico and Canada to help their faltering economies, with the exclusive rights to their oil and other resources, then China can run their industrial expansion for the next 100 years. We are already destabilized, so we may not be able to stop or compete with

---

[4] "Homeowner Equity Below 50% for First Time Since 1945," CNBC.com, http://www.cnbc.com/id/23503784, March 6, 2008.

them. We may be still borrowing money from them instead.

In 2008 the job market was registering a heavy slump, with the unemployment rate expected to reach 10% in 2009. The private sector was cutting jobs with lightning speed. While manufacturing, construction, and retail jobs kept dropping, some people stopped looking for jobs because not enough jobs were available. The experts told us to buy property because the price of homes was dropping, but what they didn't tell us is that after we bought, the prices could continue to drop. The homes may be worth less the next year, and if you have to sell within a few years, it could be at a heavy loss of $50,000 to $150,000 and possibly even more.

Jobs are still being shipped to foreign countries and we are quickly realizing the possibility of giving more control in certain areas of trade, finance and manufacturing to foreign entities that provide us with loans. If the recession gets much worse, companies could see the change from manufacturing American products to sewing clothes and making toys for the developing countries. What will the tag read? Made in the Taiwanese Republic of America or Made in the American Republic of India? Or will it just read Made in China, as they will be the ones with a stick on our backs, and our loans and notes of debt in their pocket? Are you as insulted as I am? Are you as angry as I am? Are you as scared as I am? Are you in Shock and Awe, as I am? You should be. We currently buy much more from China than we sell to them. Soon we may sell them the barn to buy feed for the horses. Everything in economics is planned way ahead, years ahead, so who planned this recession? Diabolical men who have seen it happen and experimented with it before.

The new plan for companies all over the world is becoming multinational, with no boundaries or taxes to keep their profits down as they transfer funds all around the globe. This is what was done during the Nazi invasions. Companies transferred and sold stock to their foreign partners, thereby saving their fortunes from seizure by the Nazis. It's an old trick. They could even own small countries or buy out the government there, and enjoy some sovereign power with their own banks and an independence that has no rules: another old trick.

If too many companies move their main operations out of America, as we see many have done, we may have no choice but to merge with our neighbors, Mexico and Canada, as we already have trade between us amounting to over $900 billion, approaching the $1 trillion mark in 2008. When we have no choice about it, no one will be thinking about illegal immigration because we will all be traveling across the borders to find jobs, as some do now to buy cheaper gas and diesel.

When we go to Mexico and Canada to find jobs, can you guess who will be there waiting for us? You will be employed by the same companies that laid you off and moved the jobs out of the country. There won't be any unions or health care benefits to look forward to either. Everyone will be freelance, as is being done with all the big companies here right presently. I and many more have already been put in that boat: freelance with no benefits or get another job. So get ready, because I see these scenarios coming to fruition. More Shock and Awe on us.

EDUCATION

This book is not meant just to highlight the problems we face, but is also an attempt to offer possible ideas to bring about solutions.

Children's achievements are a testament to good or poor parental skills. Simply speaking to them more often, smiling with them, and hugging them may make a huge difference in how they see the world. The world can be dark and scary, or bright, welcoming and glowing with opportunity. It all hinges on what you put into their expanding and encourage-able little minds, and how much you try to inspire them.

When children are taught that educating themselves is hard work, or an uphill battle, their perception of becoming educated is a negative one. If I think going to my place of employment is negative, then I won't get much done. Your kids are the same. At an early age I kept reminding my kids that education is not negative work, but rather a positive opportunity to learn and progress. Resisting this chance means that they may not absorb as much as they should, resulting in them missing the eventual benefits that could be offered to them.

You can have the best school with the finest teachers and programs, but if your children are not looking forward to the experience, they will not learn as much as they could. Some people don't realize that it is not the teacher who has to inspire the student, but you the parent. If students walk into that school wanting to learn, the teacher cannot prevent them. If you allow them to go to school with an unwillingness to learn, the best teacher can't help them. They will more easily join a gang in school. If you do your part to prepare your children to accept the gift of education, when they arrive at school, the teacher will be able to do a better job with the rest of the process. Education begins at home. School is not a prison, as some kids think.

Some people believe that their job is just to bring the lamb to the slaughter, or get the kid to the school bus and their job is finished, and the teacher's job is to magically get it done. Your job is to open the children's minds to the wonder of learning things. Don't force them to go to school; inspire and encourage them instead. It brings better results.

Remember, what they think about the process is as important to their progress as how many hours they study. If they want to pay attention in school, they may learn more than the child who resists or plays and then studies at home for longer hours to make up the lost ground after school. Another part of the puzzle is this: if our children think they have done their best that means they are done trying harder because the best means better can't be achieved.

That's a stumbling block right there. The word or term "best" means the end: no achieving higher, so no need to spend more time trying. They may stop trying and won't achieve more. The hare stops and the turtle wins. Instead, what I made my kids realize is they should always keep bettering themselves. Throw out the term "best" and replace it with the term "better." Anything they accomplish today can be outdone tomorrow. As technology improves, there is much more for us to learn. It's a never-ending process and that's good. Just getting your kids to understand this point alone could be the take-off point which allows them to spread their wings, and soar to a new and more fulfilling future.

While I realize that the majority of people don't have enough time in the day to be with their kids to encourage them to study, if children are taught to encourage themselves to progress, and convinced to want their education, you won't need to police them or push them to study. They will see the importance of studying for their own benefit, not studying to please you. I have seen that in my own kids, getting up hours before school to do extra studies and homework, so I write with experience.

Some people support their children when they say they can't study because of some weak excuse or even a legitimate medical condition, like ADD. I know ADD and those other diseases or disabilities are real problems, but you can help kids overcome these challenges mentally by your approach to them, and their approach to the problem. Strengthen their will to overcome it, by letting them know they can live with it and still be proud, happy and normal, rather than if you taught them to fear it, and to accept being defeated by it, by thinking they are different or lesser than the other kids. You can teach them to go around it and emerge a stronger person on the other side. I see lots of parents with special-needs kids doing just that: encouraging their kids to be their best. Everyone can do that, not just parents with special-needs kids. Sometimes my kids are lazy, and I have to tug their ear and get them off their butts. That's normal. Don't encourage them to be lazy, as success energizes them more than anything else. Help them find success; you will like the results.

If your medically ill children can understand speech, then you are already on the road to success. You can now reach inside their brains and mold a productive, proud, successful and happy child. You can use the trust they have in you, and use choice words to instill confidence, self pride, patience and determination. Often, people afflicted with medical problems make a name for themselves in the business arena, starting and doing business on the Internet, being productive and profitable members of society, and even becoming parents.

You can tap into that energy. Remember, when the human body loses some function, it compensates by increasing the efficiency of the other functions. When the body loses sight, it increases its ability to hear, smell and feel. So you have to carefully figure out what your children's strengths are and build on them. Parents know their children better than a professional, so don't depend on the doctors; this is something that you will be best at doing.

Being depressed, kids can convince themselves that they have a defect they can't overcome. If you encourage them with that train of thought, you help to make it a reality. This cripples the child mentally. When children are genuinely medically deficient, the thing they want most is for you to look at them, love them and treat them like normal kids. They want you to help them to work around their problem and lead them to success like any other kid. Remember the brain compensates, so many of them improve over time.

When you stay with them through the tough times, this inspires them to try more. They will achieve more than if they didn't try, and they end up feeling much better about themselves. It builds their self esteem when they achieve; they see themselves like any other child who has a problem. One great thing with most kids is they have a large imagination, which helps them to block out the hurdles, and focus on the task of being super and overcoming their disorder.

If they face up to their problem and learn to overcome it, then it does not remain a problem anymore, just a condition they can live with. They can bypass that condition, just like you bypassed the fact that you grew up thinking you were ugly when you really weren't: didn't we all? Every child wants to be Superman, Super-girl or super something, and your compassion and support help them to be super at overcoming fear and adversity. Just make them believe. It helps if you believe they are super also. If your child does not have a medical condition, you've already won.

Since my kids started grade school, my family has not watched TV or played video games during the week (99% of the time). House rules. This gave them more time to do things for themselves. It taught them to have structure at an early age, when it's easier for them to see the benefits of it, without the distraction of friends and the outside world. Obviously, this was quality time and it helped build the family's unity. Being a good parent is your duty, not your weakness, so be strong and just be one.

When my kids were older they had more time to play games with us, help in the kitchen, and be self sufficient without the retardation of watching TV. When they are self sufficient, it shows in their school work and their lively outlook. They also learn to cook and do other things that their friends can't, so they are considered by their peers to be great friends to have. They are not cast aside but become leaders amongst their friends. Independent kids become good organizers and top achievers in their schools, and go on to become great parents and presidents too, apparently.

The world is changing now. My son is now on his own away at college. My daughter lives at home, attending high school, and her friends are in touch with text and e-mail constantly. So now I have to change my approach, as do you. We still don't watch TV during the week...most of the time but I'm flexible now. She will be on the computer a lot after school, doing homework and e-mailing her friends...watching videos...and listening to music, all at once. That's okay. I don't need to police them as much because they trust themselves to know right from wrong and they need a little space to grow. Just keep reminding them to have a schedule or they won't sleep. What comes after that is to be good friends with them and converse with them about everything under the stars. They grow up fast and if you are distant, you lose out because soon you won't see them often, as they will be off to college somewhere in America or in a foreign land.

Enjoy constructive chats for 30 seconds sometimes. It's better than none. Tell them "I love you" 20 times a day, literally. My kids have heard that since they were born. I never stopped telling them. They often tell me when I forget to say it and that makes me feel good. To hear it gives them confidence; you are their pillar, their support. They are not scared to make mistakes. You will still love them. Love doesn't stop at the door; it has no boundaries or time limits — it's forever. When they know that, it's one less thing for them to worry about. They know you'll be there in the end.

Love is a great part of their education…in life.

Tell them you are proud of them. Tell them that sometimes they may feel lonely but they are never alone.

I understand that religions and customs vary, so I tell my children to be objective in what they believe. Look at the preachers, as they are not all sincere and trustworthy. Thousands of them are pedophiles. The church protects them even now, and has since the year 60AD, when they made laws about it; they have been doing this nonsense since that time and getting away with it.

EVOLUTION

The food we eat is now mostly mass-produced and mass-processed, filled with unhealthy chemicals. This is giving us all sorts of medical conditions that we would never have believed could happen. Our evolution is definitely influenced by what we eat, and apparently also by what containers we eat in.

Men are embracing gay lifestyles in ever increasing numbers or so it appears. It may just be that people are evolving, or admitting it more to themselves and coming out to the public about it, enabling a more accurate count of the issue. This also applies to women who are making their gay preferences known too in ever increasing numbers. The idea that this is a new development brings up the question of what is causing this transformation of traditionally straight people becoming gay, even after marriage to the opposite sex. Are they becoming gay or unknowingly born gay?

Some become gay just because they like an aspect of the gay life, such as the dress or the closeness with new gay friends. Some like the sex. Some have more fun in gay circles. Other people say that you are born gay and just found out, or figured it out. My thought is that those two scenarios are correct, which explains why a man can have a wonderful relationship with a woman, have kids, and then turn to a gay lifestyle or preference, or realize he would like to become gay because of the different sex. Or maybe he was gay all along and found out while being married. This applies to both genders.

The most important thing about being gay is that people want to enjoy their short lives on this Earth, and if embracing their gayness helps them to enjoy life, then it is good. They do not need to be foolishly exorcised to remove demons or convinced that they are not gay. Other people should not try to belittle them, as doing so only shows how weak, hateful and insecure these other people are.

When people become older and continue eating junk foods, or foods not suited for them, their physical needs change, their hormonal production changes and, as a result, their chemical balance changes, making it easy to see how and why they can make the conscious decision to adopt a gay sexual preference after their hormones guide them in different directions. Some change over and totally and fully embrace the gay lifestyle, dressing and adopting mannerisms generally associated as gay behavior. Others continue their straight lifestyle but like private gay sex sometimes, when they feel they are in the mood, becoming bisexuals openly or in concealment.

I think it can also work in reverse, where people who have lived as a gay person decide to try something new. Tired of the old boring sex and subject to changing chemical balances, they change and try to enjoy a different and sometimes straight lifestyle. I wonder if they succeed in enjoying it enough to stop the gay lifestyle altogether. That is an interesting idea. In any event, they will be straight to their new friends, so I guess it could work. Many people lose interest in sex as they get older, so it's not big on their agenda anyway, although some people continue to have satisfying sex lives into their elder years, with the addition of little blue pills.

The onset of diminished prostate health can affect the ability of men to have a satisfactory climatic experience when having a heterosexual encounter. So quite naturally they start experimenting with more kinky sexual practices and could develop a liking for one type of play or another. For example, one man may like role playing to get him interested in his female partner; another man may like to watch his female partner doing different things which excite him.

Some men may enjoy having their female partners play with them in different ways to induce their interest in her, or to help them to get aroused, as there is less testosterone and other beneficial chemicals and hormones in their aging systems. Naturally, a man can pursue those games by himself when she is sometimes absent or too busy, including gay play. These are just a few scenarios, ideas and games out of dozens that humans invent, to pique their interest in an act they have been engaging in for long enough in their lives that they sometimes become bored with it, or lose their urge due to bodily changes, medical interactions and side effects of medications.

Sometimes people have been married and faithful to one person so long, they become accustomed to the same actions all the time, so they invent games to play together. Could some people become accustomed to playing with the same sex when they masturbate? If a man masturbates, he is handling the male genitalia. While he will have pleasurable climatic feelings in the end, he may subconsciously develop a liking for handling male parts —

any male's part, not just his own — and over a long period of time may come to like doing that enough to look for a pleasure he can only get from another man's genitalia. This applies to women as well developing a liking for playing with different female parts and genitalia. I could be wrong but I don't think I am. Who knows? I await the studies.

Is this evolution toward a gay lifestyle or demeanor a natural result of human evolution, or induced unintentionally by the chemicals added to our foodstuff and medicines, which in turn affect our hormonal balances? It's both, I think. Women are slowly embracing their need to evolve into a new being: one who is a single parent and has the courage to deal with problems that are really quite overwhelming for one person to cope with. She is still evolving into that person who is as much the father figure in the family, working to support the family, as she is the traditional mother and anchor to a growing child, providing all the wisdom needed as only a woman can.

She slowly incorporates some masculine traits of old, and so blurs the line between the male and female roles in an ever-changing society. Will this also blur the line for the child, of the difference between traditional male and traditional female roles, with the advent of males exercising the use of more visible emotions to rear their kids, causing some kids to misunderstand what traditional male roles were and to develop the demeanor of a gay person? I don't know. I'm just thinking outside the box.

Trying to become tougher over an extended period of time may cause some women to change and become more attracted to other women, for the purpose of physical stimulation or social reasons, as emotions are a human trait that can cause so many chemical changes in the brain of a growing child or an adult. I think that the rise in lesbian relationships supports this to a limited but increasing extent. You cannot rule out the possible effects on the psyche of both young and old. External stimuli does cause the release of different chemicals in the brain, causing changes in behavior, much like how chocolate produces more pleasure-inducing chemical releases in the brain than sex does.

As the woman does this single parent evolution, man does the same, faced with similar needs to be the best single parent he can be. Instead of being perceived as all male or all female, the roles are merging and we could be seeing the early stages of another giant step for mankind. Obviously, men can't become women and vice versa without some medical help…yet. Bearing this in mind, the womb does have a way of producing mind-boggling surprises over an extended period of time.

It has now been learned that since 2003, in the Potomac River among others, some male small and big mouth bass are now producing eggs.[5] An Internet search of "male fish with eggs" reveals startling results. In one area, 80% of all male small mouth bass were found to have eggs. I hasten to add that other forms of wildlife live in those same waterways along the Eastern Seaboard, and some reptiles in Florida, young alligators for example, are

---

[5] Fahrenthold, David A., "Male Bass in Potomac Producing Eggs," WashingtonPost.com,
http://www.washingtonpost.com/wp-dyn/articles/A33850-2004Oct14.html, October 15, 2004.

showing some evolutionary problems due to the pollutants found in these waters. People are worried because they get this same water in their taps from these polluted rivers, and do not know the effect it will have on their babies and growing children.

Maybe hermaphroditism is going to become a more frequent occurrence naturally or because of all the medications we are taking. We may become asexual, being able to have kids by ourselves, without having to have sex with each another. Medical drugs do weird things to the population over a thousand years and can cause the growing process in the fetus to become obstructed. The child then keeps both functioning sexual body parts, including the womb. We have seen the slow evolution in animals to address different problems, which can mean survival to a species.

In a thousand years hermaphrodites may be the normal humans and a single sex person may be considered a freak of nature, or a product of medical engineering, which the parent decides. Fortunately, we still cannot see that far into the future. For now all we can do is see what we are now, and what we were thousands of years ago. Who could have thought 2,000 years ago that we would have stem cell research, gene cloning and gene transfer, DNA or gene manipulation, and the complete cloning of an entity, human or animal, in the 21st century? Who would have thought that viruses and retroviruses would have made mankind what we are today, by changing our genes over millions of years?

Why are our children reaching puberty much earlier than before? Steroids and growth hormones fed to the animals we eat, also contained in the plants we eat, are the main cause, I think. This, coupled with chemicals and medications, in the public water system, makes the problems and occurrences even more prevalent. Altered seeds that grow our foods also could create problems over extended time periods. These problems now help the organic food industry to become more profitable than it ever was. I think it is man's fault because of the unhealthy foods, so should we or our government put a stop to it, or should God stop it? Could God stop it? It looks like the industry is more powerful than He is. Money really does talk.

EVOLUTION OR EXTINCTION?

What is evolution? When and why does it occur? It is the way a living entity changes in order to survive or adapt to varying conditions. This occurs when conditions arise which threaten the entity in one way or another. I recently saw a documentary on *The Doc Zone* by CBC of Canada. It was called "The Disappearing Male." The report showed that the human male is under the threat of extinction.[6] When this happens, obviously, the human species as we know it will vanish. The remaining female population will adapt and evolve to compensate and become a new creature or die.

Are we headed for extinction? The alarming answer is yes. It has been suggested by scientists that we are now experiencing the beginning of the extinction of human beings. All living entities devise ways to avoid extinction, knowingly or not, the question is —have we?

Sperm count in humans is down by half over the last 50 years. Sperm abnormality has increased at an alarming rate. Testicular cancer has doubled in the last 20 years. It is important to note that the animal kingdom is also having similar problems, which suggests that we have a common denominator. These problems have now been attributed to the use of synthetic chemicals on a massive and worldwide scale. One such chemical is Bisphenol A, or BPA, which

---

[6] "The Disappearing Male," *The Doc Zone*, CBC TV, http://www.cbc.ca/documentaries/doczone/2008/disappearingmale/ , October 2, 2009.

was invented in 1891, and is used extensively in just about everything that has hard plastic in it, from CDs to plastic containers and even baby bottles. This chemical makes plastic products harder and stronger. It is an endocrine disruptor, meaning it disturbs the proper functioning of the endocrine system and the hormones which these glands produce. These hormones regulate our bodies' functions. Testosterone is the main disrupted hormone that is of concern in the pending male extinction.

Another group of chemicals called phthalates are also raising concerns. These chemicals — produced since the 1920s — are used to soften plastic products like rubber ducks and other toys. What is frightening is that they are also endocrine disruptors.

Parents are overcome with panic and grief knowing that for the last 40 years or more they have been feeding their children with poisoned baby bottles, and they have let their children chew on rubber ducks, pacifiers and teething rings, for as long as anyone remembers, which may have altered their normal growth. The concern is that the chemicals seep out of the products and into the mouths of our babies, a hazard that has been suspected with BPA since the 1930s. When a pregnant mother has these chemicals in her system, it subjects her growing embryo to these startling problems.

The birth of males has dropped by 50% in some places of interest: places with high concentrations of these chemicals. Instead of a ratio of 1 to 1 between boys and girls, the ratio is now 1 boy to 3 girls in some of these locations. Male sexual development has been thrown out of whack because the function of testosterone is disrupted by these chemicals. Within the last 60 years we have invented 90,000 chemicals. As much as 80,000 are in use, while only 15% are tested for effects on adult humans and almost none is tested for effects on either growing children, embryos or fetuses. The chemicals are tested on adults and not on the growing bodies of infants, so while a chemical is deemed safe for adults, the babies who are exposed are more susceptible to harm, as their bodies' resistance to these harmful chemicals could be hundreds of times less strong.

Sperm counts in most teenage men are half of what their fathers' were and 85% of their sperm are found to be abnormal, leaving 15% of normal sperm. This means mankind is surviving on a sperm count of 7.5% of normal sperm, as compared with our forefathers' sperm counts. Could we survive with any less? I think not. We have reached the edge, the brink of disaster. Long ago, sperm banks accepted sperm which had a standard volume of 60,000 counts per milliliter; that count has been reduced to 40,000, then 20,000 and they are now considering reducing the acceptance level to 10,000 per milliliter. Some birth rates in animals in polluted rivers have been found to be 90% below average, clearly showing they are affected as well.

Testosterone controls the sexual development of our male children and when its functions are blocked by chemicals, they are permanently damaged, and the hormone cannot perform the tasks of fetal development that they were supposed to accomplish. Would-be boys cannot become boys. Embryos cannot change to boys and instead become a female fetus. The result is a mix of undeveloped or changed humans with various developmental abnormalities.

Plastics enhance our lives but unfortunately, they are poisoning our unborn children to the extent of bringing about human extinction. Up until about seven or eight weeks old, the embryo is neither male nor female. The embryo grows into a fetus at around that time, and it is the critical time when it is changing to a boy or girl. Sexual hormones, in particular testosterone, then take over and help determine if a child becomes a male or, by its absence or inaction, a female. When the chemicals interfere with this process, the result is abnormal development, both physically and mentally.

Some embryos develop into a male body but that is itself a physical change. Accompanying that physical change is also a mental change needed to make the human embryo a complete male or female. Things can go wrong. Some boys may not get the required corresponding male wiring in the brain; consequently, they have a male body with a female brain — in other words, a girl trapped in a boy's body. This happens in reverse as well: a female body with a male wired brain — a boy trapped in a girl's body. We see this quite often, in alarming numbers, in our modern, chemically poisoned society.

Things do not always go wrong in that simple way either; it sometimes gets really mixed up and complicated. For example, a boy may retain a girl's genitals, or a girl may grow a boy's genitals We see this phenomena increasing as well.

Soon there may not be enough traditional males with properly functioning genitalia and normal sperm counts to carry on the human species as we already survive on only

7.5 % of traditional levels. Is the species evolving or going to evolve to a point where a person will be able to impregnate her or himself? Hermaphroditism opens that door to a new possibility. We see it elsewhere in nature. It is a natural occurrence of some species after millions of years of evolution and threats to its survival. We see asexual reproduction in turkeys, sharks, starfish, bees and other species. It is not a new occurrence.

The emergence of such sexually diverse groups of people has a profound effect on society and societal development. Some may speculate that gay people and hermaphrodites are sometimes the results of these chemical interferences in the embryonic and fetal stages of a child's development. Others may seek different explanations, including religious ones. I will leave that type of speculation up to you, as each person has his or her own ideas.

One thing is certain; we are threatened by something more devastating than any bomb, or any and all the plagues gone by, and our evolution may be the only way to survive. Since the 1970s, the drop in the birth rate of boys has resulted in as many as three million less boys being born and consequently, three million more girls and mixed sexes. With the invention of new synthetic chemicals and medicines, the problem grows even larger and finding solutions becomes more immediate, more urgent. Evolution may be our only way out of extinction, if we still have time.

FEAR

Fear sells. That's the new mantra. There is a fear of losing Christmas and a fear of losing English as our main language. We have such a mix of different nationalities in this country that it is impossible to lose English's dominance to the parlance of any other country. English is the only bridge. The media plays on the fears of weak people. Even the strong are bombarded with fears of terrorism.

The leaders and the media make the Democrats fear the Republicans and vice versa. That division made it easy to steal from and empty the Treasury, under our noses, while yelling, "Terrorist, terrorist," as was done during the Bush reign.

It appears the Bush administration and their friends were the ones terrorizing our economy, leaving us defenseless to attacks, of all kinds, from wealthy nations and sovereign funds that buy our debts and increase their control over our economy. Republicans used the fear of Bin Laden to win the elections twice. Bin Laden was not found, as I suspect he was an integral part of their plan. The constant threat of a terrorist attack had many too scared to vote against Bush in 2004. So BL was more useful to them alive than dead. Maybe someone else will find him.

Even the Republicans were running scared of the Bush administration in the end. Just listen to the Republicans in the media reclassifying themselves as Independents and

Reagan Republicans. They were powerless to stop a machine they helped to build. They have no pride left, as they had long since swallowed that when they found out their war was a fake. I call it their war because they were all for it; they lied and sold it to us while they were pushing us off that cliff.

They make you fearful of the poor Mexican. The poor, helpless Mexican who has nothing. I don't think you should worry about the poor Mexican taking your job. Soon there will be no more jobs to take. The jobs are all being shipped away — to Mexico. The Mexicans have a country to go back to, with new jobs waiting for them. Where do you and I have to go? While many around the world hate Americans for our warmongering, they won't want us in their countries. Mexicans may be kicking *us* out then. We may be the ones sneaking over the border to find a job and living in fear of being deported.

The Christian Americans insist on sticking to divisive immigration issues and are deporting the Christian Mexicans. Such is the greatness of the faithful and their fake love for Christ, other Christians and real Christianity. Remember, a religion or a country is only as great as its people. Some Christians are full of hate for their own Christian Mexican brown brethren, but they like Christian Whites from Europe and elsewhere, so what does that say? Isn't that racism?

I sense that's why there are so many pedophile priests, death-penalty loving Christians, gay-bashing Christians and substance-abusing Christians, because they don't know the truth of Jesus' teachings which knows no boundaries of color, creed or race. These folks only know what the church misleads them with — fear of most things — in order to believe in some vengeful, fire-breathing God. That also proves the people do not really believe in God or they would only do good deeds to avoid punishment. That is shocking and awful. What would Jesus do? They should try to find out. It's amazing that those who believe in evil are the ones who practice it.

FINANCIAL HOSTAGE

We, as a part of the world community, are sometimes literally held hostage by a small group of agitators who create a large amount of damage to enrich themselves. They start wars, or are in positions where they can put financial or political policies in place that are to the detriment of one country or another. They cause whole towns to starve for jobs by building highways that bypass these little communities.

While planning the highway, they will buy up the cheap land bordering the town that is bypassed and put the exit there on the cheap land — their land, where they now build businesses, rest stops and gas stations. They cause stocks in a company to drop, so the investors lose their investment; then they will buy that stock at a reduced price and make lots of money when they sell at a higher price later on. The Madoff's $50 billion Ponzi scheme is another prime example of greed and corruption.

These unscrupulous people alter so many people's lives and cause countless people to suffer untimely, sad and wretched deaths due to their selfish actions, and the wars they start and fuel. War's greatest purpose now, and through history, has been to acquire power and money. The warmongers don't care who gets killed in the process; look at who the Nazi financiers were. Some lived in America. I say, war is the absence of good or God, and the people who start or support wars are doing something wrong and un-

Christian.

The big banks and Wall Street firms that created the mortgage sub-prime meltdown have caused the whole world to go into recession, and many people will take or lose their lives as a direct result. These banks constantly hold most of us hostage by pressuring us to take the worst loans, as they refuse to offer us better ones, even though they can and we qualify. They then turn around and call you to shake you down for money, just like organized crime. They call it their "collection department" but they're just hired thugs.

These financial people need to do their jobs responsibly, saving lives and livelihoods in the process, and saving communities. Analysts caution that there could be as many as 25 million homeowners with an "underwater mortgage," before this housing recession ends. Many will lose their homes to foreclosure or simply abandon the properties. They may want to acquire a cheaper property than their current home, but by then their credit will be damaged and the banks won't give them loans. As of March 31 2009, that number is already close to 14 million in underwater home loans.[7]

We have seen a disturbing trend of shipping our manufacturing jobs to foreign countries and this is being done by our American companies. These companies used this country to build themselves up, and now they kick us to the curb and take our jobs away to foreign countries.

---

[7] Shenn, Jody, "'Underwater' Mortgages to Hit 48%, Deutsche Bank Says (Update1)", Bloomberg.com,
http://www.bloomberg.com/apps/news?pid=20603037&sid=adBYDzUMt68k, website accessed November 17, 2009.

Shipping jobs overseas is the most shameful act and totally unpatriotic. Doesn't anyone care about this country?

We are being held hostage. We have been loyal employees, customers, and supporters of these companies. They were pillaging and plundering when the going was good, and now they are not staying here to help us end the crisis. In fact, they are increasing the impact. They are sentencing us to difficult times and an unsteady future with almost certain doom. This is what we get for believing in the promises of these greedy capitalists who say the unregulated free markets are not dangerous, and are good for the country. It's obvious disciplined capitalism is the answer.

I must comment, real believers of any god will not enrich themselves at the expense of their brethren, so are these capitalists, here and around the globe, really believers in their respective gods? Their actions say no and show they are all hypocrites when they pray. Are you angry and Shocked?

Some think the architects of this recession wanted to weaken the global economy, so it will be easier to move into foreign countries and their economies, and buy foreign companies and assets, and increase their power for a cheap price. They have already plundered and pillaged the American economy enough and now totally control it; it is time for them to expand to more green and profitable pastures around the world. Someone even suggested that the architects can create one global currency, much like Europe, or a slightly different version with four currencies; North and South Americas would have one currency between them. Europe and the Asian and African continents will each have one. This could happen if poverty forces countries to remove their borders. Some businessmen are already buying cheap real estate and businesses around the world, in an accelerated feeding frenzy created by the recession.

FOOD

Highly refined and processed foods are suspected to be the major source of illness in the developed countries. When people eat a more natural range of organic grown foods, instead of a Western diet consisting of mostly processed foods, it is possible to turn back the ill effects suffered from eating less healthy, mass-produced products.

According to many sources, including an article in *The New York Times*, due to terribly insufficient testing standards and a questionable lack of concern by producers in the food industry, there is more bovine excrement and E. Coli bacteria in our foods than you thought.[8] Because of mass production, factories cannot always maintain a clean setting to produce safe food. The assembly lines are moving too quickly and they are trying to keep costs to a minimum. The companies also put defective animals with Mad Cow disease back into the food chain; parts of the defective animals are removed and what is assumed to be the good remaining parts are put back into the food chain. They do not know what long-term effects this procedure will have. They are taking a chance on

---

[8] Moss, Michael, "E. Coli Path Shows Flaws in Beef Inspection," The NY Times.com,
http://www.nytimes.com/2009/10/04/health/04meat.html?_r=1, October 3, 2009.

risking the whole society just to make money.

If the tissue of these sick animals still has the disease, it could kill millions of people. Some of us may already be infected, thanks to George Bush's lax testing requirements. Other countries follow varied procedures, including burning the whole animal. An animal starts showing signs of Mad Cow after approximately 30 months, thus our ignorant approach has been to slaughter animals before that age so no one will know if they are infected, usually at 24 months.

Thirty months are when the infection becomes detectable, if an animal is afflicted. So we are obviously eating the infected ones along with the good. It takes hours for other countries to test for the disease, while we use archaic methods, which take days. As a result, some countries test one in four, or even 100% like Japan does, while it is said the US simply eats the evidence at an early age. Are you Shocked and in Awe?

Japan found a cow with the illness at the age of less than 24 months, while we eat all of our young cows at that age. A young animal, less than 24 months, can be infected with these prions. These are proteins which cause the disease and the young animal may not show signs of infection. These prions cannot be destroyed by extreme cold or extreme heat when cooked. How will we know if we don't test but rather eat them all? How many of us may already be infected? Mass production of tainted and unsafe food is a serious problem. There are countries that have suspended importation of American beef products as a result. Indifference, about the health and safety of beef consumers, has caused other countries who import

American beef to be alarmed to the extent of refusing to bend to this country's pleas to resume importation of our unchecked, possibly tainted beef products.

There were massive riots in foreign places when they did import our beef in 2008. MSNBC reported that our beef industry was only allowed to test 1% of beef for Mad Cow disease during George Bush's rule.[9] The market for mass-produced food is so massive and profitable that the companies selling these products cut corners in safety and cleanliness to get the food to market faster. They are allowed to include ingredients that are known to be dangerous for ingestion by humans. One such chemical additive is monosodium glutamate, commonly known as MSG, a compound that's toxic to your nerve cells. Even though it has been thought to cause a plethora of health concerns including excitotoxicity, resulting in damage to your nerve cells, companies are still allowed to add MSG to the food. Is excitotoxicity causing Alzheimer's, MS, ADD, autism, diabetes, cancer and strokes? Is nerve damage from MSG why kids run around and are restless so much? We must have conclusive studies done. High fructosecorn syrup, hydrogenised oil, homogenized or pasteurized milk, hydrogenated corn oil, and half the stuff in your pantry and refrigerator containing trans-fats are suspected to be not fit for long-term human consumption in varying quantities. But again not enough conclusive tests are being done because of company lobbyists. How do these affect growing children, whose tolerance is lower than adults?

---

[9] "Feds Fight Broad Testing for Mad Cow Disease: False Positives Could Harm Meat Industry, USDA Argues," *Associated Press,* http://www.msnbc.msn.com/id/18924801/, May 29, 2007.

The big question is, what new poison are we creating in our bodies when we mix the different chemicals from the various things we eat in one or two meals? How much high fructose corn syrup is the daily allowance that is not harmful to adults? What is the dosage for children? Can that syrup mixed with MSG from other foods in varying amounts cause cancer, diabetes, ADD and autism? We need to find out; after all, your children consume these products in their snacks constantly, as most snacks are made with one or more of these chemical compounds or dangerous cocktails, which can harm them more easily while they are young and their little bodies are more easily damaged by a smaller dosage than an adult's is. Have long-term studies been done on growing children who consume different amounts to see the potential health risks they can develop? So many of their favorite cheese snacks contain MSG and other long-named chemicals. Read the labels. Is this causing some of the children's diseases that we are now seeing? I think yes.

Drugstores are checking the drugs they give you to make sure they do not interact badly with each other, so why not protect our kids from these chemical mixes in foods and candy as well? There has been an attempt, in 2009, to pull certain drugs containing acetaminophen off the shelves, because people get it from so many different medications that they unknowingly overdose themselves when taking products together. Could it be that we ate certain chemicals when we were young and that is why our offspring are born with medical problems? I think yes. The world has been using MSG since 1909, when it was patented. We have been using it for generations now, more than 100 years, and that long-term use is concerning.

Our parents may have been affected by MSG and passed on defects to us, which we are amplifying and passing on to our own kids. Hereditary diseases do not mean the past food producers are not to be blamed and are not liable. I think they are, as they caused it and started it with the poisoning of our parents and grandparents since 1910. Obviously, it is too late for direct retribution or compensation, but that can still come in the form of outlawing the use of MSG, and saving any future generation from its poisonous effects. We will actually be saving lives.

There is now a startling occurrence of drugs and pesticides turning up in the public water system. The experts say the levels are not high enough to be alarmed about, but they are not discussing the fact that the majority of babies are fed their formulas using the water from their home taps. The concentration of these dozens of chemicals, while they may not be very harmful to adults, are quite detrimental to babies, as the level of concentration is hundreds of times more than their little bodies can endure. Are there any studies to tell if there can be possible links between child mortality rates, autism, ADD, and cancers and the amount of public water ingested by babies? Can the babies acquire long-term and short-term diseases from this contaminated water? I think so.

Are we poisoning a whole young generation? Isn't this like the Romans and the lead poisoning they suffered? Some say that lead poisoning brought down the powerful Roman Empire. What will happen to baby boys drinking estrogen in their milk? Will they have changes in their little bodies as a result of this? Estrogen affects adult males and females in different ways, so how will it affect the tiny, helpless babies? Will baby girls have early puberty, early sex and early pregnancies? Aren't they doing that already?

The drug industry and food industry go hand in hand. Unsafe foods make you slightly ill enough so that the drug industry can maintain, but not cure, the effects. The same small clique of wealthy people in the top 1% of the country, who own the large food companies, and can afford to buy large amounts of stock in them, are the ones who own and invest in drug companies. So when their food products make you sick, their drug products can help you and maintain your illness, for large profits. A neat little cycle, right? This is the kind of capitalism the politicians and some in the media support.

The ingredients are enough to make you sick! Ferrous sulfate, thiamin mono-nitrate, partially hydrogenated oils, maltodextrin, disodium phosphate, and monosodium glutamate are just some of the ingredients in one of my favorite cheese snacks. Hey, wait a minute! They advertised monosodium glutamate (MSG) in the ingredients. Wasn't that nice of them? They actually told you what poisons you are being fed. Regarding food, some say the rule is, if you can't read it, don't eat it.

I guess I was wrong and it's legal to feed us with good, yummy poison, as long as they put it on the label. Companies make it known to us that some ingredients are deadly — like those in cigarettes — but they do not have to stop producing them. It seems it's not the job of the authorities to protect us either. They have a lot of stock in the drug companies, I guess. Wasn't Bush's guy involved with some flu drug company? And didn't another guy, a senator or congressman, own a chain of hospitals? Follow the money.

Speaking of Bush's guy, his name is Donald Rumsfeld and he was formerly President Ronald Reagan's guy. My editor, Sigrid, sent me an article that really exposed this individual and showed his true colors. Apparently, Don Rumsfeld was the CEO of, and afterward president of, G.D. Searle, a company that manufactured an arguably toxic product called aspartame. It is a sweetener used in many products instead of sugar, but it is said to be poisonous. It is used in more than 5,000 foods and beverages sold worldwide, and in many food products like sugarless gum, diet soda, snacks and so many more foods that your children consume. This statement is advertised on the company's website.[10]

The article on NewsWithViews.com states, "According to the top doctors and researchers on this issue, aspartame causes headache, memory loss, seizures, vision loss, coma and cancer. It worsens or mimics the symptoms of such diseases and conditions as fibromyalgia, MS, lupus, ADD, diabetes, Alzheimer's, chronic fatigue and depression. Further dangers highlighted states that aspartame liberates free methyl alcohol. The resulting chronic methanol poisoning affects the dopamine system of the brain causing addiction. Methanol, or wood alcohol, constitutes one third of the aspartame molecule and is

---

[10] The NutraSweet Company, http://www.nutrasweet.com/, website accessed December 18, 2009.

classified as a severe metabolic poison and narcotic."[11]

Aspartame is known to contain a component called phenylalanine, which by itself carries its own dangers. You will notice that some products have this ingredient identified on their labels. The FDA's own toxicologist, Dr. Adrian Gross, told Congress that aspartame violated the Delaney Amendment which forbids putting any cancer causing products into food. Rumsfeld's company, Searle, tried for 16 years to have this dangerous product approved for human consumption and was constantly turned down by the FDA. He vowed to use his political connections to obtain approval.

Don Rumsfeld was on President Reagan's transition team and the day after taking office, the Reagan Administration appointed a certain Mr. Hayes as the new FDA Commissioner. Mr. Hayes quickly overruled all concerns and he approved aspartame for use. This was in 1981. You and your children have been consuming this poisonous drug in your food, sodas and snacks since that time. Mr. Hayes retired amid controversy later on when he secured an allegedly lucrative position at the advertising company for NutraSweet. Americans are consuming between 100 and 140 pounds of sugar per year, and many try to avoid this and the obvious health risks that may occur as a result. Unfortunately in doing so, they are guided to use alternative sweeteners that are even more dangerous and toxic than sugar.

---

[11] NWV Staff Writer, "Donald Rumsfeld and Aspartame," NewsWithViews.com,
http://www.newswithviews.com/NWVexclusive/exclusive15.htm, May 9, 2004.

A WTTG FOX5 News report supports this information. Their report highlights some well known products that use aspartame including diet coke, yogurt, cookies, pudding mix, ice cream and vitamins; it shows that aspartame is commonly known by the brand names Equal and NutraSweet.[12]

The National Soft Drink Association (NSDA) in 1983 said that aspartame was very unstable in its liquid form and urged the FDA to suspend approval of the product in sodas. One of their concerns was that in liquid form, when aspartame gets above 85 degrees Fahrenheit, it breaks down into diketopiperazine (DKP) and formaldehyde, which are both toxic. To many doctors this is of particular concern when baking your cookies and cakes at home, or when Equal or NutraSweet are added to teas, coffee and other hot drinks as they are usually over 100 degrees.

Such are the blessings of Don Rumsfeld, Ronald Reagan and aspartame. Interestingly enough, the company Ajinomoto, maker and supplier of both MSG and aspartame, provides a rebuttal service aptly named the Aspartame Information Service, which during the Bush presidency issued rebuttals to the media and other interests, on behalf of the product aspartame.

WTVJ (NBC) has done reporting with similar findings and highlighting instances where the investigative bodies which approved NutraSweet were in fact funded by the NutraSweet Company.[13]

---

[12] "Fox NutraSweet Equal Aspartame," YouTube.com, http://www.youtube.com/watch?v=ELgW4KBY-o4, website accessed December 18, 2009.

[13] "Aspartame / NutraSweet - Report - WTVJ (NBC) - Part 1 of 2," YouTube.com, http://www.youtube.com/watch?v=zf5Rfbjcx5I&NR=1,

The CBS show *60 Minutes* did their own investigative reporting confirming the stories, and also highlighted the shocking find that the cancers and other health problems experienced by the lab animals are showing up in humans twenty years later. This is as expected by the many investigators who tried over the years to have the product reviewed again and banned.[14]

This product and its purveyors, including Don Rumsfeld and Ronald Reagan, are thought to be responsible for millions of people's health problems and even deaths around the world, over the last 30 years.

There is also another sweetener on the market that has been used for a much longer period of time, which contains a product called saccharin that is thought to be equally dangerous to human health. The product is marketed under the brand name Sweet 'n Low.

Whatever we have been taught since birth is what we will believe without question, and that's wrong. This applies to food, customs and even religions, as we should be curious for our own well being. Take cannibals for instance; their offspring were taught to eat people. They were happy and their culture endured till modern days. Hopefully, they are all gone now but I don't know. Look at us; some of us are carnivores, including myself. We will eat almost anything that is dead. Just put some sauce on it. I love Chinese food and they cook everything, including

---

website accessed December 18, 2009.

[14] "Aspartame - Part 1 of 2 -- 60 Minutes Segment -- 12/29/1996," YouTube.com,
http://www.youtube.com/watch?v=dDqUpuZu8mY, website accessed December 18, 2009.

snakes and scorpions!

We have now made a delicacy out of raw meat and fish. There are people who have eaten dog meat and cat meat while thinking it was some other dead animal, like beef or stripped pork. I know now because I used to eat at one of those places without knowing. How about small producers of minced meats? How can we be sure about what they are mincing to sell to us? Aren't we just another type of vulture? We've gone from dead, cooked animals to raw meat and fish. I wonder where it will end. We are an imaginative bunch.

GANGS

Has anyone seen the series on TV called "Gangland" on the History Channel, or any of a number of other documentaries about thug and gang life? They call themselves gang bangers and they are increasing their membership daily, with your defenseless kids. Defenseless because you have not given them a strong and sensible reason to not be sucked in by the peer pressure and other reasons kids decide to join (for instance, coming from a broken home or having a cold relationship with their parents). One big reason is what you tell them to believe, about God, but we will come to that topic later on.

Watch the prison documentaries and you will see the kind of life inside the penitentiary that you are condemning your children to. What's the alternative? You teaching them to become a legal thief like our banking gangsters, the Bernie Madoffs? Or a loving, misguided religious worker? Your children deserve more from you than being taught the art of religious dormancy. Sadly, they are going to the gangs in search of a future, only to be disappointed in the end, of course, as gang life never amounts to anything good, for anyone. If they quit, they die. Prison is their only future. Some people prefer to enlist in the military, but these days they are coming back in body bags for the whims of the wealthy. Wars are now fought for oil and power. Do you want to sacrifice your children for the wars for wealth?

It is so easy for any of us to lose our kids to a gang

these days. Your children are not being inspired to do anything else, as some ancient, even prehistoric religions, a bevy of corrupt politicians, a corrupt banking system, and a small group of corrupt religious zealots and pedophiles, running the largest religion and most powerful government and economy in the world, have the children reeling in fear, disgust and hopelessness about their gloomy future.

The gangs, who seem pretty spotless compared to the aforementioned crooked groups, have been expanding their operations for years and have cliques halfway around the world. These are the big gangs that we have all heard about, but there are also local, smaller gangs who try to keep the big gangs from setting up shop in their neighborhood. The kids are encouraged to enlist in the gangs in middle school and high school, so they are approached by other friends before you even suspect the dangerous atmosphere they're in at school. It is so bad that some schools in NYC have armed police patrolling and they are handcuffing kids for crimes, while on the school property. I've seen a few led out in handcuffs.

Remember, your child is usually lost forever if he or she joins a big gang, as they kill you if you leave. When gang members are rounded up, they are deported if they are foreigners, and they start new chapters or branches in their old country. This is how the biggest gangs have spread worldwide. They commit criminal activities to survive and the drug trade is the fastest way to riches. It is already in your children's schools. When our children see us unable or unwilling to do something about the corruption in the whole system, as they see bad politicians, bad clergy, bad police, uncontrolled capitalistic greed and price gouging that wreck their futures, they get angry and end up wanting to strike out for survival. Because they are disappointed in us, they form or join gangs for safety in numbers.

Long ago people would see drugs, crime and gang activity move into their area and say that it was someone else's problem. Today, it's our problem. We are the ones who stand to lose our children.

Since our invasion of Afghanistan, poppy production has increased tremendously. The drug traders are getting richer, while our kids are stealing to buy the drugs in America. How is that possible? These gangs are working for the negative forces at play in our crumbling society. The gangs, the warlords and warmongers, share a similar approach to doing their evil businesses. They enjoy doing the crimes they do, as it is profitable. It is not that they are always victims of circumstance and have to do crimes. Very few of us are. I have always done things that I enjoyed doing, some of which were not positive, but we have to improve as we go along. We have to think of the children's future now, not our own.

One hundred years ago, the church had a strong following and there were no gangs. Slowly, these percentages have been changing and now, the church has an increasingly smaller percentage of followers in ratio to the gangs, who are increasing in numbers worldwide. The trend does not show signs of slowing and this clearly suggests that the gangs will eventually have double the numbers of the church. The gangs are made up of your lost and angry children.

If we want to stop the escalation, we must find an alternative to this failing religious belief that is not successful in helping to keep our families together. That alternative is enlightenment. The new age requires a new idea about spirituality to complement the new information we learn about our past and its religions, and also to combat the new problems we see like drugs, gangs, terrorism and other things still to come, which will threaten the cohesion and very survival of the family.

When we only had the concern of poverty and tyrant rulers thousands of years ago, religion was a strong enough tool used by parents and churches to keep their families together, but now the stakes are much higher, and more "in your face" immediate, with gangs and drugs in our schools. Ancient religion is not efficiently equipped to deal with these new 21st century threats, so it has to take a back seat to a more direct approach of truth and spirituality to keep the family together.

What we learn through technology pokes holes in religious beliefs, so we have to give children something different to strengthen themselves against gangs and drugs. Luckily, we don't have to look far for the answer. The spirituality at the core of all religions is the only tool immediately within reach that can help them fight back, and they do not have to leave the religion they know to find it. Spirituality is a step beyond religion but the children can still get to it through their outdated religions — through the door, as Jesus said.

The system of policing crime in our communities has always been an uphill battle, with no good solution. The most popular solution is to put the criminals behind bars. To that end, the prison system has become a power unto itself, with more prisons being built all the time. The amount of supplies and resources needed to run the world's largest prison system makes it a billion dollar business and the good folks at the top, who are benefiting, realize that they must have a steady influx of criminals to fill the ever increasing number of new prisons.

The prison systems do their best to keep the number of inmates high, which means having a strong and functioning gang population inside, who are controlling what goes on outside, ensuring that the gangs bring in new kids, so as to maintain a steady flow of felons through the whole system. It seems some are depending on the un-rehabilitated criminals being released onto the streets to indoctrinate more lost kids into gangs. The proof of this is that prisons do not pursue proper rehab programs on a large scale. *Time.com* states that some prisons have been rumored to be selling human body organs for illegal profits. This also happens elsewhere in the world, including China. That is a new business venture that is just now rearing its ugly head. It is easy to arrange gang fights and have new dead donors to facilitate this new enterprise.

Drugs are allowed to be brought in by the gangs to keep the inmates on edge, thereby defeating rehab and maintaining the mindset of the criminal. Every action by the prison is geared to keep the inmate population growing, mostly with gang members, as they have a working hierarchy to control their members and ensure their gang enlistments increase inside and outside the prisons. Our children are the only targets who will feed the appetite for new gang members. We need to save them by giving them something to believe in that will have a stronger impact on them than the old failing religions of the past. Everything is going against your children; the system is geared to make them criminals and gang members, so be aware and try to take them back, as you are all they have and you have to support them.

GREED

People should try to enrich themselves but not at the expense of others or the country: for example, war profiteering. Sadly, modern war is more of a money-making device than the result of a security concern. There are billion dollar no-bid contracts, and paid private security companies with more mercenaries to do the fighting than our own soldiers. American contractors got reconstruction contracts in the Iraq war instead of local Iraqi contractors, which then caused the locals to join the militias. We, in turn, had to bribe the militias to not fight against us.

Many of us have turned away from helping others and allowed them to sink into despair. But these others are still part of the chain we call human, and humanity is what separates us from other species of animals on this planet. When a person loses his focus on humanity and is consumed by his greed, he becomes like a pig squealing at the top of his voice, "I want more, more, more!" Never mind that life is too short to ever enjoy the true benefits of that wealth.

There is a great deal of squealing going on in our global society right now. More stealing, grabbing, backbiting, groping in the mud of crime and deceit, in this slop of greedy politics mixed with greedy religion. Politics and religion must remain separate. They fit together so perfectly because they both revolve around illusion in today's society. They had humble, well-meaning, and intelligent beginnings and were invented to help people to create and live in a better society.

But they have been hijacked and allowed to become tools of the corporations, which now mix them together, and use them to confuse and control the population. Using these politicians and religions as tools to enrich themselves, the corporations create divisions and havoc among the people. This helps the tools to function even more efficiently. War is one of the best uses of the tools, by and for the corporations; it creates more division and profits.

The hidden casualties are our family members, who are sent to fight these pointless and sometimes illegal wars. Our children are watching, and they are the gatekeepers of the future, so be careful that they don't lock you out for being part of the corporations, banking gangsters, politicians and greedy religions. When you steal or do wrong, don't tell them it was all for them because they won't want your blood money. Children have higher, more virtuous principles than we do. Are they wrong? Should they grow up to be as the greedy and destructive are amongst us? Our conscience must guide us to teach them to do good or they will find a version of hell, as the greedy always do at the end of their lifetime.

PART TWO

GOD

The greatest Shock and Awe on America comes in the form of religion and the various religious beliefs of thousands of years ago. Mistakenly, religion undermines the progress of modern man and his stride into the future. Religious ideology resists the need to intellectually progress further than the superstitions of our ancestors. You are taught that everything is the will of God, so let it ride; do nothing to change your circumstances, as your attempts will be futile; everything is His will and He will make it change for you, and shower you with success when He is good and ready. If you succeed, then God wanted that for you, and if you fail, it is because God has bigger and better things in store for you.

You are taught whatever you achieve is given to you by God — your God, my God, The God and some other God just down the street. That's false and misleading, as religions teach you not about God but about fear: fear of an idea of there being a vengeful God watching you. Religions do not teach you that God has long hair, is white or black, and speaks with a stammer because they do not know themselves. They have no clue who or what God is or if He or She or It even exists. They blindly praise and blame God for everything. That's what I call the Blind Mice Syndrome. If you let them lead you, then that's the blind leading the blind. How unfortunate it is for the soul or the family that depends on those blind mice.

When human beings have lived their lives as they

chose to, and are now in a state of mind where they realize that they may depart the Earth at any moment, they will start to think about the meaning of life, and their purpose and achievements. They will think of the journey that they have taken, of the reason for that journey, and what was learned and accomplished. They usually arrive at the understanding that life is a journey of a cyclic nature. You are made to take that journey and taught to seek wisdom, happiness and success through your monetary accomplishments. In the end you may discover that what you sought at the end was inside you all the time, since the beginning, and not in your wallet.

Discovery of your inner intelligence, understanding, respect for all life, and the ability to humbly be happy with whatever you have are what tell you that you have been successful. These concepts are what you will take through death's door, while leaving your money behind. Jesus taught when you come to know the beginning, you will also know the end, so don't bother to search for the end but rather find the beginning — your source inside you — and live, knowing yourself.

When you acquire wisdom and humility, this may lead you to realize that there is something called enlightenment. Enlightenment is what you discover had been present and functioning in yourself all the while, albeit without your knowledge. You are an enlightened being, functioning in a physical body. When you find your enlightenment, spiritual consciousness is awakened for you, by you, in you, and it is the key to help you on the next part of your journey wherever you go when you die.

What you were taught as a child in Sunday school or religious school about death and salvation will not make much sense anymore, as you ponder your life and you near your inevitable death. When you die, you leave your body behind — you know this, so will you then seek Earthly pleasures? Strapping young men, pretty young women, riches and some kind of real estate, like a throne in heaven? No. What can you use them for when you are dead and in your spirit form? Nothing, and will they be available to you in heaven? Again, no.

I am not suggesting that you change whichever religion you follow. I am religiously eclectic, having the three major religions in my family, which are Hindu, Roman Catholic and Muslim. I also went to an Anglican school and was in the choir for three years. I took communion and shared in the Eucharist weekly, attended a Presbyterian church prior to that, and frankly grew up in and participated in all, as they have the same basic purposes of enlightenment at the core but with differing rituals. It's just that you have not been taught to identify what that enlightened core is and how to break through each religion's dogma to get there. Whether you choose to follow any one religion and way of life, a few of them, or none at all, this is not about you or me. This is about your family and your world. When you spread Gnosis or knowledge, and enlightenment in your circle, you help them all to help themselves.

Question: why not follow a few religions instead of just one, if they are all from one God? They will each teach you something different about the truth of enlightenment. All of you have friends and family in need; maybe you were guided to read this book by your higher self, that thing you call your guardian angel, your over-self, your conscience, God and other names. This may be your calling — to learn about and to carry this teaching of enlightenment further.

We do not live in the traditional black and white world of the fifties and sixties, with white picket fences, oppressed and obedient spouses, widely accepted and approved apartheid and daily problems we could deal with. The real problem these days, although happening outside your family, is affecting everyone inside your family. The happy, simple family of the fifties and sixties is no more; they are replaced with a world of chaos, confusion and warfare of a different kind. War with other countries, terrorism and gang warfare are in your face every day and in your family's future, so please don't run away, as there is no place to hide. We have to face the problems and solve them. We can start by finding enlightenment — through or without religion.

There is as much superstition associated with religion as there are facts in the stories and writings you encounter. Most of the stories have some fact mixed with fiction, culture and superstition, so as to achieve the desired impact of awe, confusion and fear about religion and, indeed about God. With that same train of thought, people tend to stop at a point of belief where religion is king and any proof or resistance given by science is the enemy, witchcraft or demon-speak. With that same lack of thought, they limit the role God plays in their lives and so too what they believe about religion. They live as though God can only see the good they do in church and God is blind to their misgivings in their everyday lives. They paint God as an entity incapable of creating more than they see in front of their noses. I am not saying there is a God, but if there was, they demean Him.

They will somehow choose to believe that God is a living, breathing person or entity that is extreme, and *He* is unintelligent enough to be vengeful, and bring down plagues and destruction on your peaceful existence and that of your family, if you don't become a slave to the religion's dogmatic way of life. They will stop at that point. They will not choose to believe the opposite is true; that the real truth is that what they call God could be so much better and so much more.

Is there one God with different religious names? Is the Christian God the same God which the other religions of the world worship? I think not. How do they know if they do not even try to learn each other's religion? If it were the same God with different names around the world, then we would all have the same set of rules to follow but this is not so. Why do we have different rules? If there is one God, then we all are misinterpreting the rules, and that is sufficient proof that we are wrong about some parts of religion and God.

One religious following can't be carnivores while another is vegetarian and another vegan, while yet another's rule is not to eat fish without scales or with shells. There are a multitude of facts which prove our misunderstanding of there being one God. One God would mean one religion, and none of the gods seem to vehemently oppose the other, so there must be no gods, but only over-zealous and ambitious churches which perpetuate the stories.

How wrong do we have to be about religion before we understand that God or the idea of God only offers us comfort in our time of need? I have leaned on that support time and again, before now. I understand what God is, and what comfort and hope is afforded to those in need. I cannot tell people who are taught to pray, to not draw upon the strength that their God will provide, to not turn away from being needy and to instead draw strength from their inner source. They were not taught this.

There are some who cannot do this and they need the idea of God to comfort them. God is always portrayed as a person with feelings, and this provides comfort when compared to a perceived empty and unfeeling universe, but the fact is you are the one with feelings and compassion; you are the one who has to constantly give, and in this action of constantly giving, you find reward in giving comfort to others. You become the god to others, a god more real than the varying religious ideas called gods, in different cultures around the world. How easy it is to see the fault in someone else's god but not your own. If it is just a matter of each religion's interpretation of God that is wrong, then the question remains, how much of the interpretations are right?

It is difficult to wrap our minds around the numbers. One multiplied by 1,000 makes 1,000, 1,000 x 1,000 makes 1 million, 1 million x 1,000 makes 1 billion, 1 billion x 1,000 makes 1 trillion. 1 trillion x 1,000 makes... That's the number of planets out there, some with life, *just in our galaxy alone*, and there are trillions of galaxies in the universe, in this one dimension we are aware of. That's how large this universe is and how insignificant religion is.

There is no religion that is important in real life; humanity and co-existence are more important. Only our survival is important against our own destructive and mischievous selves, and other challenges in the universe, possibly an asteroid hitting us and destroying the Earth. Smaller ones hit us every day. There is a bigger picture here in the universe than religion and gods. Unfortunately, man retards his progress and denies his potential by believing in both above himself. If an astronaut says that God told him to destroy the International Space Station or the Space Shuttle because Satan's demons may capture it, we would put that astronaut in the asylum and say he was mad, and we would be right. Satan does not exist in space but only in the minds of crazy astronauts. What does that say about the sanity of religion?

Mankind will believe all sorts of superstitions and stories, which a modern ten-year-old in grade school could devise — David killing the giant Goliath, and Sampson having the magical strength of God contained in his hair... Delilah cutting his hair and destroying his power, angels destroying Sodom and Gomorrah, Lot's wife turning into a pillar of salt and many more. It was easy to invent those stories centuries ago and there is no one around now to prove they were not true. Those are just some of many stories which call on the readers' belief in superstition, or for the readers' absence of the ability to think independently, in order to follow religion and religious dogma, and develop a need for the church and those in its employ.

There are many people who know more about God, religion (as it is actually a separate subject) and spirituality than I do. If you have encountered them and learned about life from them, then that was the purpose of their meeting with you, as that has now become the purpose of us all — to teach truth to each other. If you have not had the distinct honor of meeting them or learning something from them, then it means I have been endowed with that honorable task and will fulfill my mission to enlighten you, and bring you wisdom, knowledge, understanding, and ultimately peace, ascension and enlightenment.

Man's unfortunate past of being misled and misdirected by religion is a past that has changed our present and our future to something that has not resulted in the best outcome for the human family. We are trained in the mistaken ways that religion and its dogma dictate to us, and the disastrous results are there for all to see, in history and in our present time. War, with murder and mayhem, has plagued us for thousands of years, usually because of, and with support from, religion and because of religious dictates and the people who misuse them.

Because of man's willingness to fight, spiritual relief is distant, though still in your lifetime. You can start now to bring about a better future by learning about a more honorable, sensible, respectful, and enlightened way to live day to day in this fleeting existence, and enhance your experiences and those of your loved ones. Our experience and understanding of religion can be useful if used as step one, in the journey or quest of attaining and understanding consciousness, becoming enlightened, and ultimately, reaching step two, which we were taught that Jesus and other prophets achieved. There are more steps after that, of course.

Religion is not a master plan by God but is in fact just the opposite; it was a plan by man. It may have been a wise tool in controlling the ignorant population of the past, and controlling civil unrest in a time of need, but just like the old cars of 100 years ago, it has outlived its usefulness of being able to efficiently drive us now in the present, with our heightened level of education, technology and need for efficiency in everything, or for that matter, to play any substantive and meaningful role to help propel us into our bountiful future.

Mankind's failures can be blamed on his hand of destiny, a destiny he creates and changes each day: the fingers of the hand being racism, greed, hate, envy and religious fanaticism. All our other prejudices, vices and problems, I think stem from these. Without these bad fingers of choice, the hand will not function negatively. So, man can create a different hand, a better destiny with a better result: one with fingers of maybe love, spiritual freedom, goodwill, humor and intelligence. If man keeps those negative habits, his destiny is chosen or dictated for him, by the actions of his hand — his choices. You can't walk around with these negative thoughts and be a good person. You will just be a vessel of failure, eventually succumbing to your bad choices and deeds.

There is good and there is truth at the center of all major religions. They are just surrounded by a wall of ignorance, rituals, superstitions, fear and the dogma which you must all break down, break through or throw away. I now have to make you curious, if only to prove me wrong. You have nothing to lose, as gaining new knowledge or strengthening your own beliefs is not a loss. To do that, you will have to ask some questions, do some reasoning and get some answers. You may even save your children, in the process, from their friends in gangs who are trying to indoctrinate them, and give them a new family, one that exists inside and outside of prison. Saving them...how about that? That's a gain, and certainly a good thing.

To a lot of worshippers, religion and its dogma are not a necessity, just an inconvenience they must partake in to follow the crowd; it is a fad, the "in" thing. They think that because everyone else does it, they should too, as everyone can't be wrong. It is a small bet on an unseen, unsure thing, just in case there is a god. They say to themselves that it is better to practice a little religion, of any kind, than none at all, and you should hedge your bets with it just in case the religion thing turns out to have some truth in it. That type of thinking shows up true in the way we live our lives, and I may need correcting, but it looks to me that this applies to the majority of the world. We don't spend 80% of our day praying in church, which is what we would do if we thought that religion was true and the priests were right — that it was the right and true thing to do, and some multi-ethnic God was watching over the whole Earth. A couple of hours a week or per year is enough for most of us, to follow the crowd and save face.

We don't wholeheartedly believe all of it and also don't have the time for it. The kids are in school, you have to get to work and deal with all that drama going on in your daily life. Your ex has a new squeeze who is taking care of your kids and all that. We can't even take much time to cook a good breakfast each morning, hence the reason we feed our kids processed, mass-produced, unhealthy, sugar-coated cereals, waffles, bagels, jelly-filled treats on the go, and the like. We dabble halfheartedly as a precaution, in the different versions of Christianity, which has some 38,000 denominations, and also in other religions, just in case they turn out to have some truth in them. We don't want to be damned in a hellish place somewhere.

We are constantly bombarded with a myriad of daily problems. This cuts down on the precious little time we have for religion, for ourselves, for our families and for paying those bills...or dodging the pesky bill collectors. I estimate that only about 5% of Christians, or other religious persons around the world, are really into the belief of their religious and spiritual salvation, and practice their religion constantly. Those are the priests and their hierarchy. The rest of us simply look at them, wink and think they are fanatics, or just lucky to have the time and patience to be penniless and practicing religion, which is what you have to be, to become a real believer — penniless, as you have to spend all of your time serving the religion in one way or another, not running after money, as the rest of us do. Mind you, there are new groups of religious followers who now say their God wants them to be rich, another twist to an already twisted story.

We in the real world — the fast-paced, modern, civilized, bill-paying world — can't tie ourselves down with too much ancient superstitious religious dogma, so some of us decide to pick a religion or version of it that we think makes as much sense, and has as little inconvenience, as the rest of the dogma-plagued religions. The Christian religion (all the different varieties of it, in my opinion) is more attractive and convenient for many people around the world, because (1) the religion does not take away your meat products. Think of how many Christians who can actually wean themselves off meat, especially BBQ, and even strange exotic meats and fish including snake, shrimp, lobster, clams, crabs, sushi, iguana, dog or monkey meat, which many people eat around the world. And (2) does not require you to take time out of your busy day to fervently pray five or 10 or more times a day like the Buddhists, Hindus and others. And (3) you don't have to spend more than a couple of convenient hours one Sunday morning per week in the church for a quick fix, like maybe a short sermon, or a fast confessional cleansing and you're finished.

Sounds like a colon cleansing, or a car tune-up: quick procedure and you're out, and back in the race. Ask yourself, how many of us believe in flaming airborne chariots and magical miracle fixes, in this day and age of fax machines and computers? Not very many, right? Not even the pedophile preachers apparently, or they would stop their twisted and wretched sport.

There is a better, more convenient way. You won't need a church when you are taught the truth of all religions. First, I have to show you what arguments our children (yours and my two teenagers) are faced with when addressing any basic religious beliefs. If you cannot offer a realistic and reasonable explanation to them, believe me, they will think you are stupid.

You are already well on your way to losing the respect and pride your kids have in you because they are smarter than most people, including what you give them credit for. They are not accepting dogma as we do. If you turn them off mentally, it is too late to retrieve them because gangs are for life. I stress, if they try to leave the gang the members will kill them, so save them quickly before they join, as right now you can be losing them.

What is God? Did God create everything a few thousand years ago in the Garden of Eden? Was it done by magic or science, and if so, why is our galaxy millions of years old and the universe even older? Will there still be a hell if there is no God to fit into our traditional understanding of what a God and hell is believed to be? When your kid asks you these questions, what will you answer?

Is Jesus under attack? Yes, but not by me. I just got here. The attack started thousands of years ago, by people who made up religion and invented God, long before Jesus. When Jesus came along they killed Him. Why? Because He spoke and taught the truth, not the half truths you have been led to believe by the religions. He taught that we exist as part of the whole and must depend on ourselves to achieve enlightenment, and we should do good deeds for each other, whereas the church taught that God exists, and we must depend on and follow them, and serve them to get to Him. They killed Jesus and rewrote His message; this much is obvious.

There is hell only in your mind, I think, because our fearful version of a vengeful God needs a hell to complete the big picture. What about the other side of the coin, Satan? Will He also cease to exist if the truth about God were different? These are quite pungent questions and ideas that our children ponder, and the churches do not want us to bring up.

The wide-sweeping sayings, "God works in mysterious ways," and "It is intelligent design" don't work as well on our children, and their confused and uninformed friends, as they did when we were mindless kids, as we easily accepted what we were told, without question, alongside our misguided friends.

Children will ask you, does the entity or force we call God exist? The truth is there is a force but it exists in a different way from what we were taught. It is not an interactive force or form that we should worship in any way. Is there a heaven? Well, a woman's beauty could be heaven to most, so no, there is no religion's fantasy-heaven up there somewhere, with wings and pearly gates; it's all in your mind. Do the heavens from all different religions look the same? It will look like anything you want it to be, as it is all made up in your mind by you, to reflect what version of religion you have been taught. A Hindu's heaven won't have a hamburger joint but may have a franchise of "Tofu Heaven."

Can we just have goodness in our heart and call it God? Yes, although (1) it defeats the church's purpose for you to think there is not a fictional god to serve, so they would not approve, also (2) you will still be training yourself with the wrong principle of you having and serving a god, when the truth is you are not. Man's idea of God came from the need of someone to do good for others. Man suffered miserably, thousands of years ago, so he created an illusion, an oasis in the desert of agony. People needed a god, so they invented one, to help them endure and overcome the physical and mental stresses of that time: something fictitious that the Pharaohs and kings could not find or conquer. Are love, goodness and consciousness contained in our physical pumping, beating heart or are they in our minds or in our souls? The latter is correct, as you can transplant hearts. Is religion failing the world now? It always has. Look at our history of war and destruction by religious bodies. What is evil? Does it exist? Man does mischievous and wicked things, and we mischaracterize it and call it evil, suggesting it is something coming from a non-existent Devil. That is our misinterpretation of it.

If tribes don't know a mainstream god, are they living in hell? No. Does hell exist only when you know about your god? Yes, obviously. Does your god need Satan to exist? Again, yes. Hitler, a Christian, thought his deeds were right according to HIS twisted misunderstanding of what a Catholic god is, and wants and allowed him to do. He did his own bad deeds. No god helped or allowed him to.

Right and wrong are part of a concept; just look at the Crusades. Who was right, the Christians or the Muslims? They both killed a lot of each other's men, women and children. So was the murder of their enemies acceptable to or required by their gods? It was all religious misperception. Look around; it still continues to this day between some religious groups. Is there one God or Devil turning man against his brother? No, obviously the men in the Crusades and all wars had free will to fight and kill, so it was not a god's or some devil's fault, but their own.

Is there more negativity in the world than goodness? No, just a lot of poverty and suffering, which we can solve. Are the people who cause the bad things following Satan? No. Ask yourself, who caused the sub-prime meltdown that caused a worldwide economic meltdown, which then forced millions of people into poverty, destitution, despair, disease and desperation, and even to lose or take their lives and others' lives as a result? The answer is greedy people, not God or Satan. Are these greedy bankers the workers of Satan because of their avarice? No, they are just greedy. Lots of bankers and brokers are religious followers, who believe in unrestricted, free market capitalism that rewards a select few against the many. They are just hypocrites, if they are religious believers. The church receives donations from greedy people and companies, so are they bad? I don't think so. They just want and need money. How will your kids answer those questions? How will you answer your kids?

What about our political leaders? Are they and the churches just doing what they want without fear of God's wrath against them? Yes. If they don't even fear God's wrath, do they think there is really no God to fear? That's what their actions suggest. Would Jesus approve of the churches inviting the money lenders and politicians in? No. Would He be happy with them now running the churches as some do? After all, didn't He drive them out?

It appears the churches are making up their own minds and their own interpretations of the scriptures as they go, much as they have been doing all along throughout history. The fact is, if God were all powerful, then He would simply get rid of the Devil and everything would be fine. Then with the universe safe, we could all live in peace, mindlessly praising God forever, right? There are lots of questions we need to ask, and one chapter will not change eons of superstitions but the most important question is, what are the intelligent answers?

IN THE BEGINNING

First, there was the Old Testament. Second, there came the New Testament. Is there a third truth? Yes, and the truth is knocking, so let's open the door. Fear sells and the fear of God has helped the churches all along to sell misinformation, crosses, T-shirts, Bibles, and now air time on TV with new million dollar TV ministries. The same applies to religions in other parts of the world. With the help of television and the Internet, religion has become a more lucrative, international business enterprise. The churches collectively do more worldwide business than the banks. They sell fear of punishment for the sins of believers, sins against God's commandments and doctrines, but their biggest sell of fear is the fear of God's vengeance on nonbelievers.

Researching the word Christianity will give you its real history, which surprisingly, most people do not know in any substantial detail that could help them to decide how good or bad this religion and most others are to humanity's development. Christianity is one of four major religions that all stem from the teaching of Abraham. It began as a Jewish sect, and progressed or morphed to become what we now think it is, which is quite different from what it originally was. The religion has to constantly change to deal with social issues and the revelations of technology, which disprove many stories from the scriptures. Scientific proof also changes our understanding, to show how religion exists as some sort of superstition in today's world and which direction religion will go in the future, as we travel into space and learn about the other trillions of galaxies around us. So let's find out a few things, firstly the meaning of the words HALLUCINATE, BELIEVE, DOGMA, CULT and FICTION.

Hallucinate
To imagine sensing something: to imagine seeing, hearing, or otherwise sensing people, things, or events that are not present or actually occurring at the time

Believe
To think that something exists: to be of the opinion that something exists or is a reality, especially when there is no absolute proof of its existence or reality; believe in reincarnation

To have religious faith: to have a belief in God or in a religion's gods

Dogma
1. A religious belief: a belief or set of beliefs that a religion holds to be true

Cult
1. A religion: a system of religious or spiritual beliefs, especially an informal and transient belief system regarded by others as misguided, unorthodox, extremist or false; directed by a charismatic, authoritarian leader

2. A religious group: a group of people who share religious or spiritual beliefs, especially beliefs regarded by others as misguided, unorthodox, extremist, or false

Fiction

An untrue statement: something that is untrue and has been made up to deceive people

Each religion thinks the other is a cult, by them being false or misguided. So which one is right? All of them, I think. Does that mean they are all cults? A cult is just a group of religious believers, regardless of color, gender or rituals. Obviously, fiction is a large part of religion, as they all say there is one god, yet they have different rules and rituals to please that one god, and each religion says they have the one true god.

Funny play on words... DOGMA, AM GOD. The reverse of the word dogma is am god. AM GOD ...I ask who? I...I Am God. I think this is what Jesus taught. Not "I" meaning Him alone, but anyone who is strong enough and simple enough to see His truth, or His point of view and say "I." It is anyone who can understand the enlightenment that Jesus discovered and taught. It is the real truth against blind dogma. It does not profit us to be bogged down by words or by whose interpretation of Jesus' teachings, or any religion, is correct. So let us move on. In my view, religion was born out of the marriage of inspiration, desperation and delirium. We can separate the three and seek the inspired part of any religion.

Jesus taught that He had attained the enlightenment to be one with the creator, the force, the universe, or the consciousness we call God. No one argues that point, but they lose sight of it when they stop at Jesus being the only one able to attain such enlightenment. Jesus tried to show us the way to enlightenment, so that we could also achieve it right here on Earth, right now as He did. He showed us that He was as much a part of the whole as we were. Instead of bowing in fearful servitude to the whole, a whole which some of us do not choose to acknowledge or cannot understand, we should live as though we are of the whole, because we are. Be as the whole: respectable, brave, honest, kind and intelligent enough to progress past the ancient teachings and oppressive restrictions of thousands of years of delirium.

WHO OR WHAT IS GOD?

In the beginning, there was...what? Darkness and He made or gave light? That does not make much sense. Consciousness — the force — is like light, dispelling the darkness of ignorance but is the light a "He?" Is your God a "He," "She" or "It"? Is God an actual being sitting on a real throne, or is "It" really a gathering of souls or forces working together that we call God? People are so closed-minded on this subject. They think God can't be anything more than a magical man on a throne. I sense that religion was invented or hijacked by men, hence their superior status over women in this ancient concoction of ideas.

The topic of God is designed to be confusing, and that is the instrument the different religions have always copied from each other and used to control you: confusion, coupled with fear of the unknown. What or who is God? Is He a fictional savior of the tortured or is He the vengeful, playful torturer? Is He, It or She a hero of the wronged, or just a fictional tool, used by the churches and other religions thousands of years ago to keep their populations subservient, pacified, contented with their squalor and willing to please their oppressors, who at that time could have been the rulers working with the political help of the churches?

The church was seen as an essential middleman between the rulers and the population, and often would do the bidding of the rulers, to help maintain control, in exchange for all sorts of boons. Look around, has anything changed? No. The churches still work with the rulers and politicians to control you, for their mutual benefit. If you can't beat your enemy, then join him, so that is what these two great spinners of words did. They have learned over the ages to control you with their words.

We can see what God could be by seeing what He is not. A loving, intelligent God won't be vengeful, wicked or filled with darkness, confusion and despair. Remember the Bible story of the two mothers fighting over one baby? The real loving mom gave up the child instead of consenting to have the baby cut into two pieces. Likewise, in life, as with the mother, there is no room in love, for hate to exist. A real and loving God, like a loving parent, will not subject us to the suffering we experience on this Earth; the story of God constantly testing us and setting hurdles for us to overcome day after day, so we can reap our reward of qualifying to serve Him forever, does not fit into the image of an intelligent designer and parent, but does fit in with ideas of a delirious inventor.

This means we are not being told the truth, so we should understand that the opposite has to be true. The God consciousness we are taught to believe in may indeed exist, just not in the form we are taught. The force we seek as God is the source of spiritual enlightenment and goodness. Vengeance, war, death and destruction being brought down on us, sounds more like a story about Satan not God. Are we really made to fear and worship someone's idea of Satan, thinking it is God? After all, you've never seen what you are worshiping, have you? Chaos and slavery for any cause is usually associated with Satan. Are God and Satan two sides of the same coin, which is religion?

It may be that Abraham and the other elders of that time discovered the idea of a good force, but not understanding what it could be, they created this concept of God and the Devil, as that was the extent of their intelligence or education. They could not really understand the universe and all its secrets.

They were uneducated by our standards, and didn't know about planets and other galaxies even existing, so they went with what they knew. It's taboo for the churches to speak about space even now because they can't get the possibility of life on other planets to fit into their skewed stories of religion. Does Christianity address space in any intelligent way? The inventors thought it was just God and them — created in God's image no less — courageously battling against Satan in this poorly-conceived, limiting idea of the existence of heaven and hell. Their followers had no better ideas or understanding, so out of goodwill, respect, fear and blind desperate faith in wanting and needing an end to their suffering, they chose to follow and believe in the church's stories. We still do today, even though we now live in heaven, by their standards. We also now live in space. Are there demons in space now? There could be but only if they originate from the minds of our people up there. Would there be a Satan interacting with the life-forms in space? No, that's just crazy.

I ask you, are we still living in the past because of our religious misguidance, wandering aimlessly through the present and blinded of the future? Yes. Why are we living in the past? Well, that is where you have to be mentally to believe in demons and gods, heaven and hell and flaming chariots. Should we give up our evolving and ever-progressive intelligence to believe in prehistoric, superstitious religions of any type? No! If we do that, we will indeed be sacrificing our firstborns like Abraham, to the gangs, pimps and pushers who are waiting for them.

Starting with Jesus, and throughout the centuries, the understanding of the consciousness of the universe has been revealed many times before, and whereas any vocal proponents of that consciousness were quickly found out, dismissed, slaughtered or burnt at the stake as a witch or wizard to hide what they were saying, I think they have stopped the burnings now, so we will reveal it again. Where's the line separating the faithful, misled, loving priest and his friend, the corrupt politician? The politician can give you riches that you can't carry with you to the afterlife, and the loving but mistaken and misguided religions claim that they can give you something called salvation, yet they offer no guarantees, as (1) they've never been there, (2) they still don't know if it works, and (3) they do not have it down to a science. Isn't that ironic?

They try to ridicule science, so they can keep you in church, while all the while what they seek turns out to actually be a pure form of high science: dealing with the soul. Jesus' teaching is not about blind faith and magical miracles, but about a real and functioning force, and I think all forces are a form of science. Science, time, space, black holes, seeing the Andromeda Galaxy right now, as it was millions of years ago through a telescope… none of it is magic — it's real. It is intelligent science at work and it appears that tribal superstitions of religions have outlived their purpose and usefulness.

What if the religions don't understand what real salvation is? To me, salvation is not a reward you work toward receiving as a blessing for your work as a good person. The reward of salvation is not even a real thing given to you by any generous god. Salvation is just a word invented by a word spinner and used as a hook to keep you in a faulty religion. If you believe it exists, you can only get it by your good deeds anyway, not through the church, your donations or any other way.

Before "accepting Jesus" started, what do you think happened to your dearly departed? Did they get salvation? Did they go to a hell because they weren't "born again" Christians? Or did they go to hell if they were not baptized, christened or circumcised? Billions of people around the world died over the centuries without ever knowing about Jesus, baptism or circumcision. What story did the church invent to explain this? Do the rules change for them because they didn't know? Do they not qualify to be one of the saved? It's all convenient stories that change with the times, and are invented as we go along.

Some people have lost their way; they have forgotten how to be human, as they train themselves to be a servant of God, a soldier of God — and they will kill for a god. They have lost touch with their inner selves — their true selves. They live in an alternate reality, one which they create as they go along. They live outside the reality of being in control of themselves, and their actions or destiny. They give up their self control to the Bible, the churches and various cults. They are similar to a deluded person who thinks he or she is God's servant, communicates with God and is His gift to the world, all the time missing the point that he is a normal human being, like Jesus, who is more wonderful and powerful than any servant can be. A servant of a king is still worse off than the poor man who is his own ruler. A friend once told me, it's better to be a king in your own poor country than a slave in someone else's rich country. Sanity can be easily lost in the worship and delusion of religion. Even the Bible says, do not kill but the followers misinterpret that too, and kill anyway.

Religion is the most uneducated, unimaginative story ever concocted. It is grade school material and it is very inconsistent. How can a mystical, all powerful and all intelligent god have such a stupid plan? Slavery and subservience to "Him" being the order of the day, topped off with delusions of rewards of salvation, from a god that is bent on vengeful rule? It is an utterly childish story, totally inconsistent with the concept of an intelligent god. Thousands of years ago, all they thought having real power meant was to have worshipers and slaves —subservient sheep. They never thought we could break that cycle and have progress, but we did. Religious subservience is a backward concept for the 21st century.

We are going out into space with an idea befitting a caveman. In fact, we already live in space — wouldn't that have been unacceptable to religion? Even the tower of Babel was built too high for God's pleasure in that childish story. The inventors of religion wrote about the stars and were in awe of the heavens where God sits. Little did they know each star was actually part of a billion planets and stars within billions of galaxies, just like our own Milky Way galaxy.

Not many people want to think about their religion. They simply do the tribal thing and accept what everyone does, and they fall in line and follow the dogma. They do not try to go deeper into the teachings to find the history or the real message. If they did, then they would have understood what Jesus and John Lennon were saying, which is you don't need to follow a religion to make a beautiful world, and have a beautiful existence living in peace with each other. Michael Jackson started with the man in the mirror, because that's where change starts and happens, with you, through your own self empowerment. Jesus does not want you to follow Him or worship Him, but to mirror what He did and not have religion but something deeper and purer — enlightenment and consciousness. You will find it in you; just look and think for yourself with your inner, peaceful self. It's all in your mind and all about self empowerment. The Kingdom is within you, not in your religious beliefs, books and institutions.

Here is a task for you: if you stop worshiping any gods for a month and just live a good, loving and respectful life, taking care of and teaching others to respect each other and themselves, do you think God will punish you any more than He will right now? What will you lose if you tried this experiment? Nothing, because the church says that you are already a sinner and are going to hell; if anything, the Devil may like you more and go easy on you. Do you see how senseless that sounds? Will you become more evil because you stopped worshiping something? Would you become cursed and deserving of more punishment than you deserve right now as a sinner? Are you afraid of being cast down to hell for teaching good? Jesus did it; the result is He died. John did it; same result, he died. Maybe you or I might be murdered like they and others who taught goodness were. Do you want to risk it?

There are some corrupt priests in partnership with

crooked politicians, both trying to keep you confused, usually for self enrichment with money and power. Would you risk your children for them? Would you leave your children at their mercy? Wouldn't the real truth-seeking priests denounce all wars if they believed in salvation or the Ten Commandments? Yes, they would, and I caution you to look at which ones support the wars.

After all, thou shall not kill any color or creed of man, not even for capital punishment. All religions that preach support for any kind of death are mistaken, and that will be the ultimate proof that they do not believe in salvation or in what they preach. Why would they give up their own salvation by supporting any kind of death and murder in any way, for any man? They wouldn't. That's your proof that they don't believe in religion, God, or the commandments and punishment for sinners.

No god wants you to kill people for His purpose or enjoyment. Remember, His ability to perform magical or miraculous feats can solve all your problems without you murdering someone, so why do it? To the corrupt warmongers, "achieving salvation" are just empty words they use to trap you. The church and the state make strange bedfellows, but that's what they are. The genuine priests, who are good, do not get involved with corrupt politicians or support wars. Their daily routine is supporting their communities and that's how you know them. Every life is precious and can be used for the benefit of our mission here on Earth…even those on death row…so the church supporting death and war is wrong.

How dangerous is that to your family or your country, when the corrupt partners do each other's bidding for their own selfish reasons? Don't they endanger your families?

Yes. We already know these corrupt politicians by their works and greedy deeds. Your kids are sent by them to fight other innocents in wars, killing men, women and children, for the politicians' and their friends' selfish gains, and not for security purposes. There has been a history of politicians trying to start wars and conflicts all through the ages, with the support of religious bodies. It's not a new tactic.

Are you giving away your kids' innocence and trust of your protection to the thousands of pedophiles masquerading as priests all around the world, or the homoerotic, drug-using televangelists, masquerading as priests? They all cry on TV after they are caught, but are they genuinely sorry or just acting? They are good actors. I must stress repeatedly, not all priests are bad — only a small minority, compared to the size of the world clerical community. Not all politicians are bad either, but our system does help the bad ones to rise to the top, when the people do not keep them in check.

The Mega Churches are the money-hungry, powerhouses supporting war and now challenging the Vatican for the financial throne. They give you a show, not salvation. Television is for entertainment and as you know we rarely even get unbiased journalism on TV anymore. Every show the Mega Churches do is all scripted and edited before it is shown to you on TV, and meant to mislead you to believe in some kind of religion. Different regions of the world have their own shows to lure you into their religion. If a person ran up on the stage or the alter during the taping of the prayer show, and started undressing and using foul language, do you think that it could be shown like that on

TV? No, it will be edited first. It always is. The station will be charged by the authorities if they don't.

When you are shown someone on the television being instantly healed at these televised prayer meetings, by the Mega Churches, do you think it is all real? It is not. Call me doubtful. Those priests are just good actors. Why do they only cure a few select people? If the pastor was authentic, and he had a connection to a real and powerful God, he could heal everyone in that gathering: all 20,000 of them. Just think of how much in donations they collect at these televised prayer meetings from the live audience that attends, and the people who call in on the phone at home. They make a lot of money. They will even sell you a DVD copy of the show. It's just like wrestling, all made up, all fake just for your entertainment and donations.

Before television, no one had a vehicle that made religion as profitable as it is now. Globally, religion is one of the most profitable financial ventures of all time. One person donated $20 million to fix up a church in New York City in 2008. A pizza magnate in that same year built a whole city for the religious to live and work in. Follow the money; this is the kind of fervor that the religious leaders hope to inspire in those who donate.

Our children are highly intelligent, and not easily fooled or misled about religion, as we were by some priests or politicians, who should be locked up. Kids are into computers and nuclear science; ancient superstition is not in the cards for them. Theirs is the task of populating new planets, not learning how to sell crosses. When people were primitive, religion was a useful tool of control. Now religion just   slows our civilization's progress, after 4,000 years of painstakingly slower progress out of the darkness, we would do ourselves a favor by leaving religion in the past where it belongs.

CONFUSION, CHRISTIANIZATION

Some people stop at the doorway of their religions, and they do not go in or delve more deeply into the real substance of it. Jesus said in the Gospel of Thomas that they should seek and come inside. If they do they will find real truth, and should not listen to the person at the doorway telling them distracting stories of a vengeful god. They will find that religion's truth should not be a lot of fanatical ideas but as Gandhi, John Lennon and Tolstoy found out, it should be about spirituality and peace. The fanatics at the door — the church — are what people must avoid. All religions have an avenue to truth, peace and progress, both spiritual progress and progress for humanity. Bypass the fanatics at the doorway. Go deeper into your religion. The truth of peace is the same for any religion, or should be, though there are new religious cults springing up every so often that have quite questionable motives.

Should we believe what the holy book says about God? If so, which religion's god, and which holy book? Which one of the world's worshipping communities has the answer to this question of whose religion is correct? Before there was a Christian religion (the ancient version or the modern version into which it has morphed), there were thousands of years of worship to other gods, and maybe sometimes the same god with various names by different groups of people. We have seen that the Romans, Greeks and the Pharaohs had or invented their own gods.

If you take snapshots of the Christian religion after

Christ, every couple of centuries you will notice the religion changes in various ways. The main trend of senseless worshipping does not change, but you do see changes that are related to the society and its progress through the centuries. A simple example is in the 17th century, when King James made a new Bible, or rewrote and changed the old Bible. There were no issues like Roe vs. Wade and stem cell research. Religion changes over time. Even then you did not have to be reborn to get a ticket to heaven. If you knew the king, you had a free pass and if you angered the church, you were excommunicated, or in the time of the inquisition, you were killed. Now the church is concerned with stem cells, pro life, gay marriage and who is elected president.

When we look at that early time before Jesus, the people who lived along the Sindhu River, sometimes referred to as the Hindo people, generally lived with the beliefs of one god with various avatars or manifestations on Earth, much like Jesus being an avatar coming allegedly as the son of God. The word Hindu was substituted for the word Sindhu as time went by. The word Indians was also mispronounced as Hindus by the Persians.

Over generations, people who were devout followers of religion were considered saints when they died and ascended to their father in heaven, or ascended to a higher plane in the vast universe, much like we do at present with our own saints: Jesus' mother Mary, Saint Nicholas and others. We may soon make Mother Teresa a saint.

Over time people prayed to them for help and guidance, as we also do now. Over hundreds of years, worshipers came to think of them as angels, or avenues to

God, along with the different avatars like Jesus, believing they were helpful in times of distress, or that they had the power to help. This included people like Mother Mary, Saint Christopher, Shiva, Krishna, Zeus, Poseidon, Ra, and other avatars, as there are many, hundreds or thousands globally. Each little tribe had their own names for their mystical gods, and there were thousands of tribes back then and over man's history.

The Hindus, it is thought, are one of the first ancient people or groups, who are still in existence today, to have had the concept of God, thousands of years ago, long before the time of the Old Testament's "documentations." Most of the other tribes have died off. The Hindus survived through the ages and gradually changed some of their ideas, just as we see being done over this short 2,000-year period with other religions. They merged with other peoples, and in their primitive thinking came to the understanding of one supreme God, with avatars or angels, beneath or existing alongside Him. Those chosen ones were some of the more faithful of the deceased followers of the religion, and were believed to have been sent by God, similar to the story of Jesus, to do His works and miracles.

The conquerors of the Hindu people would have tried to dispel the idea of any conquered group having a working knowledge of a religion with one god as a way of life, as indeed the different groups of Hindus being conquered all had some difference in their ways of life and worship, and these conquerors would have decried the notion of these Hindus worshiping one main god. They proudly and valiantly claimed the different native tribes worshiped many gods and were confused, and they were partly right; there was worship to different gods and avatars, but they were not totally confused as they had some of the basics right, like levels of spirituality and how to achieve them with peace not war.

This confusion was advantageous to the conquerors, so that they could claim dominance for their own god and religion, and gain favor from their own followers: their conquered indoctrinated and their slaves, whom they conspired to deceive. These were the conquering Romans. History shows that they worshipped different gods within their own communities as well. As we now know, all conquerors have false gods and false beliefs; they conquer and spread the disease of worshiping death and hate, instead of life and love. They killed for pleasure and plunder, much as we see done at present around the world.

After the death of Jesus and up until the Middle Ages, the practice of Christianization was known to have forcibly started the spread of the Christian religion, which is now the world's most dominant. The Catholic Church effectively eliminated any and all threats to their establishment throughout history, in violent and bloody events. Jesus would never have agreed with Christianization, which amounted to mass murder in different instances throughout history. The Roman Inquisition was one such terrible period where torture, bloodshed and death ruled supreme from the 12th century, for 700 years, until the 19th century. Millions died worldwide. The Roman Catholic Church was the epitome of the said evil they decried.

Does that ring a bell? Are we playing the role of the Romans in Iraq and elsewhere? Was this Iraqi invasion part of the reemergence of Christianization disguised as spreading democracy? As the Hindus were intelligent enough to learn to live in peace alongside their neighbors, they were conquered numerous times, by others including the Romans. This mimics exactly what we saw in America, with the Native American Indians being conquered and annihilated, just for the plunder and theft of their land and their eventual Christianization. Did Bush try to do that again in Iraq?

To begin to understand modern religion's history, you have to first realize that the ancient Asian continent is the birthplace of the main religious concepts we know today. Where did the main groups of Muslims, Christians, Jews, Buddhists and Hindus come from? Where are Bethlehem, Jerusalem and all the other locations mentioned in the Bible? In Asia, on that continent, which was considered a single land mass in the time of the Classical Antiquity, 800 BC to 500AD.

Some names of places and borders have been changed since then. There were people all over Asia trading with each other. Travel was slow so they would spend long spells of time traveling alongside one another, learning from each other while going in the same directions, on the same roadways. This happened for centuries.

By traveling together, there was safety in larger numbers of caravans, to protect against ambushing bands of thieves. The people from China, India, Syria, Iran (formerly the Persian Empire), Saudi Arabia (formerly the Kingdom of Hejaz-Nejd), Turkey (formerly The Ottoman Empire), Mesopotamia

(formerly a combination of parts of Iraq, Iran, Syria and Turkey), Egypt and all others surrounding that general area and farther out to the whole of Asia, traveled together to each other's lands and traded amongst themselves, all the while learning from and about each other's religions, cultures and their families. I am sure they had inter-racial marriages also. During these times, religious ideas were always discussed and exchanged between people from different parts of Asia to help them understand and live in harmony with each other, and to keep trade alive, a practice that continues to this day amongst all religions and now companies trading internationally.

The older Hindu religion is uncannily mirrored by the younger Christian religion. Is that just a coincidence? Not likely. Why do the Christian rosary beads, which number 108 beads, mirror the Hindu jape beads, which are also 108 beads? Why do the Christians have a Trinity as do the Hindus? Why do they have a concept of there being nothingness out of which God created everything, as the Hindus did before them?

Observe the religious teachings of Jesus; there are Hindu beliefs in His teaching of love and pacifism, or at least the Hindus before Him had the same teachings. Jesus may have been a learned Hindu scholar or just a friend of the Hindus, come to bring the rest of the world out of the Dark Ages. Is there a problem with where Jesus learned or developed His identity and consequently His destiny? Is Eastern peace and love inferior or different to Western peace and love? Let's just say, from the Jews, Romans or Hindus, He learned his craft. Not a big deal and not important. That He came and did His work is the real importance, and we owe it to Him and our families to seek and find the real truth of His teachings.

If the writers of the Bible were "inspired" to write

about a religion, and it mirrors a religion that already exists, then are they suggesting that the older religion is the truth? Jesus taught enlightenment, a Hindu concept, as they also did before him. Are we now seeing that this could have been the dominant religion before the Bible, and was copied in small ways by the biblical writers for some diabolical purpose? For the sole purpose of making it their own created religion, which could have been used for the control of their own people?

They blur and confuse the timeline, so you will not suspect that they could have copied the religion from someone else. Does it really matter? No, it doesn't. What does matter is to move away from these frivolous distracting arguments that the church will bring up to discredit other religions. It is really not profitable for the future of a space-bound, advanced species of mankind. We simply need to do what is right for all concerned, especially our family, and that is to find the core of any religion, and try to be enlightened and peaceful in our affairs.

They may have chosen to copy the Hindu religion instead of any other religions of that time simply because that may have been the dominant one or just closer to the point they fancied, but I will not waste time trying to figure out when or why. They could just as well have decided to copy another religion or invent their own. If they copied a religion from the planet Mars, neither would we know 2,000 years later nor would it make a difference to us in the 21st century; the history does not matter. It only serves to distract us from the fact that the new religion it has morphed into is faulty, and leading people away from real truth, and away from religion's real core of peace, progress and enlightenment. The false core is cyclical worship to get to heaven.

Maybe they saw some glimpse of the truth in this Hindu version, but felt that it was not complete or to their liking, so they added a few changes of their own. There were other religions around thousands of years before Christ. Religion can be disentangled to show its invention and duplication, and therefore it may not be as inspired and mystical as they would have us believe.

The Bible and its scholars suggest that Adam and Eve's history was more recent in time than the timeline we have discovered of some of the early tribes of people or animals. Isn't that odd? Which is true? These early peoples have histories dating back to prehistoric ages. Are the woolly mammoths and dinosaurs false and never existed? Are the religions wrong about these facts? Are they spinning or twisting the information, or are they alluding that it is all false information, planted by the scientists, as I myself have been told before? Why would God start man at a prehistoric level? Did He create a fully linguistic human Adam, from dirt? If He did, are the cavemen descendents of Adam who lost their speech? If so, what about the timeline? It would suggest that Adam's story happened millions of years ago. Also did He make Eve from a rib? That's real magic, not slight-of-hand.

I ask you, who is it that is trying to keep us confused and afraid? Scientists can prove these prehistoric things are true or false, and religions only tell us to humbly believe and have blind faith that the scientists are false and religion is true, without the church being able to prove anything to us that makes sense. If religion is true, then what happened to Elijah's fiery, flying chariot? Did he just park it up or are they still using it? Because I haven't heard about it since.

Intelligence and proof should not be cast aside; the inventors of the religions are not alive anymore. We must move away from religious fanaticism and look for proof of one idea or the other, to arrive at the truth. Can they both be right? I think they are. There was prehistoric man and there is a higher spiritual force. That higher spiritual force is now you. It is now in you and exists as a spiritual part of you, as you are part of it. Isn't that enough? Learn about your own force first, the real one inside you, as it is only then you will be able to understand the rest of the truth.

If you ask various religions' leaders — your pastor, imam, pundit, priest or priestess — if they suggest you blindly follow any religion without learning about it, they all say no. They will all say that if you are blind when following anything, you will run into obstacles. So they will tell you that the only way to be true to yourself is to ask, research, think, learn and get to know the religion you are about to join and worship. That makes the best worshipper, especially if you are thinking of going to a different religious order than theirs. They will tell you that they don't want you to be there, if only to mislead yourself or others. I urge you to seek as well.

Why should we follow Catholic instead of Anglican, Presbyterian or Baptist, Seventh Day Adventist or Episcopalian, Opus Dei, Church of Latter Day Saints, Mormonism, Judaism or Haskala? These are all religions that believe in the use of the Bible, and Jesus, to worship. The Old and New Testaments are filled with information that was put together by people over a long period of time. It was created after the facts, starting 2,000 years ago for The New Testament, and 4,000 years ago for The Old

Testament with the faith of Judaism. The King James Version was compiled four centuries ago, so the Bible was being created and recreated each time. Why should we change and follow any other religion when they also shroud their core beliefs with dogma? Why not just find the core of your present religion and use that knowledge, without the rituals and dogma?

The latest and largest threat against truth is now the Mega Churches. They could be the money lenders in the church yard that Jesus chased away. He saw the future. He knew they would prevail; they would come back after He was gone to sell their products, but not in the church yard outside as before — this time they would build the church and ply their trade from inside. They would become the church and then expand to become the Mega Churches. They are selling deception and entertainment as if it were professional wrestling. They sell false healing and false salvation. They are also plying their trade at the end of a gun in Iraq, and other places, when they support the wars we get involved in.

I think what really overwhelmed Jesus with grief was not his death — He was trained to overcome that — but seeing what kind of people would come to deceive us from inside the church in the 20th century. People like Jim Jones, drugged-up priests on crystal methamphetamines, and pedophiles with their cults and communes all over the country, making underage children, sometimes their own, have sex and babies for them.

After the time of Jesus had come and gone, people started to write about Him. This began at least a generation after His death, 1st century onwards, from rumors, hearsay and clouded memories passed on from one generation to another. These writers were said to have been "inspired" by the Holy Ghost, or more recently to sound intellectually, or grammatically, correct the term was changed to the Holy Spirit, as dead people are believed to turn to ghosts.

We have dozens of these inspired biblical writers in the psych wards. Aren't we more intelligent now, so that we can better diagnose these people? Hence, us having them in the sanitarium instead of in a monastery, adding more "inspired" verses to the various religious writings.

When you look back at history, a significant number of them were indeed irrational and hallucinatory, which was considered normal for that era. Remember, these were fanatical, ignorant, "inspired" people, who saw chariots of fire in the sky and are believed by everyone else to have been credible witnesses.

Jesus preached about love and wisdom without a church or religion, so they murdered Him. Now think, how intelligent could they have really been to do that? Jesus' problem was the people of that time had a low level of spiritual understanding, so His message was hard to teach them, as they could not understand His evolved ideas.

God is the higher power and force which we must learn to understand. Jesus preached that God, the force, is you, and in you and therefore you are God; you are part and parcel of the God force. God is being good to all, and that makes you a god to your family and others that you help. Be good and be God because religion's version of God is a word describing an unknown entity, with the entire make-believe dogma attached to it. Jesus' version is a living force: that is, you, I and Him, doing what a god does, which is to rise out of the state of selfish greed and vanity we exist in, and help each other in any way we reasonably can. He had to suggest to them that God was his Father, and theirs, not anything else because these humble but primitive people could not understand much in the way of enlightenment. They needed an object in a box, to focus on. We do not. The only ones who understood Jesus were his disciples, and then only barely, so he went slowly with them, giving them specific parables to help them think, explore and discover.

The masses were "taught" by the church that they were sinners and not worth much, and needed to be led by the holy shepherds of the church and by the dogma. Jesus instead was trying to teach them to be leaders, not followers. The religions need followers. Remember, the churches had the ear of the kings and other hierarchy, who would use force to guide the people if they resisted the church, so they were forced to follow.

The various houses of worship should really be community centers, providing a forum for people to come together for various reasons that uplift the community, and to provide social services and programs. They should not be teaching about a concept or a god that they do not even value enough to seek and to understand the real truth.

With Jesus' teachings, no one would have the need for a church, any religion, or religious scholars, and some corrupt religious leaders who have their own agendas. The church could not use Jesus' free-thinking ideas or concepts to stay in control of the masses whom they treated like sheep, so they murdered Him, suppressed His teachings, invented the Bible, pieced together from various writings of the time including the Hindus and with the help of the

Gnostic movement: Jesus' movement. The rest, as they say, is history.

If the off-the-wall beliefs of magic, and the like, at that time were normal, then it makes sense that they could believe in demons. These people were haunted by their fears and mental demonic possession so often, it became the norm to see demon activity and believe in such things. It would be the easiest thing for the church to trick them to believe about the Bible and Satan. People who see or are possessed by demons are usually depressed and have low self esteem, so is it all mental delirium? Do you have to be depressed to believe that you need a god to save you from your alleged weak self?

Now that we know more, we can better diagnose the "inspired" writers as mentally challenged, delusional, schizophrenic or psychotic. These are the people who wrote the Bible, which I might add, was created by men in the church in 300 BC. And everything that did not fit their agenda or conspiracy at the time was omitted; Gnostic and other books were burned, etc. Women fell from grace, in their clouded eyes. Who can we say out of this group was inspired? The Bible was edited many times after, the last notable edit being the King James Version in the 1600s.

In the year 312 AD the ruler Constantine accepted Christianity as the great religion of that time. By the next year, it was accepted as the official religion. It is thought that he saw the profitability of having this as the official religion, and it was accepted by all who feared the kingdom, or they were killed. He thought it would have encouraged more people to cooperate with and support the kingdom than any other method. With any well conceived religion, he saw he could win over the masses. This would have expanded the numbers in the kingdom, more so than conquering them would have done.

Three centuries after they murdered Jesus, while compiling the new Bible, they also removed many leading roles that women had in the religion, made them servants of men, not equals, and ruled them like slaves, treating them worse than animals in some cases. Remember, women only won the right to vote after the end of slavery, 1900 years later. And that's only in America; in other parts of the world, women still can't speak, much less think aloud, or voice their hopes and dreams publicly, without the threat of being stoned, beaten or killed.

They loved slavery back then, and they still do now, so how could they know Jesus?

Now we know about the cell phone and microwave; back then, that would have been seen as the Devil's magical works.

One question that comes to mind is, how was the church able to mislead the population that easily, so widespread and effectively, with their brand of religion? The answer is right there in plain sight! The experts say that it is the same thing that helped bring about the demise of the largest and most powerful empire during the time of Jesus: The Roman Empire.

Remember, there were no laws about alcohol, and these people constantly drank wine as if it were water, from any age that was suitable, to the adolescents of the day. Some were highly intoxicated quite often. Some were surely crazy, but who would have known it, if the drunkard was considered normal back then? This drinking was part of a larger problem.

The main problem was that they had no way of protecting themselves from metal poisoning such as lead, copper, bronze, or ingestion of rust in their drink, and the ill effects of these cumulatively, upon the human brain and physiology. Lead pipes were used in their plumbing, which delivered their drinking water. A lot of their cooking utensils were lined with bronze, copper and lead: lead being the preferred metal, as the other metals reacted with the acids in the defrutum that was being boiled in them.

A search of lead poisoning reveals the undeniable history of this tragic phenomenon, which I think, helped bring about the age of religious modern-day worship and misinformation, spanning some 2,000 to 5,000 years ago until present day.

The dangerous effects of lead poisoning have been well documented in our own recent history. This includes various birth defects, dementia, comas, delirium, severe convulsions and even death: common ailments back then. Heavy metals in your body also cause cancers. The use of lead has shown up more than 5,000 years before Christ, in artifacts found around the world.

Lead was first thought to have been mined in Asia Minor for massive and widespread use around the year 6,000 BC because it was easy to melt, fashion and use. It is well known the Romans used it to pipe their drinking water and line their cooking utensils. The toxicity of lead was first recognized by Nicander of Colophon approximately 5,800 years after it was first used. Nicander was a learned scholar, and wrote extensively on the poisons and antidotes of that time period. He was able to see the ill effects of lead poisoning firsthand. He wrote about the incidence of lead-induced anemia and colic in 250 BC. There was also the prevalence of gout, thought to be as a result of the use of lead products in the pottery of that time.

Aulus Cornelius Celsus in 30 AD wrote of white-lead poisoning, although he still recommended it for use in certain ointments to stop bleeding, and reduce infection and inflammation in wounds, as it is toxic to bacteria.

Monks in 17th century Germany, who were wine drinkers, developed colic from the use of "sugar of lead." In the 18th century, in Boston, Massachusetts, rum was distilled in stills using lead.

What we know about the Roman Empire is that they used lead extensively. Obviously, the use of lead would spread anywhere in the world where trading was done. During the 6,000 years before Jesus walked the Earth, it was widespread in the daily lives of many people, as it was used in pottery and kitchen implements, plumbing, and water supply systems, cosmetics, decorative coloring in homes, and in foodstuff, most notably wine.

The wine was sweetened and flavored with a product called "sapa," which was grape syrup boiled in lead pots. When the freshly-squeezed grapes and their juices were boiled, it became a mixture called defrutum. The defrutum was further boiled down to become a strong concentrate called sapa. Defrutum was boiled in pots lined with bronze, copper, and lead but because other metals reacted with the solution being boiled, lead was the preferred pot to use. When boiled in these lead pots, the lead would leach into the syrup, which was then added to the wine.

Unlike the other metals used, the concentration of lead in the mixture was so highly toxic that it had the desired effect of eliminating further fermenting and souring of the wine, by poisoning organisms and bacteria and effectively killing them. This sapa was also used for that same reason, as a preservative in fruit juices, foods and meats, thereby spreading the lead poisoning to people and children who were not drinking wine. Defrutum was fed to animals, as it was thought that it improved the taste of their flesh. Women used defrutum and sapa in their cosmetics.

Lead poisoning can result in delusions, memory loss and many more serious illnesses. This unknowingly helped the people to become highly delirious, which I think caused them to be swayed more easily by the rich, delirious, influential elders of the church. Quite simple and effective on a massive scale, as most used these lead utensils in their daily lives. Had it been planned by anyone, it would have been truly diabolical, but alas, it was all done by mistake and coincidence.

Consider entire populations, for generations, thousands of years, being poisoned with levels thousands of times stronger than what we now consider to be dangerous for human consumption. These people were exposed to this daily, cooking and eating from these utensils. The children's dosage was higher as their bodies are smaller, compared to an adult consuming the same amount in food and drink.

The specific type of lead native to certain Spanish mines was found as far north as Greenland, in the dust that blew there on the winds. While the lead was being mined, the lead dust was blown wherever the winds carried it, poisoning large distant areas without anyone being the wiser. This would effectively place the lead in most open water sources in the reach of the winds that were coming from the mining areas. The lead dust tainted waters in rivers, which would then flow to faraway communities. So where the wind didn't carry the poisonous dust, the water did. The fish would have been poisoned by the lead in the water, and then the people would be poisoned by feeding on the fish.

The lead would also enter the water shed, the underground bodies of water that fed millions, and could have poisoned entire regions in this way. The tainted water and the defrutum were fed to livestock, and the poisoned milk and meat were consumed. The contaminated water was used in the fields for the crops, which would have become poisonous and then eaten. We see that happening now in the pesticides we use on our crops, being absorbed by the plants and in turn poisoning us. We also see the steroids and other chemicals in our meats being passed on to us when we eat.

It is generally believed that the widespread use of lead by the Roman Empire undoubtedly helped bring about the empire's end. The highly poisoned hierarchy of Romans could not have as many normal and healthy offspring as they should have, and we have since discovered that birth defects are brought on by lead poisoning. What a testament to its potential for devastation. It also would have caused reproductive problems for the poor men and women alike, as it did to the rich and affluent in the community.

The French banned the use of lead-based paint in the 1920s, and the U.S. did also…we gallantly saw the danger in it, too…almost 60 years later. Go figure.

Knowing that lead was used extensively for 8,000 years, up until about two centuries ago, leads me to the assumption that even the longest surviving religions' writers from that time onwards could have been affected by lead poisoning, resulting in mental delusions of interactions with gods and demons. One delusional idea would feed the next. Each idea adding to and building on the last. Their imaginations would be running wild in that ignorant environment. Give a caveman a club and see him rise to power.

Their power over God, and knowing and deciding what He wanted, was the caveman's club back then. Isn't it suspicious that all He wanted was for the ignorant people to respect His preachers, be submissive to them, and hold them in awe since they had the knowledge about what He wanted? The commandments, used as a tool, were the ultimate way to convince the masses that they were sinners in these various ways they described, and that they needed to be under the guidance of the church and its employees.

The submissive crowd could be led for years through the wilderness of poverty and despair, and bear witness to the parting of the seas. Did it all really happen exactly as they said it did? I think not, although the David and Goliath thing was not too shabby. Samson and Delilah were a stretch though, with the super strength in the hair. Sounds like an archaic Superman, doesn't it?

Mental delusions, demonic or satanic paranoia, coupled with hearsay, following the leaders or the crowd, and the pure ingenuity of the human imagination, could together be the crux of the invention of religion: all the religions that were born out of that time period, 8,000 years ago, and coming forward to the 1800s, when we stopped eating and drinking lead. It helped to increase our religious psychosis, our religious paranoia about the end of the world, and our willingness to believe anything, no matter how far-fetched it was.

Over thousands of years, generations one after the other of entire communities would have been poisoned from birth, and grown up being poisoned more each day, by this widely-used, essential metal. Even the babies and children would have been fed, in poisonous containers, milk from the animals which drank the water laced with lead, eventually causing each generation to be as much as, or more, poisoned and delusional than the last, and passing on medical conditions and defects which would then become considered normal and hereditary, adding to the increasing psychosis of whole populations of people.

The affluent in any society are known to have the most influence in the affairs of the day, and of course they are also the ones who will consume the most food and drink, due to their purchasing ability and status. Ultimately, this will result in them ingesting more lead in their diet than the poorer folk in the community, thereby becoming more delirious and more psychotic.

This suggests that they are the ones who introduced delusional ideas to their delusional hierarchy, and had these ideas followed and adopted to become laws because of their great influence by being the decision makers, the council members, the high clergy and the elite. Sadly, not much has changed; the delusional elite still make the rules..

What we now realize is that any amount of lead over a certain level, in your body, is unsafe. What these people ingested in one day of drinking wine or poisoned water, or eating tainted foods, meats or plants, could have been hundreds of times the smallest amount that our best scientists, doctors or the FDA consider safe for human consumption.

Two thousand years ago, these people believed in sorcery and witchcraft, and good and evil. They would see a meteorite in flames plummeting to Earth and they would run for cover thinking Lucifer or one of His demons was coming to get them. Can you just imagine what they would tell the townspeople? The bringer of inspired news would be held in high regard back then, like a middleman working for God. Fast forward by even one generation and that story, just like our rumors, would change and be a battle of epic proportions between Satan and God, with armies of angels and demons on each side, and flaming chariots flying all over the place.

The stories we hear are not as believable now as they were 2,000 years ago. These people were quite humble and primitive in their thinking, and they accepted the stories from Jesus' days as the gospel truth. They knew neither science nor common sense. Do you think gospel truth is different from real truth? That answer, my friends, is yes. It reminds me of a popular British TV series in the '70s called "Catweazle." It was about a wizard who was shrewd, superstitious, knew about potions and alchemy and was definitely crazy: what a good example of our ancestors, the inspired writers and the church elites.

The Bible has been rewritten more than once. Rewritten does not mean reprinted. Rewritten means they take things out, put things in and change what the original meaning was before. The blind worshippers are then expected to take it for granted that "inspired" people have rewritten it. Do you believe this? Does God really inspire these people to rewrite the Bible multiple times? Did He change His mind? Wasn't writing it once good enough?

How about these people who start their own types of Christian worship and Christian churches, like Jim Jones, the Millerites, the Branch Davidians and others? Are they genuine or just opportunistic? New churches are popping up all over the world. Are they really authentic or are they the same as each other — just doing what they want in the name of religious beliefs and the almighty dollar? The count so far exceeds 40,000 denominations, with 3,751,000 congregations (worship centers).

Their members' personal income totals $18, 520 billion, and as much as $410 billion of that is given to Christian causes. Their churches' income is another $160 billion.[15] You can see the lucrative "other" side of the coin. This is not counting other religions around the world and the finances they command.

In the early 16th century, the Bible was redone under the instruction of King James and with more than 50 of his cohorts, from the clergy to some alleged scholars of that time. They all worked on the rewriting, to make it what it is today by adding and omitting what they considered relevant to the teachings that were needed at that time, to bring about the specific goal of complete rule and subservience of the peasants, by the king and the church. How much did they change, omit and add? No one knows.

The New Testament is a different book than the Old Testament, with a different God. This new God has a new face, a new behavior, with new stories to keep followers confused, and psychotic believers of miracles and demons.

---

[15] Gordon-Conwell Theological Seminary, "Status of Global Mission," http://ockenga.gordonconwell.edu/, website accessed November 17, 2009.

Of course, as with all religions, not all followers are psychotic. This new God does not show Himself and has been silent for centuries.

While it took centuries to write and put together the Old Testament, the new one was invented in a short enough time, done by one man in his lifetime, one king…it is an invention by King James himself. He was at that time, bringing man out of the world of cannibalism and blood sacrifices, in a noble effort to help the tired religion to evolve. What a dirty word evolution has become, by the followers of an evolved religion who do not believe in, or support, evolution.

If you translate something written last year to what you think it means today, you will lose some of the original ideas, concepts or meanings; you can lose the gist of it. King James had translations done from various writings 1,600 years after the murder of Jesus, and I'm sure, he added some things. How accurate could they have been after so long? Did he use "inspired" writers and scholars to piece together this latest version? Were they all living in the same compound, all waiting for when the old God changed His mind and wanted the Bible rewritten? I think not. They just followed James' orders and ideas, while James was actually following his predecessor's orders. It was not divinely commissioned.

They all believed in ghosts and demons, so how intelligent or correct could they have been? How rational or fanatical were they, in that age? They burned people alive for witchcraft, remember? They did not just take the old Bible, and copy it or reprint it. They rewrote it, made a new one and they threw the old one in the garbage. We see here religious evolution in plain sight.

People don't believe in devils and witchcraft in this modern age, do they? I think not. But you do...if you believe in the Bible or religion. I know about the Wicca practitioners who are allegedly the modern-day practitioners of their magical craft, but I do think we all sanely believe that wizards, witches, demons and Moses were all make-believe. There are movies about wizards and magic right now. Do you believe they are real, too? No.

There may even be a connection of the Wicca practitioners to the Gnostic movement of Jesus, who had to survive, hide from the law and the early church, and provide a vehicle for their teachings to live on; and it is rumored they did so, by way of various underground alchemist movements.

Even Mother Teresa puts religion in a new light by her own experiences, in our modern times, and most persons think she was the epitome of her religion's kindness. Her writings showed that she never found their God, or so she thought. She did not find the God she was taught to look for, the one she was told had existed, in the form she was taught that He existed in.

The truth is, God-energy does exist. It is just in a different form, quite simply. How difficult is that to understand? We are intelligent enough to understand this now but our ancestors weren't. The spiritual force we call God may exist, just not with arms and legs, sitting on a throne in heaven. You can call the force that some call consciousness, by any other name you choose — God, Satan, Zeus or even a toaster. It is still the same force and the name is not important. It is without a gender and we are each a part of the whole that it is. We are a drop in the ocean of that energy. The people who invented religion did not understand consciousness, or maybe thought it just did not serve them and their thirst for riches, power and control. Why it was made up is less urgent an issue than finding out what the truth really is; that distracting answer as to *why* is neither important, nor able to be uncovered. The most important thing remains to find the truth and teach it to our children.

You may not believe this, but the truth is that none of us good religious people knows anything substantial about God. What we think we know comes from very questionable sources and has changed a lot over time. Although some of us may know the way to enlightenment, what most of us know about religion is what has been made up over the years, and taught to us before we were old enough to know better. What is written in the Bible is called the Gospel truth, which varies from what I believe Christ's messages really meant. So do you believe King James and his cohorts?

Some authors suggest that Jesus did not have a virgin birth nor was He resurrected. Be that as it may, I am going on the adventurous assumption that He did indeed exist. The church doesn't appear to know the truth of what Christ meant in His parables, or I think they would have released it. Just take a look at how many different Christian churches or denominations there are. With truth, there would be one Christian church and one denomination, right? I sincerely think that only the Vatican, if anyone, could have had this understanding of Jesus' true meaning, and suppressed it if they did have it.

That would mean the popes, each of them, were privy to the information but allowed it to be hidden, if they had indeed understood it. Had this happened, it may have been because they were of the opinion that the time was not yet right for the world to know Jesus' truth, or they realized they would lose their followers and the billions they collect in donations. They may have released it in their own time, in the future, or kept it hidden as long as possible to maintain their followers and donors. We simply don't know.

But it appears the great consciousness decided it to be now, rather than later, so it is being revealed in many different ways by different sources, including this book. To decipher what Jesus meant required as much intuition and imagination as is needed to believe in religion. But even if the messages were deciphered before, it appears people may not have been able to understand it or trust it, and some form of proof and common sense in the form of tangible evidence was needed. The proof can be in discovering what is false in all religious teachings.

The people misunderstood the truth. I don't blame them; they just couldn't understand that high spiritual level or state of unselfish being that Jesus was in, and was a part of. The real truth from Jesus is that God is good, and good is God. Let me explain — when you have good and peace in your mind and in your being, in your inner self, that is your manifestation of God, or Nirvana, or Enlightenment and that should be enough, for regular humans at least, if you even choose to want to call it God or something else. Helping an old lady cross the street in God's name, or just for Goodness' sake still means she crossed by your help and kindness, and it is not a miracle connected to some God; it was you alone.

Do not hold the form of the sinner inside you, and then go looking for an external force to worship and to save you. Your inner self is that force. Do good deeds for others and yourself. That's all God is to regular, clueless, innocent humans. Goodness is man's greatness and man's greatness is his goodness. If you are looking for a miracle to make you understand enlightenment and God's love, then that miracle is people helping each other to grow and spread eternal, unselfish love. That's all, no miracles or magic. Jesus said as much, taught as much and lived as much, and I am sure he didn't multiply those loaves of bread, and those grilled or sautéed fishes for the alleged crowds. No one even mentioned if they were spicy or had onions, so were they raw? Obviously, it was made up.

When it comes to the subject of God, we are still living and thinking as if we are those people in the past. We have not progressed, mentally, in our understanding, to get past the veil of make believe. We just invent new rituals, like being born again and various things like that. Look around the world; you can see how many rituals we have invented through the years.

When we constantly do good, we are cleansing and empowering ourselves. The selfless feeling, and the understanding of the action of doing well without reward, will scrape away the dirt of our prejudices, helping us to let go of our greed and do more, for less reward and fame. When our minds and souls are being cleansed in this way, they are made receptive to the intuition and inspiration of consciousness. When you do good, you receive your inspiration from the source of spiritual enlightenment, which is your inner self, but only as much as you can understand and ingest. You can't feed a baby a gallon of milk. We must learn gradually.

You don't have to believe in the idea that we are created in the image and likeness of God to know that a force of consciousness exists. The idea of God looking like us is truly ancient and unimaginative. You do not have to limit the existence of your God to a certain way of thinking, or being of any ideology, as written in the Bible and other religious texts. To confine God's existence in a box of biblical imagination, and having parameters of human insecurities; of Him being a vengeful God, and to put Him in a cage of "inspired" ideas by delusional writers, so that you feel you can now understand Him and His infinite truth, is neither wise nor fitting for something that is presumed to be supreme.

If you are taught that God is infinite and supreme, how then can you understand the concept of what He really is, when you don't even know who, what, or where He is? You are the baby trying to drink the gallon of milk when you have not even drunk a glass. The supreme truth must be learned and understood in small doses. Doing good helps you learn.

Dogma does not teach you. It bends you to follow rituals and psychotic teachings of miracles and devils. It has even broken some with a weak will. Look at how many religious fanatics there are around the world, in all the big religions. You can only learn about being good by living it. Nothing else will teach you about the rewards of good — only life and living it, doing it. Reading about it will not make you a good person. You have to live it and be it.

A simple thing, as life and existing elsewhere in the

universe are not addressed by the church but you expect to understand a supreme God? That's not making sense. I say this because if you understood the vastness and complexity of the physical universe, which still has boundaries, you would realize that the vastness of a spiritual universe and existence, which has no boundaries, is too large and infinite to be contained within the rules, in the Bible, of what a god must be.

To begin with, we name or describe the consciousness with a word — "God." To name something means to capture it, define it, restrict its parameters, encase it and reduce its essence in some way, imprison it in a jar like a butterfly. It makes the force a finite object or thing, when what we call "God" is really supposed to be infinite. "God" is something defined, finite and limited, but spirituality, enlightenment and consciousness are infinite and unlimited.

Zeus was a god. So was Thor, and so *were* Jehovah and the rest of them. They were just names really or they would still be around today doing magic…none are and the world did not end recently in the year 2000, as they all proclaimed it would, just as they had been saying since the 1800s. Nor will it end unless we let the religious fanatics have their way.

We say "God" and expect to see something corresponding to that term, like a man on a throne, or a puff of smoke, a burning bush with a thundering voice, or a king looking down at us from the heavens. We expect something. Spirituality is not a being. Consciousness is not a living person with parameters and restrictions; it is a state of being. Being alive is a state of being, not something tangible like a stone. Whether folks choose to believe it or not, they are in a state of being because they are alive. So are germs and animals, and consciousness is what separates us from them.

So too what we try to capture in the term "God" is actually a state of peace and existence, not an object that we can interact with. That misconception of an object or person started the ball of misunderstanding rolling eons ago. People are looking for something that they can touch or hold, not a frame of mind or a reflection of awareness, hence the burning bush idea.

Do you own your home, wife, children, shoes and car? No, the term "ownership" on Earth is just an illusion, just like the term "God." What we think is real or important on Earth is not so real that we can take it with us after death. That tells you that there are social ideas, like religion or culture, or preferences of foods, music, sex, love and ownership of money, things and climatic seasons that are not relevant outside of Earth. In your real and spiritual form, these things are not going to be a reality for you, as you will exist in a non-physical form, somewhere else.

When you consider that our Earth is like one grain of sand amongst all the grains from all the beaches and deserts around the world, then you will have an idea of how gigantic the universe is, how small the Earth is in the universe, and how huge the consciousness is, to be existing throughout the whole universe. Also, you will realize how insignificant, unimportant and senseless religion is in the vastness of the universe.

Our misunderstood little idea of God in a box is exactly that. Acquiring consciousness and enlightenment is like trying to grab light with your hand. It exists but not in a form you can touch or hold, yet you can see it so you have proof that it is there. You recognize it in your mind and with your senses. So, too, you can find that force of consciousness inside you, and use it if you learn how to.

That understanding of what He, She or It could be, and is, must be the first step in your journey toward the enlightenment that Jesus and others wanted us to accomplish. Is Jesus really under a rock or in a piece of wood? Is God really in the eyes of your newborn, or in the beauty of the butterflies on the lake? How about in the rainbow over the waterfall? Yes, but you have to be re-educated to understand the full extent of it. "God," or the consciousness, is really a life force, for you to be part of and become, not an object for you to worship or use.

God is not the mayor or steward of your town, or any other in the universe. You are, so you have to take care of your own town, your own family. Don't pray to, or wait for, or enlist God's help. Your prayers are just words blowing in the wind. All of nature is part of an active conscious force, which exists on Earth and in Earth. Earth, in turn, is a small planet among many in our solar system. Our solar system is just one of billions in our galaxy, which in turn is a microscopic part of an estimated 50 billion galaxies in the universe. That universe has levels of spirituality, made up of each individual thing, planet, animal, human, other life-forms, and other things and beings in other dimensions which we cannot see; and it, the universe, is part of the true spiritual consciousness which exists. That complete **system** of spiritual existence is certainly much larger than the God in the Bible or any god in any scriptures.

Everything alive in the universe and on this Earth has a life, and has some form or level of consciousness. For example, one version of the story goes like this: A guy married a girl and moved to the richest part of town, with sprawling meadows and dozens of mountains for endless miles, farther than the eyes could see. The weather was forever warm and marvelous. It was always perfect. They had many kids and they were happy. One day a large object came down from the sky and scraped away all the mountains. Soon after that a flood came and washed everyone away, and killed everything. Then the person spat the mouthwash out and began getting ready for work.

Do you understand? There are bigger things than us that we can't see, forces that exist and function alongside our own existence. The bacteria in our mouths have a short life and existence of their own, every day, as do we. Like the bacteria, we live for a few short years while not seeing the bigger aspect of life going on for eons in the universe and in different dimensions outside our own. We do not see the forest because of the trees.

You do not know what the astronauts are doing in space right now, but they are there and they are working, while one galaxy is pulling away from another and having a gravitational effect on it, which may cause it to crash into some other galaxy in a solar system like ours, and destroy them all. This could destroy billions of planets, and billions of life-forms, just as is happening in millions of other galaxies and solar systems right now.

How important is the existence of an animal, a human and a bee, compared to the crashing solar systems, happening in the universe right now? Not very important, so how important are the ideas of the group? The animal wants a fruit, the bee wants nectar and the human wants to see a god. These ideas are nothing. The only thing that will survive the short chaotic lives we glimpse is your enlightened spirit, your consciousness, so that is what is important and must be cultivated by all in the group: the animal, the bee and you.

If you gave God the ability and said He is magically infinite, couldn't He choose to exist as one entity to you, so you can understand Him with your limited, unopened mind, when His real form is something else, something greater? You tell your three-year-old that you are his parent, but you can't expect him to understand that you are also a hedge fund manager, a spouse, an in-law, a friend, a sailor and a CIA agent all in one. What would he do with that information? He won't understand it all. Same here — we are told as much as we can understand. We must keep learning and evolving: drinking milk, glass by glass, slowly, not the whole gallon all at once.

It's like being able to hear sound. Until the discovery of the microwave, no one thought sound could be used to cook food. What would they have thought about that information 2,000 years ago? In the same way, we really don't know about God's true form, and you can name or call any entity God. When we let children listen to classical music when studying, the sound somehow helps them learn, remember or understand more things, by one process or another. Maybe it relaxes their senses or stimulates different parts of the brain. It may even help release different hormones that help the brain to increase comprehension. This little we know about sound or the consciousness we confusingly call "God."

So how much can we really have known about the Light, the Consciousness, 2,000 and 4,000 years ago? We are not following a new consciousness, one which was discovered in modern times. It has been here all along. Although we are inundated with religious ideas that are thousands of years old, they are not as old as the consciousness of all life in the universe. As far back as the 17th century, different groups, including some people of the Jewish faith, tried to bring forth the understanding or concept of enlightenment, and God Consciousness

without religion, to the public arena, but were largely rebuffed by the mainstream religions, which did not think it a matter that their followers should be aware of, for fear of losing their favor.

It's like a community leader who heads the Catholic Church in my area. He does helpful things for everyone, of all religions. He does not ask what religion you follow; if you need his services, he is there for you. He is not doing the church's work, as he probably thinks he is. He is doing *his* work, just in a church. The doing of good is done by him for others, and I'm sure he would do it even if he was not the Father in a church. We can be the same; do good works, out of church. Don't think about goodness just in church on Sunday, or on behalf of a religion and its dogma; do it for others for free, not for any recognition, reward or fame.

Man is at a level too low spiritually to see or understand God's forms or existence, so for practical purposes, God does not exist to us — what exists is just a misdirected idea of what people want God to be: in other words, our idea or version of God is the product of religious psychosis coupled with religious paranoia in a seemingly neat nutshell. Don't misunderstand. I'm not saying a god doesn't exist at all. It's just that we are not enlightened enough to see or know much about an actual god force, so humans made up one. Mother Teresa kept searching her whole life, more than 50 years, for a god she knew nothing about and never found it...and she was a nun.

If she had been taught that God existed in or through her good deeds and good thoughts, then she would have realized that she was with the God Consciousness all along. She was not educated enough in the real way to understand enlightenment, in order to find Him (or It). It's like that footprints in the sand story. You don't know about the force that is sustaining you and carrying you through life. You don't even know it is there. You think it is someone called God, when it is something totally different.

It's not the tires that are driving you around; it's the car. The tires are just part of it. Similarly, your idea of a god is just a small part, a tire of the larger vehicle which exists, with each religion having one.. Now if you look at it, the tires and the cars are good because they are the vehicles or the means that gets mankind on the road of consciousness, so use them as such. Use religion as a stepping stone, to learn and understand the truth. Don't just worship the tire.

Enlightenment simply means seeing and doing things through your inner self, rather than your outer self, which is contaminated with human senses, like religious psychosis and paranoia, prejudices, greed, jealousy, racism, love of money, fame, power over others, and so on. We must seek goodness not God-ness, and consciousness, not consistency and comfort in our continuously changing lives. We work hard to buy things that add consistency and comforts to our lives, without selflessly trying to do good for each other. To see God we first have to see the good in ourselves, and then in others. You can't bring good to others if you can't first find it in yourself.

The fear sellers try to fool you into thinking there is a fast-track way to something called salvation, just by praying, giving tithes, being baptized, accepting Jesus, not being gay or supporting gay marriage, not using contraception, being christened or some combination of these. That's just being lazy and gullible. You can't snap your finger and be saved from your prejudices; that is wrong. You can't accept Jesus or anyone else, and become a good person. We see that in most worshippers. You can't be christened or baptized, and become magically good. You have to work for it, deserve it or you can't find it. What if salvation is not a prize in the sky, but really means being good and becoming conscious as a result? That's the real saving — of yourself; being saved is becoming enlightened, and this will save you from your greedy path of achieving the nothingness of your Earthly riches.

It is in the doing that you learn and achieve success. You can't choose not to study, and get an education or high grades; you have to do the work to acquire the knowledge of the specific subject you are trying to pass. Learning carpentry won't help you pass physics. Likewise, you will acquire the knowledge only when you first do the work. While doing the work of goodness for others without reward, you will slowly be cleansing your dusty mind and soul, and through that work, you will learn about and acquire more and more enlightenment. Soon you will become a person who can give up all your wants and prejudices, or at least control them, and this is progress that you can measure, and take with you when you die. When your children learn this from you, won't they become better persons who you will be more proud of?

Jesus just taught about goodness and love. He didn't set lofty goals, and give commandments, but one suggestion; do unto others. He kept it simple. Be without sin and then you can cast stones. Cleanse yourself first, the inner self, not the outer self. People in His time were so dismayed, and in so much poverty, pain and desperation, they were only focused on their outer selves, their outer pain, and their outer thirst for relief. He tried to show them that their thirst and quenching came from within, and when that was done, the outer problems were nothing, temporary, and could be used as an opportunity for growth.

He may have realized that this was all our ancestors could comprehend. The enlightenment from selflessness, which He taught, has been held back and manipulated by the churches for 2,000 years. It is not difficult to be selflessly good and enlightened, not even in this present age; in fact, it's easier, and people won't burn you at the stake or stone you if you do. On the Ed Schultz radio program on November 4th 2008, I heard one of his audience members say she recently became blind, and did not take food stamps because she did not need them. She was helping in her little way, by not being a financial burden on the state. You can do unselfish things, too.

Don't believe in demons. Believe in yourself. Don't teach your children to believe in demons, Satan and hell. If you are teaching them to be weak like that, you are putting them in danger with such poisonous thoughts because you can lose them in the end to the gangs, who will show them a more desperate kind of truth and relief: one that entails stealing and killing to survive the rise of gas and other prices. Gangs drive, shop in the malls and eat more than you think. Teach your children to empower and believe in themselves and you may be able to avoid this devastating future. The youth in our society are not believing in fantasy and antiquated stories about some delirious rapture, while their world is crumbling around them, with recession and war at the forefront of the threats to their future, and the children they want to bear.

In the 1800s, the Millerites believed that nonsense. Look at what happened to them as a result. These modern-day Millerites in the churches, who are telling you to believe in demons, to believe in their misunderstandings, are the true downfall of man — not religion, but gullible or nonchalant people who invent religion, twist it and believe in it, while they prevent man from progressing past the fears, dogma and inhibited psychology of those who lived under different oppressive circumstances thousands of years ago.

One may argue that we are living under similar oppressive circumstances now, but actually, all we have to do these days is vote to get change, and be alert to keep the officials accountable. Back then if you spoke out, you died. Also, our lives are filled with conveniences they would have thought only Satan could provide. Believe me, air conditioning is not an oppressive circumstance. Neither is hot food from a microwave oven. We are more distracted by the vanities we run after than the well-being and future of our families. People are not even that interested in voting for the betterment of their family; that's how uninterested we are. They vehemently vote about gay rights and stem cells, and are not as concerned about their family's future. Not even 50% of the population votes in our elections, so I guess uninterested people reap what they sow — bad politicians, bad policies and wars.

Ask yourself, why do both sides in any war say that they have God on their side? Is the great God really on one side or the other, or both? I think not. Why would it have mattered to Him who we fought or who won? We will all die and join the great consciousness anyway. Do you think He would be happier if you bought a red bicycle instead of a blue one? That's how silly this kind of thinking is. Religion makes us jump through hoops and it takes away self-empowerment.

Do you believe that we are created in God's image? If you think this, then you must realize that we are encased within this material body and what you see in the mirror is not God's real image. That real image, our spiritual self, is contained within the body and we cannot see it, just the same way we can't see God or the energy in a battery.

What's the difference between God and Satan, if both of them cause you pain? If one pain is a test, what is the other? Is it a reward or a punishment? Why would God allow Satan to "turn man against his brother, until man exists no more?" That's just not smart thinking on our part to believe that makes sense. It is usually when we are in pain that we seek God, or His help, so is it God that's really causing us the pain, in order for us to seek Him? It's all a never-ending, cyclic, fanatical story meant to keep you confused and controlled. Maybe it's us just chasing our vain pleasures that are causing people to be unhappy. Are we just subjecting others to our religious psychosis? Just imagine if John Lennon's words were true, and there was a world with no dogmatic religions or religious psychosis. What if all the imaginative clergy were scientists? We would have been space explorers seeking out new worlds in new galaxies, like in a TV show right now. We would have invented the cell phone 1,000 years ago and walked on the moon before that.

The various religions can each be seen as a story that reflects the imagination and understanding of primitive minds or a delusional group 6,000 years ago. I classify that group as religiously psychotic and paranoid. Some of these people had the intellect and progressive demeanor of a stone, compared to the intelligence we now possess. It would really be a shame for a modern person, or group of people, with all the gray matter we have acquired through the centuries, to go down that road of paranoid, nonsensical biblical thinking, with demons haunting us at every turn. The inventors did it all to save the sanity of the people back then, as they lived in the most difficult and oppressive of circumstances, and that was honorable and needed at that time. I thank and applaud them. Through the years though, that reason has changed to the quest for money, power and control. We should wise up and follow the money.

Why do they still teach religion, in the 21st century? Same reason as before — money and power; apparently, nothing's changed. Do they know the truth? I don't know if any other church knew, but as I said before, I suspect the Vatican knew of Jesus' real meaning in His messages, or should have figured it out. It's right there throughout the Bible. Thou shall not kill and do onto others... Aren't those the only two guidelines we need to use? Throw away the rest of the books, from all the religions. We only need those two guidelines. With them you won't even need the psychosis of religion and its dogma. Please understand, I mean not to insult but to inspire.

You can know the truth by looking inside yourself, not outside at the church. The church can be a different player in the community, a guiding light in social affairs, bringing people together, just as people think they do or should be doing, but right now they are part of the political partnership starting wars and fueling them around the world, and that is dangerous.

Our innocent children are the ones being sent to fight wars. They are not even old enough to drink alcohol, but they are deemed old enough to be sent to fight, kill and die. The church then moves in to pick up the pieces and get converts. This mimics the conquering powers of days gone by. They conquered, and sent their churches to convert and pacify the primitive minds, or be killed during the process of Christianization. Have we brought Christianity to Iraq and Afghanistan as yet?

Is war a test of man by God? No.

Does God allow us to become ill because he wants the drug companies to make profits for the investors who pray to Him for good returns? No.

Was Mother Teresa an evil woman who could not find God? No.

Did the Native American Indians worship the wrong God, so He let them be brutally raped, murdered and wiped out? No.

Do you believe a 9/11 event won't happen again because our leaders are Christians and their all-powerful God has their backs? No.

Should I expect my children to believe the story that Jesus died on a cross to wipe away our sins and save us? No. Save us from what?

Was He murdered by the church to hold on to their power and following? Yes, He was murdered by the church because he preached that you are your own God and don't need the church: just be good to everyone and live in peace with love.

Should I expect my children to believe God put all His bets on us and didn't make millions more worlds elsewhere in the universe?

Are we a backup? Plan B or C?

Are we the failed version? I hope not.

Our children are not short-sighted and gullible to believe ancient religions, so wake up. You are losing them!!

People who look for God's help are not seeing who they are and how capable they really are. They are greedy. They are not content with what they have, which is life, peace, health. That is all they have; that is all they need. That is all they were born with. They can achieve the rest for themselves. Why do they look for a god to give them what they don't need, like winning the lottery? Do they actually get it? No. I pray all the time to win it; believe me, prayers don't work. We can't take anything with us when we die anyway.

If you believe in God, then God deserves more than selfish prayers. God deserves good deeds to others as the expression of gratitude. Hatred of gay people and others are not an example of gratitude for life. The churches trade in weakness and fear, through the paranoia of God watching your every move, and listening in on your every thought. They are conducting a profitable business. The marriage of the church and the corrupt politicians is a natural thing now. It was then, as well, when religion was invented. Jesus exposed that fact.

The church and the rulers did each other's bidding, and caused Jesus to be murdered. Why? To retain the vast power they had. Ancient, ignorant man's imagination made him suffer from paranoia, which has now been accepted as normal and expected by the faithful. Whatever you do, you are taught to be paranoid and think that God is watching you, listening to you, like a security guard does. Delirium and paranoia made a powerful combination which effectively brought about a need to have a god.

The saying goes, "Show me your friends and I'll show you who you are." The good priests are easy to find. They will not align themselves with the bad politicians, and vice versa. You will find them in the community centers helping the needy. The churches that are aligned with bad politicians are just fingers of the same hand, the hand of corruption. Sometimes they may not approve of what each other is doing but it is rare for the fingers to lead the hand, so where the hand of corruption goes, its minions, the fingers, have no choice but to do its bidding and get the job done.

So, don't follow the church or politicians who show corrupt ways. Work with the ones who show good works. By their actions you will see their compassion. See through their actions if they are good, and if they are someone with whom you want your family to work, not follow, for the betterment of a greater society.

I do not let my Chinese, Indian, Jewish, African,

Punjabi, or any of my other friends think that I feel superior or inferior to them because they worship in different ways to me or each other. I accept all invitations to attend and worship in their houses of worship. I am a Christian Hindu Muslim, with a Jewish heart and Buddhist bones. I worship by doing good…most of the time, anyway.

Believing you are weak makes you weak. The thought counts; that's where the actions and self-empowerment originate. Society fails over and over again through time, because the people fail. Why? They fail because they are taught to believe in something other than themselves, and to accept failure as God's will; you will succeed when He says you will.

At every turn, whatever they do, they are taught to say, "Thank God," "Praise God," "Saints be praised," and so many more God phrases, giving thanks to everything but themselves. They do nothing but pray and praise, so they get nowhere, while the good bird that goes out and works gets the worms. The Good Samaritan leads the way to freedom: freedom from religious bondage and human suffering.

Slaves also had to praise their masters. All these "praise" phrases reinforce the notions that we are watched over, controlled, answerable and inferior to a higher power: that we are fed by this vengeful master, and we must bow and cringe in fear, and worship the eternal presence of Him. That's not so. Do you cringe in the company of your parents? You don't or shouldn't have to. Yes, you are thankful for life, and your thanks must not be manifested by praise and empty words to gods. Who are you trying to fool with empty words and no good deeds? Wouldn't the gods see and know your words are empty? Your appreciation must come from your daily life of doing good things. You have to use this life for the noble purpose of human progress. Don't tear down your fellow man; lift him up. He's your brother and in turn, you will be lifted up by him or someone else, higher than you could climb by yourself. I am helped and lifted by others for free, without payment. It is a ripple of doing good things.

Some religions teach you to be paranoid, to expect and look forward to the rapture, the apocalypse, or Judgment Day. This is the day you die, and you are trained to accept defeat and to accept your death lovingly; you will also be subject to some kind of judgment. Well, if this were true, the magic number from Revelations, Chapter 7, of 144,000 persons to be the "saved" who go to heaven is faulty. The dogma they hold fast to is making you look favorably toward death, inspiring in you the hope of working toward a goal of becoming as religious a soul and church-going donator as can be, in order to get into the 144,000 elite group, when you are lucky enough to meet your long awaited death. Is that sane? They promise it will be a sweet death, blissful even, an enjoyment beyond imagination, as you will be in the elite club, the chosen few, the saved, the 144,000. You will be swept up in bliss. Just put your money, your admission fee, into the collection plate.

We are so sinful by religious standards, not even the pope will pass that test to get into that club. This could be called your training for your suicide mission, marching triumphantly and willingly toward death instead of bravely and excitedly driving through life with the pedal to the metal. If you think favorably about death, pretty soon you will be at ease with it, receiving it and giving it, and you will welcome the rapture; then you can join those around the world who give in, and start and support wars to quicken the arrival of Armageddon. Haven't you noticed that murder and suicide come easy to some religious, delirious people who support wars? Do you want to join them in their support?

Also, have you thought of how they came up with the number 144,000? When they were putting the dogma together, I don't think that they thought the world would have six billion people and counting. If they had, they would have set the number in the millions, but they were making it up as they went along. Maybe the pope will change the number to a higher one. We'll see.

We humans are all too immersed in our existence on this Earth to pass the sinner's test. Thank God, that there's no God's judgment to worry about, to poke fun there. God is not here or there somewhere, and interactive as a video game. The system you go through after death is not important; what is important is to know that you are here to fulfill a mission of living a life, any kind of good, unselfish life, free of religious retardation. Learning religious dogma is not necessary for you to live an enlightened, selfless life, like Jesus did. It is simply a retardant. In fact, it is dangerous; you can become religiously psychotic, if you're not careful, or do not get help from enlightened sources.

A mental and spiritual lift is something you can't buy at the supermarket or at church, but you can still acquire it, if you do good things in your life. It's like washing your car often. It's more pleasant and uplifting for you to ride in and drive a clean vehicle; that's the same with your body and spirit. When you cleanse your body with good thoughts and deeds, your spirit, your inner true self, is much more comfortable riding and driving inside your outer self/body.

The inner self is less distracted when not addressing issues of the body, like greed, racism and hate, so it can drive much better down the road of your existence on this Earth, your journey of life. This will make you reach your destiny much more fulfilled and peaceful, having helped many others along the way. Who says there aren't heroes anymore? You can be, first to yourself, by deciding to improve, then to your family by your action of improving. Later on, this improvement should and usually will increase to helping others to improve themselves, and they will also go on to help others.

How does medical care and intervention support or negate the belief of God? In the past, a person at death's door was considered a recipient of God's blessing of being recalled by Him. Everyone says that the dearly departed have gone back to God, He called them back and we should be happy for them. So why are we not happier with death and are not rushing to die, instead of trying to stay with our families?

If the dead have been recalled by God, regardless of how they die, then the paramedics are not doing us any favors. They are actually doing a bad thing by saving us from death, aren't they? The lifeguard who performed CPR on your child, is he doing an evil thing by saving a drowning person? The surgeons who operate to remove something which will cause your death, or cure our cancers, are they doing something against God? Does God punish us for saving lives, or going against His wishes and curing ourselves of a multitude of diseases?

No, we have to preserve life and God has no role in

that. We have to help life to grow, not take it by any means, including wars. The inner spirit is there to guide your brain to do what you came here to do, which is to do good. You may be resisting and doing bad things, but you will improve with age; most do. You did not come here to die. You came here to live, and life is greater than money and power, as these are just temporary illusions that do not keep us really happy. If you lost them today, you would be unhappy but you would survive. You can't lose your good deeds or your happy spirit, so that is what you should pursue.

I think that anyone can see that the thought of a god running things on this Earth does not add up. Were you saved from an accident by the hand of God performing a miracle on you, or because of the good, coincidental, split-second timing of events that caused you to survive, without your input? You may think that a split-second escape can only be a miracle from God, but that is opinion, not fact and with or without you or God, life goes on at split-second speed, here on Earth, and everywhere else in the universe, that you don't see.

I am spending a lot of time on the issue of religion because I think it has been the one largest single hurdle to mankind's progress, all through time and all around this world. I know that to many of you, the idea of a better and deeper understanding of your own religion, and becoming enlightened through it, is new and could be confusing, so I spend the time, and I want you to be skeptical. Don't just stop at the door of your beliefs and rituals; start to look deeper into your religion, to find the core, where you will find consciousness.

You will discover that you do not have to kneel to find your inner self. All religions teach goodness but no one needs to be controlled by the dogma, ideology or the purveyors of the church. Many people will read this book, and even though I am speaking of one subject, religion, not everyone will get the idea of self control. This is why I constantly present the argument from many different angles, as each new angle will help other people to understand the simple truth: that you are your own best friend and companion on this journey. Take good care of your friend, Jesus said.

Why would God let us invent and use the atom bomb? Do we really think God would be so vengeful or shortsighted? Are we letting God exist in a humanly-conceived box of confinement? Do we even know exactly how many people we killed with the A bomb? Were the black plague, flu epidemics and pandemics a punishment or experiment by God? That He didn't prevent them does not make sense. He did not help the Holocaust victims, so does He exist on Earth? No, not in the interactive video game way people have been misled to believe.

I think there are gods in every level of life; insects are gods to plants, as much as we humans are gods to insects. So, was ancient man just interacting with a more intelligent being? A god can be anything, including a delusion allowed to simmer for thousands of years and supported by thousands of people, with some over time injecting their own twist of understanding into the mix of dogma. Tribes all over the world have things and ideas they worship. We are just a bigger tribe living with a bigger illusion. The tribes think they have a god. We think we have a bigger, better, real god. It is a delusion and an illusion that has been built up, and continues to be built on, by well-meaning people who needed something to believe in when they stopped believing in themselves. On Earth, we are the gods here, and we are charged with the responsibility to do good for each other and the planet.

Look at the fish in a tank; whatever they think about us, we are not their gods. We are like gods to them but they are just a source of enjoyment to us, like French fries or a dog. Careful though, if you are in China, a French fry may be a dog, just a source of food. The fish are intelligent enough to survive, build homes, raise families, avoid danger, and find mates, and are smart enough to ensure their continued existence without the destructive force of man's pollution killing them. We have established that they communicate with each other, much like whales and dolphins do.

We even train sea animals to save people or help in various ways in a war setting, like finding bombs underwater. Remember Flipper, the dolphin? He was highly trained. Are the animals praying to us? Are their leaders telling them they are created in our image? We don't know what they communicate about, but still you can see how ridiculous it is to think there is an interactive god in their lives or in our lives. Maybe the pythons or the lions think we are just a food source to them, and we are their walking French fries. Does that make them our gods? No. What does your god look like? You don't know, do you?

In the year 2009, we find ourselves preaching fanatically about a god invented 6,000 years ago by what may have been illiterate people, for their own reasons and uses. These people meant well, but were so ignorant they would have thought heart surgery was a trip to the Devil's lair, and that they were seeing what the Devil does to bad people when they die.

Being in a state of ignorance made them invent a god to diffuse or allay their fears and misunderstandings, and cope with their harsh living conditions. Education was not something that was given to most people of that era, so they had to accept whatever they were taught, as gospel, as law. It was something they could not disprove or disagree with; it was all they had, and they would have been cast out, stoned or even killed if they did not fall in line with everyone else.

Their level of education is surpassed by our third and fourth graders now. Would you believe third graders and call the TV reporters if they said that God speaks to them all the time? No, but you would carry them to a doctor because they may be sick and delusional. So how come you believe the 6,000-year-old, mistaken, misdirected, delusional, beaten-as-slaves third graders?

It's like a human teaching a dog or pack of dogs to live together. The animals will learn what the master teaches and they will do what they are taught. Likewise, humans who allow themselves to be led by religious leaders will learn to become weakling worshippers, and will become members of a sect or cult that believes in their own weakness, and needs to be lorded over by an unseen God, and of course, well-meaning, or opportunistic clergy. Think of it, wasn't Christianity a cult-like movement after Jesus' death, until forced into acceptance hundreds of years later? Fast forward that and here we are. In America we have so many cults and psychotic sects thinking all sorts of weird ideas about their gods. Look at the Waco disaster, and the other polygamist sect that had the authorities remove more than 430 of their children in 2008, some of whom were being raped and having children themselves, fathered by variously-aged perverted men and pedophiles. They were exchanging their under-aged daughters for someone else's. Everyone was having a merry time. Some of the children are believed to have been victims of child sexual abuse since an early age, even before puberty.

In the end, I surmise that there is not your God — there is only you. There is not your God — there is only me. There is not your God — there is only your son or daughter. There is not your God — there are only your family and friends. There is not your God — only the well-meaning priests, and a few corrupt priests and politicians working together. Until the time when we become enlightened enough to find the truth about the real God Consciousness, there is not your God, or any God, for us, or Mother Teresa.

Mahatma Gandhi found the God Consciousness of the universe, and he defeated the British occupiers without a sword, but with something more powerful: peace. That's real truth — inner spiritual courage, determination to do good, understanding the laws of the universe, and the confidence that we can improve our lives and everyone else's, if we just harness the power of peace and share love.

Can you get to heaven while fighting wars? No, that's murder. Doesn't the Bible say, "Thou shall not kill"? Remember, I am not telling you that God does not exist because everything exists, either physically in this world, physically in another part of the universe or even just in your mind. If you think there is danger or evil somewhere, then in your mind you are right, and therefore it is true to you, and maybe you can convince others to believe it too, without giving them proof. They are willing participants in believing you; they may have as little or as much understanding, or be as correct or as delusional as you. So religion is real, to you and many other people, but is there life on other planets and does your truth about God apply to them as well? Did God create others in His image on other planets or just you? Let the pope and all other religious leaders make up an excuse to answer that.

Are you curious or insulted by my ideas? Do you think there is truth other than what you have been taught? I think we are being misled and that is the real Shock and Awe on us, our country, our species and our families. We have modern-day oppression of truth, whether we are aware of it or not. If I make you curious or angry enough to seek the truth, just to prove me wrong, then you'll be better off and so will your family.

I saw a sign which asked "Where is the Messiah when we need Her?" Yes, people have differing views about God and want help and relief, but they are clearly not finding it, as they are looking for the wrong comforts. After helping thousands of children, Princess Diana suffered a horrible death. Where was God? If she and Mother Teresa could not find it, I feel certain that it is proved, God is not interactive and we won't find it either.

PROTECT YOUR FAMILY.
DON'T WAIT FOR GOD.

God Consciousness exists for you only after *you* exist to you. You cannot reach enlightenment through a church but only through yourself. If you have not found your inner self, how can you find consciousness? You are not insignificant — you are more important to yourself than you are to your family, friends or religion. Only after you find yourself will you be able to function, find truth and help others.

So what do you do? Until you make other plans, or arrangements, about God's help, you've got to protect your family, while you try to find yourself. Protect them against the gangs that want to indoctrinate your child and turn him or her into a criminal, going to jail and doing drugs, and destroying the future of your other children.

You've got to protect them from the greedy, unscrupulous and corrupt people who work in the banks, who give bad loans and then foreclose, who take away people's homes and destroy families; the greedy, unscrupulous people who support and work in their collection agencies; and those who harass you from morning to night to force you to give up, all for the almighty dollar.

You've got to protect them against the crooked politicians who support these corrupt banks. You've got a lot of problems, too many for a non-interactive, videogame-type God to solve for you, so I think you'd better be the hero, and show some strength to your children and family. Step up to the plate and solve these problems yourself. How? You have to keep voting, and calling and writing your elected officials often. Help to make them accountable for their actions and decisions, force them to clean up the neighborhoods. They can control police brutality better than you can. Stay active in the affairs of the community. This is also a good function for the church.

There are millions of people with children suffering from cancers and illnesses brought on by an unethical food and drug business, and the lack of regulations for the industry. These sick people need help more than you do. Your problems can be solved by you; theirs can't and they have to depend on a broken and corrupt health system if they stand a chance of living to see tomorrow. So help yourself.

You've got to stop cowering and wallowing in self pity, in hopes that some God will ride in on a flaming chariot and whisk you away to heaven. Will your God in shining armor solve your problems, and make you win the lottery or find a big bag of money because you deserve it and He owes you? Most people think lots of money will solve their problems and may even help them buy salvation by large donations. Do you think you are so important that God can't do without you, and He needs you, as you are the best thing to come along since sliced bread? No, you know better. You have to willingly become deserving of enlightenment to find it, as it exists all around you, in the good tasks you can perform, and thereby cleanse yourself with your good actions.

Some people have sanity attacks and want to leave a religion and seek their inner self, tap into their inner strength, but they have built their lives around the church and religion, and don't know how to leave. They think they will feel ashamed and they will let down the people around them, including their families and relatives if they leave, or that they will be looked upon as traitors or ridiculed for doing so. They know so little about God that they do not know what would happen if they leave. So they choose not to wake up, and to not have courage and break the cycle of misdirection, and find truth; they elect to hide their true feelings, and secretly question the religion but do not do anything about it, and continue to allow their loved ones to be misled by it. If Mom or Dad queries dogma, the kids might also, so do it.

Some people's leadership characteristics have been oppressed for so long, they are comfortable being sheep, running away from their duty and running with the flock. They choose to stay in religious bondage and dogmatic slavery. The good news is, they don't have to leave the religion, as they can help people anywhere they are. They don't even have to tell anyone. They just have to stop believing in the dogma of the religion. We all can. Strip the dogma away, with all the rituals, and seek a higher and closer understanding with the same non-violent consciousness called God, which you seek to find in any religion. You have to find the real Jesus, and all the other names of the consciousness you seek, and that can be done privately, without leaving the religion if you choose. If you stay, you may even be able to help others to find the source of truth. Also, stop the name calling. God doesn't have a name or a religious cage to stay in. That's just incorrect...dogma. God is not an object but that is what we are taught, with a name; that God is an object or an explainable thing. You will not learn the whole truth if you are told about it. You have to find it on your journey of peace.

You may ask how it's possible to find God. I will tell you. Pretend that there is no God and don't think about God. Thinking about God distracts you from doing what you must do to find God, so you will not find God by trying to search or worship or pray. Also you do not know God, so how will you know if you find God? You won't. All these things prevent you from doing what you need to do, which is simply to be and do good. God will not want you to do anything else but do good things. That is all you can do to become deserving of the knowledge. When you do good things, you are on the path, and you will find God and Goodness while on it. Good is the work that must be performed to find the truth you seek. Remember, God is not an object in a box that you can purchase with donations or hold with your hand.

Pick yourself up and get out of the gutter of selfishness, self pity and failure. Solve your problems and stop failing your family and your community. Find that inner strength. When you fail your family, they go out in the community and they carry your doom, gloom and weakness with them, so ultimately, you make them fail. They carry your failing religious teaching, as well. It's your fault. Be an example that strengthens them, inspires them and makes them feel pride in themselves and you. Find the truth to teac to them.

You are sitting there waiting for a god to fix your business and the family is sitting there waiting on you to fix things, so you end up disappointing them. You become nothing but a failure to your family and the world. Believe me when I tell you, your family won't wait too long. Your kids will grow up and leave, and your spouse will see through you and leave you mentally, physically or both. You then end up at the bottom of a bottle. When your kids grow up and leave, you want to know that you are sending them in the right direction to success, not to join some gang or become a convict.

If you were God, would you want everyone to sit around, waiting for you to come around and solve their problems, like you are some sort of slave or the hired help? If you were God, you would say that you don't need this bunch of worthless, lazy people. You won't even go near them. Newsflash — God is not coming. God is an instrument being conveniently used by the church to enrich itself; enlightenment is an instrument to be used by you to enrich yourself, and the path to achieve this is to be peaceful and to do good, so it is a worthy endeavor. Peaceful: thou shall not kill.

Public figures speak about God as if He or It is real but they don't believe that, because their actions show and prove that they do not fear His punishment, as they rob us like regular bandits. Action speaks louder than words. They just say they are Christians to be in the group, in the clique, appearing in the know, fooling everyone who has enough low self esteem to think they need a god for a crutch. Your kids don't need a crutch; they need a parent because they can do crime by themselves just fine, if you don't inspire them.

These superstitious and misled people are the target of unethical public figures, from politicians to priests, from radio talk show hosts, to TV show hosts; some of them are liars and fools leading others, the blind leading the blind. Lying is never part of the truth, so we must stop lying, and living a lie, in order to be reunited with the truth of real God Consciousness, when we go to the hereafter whenever death transforms or releases you from your human form. People live as if they will be here forever. No, we will pass on and be there forever.

Some misled or corrupt priests say that God struck us with AIDS and Katrina, for our bad deeds, and some Christians agreed by staying silent. Well, if that were true, why did He let children be born with or become infected with disease? Are unborn children punished for the deeds of their parents or have they come here with baggage from somewhere else? Is He punishing us with a recession because we are deporting millions of illegal immigrant children? Don't forget 12 million illegal immigrants in most cases means two parents and a few kids (on average we are deporting 4 to 6 million kids). That's a lot of tears and grief to fall on us. Those numbers remind me of the Holocaust and the annihilation of the Native Americans. Weren't religious people involved in those incidents also? What about the doctors and nurses who are infected with AIDS in the course of their jobs? Are they evil, too?

Jim Jones, Jimmy Swaggart, Tony Alamo, Ted Haggard and countless other priests swindled many people along the way: their parishioners. Are their parishioners really saved? No, but they were used. God is really just a game to them, the object being to get rich. These religious shysters on TV, not the good priests, make things up as they go along, and bend the facts to fit their twisted translation of religious doctrines. As their twisted versions become more accepted by the willing, uninquisitive and carefree followers, they are transformed into fact and history.

This is how the Bible, and other religious books and teachings came to be; it wasn't magic and miracles. It was just the power of mind control wielded by the privileged and those perceived as knowledgeable — power to convince the meek, frightened and oppressed to kneel, and power to bring about a system of control of the masses. This power commanded and ensured the unwillingness of followers to question the purveyors of this fine tradition, of seeing gods, and the ability to maintain an atmosphere of suppressing the disbelievers.

This power was always passed down to a hand-selected, elite few, like-minded individuals, who in turn took over the mantle and carried on the tradition of control, changing dogma and implementing new ideas to keep the population in fear and awe of gods, who would be generous when they and their priests were worshiped, respected and held in high esteem. But these gods would be angry, spiteful and vengeful when ignored or not praised, and the preachers not revered. The punishment to non-believers and their families, throughout those turbulent times, was being put to death in various ways, by the church, politicians and kings. Also, being threatened with excommunication or being ostracized, if you resisted, was a real scare to a humble peasant. If that didn't work, I hear stoning and burning at the stake were chic and in style all year round.

The Anglicans say they follow Christ and believe the Bible; so do the Roman Catholics, the Presbyterians, the Baptists, the Shouter Baptists, the Mormons, etc. Many

Christians say that other Christians are wrong and they are right because they each do something differently to each other, so is that proof that all are mistaken?

If they were all correct, then they would all be together as one, saying the other religions of the world were wrong, like the Hindus, Buddhists, Jews, etc. I think they do that now anyway; that's the one thing they all agree on: suppression of other religions, subtly. They consider anyone who has not accepted their type of religion to be doomed and damned, even the different denominations of their own religion.

That is just more manipulation and mental reconditioning, using fear as a tactic of control. That is proof to me that they are all mistaken because they are all singing the same old song of doom and damnation, just in a different language around the globe about a different god, which begs the question of how many gods are there? Truth be told, they can all find the conscious force they call God by stripping away the dogma of each and every religion; then they would all be right, in any language. When they discover that force, I think they will stop calling it "God," as it is a force. People use the term God to mean something singular, with human-like goals and ideals, and it is more misleading than good to do this.

Few religions understand and teach enlightenment. The Hindus and Buddhists do in their own way, although they still have some dogma in both. I'm sure there are also others that teach enlightenment but the main religions don't. It is a threat to their control. They have rules to follow in order to attain freedom. Does that make sense to you? What kind of freedom is that, being subjected to religious bondage?

They are many different religions with different rules, so there must be a hundred gods. Each group invented a different view of their god. Within each group, they are even more splintered, with members having different views of what they think God should be and the boundaries He is kept in. The Christians are splintered in thousands of different sects and denominations with differing views and beliefs, and the other world religions also have the same occurrence. Is that blind mice running in circles? Sure.

Why do gods allow eating some meats and not eating others? Gods didn't make the rules; different men did at different times in different countries — all manmade rules, not made by any god. Why do some gods allow pre-teen marriage and some don't? Again God didn't decide; man did. Who wrote these religious documents? God didn't, man did. Who inspired the writers: God or man? If God, then which God of which country, as all the religions have writings that mirror each other, with strong differences?

Remember the term "lost in translation?" That most certainly applies to some of these religions, which have over the centuries morphed into cults that are stranger than fiction, after their writings were translated, adopted and are forever adapting to modern societal changes. They are still making it up as they go along, as now they are the authorities on abortion, stem cell research and gay marriage rights. Did they have those issues 4,000 years ago? No.

So Moses parted the sea, Jesus turned water into wine, and someone blessed us with cancer and AIDS. Did He bless us with nuclear radiation poisoning, as well? No. It's all in the mind and manmade. It's what you choose to believe. None of it is a real religion with real gods: only man's imagination on steroids. Truth is not a changing religion but a non-changing reality.

Apparently, we are still primitive enough to believe in magical kingdoms with angels, The Garden of Eden, naked people and a serpent who gives away free apples. The media is also now the religious voice of the people. I'll give you three guesses as to which people the media represents. The powerful churches and wealthy people, of course, just as it has always been. Not much has changed; we just have cars instead of horses and planes instead of flaming chariots. The pursuit of power and money still exists much the same as it did back then.

While observing the growing habits of my five-foot plant, I noticed that as I had it placed by the window, the plant grew slowly and toward the window, distracted by trying to get the direct sunlight, but when it slowly grew upwards and was able to pass the window, the growth rate increased and the direction of growth changed from sideways to straight upwards. I can only deduce, correctly or not, that it is now gathering or feeding off the energy all around it, instead of being distracted by going toward the window.

This leads me to draw a parallel with the churches and their religions attracting the people, and causing our inner and spiritual growth to slow down, become distracted and go sideways, and if we were to gather the energy around us and grow that inner self instead of going sideways toward the religion, we would progress faster to the real source of truth, light and consciousness that we all seek.

The window was at a lower level, and when the plant passed it, it discovered a better, faster and more efficient type of growth, without the distraction of what the window offered. Each level has a different consciousness and state of being. Just as when we die, we go to a different level. Jesus' teachings and philosophy show this to be true, as He said, "I am not of this world." He had ascended to a higher level.

People are now becoming curious about what is there after we die. I ask you, what happens to a plant that gets too much sunlight or water? It cannot use it, just like us who are not conscious or enlightened enough to understand the forces we exist by. We can't use or even comprehend that information about the journey and work we will do after we depart from this Earth, without enlightenment.

That's one reason why most don't know what the truth is. They can't understand it or realize that it is so simple. I suggest that people learn more about doing good deeds for others. Then they will understand what Jesus meant. It is more important now to become enlightened than to figure out what happens after you attain consciousness. That understanding comes with enlightenment anyway, and it's not a truth that will change with the wind, as these religions do. The truth remains the same always.

CHRISTIANITY AND JESUS

Who is Jesus? He is the source that Christianity was incorrectly modeled after. Was He born on December 25th? No. Was a star placed there to guide the wise men? No, that solar system was always there. Where did He study during His missing years? Many differ in their opinions. Were all His miracles done by magic? Again some differ in their views. This alone can demonstrate that some things we were taught may not be completely accurate. It is said that we should trust no man. Jesus cast doubt on the truthfulness of the Pharisees and the scholars, who I believe had a great deal of control in the writing of the early Bible, and the rewritings through the ages. The question that remains in light of this is, what is the real truth?

Christians are taught that blind faith is the only good faith; that's not true. A God, like a good parent, would want smart children. The churches mistakenly teach that God wants blind, gullible followers, as they themselves do. If you question the churches or doubt the religion, they will say you are wrong. I think the purpose of your children's brain is to question. Aren't you proud of their ability to use reason to guide themselves through life, in your absence, and keep themselves out of trouble? You may not know it but peer pressure causes kids to do things they shouldn't do, because you, their parent or elder, teach them to be gullible and not question. This will allow them to become followers instead of leaders, and when they follow criminals, what do you think they will become?

Many Christians choose to blatantly condemn any other religion as wrong, as idol worshippers, as witches and any other name that makes them feel good about their own religion. I won't say that their critique is bad, but it is not good since they do not recognize the real truth of consciousness in the core of their own religion, but only believe in a cheap, knock-off, dogmatic version.

Jesus was missing from the age of 12 to the age of 29. Where was He? It is said that He spent some of that time in India learning what He needed to know, from the gurus and monasteries He visited, to establish His ministry. That could be a rumor; I was not there. Maybe He only spent the summer, a couple weeks, as the message was not hard to get. Anyone who can prove otherwise is welcome. We do know that the peoples of the East traded with each other, and taught each other, so it was easy to pick up each other's ideas and teachings. Practicing self control is the hard part but he could have done that on his own after learning about it.

If other forms of peaceful religions that taught enlightenment were wrong, Jesus would have said so, and King James would have been only too happy to include that in the Bible. King James elected not to say that Jesus taught that all other religions teaching enlightenment were wrong, and this is important. It is not only important to observe what was said, but also what was not said, and Jesus did not say it. King James decided to have the Bible redone to reflect certain ideals and totally omit others, but he still did not write that Jesus taught or said that all the other enlightened religions were wrong.

What Jesus did try to do was teach His flock a mild form of enlightenment: His flock being anyone who would listen to Him, as people were all lacking in understanding, self control and knowledge, in His eyes. While Jesus was teaching, would He have turned away anyone from another religion who wanted to join Him? No. Did He tell them His religion was better? No. Did He even have a religion for them to follow back then? No. He taught that truth was going directly to the source, through self control, without a religion or church in between. This is simple and truthful.

The idea that Jesus might be teaching some variation of Eastern culture or religion was unacceptable to the Europeans, and still is. They wanted their own religion and largely reinvented it, with King James using the earlier versions of the scriptures, erasing things that would not fit nicely into their perfectly thought-up religion. In their primitive way of thinking, of always trying to conquer everything, was this just another pathetic attempt by the hierarchy in the 1600s at trying to control the populace? Yes. Control resources and economy, with the reinvention of this super religion! It has come to pass, up until recent times, when in the last 40 years, with the growth of massive multinational companies, the church has had to take a back seat to bigger business or at least share the throne. Until then, the church was the biggest business in the world, the only game in town. To some extent it could be said that the collective churches still control the world's purses, just with the sheer size of their combined real estate equity and donated income.

The church wielded more power than kingdoms throughout history, and still does. Kings and kingdoms come and go. Each new power would quite naturally fall in line behind the church to rule the masses. If the churches wanted, they could have overthrown any king, even King James, so he also had to keep on their good side and keep them happy. Dozens of bishops and scholars of that time, around the year 1611 AD, rewrote the Bible, because there were other versions, but they wanted to make the Super Bug of all religions. King James was instructed to rewrite the Bible by his predecessor, who saw the need for a new direction with the religion, to revamp the waning religion and dwindling hopes of the masses.

How can we tell that the real truth is different from what we have been taught? Simple: if a church is working with corrupt politicians against the best interest of the people, they are not the conduit to godliness and will not bring truth. Look around, does this world of recession, greed and war look like religion, which has always been in control, is the way? They, the church and their corrupt politician friends, are who led us here, to wars and recession.

Remember the vendors in the churchyard? Jesus chased them out. They are back, disguised as televangelists, churches, and cults still using the churchyard to sell their wares, just as they did in Jesus' time, except they now own the church and the premises. They have radio programs, and they have their own newspapers, TV channels and Internet sites. Sadly, some people who are trying to be good are unknowingly attending these same corrupt churches, and think there is nowhere else to go to worship. Usually, this is how new churches are formed. This is okay but the message has to change.

The miracles Jesus performed are some of the skills

learned, practiced and known by only the highest of Eastern holy men. What some thought were miracles were simply high forms of Eastern healing methods used by enlightened men. Some of the miracles quoted can just as easily be embellishments planted by the church to discourage the suspicions of Him not being sent with powers from God. If Jesus was thought to have revived a dead person, then there would be no question of His powers from God, so why couldn't the church or King James have made it up? Who here can say it did or didn't happen? No one who was there then is here now to say. Such is the game of deception that is played on us, to be blind believers.

What is important to note, the point they missed, is that His real greatness was His teachings, not magical healing stories. His teachings of love, humility, self control and service to others are His real magic, and they live on. Acquiring these is the only way you will become holy, become pure, elevate yourself spiritually from the animals we may be, and be one with the truth, because the force you call God is within your thoughts and your being, not in a church somewhere. Not enclosed within four walls or in stories of magic.

There is not much honesty, integrity and respect in this world anymore. There is much more greed, hate and despair plaguing the seed of mankind. I think I may be one of many that now have a duty to try to help restore man's legacy or destiny. We are all the appointed stewards of our children's future and we have not secured it, but have left it to be blown and be battered in the winds of unchecked, undisciplined capitalism, globalization and plain, unsweetened greed.

We can't try to change the destructive course that our

children are destined to go down, caused by our greedy ways, until we first change the destructive ways we have allowed ourselves to succumb to internally, spiritually and mentally. We have become accustomed to lying, cheating, stealing and being surrounded by death. Those who do it best are rewarded with the biggest jobs and best salaries. If we do not change internally, we can't bring about change externally.

There is an old saying that goes, a liar is a thief and a thief is a murderer. The liar, when he is caught by the homeowner at 2 a.m. stealing in his home, will murder the homeowner to get away secretly. So the liar is a thief, who then becomes a murderer. We have become a society of liars, and we are willingly allowing the thieves to invade our homes and steal our most prized possession, which are our children.

They do not even have to murder us to get away, as we don't try to stop them. They are stealing our children's hearts, minds and their futures. If you can't understand how and why, I will tell you. They are stealing the children's hopes and dreams. The children are being taught that becoming a liar and a thief like them is good, to avoid ending up impoverished like us, their parents. The children are depressed when they see us suffering to pay the bills, with a dwindling income, amid rising gas and food prices, and the companies making record profits. You can't buy them the simple things they deserve, as you have to buy food and pay the rent instead. You must change this future, as the future is what we make it; it is in our hands and not predetermined.

To change this awful future, you must first change

within, and realize that you have been misled by dogmatic religion, and have compromised the bright hopes and future of your family in the process. Reconnect with your inner self. Be calm and still, and you will feel your inner spirit calling out to you sweetly, peacefully. Meditate. Visit yourself. Travel inside yourself and reunite yourself with your most sacred possession — you, your soul, your inner peace, and your inner, unselfish love of yourself.

There is no need to seek a god outside of yourself, as the seed of that consciousness, the source of that universal love, is already inside you, buried under deceit, hate, jealousy, vanity, racism, religious misdirection and greed. No one can take away your spirit, or its voice, which is called your conscience, but you can smother it, until you can't hear the voice anymore, as it is drowned out by our overly ambitious scream of wants and craving needs.

Lots of preachers don't want to reveal this truth to you, as they will lose you, so they have to teach you to beg God. To be weak and dependent upon the church, which I think was also King James's plan. Taxing or tithes by the church is now, and was then, one of the largest money-making ventures in the world. He also needed a way to keep the peasants in line, under control, submissive, and donating what little they had to the church, which I suspect would then be divvied up with King James in taxes. This practice kept them poor and him in power, thus giving unto Caesar what was Caesar's, (or unto James what was James's). I suspect Jesus did not say that line about Caesar, and King James put that in the Bible himself; If the population remained poor, he had more power over them. We see the same thing happening in today's society, with the elite and their multinational companies trying to destroy the middle class, and keep us all poor and controllable.

The church is not the arm of God Consciousness; you are. A god did not put you here to beg. Jesus never showed you to be afraid. He showed you to be strong, develop your inner courage and acquire self control, so you will have faith in yourself and face the tasks at hand. Don't run away and hide behind the church, scared of the future; when you run away, you leave your family behind defenseless. See what happens to fatherless kids in broken families; they stray and get in trouble.

What's the worst that can happen if you don't become like them, and do not lie and steal? You may live a poor honest life, having the respect of your family, and then die of old age. Aren't we dying anyway? Death, to an enlightened person, will only be a door to a better place, one step closer to your God Consciousness. Death without enlightenment is what you have now, and this will lead you to a slower route of attaining consciousness, but there is no hell waiting for you, so fear not.

Look at your priests not with hate, but with love and sympathy because the majority of them came to this path of religion out of love for you and the world, and were just taught the wrong thing themselves. Some come for money, but you can see the good ones by their deeds. The ones with expensive cars and mansions are up to no good, as that money could have fed the poor. The good souls, good priests, willingly and lovingly offer to you the guidance that they have been taught, with the specific task of teaching you love and faith.

They are wonderful people, who only want to help you, and you must treat them with love and kindness, as that is what they deserve. The road they chose is an honorable one; they were just armed for the task with the wrong truth — the dogmatic truth of a greedy, primitive church. We have grown since then. They are as much the misguided as you were before reading this, so let's move on with love and understanding. The crying and lost children are waiting. Change inside, so you can then change outside.

Is this culture of blind faith a measure of how misguided and weak your children will become? *No!* Remember you are their teachers; teach by example. Just as Jesus was a teacher, do as He did, and be as He was, humble and wise. Speak of tolerance, not hate and war. Speak the truth to the children, and don't deny your greatness to lead them well or their ability to understand. Believe in yourself and in them, and do what you know is good. Be humble and you will learn true strength. If you think what I am saying is incorrect, you owe it to your children to find out and teach them the real truth, not twisted or half-true stories made up from the dogma of the various religions we follow.

It's easier to crush someone than to apologize to them and be humble. I have crushed my own children many times, instead of being strong and humbling to them when they were right. Many parents make that mistake but we have to try to improve, and understand their intelligence, and we will become stronger ourselves. Be strong enough to apologize, and move on with love and humility. Tell them you love them 10 times a day. I do. That gives them confidence. They will not look for approval from anyone else because they have yours. Yours is the most important and the only one they seek.

Listen to your children and your inner self, not the rich televangelist swimming in your money. Your children will think you're weak for following the empty words of televangelists and their ilk. They will soon realize that the money you gave the church could have bought them new shoes.

Are you not trying to buy salvation with your donations while your family survives without you or with less? Trying to bribe whom? God doesn't need money. He needs you to get another "o" to make you "GOOD" because you already have "GOD." He's in your mind. He is an idea and He does not need your family's money; it is only the church that needs the money. There are people who go to church on Sunday to ask for forgiveness, but the rest of the week they don't want to offer help or forgiveness to anyone. Your donations don't buy forgiveness.

King James purposely hid a lot of the scriptures from you, but that is just the past, not your future. Don't live in the past; don't consider the Bible and the church to be more important than your family. Don't worry about the church. The church survived for 4,000 years. They'll survive now. Your family won't survive at the hands of the global multinational companies, who harvest us, run our lives and have your family's fate in their greedy hands. King James left out the good parts of the "Good Book" because he wanted the primitive people of that time to be under the control of the church, and by extension, him. We live in different times now, so we must change with the times and seek knowledge. We don't need King James anymore or his ideas.

We have the Internet, cell phones and airplanes now.

They are not forces of Satan, I assure you. It's not witchcraft; we're just smarter, more technologically advanced. So we must stop thinking like suppressed peasants of the Dark Ages, cowering behind the church, as if we're hiding from the king. Your children will see you as weak, and unfortunately, to our children, we can become the bad religious fanatic dashing their hopes. If your children's safety did not depend on it, I would be laughing too, just like the televangelists and politicians, who are laughing all the way to the bank, and making you look like a person from King James's 16th century.

Jesus was said to have learned skills which Eastern culture is known for, like high forms of yoga and meditation, controlling your body, stopping your heartbeat, stopping your bleeding, becoming a controller of yourself and others at a cellular level, as healing the sick, without tools. I do not doubt that Jesus did those things; they are still done today. Try learning Reiki. It's just one spiritual healing practice among many that I have learned about.

The power of the mind is indeed amazing. Research the Russians, who did experiments during the war on mind control, studying the effects on objects, bending metal objects, reading minds and so on. Look at hypnotists; it's not magic but one of many ancient practices. Do you think magicians are real? No, they have good knowledge, and control of their mind and yours. They are illusionists. How can a man fool a lie detector? With the power of his mind, he can fool the machine into recording that he believes what he is saying is true: his truth, after he has convinced himself that his lies are the truth.

Religion is someone else's truth and you then have to convince yourself that it is your truth. Why? Because it goes against your conscience, which is telling you to doubt and question this strange idea called religion. Your conscience knows the real truth but you don't, so you trick yourself and force yourself to believe the half-truths of the religion and you go against your conscience.

You know that you have questions and suspicions about your religion, but you do not follow your gut, your conscience, and that makes you a good follower. A good follower of the religion is a bad leader of the family, as you convince or force them, your defenseless family, to become defeated by, to submit to, to kneel before in shame, to be broken by, and to follow, religion. You force the idea on them, that they are lowly and need to bow to the authority of God, and that they are not worthy of anything else. They are taught that they are only to lead their own family, within the prison and restrictions of your God. That is not real freedom, but something else, something deficient of truth and true freedom.

Monks in the Himalayas do things that people are convinced are magic, but they are exercising proper control of their mind not just their brain. Mind and brain. Yes, they are different in varying degrees; mind, body, brain, spirit, soul are different from each other. It is said that you have four bodies: one is physical, one is spiritual, one is emotional and the fourth is mental.

Practice yoga, meditation or just peacefully sit by yourself; you can learn a great deal about yourself and others, including Jesus. It comes to you. Who is to say that Jesus was not trying to teach Eastern culture in a different way? Remember, His story has been changed to reflect the views of the writer or historian, through the ages, and then lastly the views of King James and his subordinates. Maybe they chose to delete or change His true history.

It is not only important to listen to what He said but also to understand what He didn't say. Did He say or express the opinion that He thought the Eastern religions or cultures which taught peace were not to be followed? I don't think so. He did that for a reason. These were the religions of that era that saw the real truth as He saw it and they taught peace. He learned it from them and brought it to the world. Gandhi showed you the effectiveness of this power; he defeated the whole British Empire. Some just want to be lazy, follow someone in the church, and let him do the thinking and leading; anyone who says he knows about God develops a following and starts a new denomination of the church. It's now a fad.

GOD CONSCIOUSNESS AND AWARENESS

The million-dollar question has always been, "What is the meaning of life?"

It is an easy one to answer and an even easier one to understand. You have a soul or spirit that is everlasting. It cannot die. You, the real inner you, your soul has been alive and existing long before you got here. You came here to do some special work. That work is designed to help you to do and learn specific things that you couldn't do and learn when you were elsewhere in your spiritual form. A form as Jesus had, after death, being not of this world. That's the simple answer.

Instead of believing in a religion, believing in your own power is enough of an achievement. Self empowerment is good for you. As you develop more understanding about enlightenment, you will discover the answers to your myriad of new questions. Questions are good, so have them. Finding the answers will help you grow. At any rate, you came here for a short while, compared to your real spiritual lifespan. You may live to be 20, 40 or 80–years-old here, and then you die and go home. When you get there, that is when your real work starts, again. You will take what you learned from this life to help you carry on in the next.

Christians and other religions may think I am saying that they will be reincarnated into this world. I am not. When you die, do you stay here on Earth? Did Jesus? No. You go back home to your real existence, elsewhere. You are here going to school. You are away from your source, your real existence, your real home. School here on Earth lasts for as long as you live. When you die, you graduate to your next class. Eventually, you will finish school. How long that takes depends on how fast you learn but that is not our concern right now; you have to crawl before you can walk, so the hereafter is a subject you cannot understand right now, as you are still confused by religion.

When you go back to what you call your God, the force, or the consciousness, then you will start to do the next class, job, life, or whatever other name you want to call it. When you are in an elevated state of consciousness, you think, feel and exist in a higher plane, and as a result, you cannot experience the lower level feelings and thoughts that you need to learn by. Hate, jealousy, physical pain, pleasure, sex, comfort or discomfort, homosexual issues, drug addiction, loss of loved ones, violence, racism, greed, selfish love, sadness, heartbreak, anger and disappointment are just some of the many tools we use to learn our lessons.

We can't experience these in the spirit form, in the same way that we will on Earth. Reading a book can't make you feel the sensation and anxiety of claustrophobia. You have to experience it. To feel like a drug addict you have to become one, or you will just be on the outside looking in. Feeling it is the key. Reading about it is not the same. Knowing it in your spirit form is not the same. You have to live it.

Coming down to a lower, carnal level on Earth is the best way to achieve this educational process. The emotional tools that we use to experience things as we get older teach us different aspects about life, in this university of life that we call Earth. When we are young and we lose a ten dollar bill, we may feel angry, but when we are older and lose it, we may feel calm, and think that the person who finds it needs it more than us. Or we may avoid being angry by remembering that we still have twenty dollars more. We can't take our riches, or any physical thing, with us when we graduate, and learning to give it all up is also a learning experience. It's like a video game. You leave with nothing except what is in your mind.

The various religions rewrote this story of our existence to insert themselves as the middlemen between you and the Consciousness. They twisted the truth, so that you will think you need them. If they did not do it intentionally, they may have just misunderstood what they were doing, and are actually helping to create an arena on Earth for us to learn in, with all the chaos and spiritual retardation they create. You can find consciousness like Jesus did, if you throw away the dogma and rituals. The middleman churches should do a different job of community development instead of community control, of helping us to seek the truth, instead of leading us in the wrong direction.

Any religion that teaches you that killing is acceptable for the right reasons, any reason for that matter, is misunderstanding something basic about our existence in this world. We were not sent here to kill each other, for any reason, at any time. Most religions encourage killing and murder for certain reasons, or at least the followers do. Whatever those reasons are, it's wrong to murder. Murder is not what we are here to accomplish. When your government, church, temple or mosque asks you to kill, you will be betraying humanity and morality to obey them, and going against the real consciousness and rule of existence, which is simply this: do not kill. You do not like it when your own child's life is taken, so do not take another child's life.

Even if you don't know where you came from, and the real meaning of life, that rule of "do not kill" is just common sense. That's the whole story. Even Hitler should not have faced the death penalty for his crimes if he was caught; our taking his life or any other lives would not have been good, as his executioners would have been committing murder and him spending his life in prison to reflect, regret and be an example would have been better. All prisoners can be rehabilitated. If we put enough funding into prison rehabilitation as we do into war and policing, we could achieve a much better outcome for society.

Even "Tookie Williams," who started the Los Angeles Crips gang, began to help society and give back, while he was in prison. He wrote a book about the harm in joining a gang, and in doing so discouraged scores of your own children from doing just that, and saved many kids and their victims, who would have been destroyed by those kids, your kids. Some people eventually fed their hatred by killing him. That was so wrong.

He was just then becoming beneficial to society and to your kids. Just think, the next child gang-banger who shoots a person could have been saved by the guidance of Tookie. He has caused more deaths worldwide than Hitler did, as his gang keeps growing and continues to spread destruction around the globe. His connections in the crime world could have helped turn the tide against gangs, but we threw that chance away…we executed that chance when we executed him, with our religion of hatred.

Jesus taught that the god you need resides within, in your mind, not outside in a church or in the sky. Who will you find in a place of worship? Lost people like us. What will you find in the sky? You will find birds and insects. If God is a thought, idea and concept, or real, where will He be found? Jesus said everywhere: in a piece of wood, under a rock, wherever your mind is in that moment. If you are thinking about looking under the rock, you will find Him there. If you think of looking for Him in a piece of driftwood, you will find Him there because He is a thought in your mind, traveling where you travel, seeing what you see. He's not in a human form. "It's all in your mind" is the phrase that comes to mind. My kids are tired of hearing it, my signature phrase. People are now seeing religious icons in foods, clouds, plants and everything else. Now that is funny.

It's like when loved ones die. For a while, you feel that you experience them wherever you are, in different places, or familiar places they liked, as if they are going with you or coming there to meet you, and are there with you just like when they were alive. Some think their loved ones are really there with them, as you feel their presence, even though no one else can see them, and no one can say if that is real or not. It is a real thought and feeling in your mind though, to you, isn't it? Yes. Just like your version of your God is real only to you, no one else. Everyone has their own version. Your God may not be as vengeful as the church says He is. He may even have dyed His hair and wear a nose ring.

Why do you say you suffer a broken heart? That's not true but the whole world says it. It started as just a clever saying; now the world believes it has some truth. You don't love with your organs, your heart, spleen or your kidney. You do it with your mind, that thinking and feeling brain that puts every thought and feeling, sight and smell together, to make up your world only and no one else's. Yours because you see it, smell it and taste it differently than everyone else; that's why everyone's different. Your mind makes you eat food with different tastes and smells, and tell them apart in the dark. That's why you can convince yourself that you can't kick drugs or alcohol, when you really can...because of your mind and its negative conditioning of believing it can't.

In your mind God represents something, and that something is HOPE. Hope is a thought inside, instilled in you to give you determination and the courage to survive against all odds. Instilled by whom, you ask? Instilled by your mother, her survival instinct, transferred from her DNA to your DNA. From your ancestors living in caves or huts who had to face insurmountable odds and dangers just to live. Hope is linked to optimism. It's a feeling that you can improve the outcome of a situation. Hope is a survival instinct that man tried to capture in words and pass on in ideas. Having hope is a glance, an unsure and fleeting glance of an idea and concept that hints your survival and improvement. It tells us apart from animals who don't feel hope or just don't know English… We've discovered that animals have families and language, too.

You think God is in human form and we were created in His image, but that's wrong. We are self destructive; God simply would not be. That tells how different we are to God. The religions convinced you that it is complicated and needs rituals, baptism, communion and christening. They persuaded you to not think for yourself, but to instead follow scripture.

Think of religion as a governmental policy that was started for the ancient and uncivilized people thousands of years ago. The new government has moved in and it is now time to change the old policies, as they are not useful anymore. The new formula is consciousness. We need new policies and formulas as we progress — solar and wind energy instead of foreign oil. As we explore the universe, it becomes apparent that religion is too small an idea to apply to the vast universe, and magical religions have no place in it.

We are self destructive; magical religions are not stopping our destructive ways. They have failed us. Yes, if we live as slaves in submission to magical religions, we may be less destructive but that's not real freedom of spirit. That's mental and religious bondage, and a form of the "Stockholm Syndrome," believing that something restricting you is giving you real freedom. All you are really getting is a false perception of being free, because you still fall under the rule of the church. If you understand this, that's where the reality takes over and you start seeing a different concept of what is real. A real God would not allow us to destroy others, or the Earth with wars and famine that we could alleviate or even eradicate.

Can you decide who you know, that can prove God exists to you right now? Not a history story from any religious books, but give you proof? No one. Not even Jesus chose to show people who or what God is. He just said things about His source, His force, but He never described what God was or is, or even if He was a singular or collective force. He called it Father to keep it simple to understand, staying close to what they already believed, so they would still get an idea of the direction in which He wanted them to go. He was not telling them to worship the moon, animal or other objects; He had to establish to the people that it was not an object, without losing them on a description of the consciousness that he knew they would not understand. Your 10-year-old can't understand it either.

My children's expressions, the love I feel for my family, the feeling of doing something good without reward, the happiness I'll feel when I finally win the lottery. These things are not God's things; these are man's things. Man's thoughts, man's fears, man's joy. Not God's but man's. Man has the thought or concept of his God in him. I can't tell you if it is true the other way around — if man is a thought of any gods, as they don't exist as you think they do. Your computer can identify you but it can't hug you. The God Consciousness, likewise, is not as interactive as the churches led you to believe. There's no God to bless you, save you or hug you. You need to start thinking for yourself, so you can see the truth and feel how right enlightenment is, for yourself. Learn it and teach it to your kids.

Have you ever seen how a swarm of bees live? They have a set of scouts that go out and find different sources of honey. They come back to the hive and are faced with the problem of how to get the hive to move to the source that they found.

That's the problem our priests have — how to get you to go to their churches, where they think it's best for you, obviously the one they work at. The bees start to dance as only bees can; the ones feeling more convinced that their own source is the best will dance the strongest and the longest. The priests start their song and dance as only priests can, and the ones convinced of their source being the right one dance the loudest and strongest (all 40,000 and more denominations of them.)

Eventually, the hive has an easier time deciding which scout to follow to the new source, usually just the longer lasting, loudest and more vibrant dancer, and they will relocate the colony there. Eventually, the masses have an easier time of seeing which preacher is the more convincing seer, usually the loudest and most sweet-talking, fear-mongering one, with the most convincing arguments for his denomination or brand of magical religion, and they relocate their family to that religion or sect.

These preachers move on to start new churches, just like the new Queen bees do. But there is a whole world outside theirs that they don't even know about, both the bees and the preachers. The church and the swarm are identical, aren't they? Neither used God's help to do their jobs. He was not sitting there helping them. This is a lesson we need to observe. Life goes on the same with or without the idea of getting help from God.

Just as the bee industry has been overcome by the highly aggressive African killer bee, which makes good honey but kills a lot of people and other animals, and eradicates other types of bee colonies, leaving only African colonies, so too do the main religious colonies have that effect on different world religious colonies, infiltrating and taking over other religious communities over a period of time.

Don't the churches go to the immigrant communities and countries to help them, teach them and convert them? Yes. Eradicating the old religions and replacing them with a new type of cyclic redundancy/hocus pocus? A 2.0 version? Yes. That version is called the practice of Christianization and it entails doing anything to force the natives to accept Christianity as their religion, by any means necessary including war and annihilation. Christianization started after the death of Christ and continued well into the Middle Ages. Consciousness is the version 3.0, without viruses; you don't need 2.0 dogma, war or death.

These converted colonies usually have their place in the grand scheme of life but just as we are not the gods of the bees, so too there is not a god over us, only perhaps a godly concept in our minds. All in our minds where our imaginations run wild, as they were meant to do. Creating concepts of ghosts and goblins, gods, devils and demons. Can you imagine if people shared those imaginative religious thoughts about needing a church and a god, with the masses, what kind of twisted, warlike world we would have? No need to imagine, just look around. They did that very thing 4,000 years ago.

Can you picture what a better world we may have had if our ancestors weren't distracted and disabled by religious dogma and stupor-stitions? Let's try to move on, up the ladder of peace and progress. Use your religious beliefs to enhance lives, not disable and destroy them. The God Consciousness that we seek is truly there. Some call it the universal consciousness: Krishna, Christ, Allah and the God of Abraham. It's all the same concept of believing in an unseen force, which is fine if done without superstitious and religious dogma.

What is consciousness? It is spiritual energy. Where is it? In your mind and soul. The consciousness is so vast, it needs a space as unending as the whole universe to exist, so you can even say that the universe is, or houses, the consciousness because you cannot travel anywhere in the universe and not be within this great consciousness. Even as Jesus said, under a rock. It's in your mind, all the time. It travels with you as part of your great spirit, your soul.

So where does it start and where does it end? It is impossible to find the edge of it. It is everywhere in the universe. It is as free as a thought. That's how simple it is; it is all the air in an inflated balloon and you cannot find a space in the balloon that does not have air. The universe is inflated with this consciousness. The air and the balloon act as one, even though they are separate entities. So, too, the universe with the consciousness within it. Can you travel the Earth and find a place without air? This is exactly the reality of consciousness. We are living in it all the time. We are enveloped in it, like a fish in the ocean.

Jesus alluded to the all of His Father because isn't It, the consciousness, the forces in nature, the father and mother of us all? Move away from the eccentric fairy tales and see the light, see the truth and see the way — a simple way. It is a truth that you have to seek out. I say to you, for us to realize the consciousness, the God we seek, we first have to gain humility and we have to seek to be humble unto our family. The human family. It grows from that seed of humility.

Teach your loved ones the truth about universal love. We have to first be good to then behold a god; God-ness or the consciousness will not be revealed to us in our greedy state. We have to love and give, we have to live like a god unto ourselves and others. Taking drugs and getting drunk are not being a god onto anyone. I don't have to explain how to humble unto others. You know how. Only then we will learn to be calm and peaceful, and have humility. Only then, did Gandhi singlehandedly defeat the whole British Empire.

It is then only we may head in the right direction to the truth, which is unselfish Goodness, or the universal consciousness, a force that is the highest science, not religion. If you see the consciousness as being a god unto you, calling it that name is wrong, but it is a step in the right direction to at least begin understanding enlightenment and the high science of our existence, without religion. So call it God for now if you wish, while you are still learning. In time, you will understand it is spiritual consciousness; a force, and not a god, and you will stop calling names.

Does not one drop of ocean water contain the very ocean within it that it came from? Every chemical of the salted water is in every drop. To the living organisms in the drop of water, it is the ocean, and the life-giving force feeding them, even if the drop of water is in a spoon, a bucket or back in the ocean. So too, is the great consciousness contained in you; you who are a part of that great universe of consciousness. You are a drop of this ocean of consciousness. Instead of the drop being in a bucket, it is contained in this human body that you occupy.

Consciousness is what we seek. Though consciousness is what we are, we just don't see it and have not been taught to seek it; we are not aware of it. We do not need to find it, as it is not lost; we are. It is here, all around us. We just have to recognize it. We are comatose. What is a person in a coma? Is he not a living person without consciousness? Without awareness? He breathes, his heart beats, his body lives. But he is still in a coma, so also when we achieve and realize the truth about the consciousness of the universe that we call God, we will come out of our coma and truly live. In the meantime, our dearly departed think they are heading to heaven or hell. Do you know where they go? We owe them that, to find the truth, to find them. Where are you sending your own children when they die? Find out.

We search far and wide for the spectacles on our face, when all the time they are sitting on our noses. So elusive is the search for consciousness, we can look through it like spectacles, and not realize that it is there, it is us, our spirits existing separately inside our bodies. When we are able to see that, then we can look at it instead of cluelessly through it. Only then we will know it is there. Consciousness is what we seek but it is not outside of us. It is inside, in our spirit. We don't have the awareness to recognize its existence. So we cannot see it.

Through the good that we do, we can find the key inside to unlock the door in our minds that leads us outside our cage of ignorance. We are ignorant of consciousness, unconscious of It, the source. Forget the distractions of if God is a He, She, It or Them. Forget the distractions of our ancestors, all the dogma and rituals that the churches have taught us. We are more intelligent now than the builders of religions ever were. We can think farther ahead. We have superb comprehension. We can see and determine our future in more ways than the inventors could see theirs, because they had a really short lifespan if they did not fall in line with the king or church. We are superior in every way and we need not follow the ignorance of blind dogma anymore. Let us lead our loved ones to true consciousness and enlightenment, and be free ourselves. We owe them that.

What is the consciousness? It is a state of understanding, of awareness, and also of being. Being in a state of enlightenment is understanding the true God-ness, or force or light. It is understanding that we are not here to serve what we think is God, Christ or any other entity, but to realize infinite wisdom and enlightenment, becoming aware of the presence of the light or consciousness within us. A drop of ocean being the ocean. How simple.

The force you call God can be thought of as your center, and the center of the collective consciousness, which is made up of... us: you and I. We are what make up the great consciousness. We are the drops that make up the ocean of life, while we are calling the ocean God. We are also the winds of change, as we can effect change in our surroundings and ultimately in the universe, by learning or not learning the truth. Each has its consequence. Each will determine where, in what direction we carry mankind. Can you have a book with no pages inside? No. We are the pages of the book.

Can we see light? Yes. What kind? White light. Can we see colors? Yes. How? Where does the colored light come from? From the white light. When we put a prism or filter in front of the source of white light, it separates the light into the colors, which when combined, make up the white light. Consciousness is the white light. We are like the separate colors, which are combined to form the white light. We come from the light. We exist in the light. We are the light.

Jesus said God is the light, using the term "God" instead of "Consciousness," so people would comprehend what He meant. Jesus said that He also is the light. So they were both a part of the light or consciousness. Can't a son be a father and husband also? So too we are all part of that light, and children of the consciousness, and as gods, we bring the light and truth to others, and to darkness and dark dogma devoid of truth, all at the same time. We can say "God" is a bringer of light, not a heavenly magical person. We are gods in that context of bringing the light of wisdom and enlightenment, not superstitious magic and miracles. When Jesus told them He was a king, they said sarcastically there can be only one king, although they knew that was untrue and you do too. We are all kings. We are all gods, a drop of the whole.

Jesus did not need us to serve Him, but to follow Him by doing what He did, following the path He took, learning the truth as He did. To follow Him does not mean to serve Him or His "Father," or our source; He meant for us to follow His actions, His course, His example, His path of becoming conscious and thereby, when we achieve this enlightenment of consciousness, we can bring it to the universe around us, building the consciousness, making it stronger, making it grow.

Follow His path of becoming conscious and enlightened, and understanding the truth. We are not slaves to any religion but spiritual beings existing in human bodies, sent to build the strength of the consciousness, in the universe around us, in our communities, in our families, on this Earth. Everything else grows by that strength, that energy which we send out, the light that we shine through the darkness of ignorance and superstition, to dispel, disperse and dissipate them. When we kill someone, we simply release the spirit inside that body, and he or she goes back home, and moves on to begin a new existence elsewhere.

Jesus had a problem, same as the prophets that came before and after Him. The problem was, how do you teach the consciousness to an ignorant, primitive and superstitious world, which is devoid of any understanding of spirituality and consciousness? Can you? No. That may be the answer that made Him cry, not his crucifixion, as His temporary shell or body was not important enough for Him to be worried about. That, and leaving the friends and loved ones He had become attached to. He realized the mission, a purpose, as we all have, and He saw the futility of that mission succeeding with the ignorant, simple-minded population; that would make anyone sad.

Our mission, as was His, is simply to grow the collective consciousness. Our problem is, although we are more educated and can understand consciousness, we have not given up the primitive, mindless superstitions and dogma, which have developed over the last 4,000 years and taken strong root. He saw that the world was not educated enough to understand the real truth then. He realized it would take many generations before that could occur. So what could He do? Plant the seeds. The seeds of knowledge. How? His life, His teachings and His crucifixion. That is how intelligent, unselfish and enlightened He was. We have to do the same, planting the seeds of knowledge. I do right now and so should you.

That is the limited story of what is told about Jesus. He planted the seeds of becoming conscious, by doing, saying and teaching what He did when He was here. He could have found a different way of doing things but He knew that over time, it could be lost and forgotten. Written parchments may rot away. Becoming a martyr for the cause and using the church as the vehicle were the only ways to keep the ideas around long enough to be rediscovered. That and a sheet of copper. His mission is being fulfilled now. His seeds are bearing fruit and the secrets that were hidden by, and carried by, the church are unfolding and coming to light in this generation, aided by the discovery of the Dead Sea Scrolls. What about the sheet of copper? Well, Jesus' disciples were not that stupid. They knew parchment would rot over time, so they recorded the message on scrolls; rolls of parchment, and also on sheets of copper, as copper would not rot and would hopefully survive until we found it. We did.

He knew that the church would, after His death, use the crucifixion for its own purpose, but that was part of His brilliant plan. A plan His disciples injected into the bloodstream of the church over the years after the event, as they helped to create this new Christian religion. He knew the opportunistic and greedy church would survive, and as long as the church became the vessel to carry the word, the story, it would endure for thousands of years, as long as needed be, knowing that it would be generations before the truth would be uncovered and discovered, or maybe released by descendants of the disciples. He needed the church, the same church that He purposely set up, to have

Him crucified. They were pawns in His plans. The church did exactly what He expected them to do. That's why He answered them the specific way He did, telling them He was a king. It was to set His plan in motion and have them crucify Him.

History proves that He was right. They did crucify Him, and they did take His story and use it for their purposes of controlling the masses. They did unknowingly carry the word, the story, the truth, their two-edged sword, the future seed of their demise, for centuries: until now. It is now revealed. Thy ironic will be done, Great King.

This is what being enlightened means. He was enlightened; that's why He could make a plan like that, which would carry the world to consciousness. Is He presently doing the same thing, in the higher level that He exists now? Interesting question. Has he done it somewhere else before? Are we just in phase two of His plan, by discovering the scrolls? Yes. Could the delirious masses at that time understand time and space, solar systems, quantum physics, string theory, black holes, quasars, other dimensions in time and space, or the existence of the universe? No. What about understanding the collective, universal consciousness? Never in 2,000 years, but 2,010 years? Yes, we can.

Can there be a Devil in the consciousness? Well, one can say the absence of light is darkness, so too the absence of consciousness can be ignorance. In this ignorance of the truth in our Earthly existence, there can falsely exist the idea of devils, with demons as angels, and a whole hierarchy can be added to them to make up or conjure in one's mind a vision or an instrument that can be used to trick or control the masses.

A vision so bad that it demands absolute adherence to whatever the inventor is suggesting, namely religious surrender to avoid eternal damnation. We have seen this: the horror stories which the lack of acceptance of these religions will bring upon the unwary victim. It's happening all around us. This puts such a scare into the worshipper that he would bow and cower in subservience to magical religions and be blessed, with inclusion in the church or group or cult, and hope to find salvation after seeing the light and being reborn, and accepting the bent and twisted truth of the church's stories.

Are there many truths or just one truth, hidden or overlooked? All religions can lead to truth if they lead to the infinite consciousness. In that way they will just be different fingers on the same hand. Unfortunately, most just lead to a fictitious heaven with pearly gates, winged angels, human pleasures, thrones, flaming chariots and a hot car for me if I get there. I wonder, now that we are so educated, have the flaming chariots turned into private jets carrying crystal meth-using, gay-bashing, and outwardly homophobic yet secretly gay priests? Have they already found their version of heaven, right here on Earth?

Does one religion's worshipper weigh more than another religion's worshiper on the scales of truth and consciousness? No, just as our Earthly bodies are nothing, our Earthly religions are the same to each other and our souls have no color, race or any other affiliation.

We have to look at what is expected to be gained or achieved from each religion. Do they follow a path of subservience to an individual, as the Christians following Christ, or to a group, as when one joins a cult, gang or church? The worshipper is distracted by trying to please the god and the church, instead of trying to gain spiritual freedom. You don't always have to selflessly give without reward, as the reward you can receive may be peace, strength and inspiration from the universe — picture yourself absorbing rays of light and good energy from the universe.

The worshipers are focused on prayerful bondage, with the hope or promise of a reward of being saved if the follower deserves it. With Christians this number is restricted or predicted to be 144,000 saved, according to Revelations, Chapter 7, and the rest of the world will be damned to hell by fire. Now that is a problem because if you counted all the good priests and priestesses globally, excluding the pedophiles, drug addicts, and con men who steal their churches' and congregations' money, you will still have more than 144,000, which means there is no more room at the inn, and the damned who are going to hell are you and me: we, the people.

Some of the rules for achieving the reward are okay — love thy neighbor, do not kill and so on, but the reward itself is what is misleading. How can you reach the heavens if you don't know what the truth is, and all the clergy fill up the flights going there? There's no room for us. This is proof that they made it up, as there is not even enough room for all the good clergy. The inventors could not count that high. And they hadn't invented the terms billion, trillion and gazillion yet. So they settled on a number they thought was sufficient. You…we, will never get to heaven. It's a small place; there is no room.

When people do not know the real outcome of their worship, that is not a good thing. Your children are not fooled and this is how we lose them. Worshippers from different religions are promised different things, when it should be only one outcome from all religions. What is that outcome? The enlightenment of the soul. Is the soul even discussed as the real center of religious worship? Not by many, if any. Remember, the soul makes up part of the force, part of the whole that you think you worship as God. The objective is to be a *part* of the whole, not worship it.

Worshiping is wrong. Okay, I said it. Why? Simple answer, what are you worshiping? God? That does not make sense if you are a part of the whole that you worship. Does that mean you are worshiping yourself? There is no God to worship. God is just a term to describe a force, energy and an idea that the ancients had. You come from the whole. You are part of the whole, therefore you are the whole. Can the ocean worship the ocean? Can you worship yourself? No. You can have a large ego but no sane person worships himself. Worshiping is wrong and misconceived; it is only for primitive minds, like the cavemen. Your action of service to your family can be said to be a form of worship, but that's different. You are selflessly serving them with humility and love as you should, and that's good.

A process of living, a way of life, is what the religions try to teach and follow. Though some of them know about becoming enlightened, they still teach us to go through a middleman, like Krishna, Shiva, Buddha, Laxmi, and even Jesus Christ, to name a few. These were the prophets who came to the people when they were in need before. I object to any kind of worship. Even worship to your family can be destructive if not done properly, as they will take advantage of you, think your kindness is weakness and walk all over you.

The real truth is simple. Feed your soul good thoughts, words and deeds. Feed the same to those around you. That's all; you don't need to serve the church's demons or go through anyone; just be as righteous, honest, and unattached to this material life as you can. It does get easier over the years. Eventually, you end up as devoted, humble and enlightened as Jesus. Serve mankind instead. Serve your family instead. Serve your spirit instead. Mind you, don't give up your money or fame. You need to buy food. Artists like to eat too. Just don't worship money and fame.

When we allow ourselves to be controlled by our vanities, instead of controlling them, then we are not as clean, enlightened, educated with spiritual knowledge, and peaceful as we need to be, in order to be involved with the higher power we wrongly worship, regardless of the names of gods that we use.

As with everything worthy, enlightenment takes some getting used to. You must be patient with yourself. It takes years, not days. It is not a reward you have to fight to get, but a journey you must happily embark on, patiently. Patience is something that you cannot rush. You have to relax to gain and use this patience as a tool to help you become enlightened.

It's like learning a sport. You take your time and enjoy it, and you become accustomed and better at it. If you rush and don't enjoy it, then stop and try again in the future. What's the hurry? You have your whole life ahead of you to do it, and if you die before, you will still get there. It's like finding religion in prison. You have the time, while doing time, so take your time. The enlightenment is always there waiting to be discovered and attained by you. It won't run away.

Compared to those in Jesus' time, we are all rich. It is true that the richer a person is, the harder it is to give up the attachment to material things and achieve enlightenment, but that's because they impatiently expect to give up the attachment in an instant, and they expect to give up their riches as well and become instantly poor. When they think of detachment and letting go, they feel sad and it is a shock to them.

That's natural. So then, let's not do it immediately. Take 60 years; that's easier. If you decide to do it over a period of 60 years, it doesn't matter how rich and greedy you are. Over those decades, you can gradually let go of the attachment to everything, mentally, at your pace, putting all your concerns to rest, like providing for your family, life insurance and the like. It does not mean giving up your riches, just your mental and emotional attachment to them.

To those who don't have 60 years to spend on this mission because you have a terminal illness or issue, you already understand the reasoning to give up all the attachments. That does not make it any easier but there is more urgency. It's not as important to try to keep the riches with you because you will lose them soon anyway, when you die, so give them to family. I expect you have already matured to the point where it may not bother you much to leave riches to your family or charity; just leaving is the sad part.

To highlight the fact that we can give up greed, I am reminded of a story about an Indian Prince, Siddhartha, who gave up his whole kingdom, his riches of mountains of gold and jewels, and started Buddhism. He was the first

Buddhist. He became the Buddha. Poverty is thought to be a burden to some, and an opportunity to others, especially those who seek enlightenment instead of money. You can seek money from religion, as the churches do, instead of seeking enlightenment, but that never works out well in the end, as you will die and leave it anyway. And the lifetime and opportunity that you had to do real learning and teaching will be lost; slipped away and spent.

That's the real problem. You waste the short time you have, or your family has, when you do not do good works to become enlightened. When you let your family worship gods, and follow religions and vain things, when they die they will have wasted their lives. That's the real loss; your opportunity to progress is gone, over, done, lost. On to the next life, but sorely lacking because you did not make gains here in this one.

It's possible to become poorer than you are right now, without wanting to. Millions of people are now going through foreclosure. If you don't have a family to take care of, why try to join the money race again? Stay simple and find enlightenment. Everything has a bright side, if you use it as such. Work for enough money to have a humble, fulfilling existence, and try to grow spiritually. Don't grab for more and more money, and be distracted by greed.

When our landlord told us that we had to move, as he needed the apartment for his sister, we were not happy. That move made us buy a house, so it was good in the end. Then when we decided to sell it, years later, we took an apartment by the ocean: again, a happy turn of events, turning lemons into lemonade. Our family is much happier, as the kids are growing and have the need for different stimulus to learn about and enjoy life. A different area, by the beach, or near the woods, or the mountains is a nice change.

Remember the example of the master who went away and left money with each of his three slaves? This version says, when they saw him again, the slave who invested the money and made a profit was able to give the master something, profits, and the slave was important to the master in a more significant, unknown way; he now had the experience of running the master's affairs, so the master was able to give him his freedom and make him a partner in the business.

The slave who invested the money and lost it was still of great importance to the master. He was given his freedom and hired as an employee of the business; even though he did not make a profit, he did the right thing. He worked to try to make a profit, as it is a free man's purpose in life to do, to try to progress and make himself better while not hurting his fellow man.

A free man has the gift of opportunity to do something, and should not be lazy to sit and do nothing. Not wasting the opportunities encountered, but earning more opportunities to do more for everyone. A productive person in the community strengthens that group, and the productive people in that community can now take that strength and go out to the farther communities, and strengthen them. The ripple effect takes place. Everyone helps his community and goes out to help others. That started with you and you are the master who brings this blessing to those people.

Back to the third slave, he was fearful and concerned with losing, and with what would befall him if he lost rather than made a profit, so he didn't invest it. He knew the master would be angry if he wastefully spent the money, so he put it under his bed. With the money safely hidden, he became lazy as he did not have to think for himself to invest and survive.

When the master came back, he told the master what he did and the master was angry. The slave asked why he was angry and the master explained that he had mountains of gold; why would he need the slave to keep the safety of a handful of money for him? He didn't. He gave the slave an opportunity to invest the money and better himself. He did not need a guard for a small amount of money. The slave was meant to use the resources the money could bring, to make a success of himself, as did the first slave. He saw that the slave was sincere about his love and care for the master's property, so he gave the slave his freedom, but not a job as he did not show courage but fear. This is also our predicament.

Now that story is important because it is used to illustrate what we should do with the opportunity of life we have been given. Life is the money; it gives us the opportunities and resources to do better with ourselves. We then return that which we gained, the profit, of our spiritual growth, to the larger community. This is both the area where you live and also the universal consciousness, which you call God. If we take the knowledge and use it to profit the soul, then we are doing what we were meant to do. We are investing and we will profit.

When you take the opportunity, and spend it worshipping a god or following a religion, and are lazy like the slave who put it under the bed, then you are not using the chance to do your job of bettering yourself. You do not add to the community or the consciousness. These people usually become selfish and a burden on everyone. When you misunderstand religion, this is what happens. You are not using the knowledge to progress. You are not even going in the right direction toward consciousness. You have put your job aside and are just following the rules of fear, the dogma of the religion, not making spiritual profit, and not staying free. You have given up your freedom and adopted religious bondage. You have stopped thinking and are letting others, and the church, do your thinking for you.

Following and fearing the religion to become blessed or reach God is not the way. It keeps you confused. When you get there, what is the reward or profit you bring back? Nothing. You bring back only what you started with. You took the life and did not earn or multiply the good with it, so you, like the slave, have no reward to present. Religious following is like putting your opportunity under the bed. Your enlightenment does not grow, as you do not help to increase consciousness in the world. You become selfish, fearful and useless since you wasted your opportunity on Earth.

Enlightenment is your profit to give back, and achieving it gives you your freedom from religion, which in turn is your reward in one beautiful package. Profit, sharing, freedom, growth and reward, all in one. Who could have a better plan? Don't be the lazy, fearful slave. Don't follow religious dogma. Know that there is a consciousness, and invest the life you are given to bring the profit of courage and enlightenment to yourself and others, and you will be able to take that enlightenment back to your source. That's what everyone wants. That's your duty and your reward. That's your riches for the next journey.

You have the gift of life to invest. If you sit nonchalantly and follow the religion, you do not get a return on the investment. Someone else could have come in your place, who would have had more courage and done better. So don't waste the space, as someone else could be using it. The line is long, waiting for a space to be born here on Earth.

I must also say, there are not only followers in a religion. There are also seekers: good people who are being told in various ways by their higher selves that there is something special and spiritual missing from their lives. Sadly, not knowing better, they naturally think religion is that missing piece.

They try to find this missing part by shopping around in different religions, like going to the mall to shop. It can be expected that there will be a lot of people attending the house of worship, closest to their home base. That's how most religions get followers. It's not that the brand of religion or the denomination was the right one; it was just the most convenient one, or one with a convenient location, or the one where their friends and family go.

Religions are frequented by people who are seeking an answer to their questions. They are not necessarily fanatics who are bent on religious bondage and blind faith. Some are curious and are indeed searching for that missing link to spiritual enrichment and enlightenment. These seekers will be sometimes misled into thinking that this cyclical way of fear is the real truth, and sadly, they are trapped in the wrong store. They will go home with the wrong goods and no refunds or do-overs. I have heard that losses of all types, bad things or wrong things, are really opportunities in disguise, so you can still use that negativity of the bad or wrong to find the positive truth of your higher self.

"Tragedy is a tool for the living to gain wisdom." (Robert Kennedy)

Religion teaches to just sit there, follow the rules and be in bondage. Some go to church on Sunday, and commit fraud, kill, rape and steal on Monday. They do bad things but they are good followers of the churches, good believers in fearing God and generous donators, so they are told that they are going to heaven. They would be locked out of heaven, if there were one. All the nonchalant, blindly faithful could end up in hell. A personal hell because that's what failure and fear is to a person who wastes life, and of course, you know that it does not exist for the enlightened souls.

Being enlightened means truly being free from the rules and fears of the churches' religion, which misunderstand and misdirect our purpose here. Our purpose is not to serve, but to profit spiritually and help that consciousness to grow; serving the religion does not make you reap the rewards of enlightenment. It only pushes you deeper over that abyss of bondage, by religion and religious leaders who don't understand their true purpose, which is to educate the people on their way to find enlightenment and become free of ignorance. Hell is failing yourself and humanity; it's your personal hell, having no profit to give to the greater consciousness.

The churches are good. They just misunderstand their true purpose. The church leaders, those who are humble and try to show a way of spreading goodness and love, instead of supporting violence and death, are doing the right thing. They just need to learn the truth about God, consciousness and true existence, which does not need subservience, just enlightenment. So don't leave the church, just use the churches as Jesus did. Use them as groups to bring about enlightenment, and build strength and cohesion in our communities. Make the churches what they are meant to be — vessels to share love, and teach enlightenment and goodness.

Everything has levels. Health, disease and sickness, financial trouble, job seniority, happiness, etc. The CIA is a perfect example. Each level that an agent passes through takes him to a different and higher level. The military, religions and church hierarchies are the same. The regular priests, who are my friends and love me as a brother, cannot meet the pope tomorrow if they wanted. Why? They are not at a level high enough to meet the pope. Can you meet the president tomorrow? No. So you understand how the levels separate everything.

If you ask the church what's next after you die and go to heaven, they won't be able to tell you. Do you just hang out in heaven having sexual orgies with virgins, or driving hot cars or flying around heaven with a new set of wings? I don't think so. Let us be clear — there are no virgins. In the spirit form, you do not have genitalia. There are no women or men waiting to have sex with you in heaven, or anywhere else, because they don't do that in the spirit realm. They have no sex organs. When you die, sex will be the furthest thing from your mind.

I ask, where is heaven, and when you get there, will you still look the same as when you die at 80 years old, or will you look like a hot 20-year-old, who is as attractive as you ever were? What happens after you take your supposed seat on your throne on the side of God? Do you sit there forever doing nothing or do you help God to rule the Earth? Think about it. Billions of people died before you. Are they all sitting on that crowded throne, helping God to rule Earth? I don't think so.

It all has to do with levels. When you pass through this level, then you go on to the next. That's the problem that Jesus faced. He could not tell the people of that time the truth — they were too primitive to understand; some still are— so he had to tell a story that they could understand. Jesus said that He is everywhere. How can you find consciousness everywhere you look? It is because you are the blood cell living in the body of consciousness, which is the universe in all its different forms and dimensions.

We are the blood cells, and the consciousness that we call God is the body, together making up a whole entity. Look at the bacteria in our bodies. To the bacteria, even the body is not known to it. The body is like the size of the universe to the microscopic bacteria. More so, the Earth becomes a super large universe compared to the body. And the real universe we see at night does not even exist to the simple microscopic bacteria.

Everything alive has a level of consciousness that applies to it, which enables that life-form to exist and function. There is a consciousness at the level of the microscopic organisms. There is a different level for plant life. There is yet another level of consciousness for animals. There is a level for humans, a higher level to which we ascend when we die, and there are levels after and above that. There are other levels of consciousness throughout the entire universe, as there is life in various forms elsewhere. It's simply like different governments for each country, and different levels of state and local government, all around the world. All life has its own existing consciousness. We don't need to be concerned with life outside Earth but we should not be fooled into thinking it does not exist.

We humans have our own place in the consciousness. We are the size of the bacteria in the grand scheme of the universal consciousness. How important are we? The most important because we have influence at a micro level of the vast universe. Think of a bad bacteria outbreak; it can kill the whole body, so we are as important as good bacteria is, to keep a good, working relationship within our part of the universe. The healthy body can now go on to do great things, things the bacteria did not even dream were possible. I'm watching the Olympics in China right now; do you think the bacteria know about it? No, but they are responsible in a large way, for not making the competitors sick.

What would God do with all of us after we converge in heaven? Recycle us? Obviously, there is more to do but you have to pass through this level to get there. When you arrive, you will be given a higher, second level to go through. When you get through the second level, you will be given a third level. Each time you attain the consciousness of that level, and learn how to free yourself of the problems of that level, you will advance to the next level, somewhat like a video game, until you reach the highest level.

You are climbing the ladder to success and purity. Each level allows us to strip away our bad ways, become more pure and learn new things. The more pure we become, the higher we can rise, so that we can do more for and within the consciousness. Life classes. Promotion. Success. Purity. Wow, we do have a purpose.

What will we look like at the higher level? Will we have a human form or will the system have us shed our human, physical body, and look like a spirit, or is that the third or even the seventh level, similar to the "Holy Spirit?" That is not important right now, is it?

There are millions of souls, past and present, doing work for the consciousness. We are all working for that force of energy, the great power, the great consciousness, the Great Assembly of Ascended Souls... whatever you want to call that which makes the whole, of which you are a part.

I and others can have the knowledge of the truth on Earth, and what has happened and what will happen to us, if only we seek as Jesus suggested. But we still can't achieve it as Jesus did, or I should say, most of us can't because we have not let go of our vices and vanities that weigh us down. It's even harder now than it was in the poor times that Jesus lived because we enjoy life more. It's more fun and we become attached more easily to the comforts of this life. Back then, they were suffering and begging for relief. We, on the other hand, are really enjoying being alive. We still enjoy being jealous and hateful, conniving and obtrusive in each other's business, getting even, and being able to buy things and shop till we drop.

We are trapped in this primitive way of fearful thinking. We are still shortsighted, looking at the church for guidance, wisdom and salvation. The church can't give that wisdom to you because if they do, you won't need the church after that. Likewise the drug companies do not want to cure you, as you will not need them after. So cure yourself of religion.

Think of how the world will change with enlightenment. No bank to threaten you, no wars to fight, no missiles to invent, just humanity going forward, as Jesus said we could. Just as all the prophets said we could, if we had courage. If we had courage to "Let go and let Go(o)d," this generation of humans could ascend rather quickly. Peace and love could prosper.

Why are there wars and famine? The only reason is the church's reluctance to teach the truth to their priests. These priests are the best of us. They all started out in the church trying to bring their fellow humans into the light. Some priests have fallen by the wayside only because the church let them fall. Had the church taught them the truth, they would not have fallen. The hierarchy of the church is to blame for their downfall, not the priests, our brothers and sisters. Now that the truth is revealed, we can all become the best we can be. When people know the truth, they will not have the need to blow each other up, steal each other's riches and invade nations to steal their resources.

Why is it that the religious among us are the ones who always want to kill each other, and fight or support wars? That's because they don't know the truth about the core of their religion. They are not really fearless humans who are in control of themselves; they are just religious followers, people who have given up and just relax while they expect a non-interactive God to do all the work to save Earth. Well, God is not saving Earth or your family, from man's greed and this recession — that's your job.

Do you want your family to be enlightened or religious? Apparently, the religions don't want you to be both but I think that we can be both. They do not speak the truth about peace, as their actions prove different motives. Religion's purpose or action should not be to kill each other, or to teach and encourage fear, death and lawful execution — but life. If both warring sides of bordering nations knew the truth, they would not even have a border in each country. This is proof that their understanding of the truth is wrong, as religion teaches fear. The great consciousness needs us to do the work we were sent here for: to achieve consciousness and enlightenment, and help each other to ascend, not spread fear.

We are too great a species to waste away fighting wars. There are billions more souls who have to come into this world, as many have also already come and gone. We are here to clear a path for them, not bring them here to fight wars. When they are killed in battle, they have gone without completing their mission. When they are made to kill in battle, they are not doing their job, as murder is not the mission of their existence. Also, the person who is killed is prevented from completing his job.

When we teach our kids to lie and steal, as our deceptive leaders and bankers do, we stall the progress of the human race. We've turned into a world of thieves and we suffer by our own hand. We are getting a taste of our own medicine. The more we destroy the world, the less we are left with. Dying by our own hand; that's ironic. We teach our kids that it's okay to steal. Just don't get caught. Dishonesty is a way of life now, in every business. Honesty is a lonely ideal.

We have turned this world into our own personal hell. We, to some small extent, had a hand in this misdirection by the church. How? We believed them and trusted them, as we were gullible and not looking for the truth, which was and is closer than you think. We just blindly accepted what was told to us. Remember, this started long before Jesus walked the Earth. This was a time when man was mentally primitive and simpleminded. I think we were not to be blamed at that time for following a religion, and we should just feel sorry that it happened and move on. We are smarter now, so there is no reason to still be fooled; in fact, we can only blame ourselves if we continue to be fooled in the 21st century.

We have to find proof of the truth. So where do we look for it? Inside our minds; that's where our intelligence exists. Our common sense is what we must use to survive, to protect our children, and to guide ourselves out of ignorance and away from trouble. We can put our imagination and common sense to work, guided by intelligence, and I guarantee that we will slay more than just mammoths, as our ancestors did. Wasn't that impressive back then, though? Slaying giant mammoths with primitive means? Even then, we were a force to be respected.

Does the heaven idea appeal to you? The virgin thing — the pearly gates to enter — the wings-on-your-back — the sitting on a throne thing? Ask yourself, all these religious ideas of heavens, are they true? I don't think so. Do you think that any one of these ideas will be a sensible enough answer to quell your confusion or your suspicion about religion? Do you think they can be combined to convince you to let your children believe in such things? I must say, not my children. I tried that.

I have sacrificed too much of myself to let my children be misled by some pedophile who has fantasies of my child and him floating around in the clouds in heaven together, or behind the pulpit. Your family is being threatened. They are your most precious asset. You have to believe that; they are more important to you than you are to yourself.

Don't try to save yourself: save them. Will you go into a fire while trying to save them? Most likely, you will, without a second thought, right? So save them from misdirection, misery and mischief. Save their minds. This in turn will help them to save themselves. With the truth, not stories. Don't worry; it's a beaten path. You'll see it. You can't get lost…again. You already are lost now anyway and you can't be lost twice at the same time, so you have nothing to lose by trying. The church says you are not going to any heaven right now in your allegedly sinful state, so you have time to try.

You can only find yourself and return to the light. Find out and you will find out. Seek and you will learn. Then lead your family out of darkness and into the light. You can be their light. They will be proud to see your shining example. Lead them or lose them — that's what it comes down to. There is no freedom in religion, as it is a cycle of control and subservience. You are only free to follow the dogmatic rules and be ruled by the elites in the religions. See for yourself if you are not made to follow the rules. There can be freedom from religion, if you desire the truth.

To me, the stories and deception don't add up. So I search inside my mind, and I read and do research, and you should, too. Use your intelligence to decide what is right or makes more sense for your children to follow. Why do the churches have to explain and convince you that their religion is the truth? If it were, wouldn't you feel that inside and not be confused about it? It's not rocket science. Your higher self is warning you when you feel doubt, so trust your instinct, your conscience, your gut, your sixth sense, not them and their questionable ideas.

You have to protect your family from lies and misdirection by questionable people who think pedophilia is not worth solving. They just moved the child molesters around to different churches for centuries, like a shell game. These people think your family is not deserving of protection by the church or you. How do we know this? By their actions of keeping it hidden since 60 AD, which is when laws were made by the Roman rulers to address the issue of sexual problems in the churches, from that time onward. Seek the proof; you will find it.

If the preachers were to face their God, and He told them that they misled you by misinterpreting what He wanted, and this is not what He wanted them to do, what do you think they will say? They will say that they just told you their understanding of what religion was, and you were too lazy and nonchalant in your concern, and freely decided to not think for yourself and freely accepted their misguided version of the truth. It is not their fault that you followed their words; they didn't force you or put a stick to your back. You should have thought about it for yourself, and come up with your own understanding of what religion is, and what the churches and God each wanted of you.

You had better start thinking for yourself. For your family's safety. Lead them; don't mislead them with other people's ideas. Your brain is working just fine. Start using it. Kick the tires and take it out for a spin. It will surprise you.

Gandhi, Buddha and the Dalai Lama had it right — by the way, the Dalai Lama is still alive, so you can see what he teaches and go ask him or read his books. The only way to rise to your heaven is a path of peace. Any religion that supports killing others for any reason is wrong about their understanding of killing; it is never good or needed. Murder is the only term to describe the act. Killing makes you a murderer. There is no good way to kill, except self defense. Pre-emptive self defense does not work, as we have seen that men are willing to start wars, and inflict mass murder and destruction under the pretense of pre-emptive self defense, and finding WMDs.

Human feelings and standards will not be important enough to excuse you from the action of murder. Even revenge or capital punishment is still murder. We will not have a human judgment after death, or any judgment to be more specific, as you will just move on to another class, carrying with you only the experiences you learned, and the currency of deeds done in this life, to use as tools in order to survive the next life, at whatever level your past deeds determine you should start at. If you did not learn to use peace, love, patience, compassion, common sense and so much more, then you will be at a disadvantage, and your new task may be to become a victim, in order to learn.

It must be said, that I believe abortion is not murder. I learned this from someone who is quite experienced in the spiritual world. She is called "The White Buffalo Woman" and you should read her books. Her name is Eve Kerwin and having personal sessions with her has been invaluable to me. I learned that the spirit does not enter the unborn child, and it is only at delivery that the spirit enters and the process is complete. Before delivery, the fetus has no spirit and is therefore not a person, but just a growing mass.

Regarding euthanasia, you must understand that most of what you experience in this life was more than likely planned by you before you took your material body in this life. It was you who decided to take these challenges and experiences to learn your own lessons of poverty, jealousy, hatred, devastating loss of family or property, drug addiction, being born deformed or having missing limbs, being very rich and many other scenarios including the conditions that lead to euthanasia.

When a person is in a medical condition that requires euthanasia, most likely you planned it and it is up to you to determine if you want to be euthanized or not, if you think the pain or discomfort is too much to bear. If you decide to be euthanized, it is not wrong. If someone, or your family, decides to do it because you are incoherent, it is not wrong. If you are coherent, and you ask to live and bear the pain and consequences, that is your decision.

While you are in this bad physical state, it is important to know that your spiritual life still goes on. Your spiritual self feels no pain at this time and if you stay in your bad state of suffering, you will simply be learning and experiencing through this, what you had planned to experience all along. Some people plan to get this type of suffering to live and experience that which they could not in their perfect spiritual form. It is in our most difficult time that we learn the most, so some people have learned to harvest precious lessons from these trying ordeals.

There may be many reasons why this type of advanced

planning is possible, and one such reason is to experience what a previous victim of yours may have had to endure by your actions. That being said, I am sorry for George Bush and his cohorts; they have a difficult time ahead.

Good deeds can save your soul, not good prayers. So there is no way that the supporters or partakers of any war will be clean enough to stay out of hell, by your standards, if there were a hell. If you want to think and live by your religious standards, remember the commandment "thou shall not kill." Remember that by my standards there is no hell, only peace and levels of enlightenment. What about killing in self defense? You can't enter people's home to steal, then kill them when they discover you and claim self defense. So you will determine if it is really self defense. You can't go to or stay in a confrontation or a fight when you can leave, then claim self defense after you murder because you could have avoided it by leaving. You decide your own fate, as it is determined by your actions. You can win a self-defense case in a court, but how can you fool yourself, when you know that you could have avoided killing in some way?

Creationism is not complete. The answers are right around us, within our eyesight, but not yet within your understanding. An easy example that you can relate to is salt. Everyone uses salt for their food and to melt the snow on their driveway, but some people do not know that eating too much salt can raise your blood pressure, which is bad if you have high blood pressure, but good if you have low pressure and know how to use it. Also, rinsing your mouth with salted water is beneficial to strengthen the gums. Some people use salt to purposely control their blood pressure as they get older and their bodies do not function properly. You are only told some of the properties of salt, as you are also only told some of the truth about religion and God.

You are given some of the ideas surrounding the religion, such as ways to worship, do's and don'ts of the specific religion, and even the miracles magically performed. The problem is, you are not given all the information and you are taught that it is all done by a god, as cited by most religions. People choose to believe that this is the whole story and there are no other theories, facts or explanations that make sense. This is because they are looking for the lazy, relaxing convenience of religion and not the truth. The simplicity of Sunday sermons and confession is convenient. They don't have to do and be good 24/7. Jesus showed us how to become enlightened; just do as He did but don't worship Him.

Like the salt, we are only aware of some of the properties of a god and religion. Can the real God be a multiple set of batteries interconnected to create a larger output of power than one individual battery or entity could produce? Yes. We do it all the time. When you have enough people, you have a stronger voice, force or riot. Can one person be a large manufacturing company? No, you need multiple people to do all the jobs. Think of when our minds and good deeds combine on this Earth; we can do unimaginable things for our spirituality, which is what you are searching for, in religion right now.

This is new to you and you may not get it too easily, as your mind has been brainwashed since you were two years old. Souls can connect, combine and cooperate in different ways to make up the greater consciousness and enhance it, bringing more energy to the universal consciousness we mistakenly call the one entity of God. I only say mistakenly because the term "God" brings baggage with it, of being one magical entity, not a larger collection of real entities. If we called the consciousness by any other name, or considered it to have a gender or human form, it still will not change. It will remain the same, so our calling it God does not change it from what it really is. These terms and names just wrongfully influence our ideas of what it is and that is not good.

Just as the invisible glue holds the legs of the table together, so too our individual consciousnesses all combine, to hold the expanding spiritual universe together in one fantastic consciousness. We are the individual drops that combine to form the vast ocean of consciousness. People may not understand this, as they have been taught to think in a certain way, leaving their minds closed to new ideas and only believing religious dogma. Shutting out new ideas, and accepting magical beings, fear and miracles, in this 21st century, is a follower's cross to bear if he or she chooses not to learn.

I have spent a lot of time telling you about the existence of God and consciousness because it is a subject that is grossly mischaracterized, and the fear about the fate for non-compliant worshippers is engrained into the character of the various religions. A one-paragraph explanation of the true God Consciousness will not break down the wall of fear: of God and dogma, and sometimes fanatical retribution that religious followers are plagued with, for non-compliance.

We are torn between truth and dogma. We have been

mentally conditioned to think of God as a foolish person who will exact revenge on non-believers, rather than there being a system, a force, an energy, or some combination thereof, that is in place performing a specific function of bringing about the continued spiritual progress of living beings throughout the universe.

There are many people facing their own fears about their worship. They face questions from different sources, including their kids, about the subject of religion, and spiritual truth will help them to understand more, open their eyes and get that first breath of reality, like an ocean breeze. As all people and religions are different, one question will not burst everyone's bubble of delirium, so I ask many different ones, from different angles, because each one will register, or have meaning, with each different person. My purpose is to debunk the myths about religion and show you a clear path.

The best of us have not been able to find this elusive God but thankfully, we have evolved the intelligence to figure it out. Just start thinking about it. The more you question all religions, your brain will find the answers you seek — the answers that make sense. Trust your instincts. You do not know how your brain works, so do not doubt that it can find the answers. Have you ever thought that the church was placed here and purposely meant to confuse you? Maybe they were but if so, why? It could be that we have to start thinking and questioning enough before the door of truth is opened to us.

This could suggest that the work of continuing to become enlightened in the different levels after our death is so difficult that there is no hope for Neanderthals like us, who like to relax and don't do much thinking, to achieve anything at the next level if we are not willing to search for answers to blind dogma and magical gods right now in this life. The church may be part of the plan by our conscious collective to purposely confuse us, to get us to think. It's a brilliant plan and suggests that there are bigger ideas in play than restrictive Earth religions. Remember the saying, the bigger the lie, the easier it is believed. How easily we believe that a religion is the truth.

So we must stay here, in blind servitude to the church, until we open our eyes to the truth. We are left running around, destroying each other, while kicking and clawing our way to monetary wealth and foolishly leaving it all behind. How smart. We are blessed for a second with love and a family, and then we set about running in the rat race to maintain the family and pay bills, and in so doing most of us let ourselves be distracted from the one important thing in our short existence: our families. So we build a bigger, business-oriented world that pollutes and poisons our offspring and our hopes for their bright futures. Eventually, that form of unchecked greed ultimately destroys the very ones we love, with diseases caused by a polluted world, and the vanities that we have become imprisoned by. That's ironic.

We are the inmates in an Earthly mental asylum, which we live in with delusion. We, the inmates, run the ward. We have to improve and cure ourselves of our insanity before we can release ourselves into the real society of consciousness, by becoming enlightened. Enlightenment does not mean giving up our prejudices, vices and vanities, but just learning to empower ourselves by controlling them. We need and use these prejudices to enhance our experiences and expand our intellect; they are the tools we use in this school of life to learn about, to feel, and to understand life and our existence, so we should not throw them out. Remember, problems are opportunities in disguise. When we learn control of our senses, we are better equipped to move on to a higher consciousness. It makes more sense than a magical god, and lazy religion, doesn't it? As a matter of fact, we do that in our daily lives and jobs now, when we strive for a promotion.

We see light, not realizing there are different colors combined to form the white light that we see. When we separate the light, it is only then we see the composition is of multiple colors. So too everything is made up of multiple ingredients, like a cake or a car. A car is not one product by itself but many parts put together. Are we gods to the cars we assemble, or to the children we produce? No. Just as the prism separates the light, so does our prism of caste, race, greed and envy prevent us from seeing the real truth of life and existence on Earth. We see one white light, not the colors behind the scene, just as we see one God or one concept of religion instead of the truth behind it. We see life through false prisms of prejudices; rich can't marry poor, white can't marry black and so on, and that influences us to not see the real truth behind the dogma, behind the religious servitude and behind racist agendas.

You have to find out what makes more sense. Find out what the real truth is to teach the kids. Right now you show them that you prefer to be led by a religion that they think is not completely true. If it is true, this is fine, but you must know if it is. Do not just blindly accept the dogma. The children will not accept unintelligent, blind following of any religion. How can you prepare them for space-age living with cavemen-like ideas of religion?

If God created the world with Adam and Eve, a few thousand years ago, where does oil come from? How was oil made under the ground? Did God do it in an instant as with the Garden of Eden or did dinosaurs and bacteria and pressure do it over millions of years? Does this prove that the Earth is billions of years old and not thousands like the religions say? Yes, and we understand oil, don't we? Why are there meteors and comets flying at us? Is God playing a video game? How was Jesus conceived? Did God do some magic or artificial insemination procedure to make Mary pregnant? If you believe Mary was a virgin and was impregnated by God, then you must believe in miracles and magic, but our children do not because they see technology — they can explain what a cell phone is and how it works. Abraham, Moses, the Three Wise Men and Joseph couldn't. A cell phone does not have a demon inside... believe me... on the other end maybe.

Can they believe the story of Adam and Eve, living in a Garden of Eden, with an evil snake and a magic Tree of Life? That sounds like a cartoon or the active imagination of primitive people with no education. The children are not fooled. Jesus performing some miracles but not others is confusing to them. Why turn water into wine but not cure all the sick children, and all the lepers, which were a major problem in that time? The tale of Lot's wife turning into a pillar of salt *really* needs to be taken with a grain of salt. Likewise with the mystical destruction of Sodom and Gomorrah — lots of salt needed there.

If religion's point is forgiveness and it is a necessity of Godly worship, why can't we have forgiven Iraq for the

September 11 attacks as they had nothing to do with 9/11? We could have turned the other cheek and found another solution. Our retaliation against countries has caused more deaths on both sides than the actual event of September 11th: more than one million deaths. Where's Jesus in that equation? We are damned by our actions and support of war, and the murder of millions instead of forgiving. Aren't Bush and his gang practicing Christians? Why didn't they forgive? Are they really good Christians and God is telling them to kill? That kind of thinking could start a nuclear war, an early Armageddon..

They are lying to us when they say they are Christians and believe in God. We are lying to ourselves and our families when we say we are good Christians who support war. Our children think we are hypocrites by our actions. Shouldn't we go to hell for going to war instead of forgiving? How could you be "saved" and follow some of Christ's teachings and not turn the other cheek? That is being a hypocrite and a coward. Are we not our brother's keeper? When we say The Lord's Prayer, and we say, "Thy will be done," I ask you, whose will is war? Is it ours or God's?

Are the TV and radio talk show hosts leading us to hell like pied pipers, by encouraging us to support war instead of being smart Christians and finding solutions? Forgiving does not mean giving up; it means we should find better solutions than war. Solutions which do not send your kids to die are smart ones. They are telling us that our false pride, of needing the upper hand in the world with our war, is more important than our souls remaining clean, so we cannot turn the other cheek, and solve it another way — we have to kill. So we should go to war and go to hell? They are tricking us when they are supposed to be good Christians and know better. Do they even believe in God as they say? No. Their supporting violence is not Jesus' way, so they will not be "saved" and they know this. Our actions determine who we are. You doom your own children with war and death.

What are they not telling us about religion? Do they know what their God will do about the war and about the soldiers sent there to do their jobs, which is to kill or be killed? Does their God want the inevitably disastrous results of war? So far, we have more than 4,000 soldiers and one million Iraqis dead, and more than two million people displaced. People will now want revenge against us, as what we sow, so shall we reap. I can tell you, no god would want so many souls to be lost to this world. Some things make no sense, and that applies to blind faith, war and any god who allows them.

Are we creating homegrown terrorists from some of the surviving families of our dead soldiers? Was Timothy McVeigh just an example we ignored? A real God would not allow this to happen. A better understanding about the real consciousness can save us from ourselves. What is the shining light in all of this? Well, think of the faith we put into worshiping Jesus and a god we created largely out of misdirection. That was good practice, so now we will be able to better appreciate and understand the real truth, a bigger truth about consciousness, and to be a more productive and inclusive part of it. This is a truth that we *can* teach our children about, and we can still call it God…or ice cream.

Our children really can't believe a god is sitting there

watching man destroy the same Earth that He lives on. If man were destroying himself alone, then God may not have intervened. As we all know, man is destroying all flora and fauna, all plants and animals, so obviously if there were a god as you envisioned, He would surely step in and stop man in his destructive quest. Just look at how we protect and care for our pets, instead of the beggars and even some of our children. Wouldn't a god also take good care of us, who are His children...or His pets?

That alone proves there is no god sitting there directing a play by play between us and an immortal Devil. People must connect the dots. They think God and the Devil are playing a video game with a set of rules they have to follow. A real god would not have a set of rules He is restricted by, like the rules set out by the Bible.

These rules and religions make it so easy for people who are bad to each other all week to go to church on Sunday to beg for forgiveness, accept Jesus and be "saved".... every week, like some sort of weekly, forgiving ritual. What about the confession thing? They fool themselves thinking God is foolish enough to fall for these rituals. What does being saved really mean? It appears that we are still stuck on primitive ideas and fears.

Many people are haunted and terrified by religion. They are running down a long road, pursued by devils and demons, all the while running toward a vengeful and punishing God, who may very well be worse than the devils themselves, as He only promises slavery and hard labor in various forms of worship to Him.

Remember in the '70s, when rock music was thought to be the music of the Devil? It was said that if you played the records backwards, you could hear the demons speaking. Parents were so superstitious and feared the Devil so much that they stopped us from buying records and listening to rock music, even on the radio. Those are the same people who promote religion and blind fear in something they know nothing about. I think we should replace the word "faith" with the word "fear," as that is what is going on in religion. Blind faith is more accurately blind fear.

Look at the dutiful worshippers; they are all living in an alternate reality, believing everything is heaven-sent in mysterious ways. Some do not even accept medical care, but prefer to die or let members of their family die, for want of blood transfusions and medical procedures. These people are the same ones who get a job as a pharmacist and then deny others when they come to get a prescription filled for birth control medicines and the like. Some do not even sell condoms in their stores. They prefer people be denied the safety of protection from STDs. Some take their loved ones out of the hospitals and try to pray for them to overcome their medical problems. Sadly, many people die as a result, including little children, who don't have a say. That is a sad example of fanaticism and the lengths people will go to, to prove the validity of their baseless beliefs in religion.

How curious is it that all the different religions share the same heaven and hell? Obviously, each was made up to copy the other. It is plain to see that the whole class copied from the one child in the class who invented religion. That is why everyone has the same idea: hell, heaven, vengeful punishing gods in a cage, demons, and a scared, confused, ignorant and paranoid population, all running around psychotically screaming the Messiah is coming and the Devil is already here.

I have come to realize that in all religions (Christian, Hindu, Buddhist), and all others, there are the cultural trappings that have evolved out of each religion's and country's long history. Some histories are longer than others; that does not matter. All religions have cultural dress, foods, places of worship, deities, preachers, religious leaders of all names and descriptions, and rituals that actually prevent you from reaching the real consciousness of your religion, which is hidden — concealed within the walls of these cultural trappings. The leaders are quick to say that we have to do this or that procedure and ritual: fast in this or that way or not at all…dress in this or that way, or you will not get the full benefit of your religion or reach heaven.

The only thing these practices and rituals do is distract you from reaching the consciousness which you seek. If you find favor in the church, does that mean you have found favor with your creator or are now farther from Him? Are you now an enlightened person like Jesus? No. It means you are pleasing to some puppeteers in the church and not to any real creator that exists, just an imaginary one made up to fool you into needing the puppeteers, and the different religions and the churches they operate from.

If you keep yourself in the state of a deranged animal, how can you raise your consciousness? You are the same inside and out — nothing else. It will benefit us to remember that what we do also determines who we become and vice-versa. I am not a saint, but I still do good deeds and think for myself, and so can you.

How can some religions allow the consumption of

specific meats while others don't? Muslims don't eat pork, Hindus don't eat beef, and another religion does not eat shell fish and fish without scales. This shows that religion is not complete as it is contradicted by each other in even the most basic ways. When flesh is well cooked, we do not know what type of meat we are eating. We may be eating minced dog, cat, and other unsavory products and probably are doing so in foreign lands, and in local restaurants right here in America. When I was younger, for years I frequently dined at a restaurant which was later discovered to be serving dog meat. My friends unknowingly ate cat meat. Serving domestic animals is a common practice all over the world, including illegally in America. Does religion condone this? Which one?

There is a tendency to praise a god who can stay in a box, or cage, and conform to the limitations we set for Him. There is the so-called heaven and there is our Earth, and we need only concern ourselves with carrying out our mission of doing good things and learning self-control here. We don't have to be concerned with heaven or what happens when we get there. God would not introduce our destructive race to the other harmless races of the universe. We will just rape, murder and conquer them as we did with the Native Americans and other natives around the world, won't we?

If God allows man to turn against his brother, till man exists no more, will He just make a new man? Is He the partner of the Devil, working to keep evil in the world? If the Devil is getting stronger, why doesn't God defeat Him now before it's too late? After all, aren't the consequences supposed to be bad if He doesn't? Or is Satan in a cage of human rules also? Is God restricted by some cage of Godly restrictions or rules that He powerlessly has to follow, so that He can't defeat the Devil? That has to be a scam and so easy to debunk.

There is a whole universe out there and that is where true reality exists. This small planet where we live resides inside the larger system of the real spiritual universe. We live here by our own set of rules, prejudices, and differing sets of religious ideas, having no control of reality, so prayers do not change anything.

When someone taps into the great consciousness, what they learn, they can't explain to the unenlightened people here, so that's where and why the God concept started. Thousands of years ago, primitive man tried to explain the consciousness they discovered to themselves and others. The God concept was as far as man could understand. When Jesus told them He was not of this world, they mistook it for magic. When He said this they mistook it to mean he was in the spirit only after His death, but He — we — are not of this Earth, but from outside this Earth, just here to visit, right now, not after death. We are great spirits here on Earth, even as we are just occupying our outer physical bodies, at this moment.

Is there one understanding that fits everyone? What's the difference between a Roman Catholic, a Presbyterian, an Anglican, a Mormon, a Buddhist, a Hindu, a Hare Krishna devotee? There is no difference, just the different prejudiced names they and all others choose to sort their groups, gangs or cults into. Did slavery make the owner better than the slave? No, it was just arrogance that made them think that they were better, same as the religious.

Those religious terms, groups and names are just

cultural trappings. Truth has nothing to do with cultural trappings, or when you worship, or how you worship, who you worship or why you worship. There are religions and cultures that teach that women have to worship in one way or another or they will suffer the consequences, which may include being shunned, stoned, raped and murdered.

Do these people realize that what they teach the young will change the world for everyone? Who is the one with the right religious idea? Would Christians follow the Eastern teachings? Jesus did. He became enlightened and did not live in denial. People follow one teaching or another, just because they want to belong to a group, religion or cult. They are scared of being alone. They are not thinking the process through to find out what makes sense. There are so many religious rules and stories that are misleading to us, yet people selectively ignore certain things because others do and follow religion incorrectly, regardless of the outcome for their families.

We are all the same. There is a black group of people in South Africa who claim that they are descended from one of the original tribes of Jews, settling in Africa at least 14 centuries ago. They were not believed, as they looked exactly alike to all the other peoples of South Africa. They are the Lemba people, one of the 10 lost tribes of Israel. DNA testing proves them to be right. Over the centuries their features changed, not their DNA. It shows that we really are all the same group of humans, just very large in number and dispersed around the globe, so we should have one truth. I think that truth is discovering enlightenment.

If Adam and Eve were the first two people, and their sons, Cain and Abel, were the next two people to walk this

Earth, then how did Cain go to the land of Nod to get a wife? They were the only four people alive at the time, so Cain could not have gotten a wife. Also how could they populate the world?

The only female person alive was Eve, so was there inbreeding? Did that one family really populate the world? It is apparently all just deception, fear-mongering and misunderstanding stacked one on top of the other over thousands of years, coupled with the nonchalance of the followers and seekers, and their unwillingness to question. How do you feel about this? Are you okay with your children believing this? Do you want shortsighted, gullible children?

GOD AND RELIGIOUS ILLUSION

Everything that happens is good for the universe as it helps the growth of consciousness. What aspects of life you do not like you can change, and make it better for yourself and the universal consciousness.

Neither religion nor the church is the answer. Mankind interacting with the universe is. Look within, go within and see the outer universe when you look back out from your personal vantage point. The body can travel and experience the universe physically; so too the soul can do so spiritually.

Atheists do not believe in God, so what will happen to them when they wake up each day, eat, get married or die? Nothing different happens to them than happens to everyone else. Why do they not suffer more, or all die painfully and go to hell? They are not as unhappy, and cursed or lost as the church wants us to believe they are. Also, they are happy to not be tormented by the religion's rules, rituals and perverted priests.

They do not suffer and neither do we. We live. We all live. Ancient man needed to see a god to save them. We can see a lot more. We can see the universe. The church tells you that we suffer so we need the church, but we don't. No matter what we are or what we do, we live. Even murderers, thieves and their friends live happily, some with monies stolen from our treasury in no bid contracts. That is what we were meant to do: live, not serve or worship. Those who embrace the truth become enlightened and conquer fear.

The kingdom is inside you and all around you.

Religion could be a way to connect to consciousness. That could have been one reason why it was introduced to the world, to help us to connect to our center, where the force resides. Religion was meant to help us to grow spiritually. Unfortunately, many of us have not been taught this. Instead we were taught to worship ideology and dogma. We don't need dogma, rules, rituals, incense, crosses, holy books, robes, hats, pictures, statues, alters, temples, churches, or anything else religious to connect to our center, or the inner force we call God.

When we go to church, we are simply doing the same as going to a gathering, party or meeting. It is supposed to be all in the name of God, and that is okay only, only, only if we understand that it is not necessary. Only after we understand that we do not need the institutions to find and connect to our force of God Consciousness, then it will be okay to attend. It's all in your mind, not in an institution, church or temple. We are trying to increase our spirituality, to have a better and stronger connection to what we think is truth, and we don't need religious misdirection to do this.

Religion has changed and morphed from a teaching to connect to God Consciousness, into a power all unto itself, where people are misdirected to using and needing the church as the middleman to get to God, but are not shown the true way to do so. We are not taught the truth — that Jesus wanted us to follow *His path*, not Him.

There are the major religions and they are good to be a part of, if we are lonely, in need of company, and have the willingness to strip away the dogma to find the truth. Any one of them will be fine in that case. There are cult-like groups that should be looked at very carefully before we get involved with them, as they mostly trade in Earthly pleasures, which is also fine. There are also organizations like the cult of Jim Jones, who killed over 900 of his followers in a camp in Guyana.

There is more illusion in religion than there is truth because the truth is short and simple. There is the physical universe and the spiritual universal consciousness, and we are part of it. That's all. That's the simple truth, short and sweet. Then the churches come along and try to confuse the public to join one group or another, dance this way or sing that way. They trap us by creating all sorts of illusionary ideas that are quite imaginative, and usually entrap those who are confused enough to fall for their stories. You don't have to be a part of a church, group or movement to become enlightened.

Not many, if any, of the spiritually revered people were part of a church. Jesus, Buddha, and others all became enlightened by thinking, not cowering in fright and in shame of their sins, in the corner of some religion. The religious beliefs were invented around them and enhanced after their deaths. The myriad of exotic and imaginative ideas and procedures we have to follow are quite funny if you take a good look at them.

There are so many amusing rituals and superstitions that it would be laughable, if it were not so sadly misleading to people who do not understand what they are getting into, because we all are genuine in our efforts to find the way to goodness and peace. We would not be going to worship if we did not want to be good souls.

So I commend you, my good human family, because

we are all trying to make this world a better place for each other. I love you all, as I am sure you love each other, and I really feel loved knowing that there is so much affection and caring in this human family. I am filled with pride that I am a part of this human family and I feel joy just being alive alongside you all. This is what it is all about and we do not need the church to be this loving to each other. I live in New York, a very expensive place, but the love and concern for each other transcends the difficulties, and in this, I see humanity's greatest achievement: peace, unity and love.

We on this Earth have the brightest future in this universe, not because we have gods who bless us with ignorance, fear, famine and wars — those are all manmade — but because we have intelligence. We have evolved to be a force second to none. We can compare ourselves to anything intelligent in the universe and we will be competitive enough to be proud of ourselves. We also have imagination, and the common sense to survive and beat the odds when faced with adversity. We are capable of compassion, and we have the know-how to use our brains, feelings and emotions together, to make decisions. We can't be beaten, except by ourselves. Our obsession with superstition and belief in magical gods has been our undoing for thousands of years, hence the reason we are just now heading for the stars. That process should have taken place 10 centuries ago, but was retarded by our myriad of beliefs, prejudices and personal greed. The future waits.

There are terms like "saved" and "believing" and "following" that can really do damage to people's minds and our little Earth. Throughout history, followers and seekers have been mentally conditioned to believe they could be saved by different religions and their gods, as if there is some pending doom approaching. The ones which teach that we have to be a part of the religious flock are misleading us. All we have to do is learn about the real force of the universe.

It is as real as the force that cooks your food in the microwave: the force that will blow your hair at the beach or that thought which makes you smile or understand. We can't tell our kids that they will die and go to heaven or hell because it is not true, and only serves to confuse them into becoming despondent and self destructive as we ourselves have become. We will lose them. I think if my kids stay with me, but believe in different religions, then I have still lost them, because they have left reality, spiritually, and have begun to live in an alternate reality, one that doesn't exist, with demons and probably even fire-breathing dragons and flaming chariots. They will be no better off than in a psych ward.

Everyone says they want guidance but the question is, what kind of guidance are they getting? If the message they get is seek and you shall find, well, that's simple to do. The problem is, some people are not encouraged by the church to seek; nonchalance is common and they end up learning to cower and follow. Prophets like Jesus did not follow. They each broke the walls around the religions of their times and found enlightenment. If they had followed, I would not be speaking about them right now. The force that you seek is right around you, and inside you, all the time. It is you. You have to want to find it, for it to be revealed to you, by you, for you. You will discover it.

Your God Consciousness is a presence that is the air around you all the time. You breathe it in and it energizes you. Then you deny it and think you need someone to guide you to it. We are like fish in the ocean, looking for a mouthful of water; you get it without knowing it. You feed on it.

Life is not only based on the past, but also on the present and moves toward the future. We can not only live with the ideas and religions of the past, but learn new ideas as we gain intelligence in the present and use them to help the future unfold with splendor, as we take our rightful place in the universe. Love comes from you, from your inner self, not a religious scripture or verse. We are the ones who make this world what it is, not a scribe or politician who has lofty ideas and is trying to fulfill his egotistical yearning.

Mankind can make great things. We have wonderful ideas but firstly, we must realize that we are great. We are not sheep, so look no further than yourself to find greatness. Do not look at a book or traditional rules but look in the mirror, and inside yourself and you will find the greatness of mankind within. This world is crying out for a way to move forward and we are the ones to make that way possible. We must empower the children to boldly go into the future, not cower in the past. Do not forget the old traditions but do not be ruled by them. Make new ones, sensible ones, new traditions to help your children's future bloom, not be stifled by old misconceptions.

Even out of the darkness of ignorance, the light of truth will emerge to shine on us and bring a new dawn. Many have let their misguided greed and love of money rule their destinies, to the detriment of the world around them. Yet still, the pain they cause dies with them like old slave masters, and a new breath of hope is blown in on a breeze of a new era: the peace after the war, the calm after the storm, and the promise of a new start and a brighter future. This new future starts here, starts now, with us and continues with our children, ushering a new age of peace and understanding. Enlightenment is the breath of a new beginning and the tide of change, which a deserving world needs, to pave a new way for our children. We have let them down long enough, made them victims of our greed, our religions and our self destruction. Has the Apocalypse come and gone? Some say yes. Bill Cosby said on an interview, the four horsemen have gone. We now see a new dawn and standing together against war, we see the Antichrist of mankind, hate and greed, is being defeated.

We were not born with our own religious ideas and society's ideas of right and wrong. We had to be programmed, taught, brainwashed, and convinced to believe, and now you have to reprogram yourself to escape the grasp of religious misunderstanding. The condition of being human and the condition of being religious are uniquely temporary Earthly illusions and Earthly delusions, which were not meant to suppress our true inner selves, but meant to magnify our greatness through education and understanding of self control in the different states of existence of life, here on Earth and elsewhere in the universe. Each cycle of life we go through is a lesson, a class attended and a lesson learned, felt, lived and experienced. We are not meant to be deluded and to misunderstand why we are here, in a cage of delusion, but we do.

Religion is a cage of illusion. To see what life is in the cage, you have to look in from the outside of the cage. If we cower, and think like the ancients, we will not go further than any religion decrees, and we will continue to retard our development as a space-bound race, as a conscious and enlightened race. We are told not to seek any consciousness or understanding, outside the rules and boundaries of the religious cage. As an inmate, how can we see the truth from inside the institution? Most can't.

There is no evil in the world, just in our minds. Aren't *we* the evildoers when we kill each other for different reasons, for oil, politics, religion, immigration or racism? When we do bad things to our women in the name of religion, or to children under the guise of religion…when we conceal the ills of the wrongdoers and pedophile priests who abused these children…when we protect and support the church leaders who hid these criminal priests…when we support the abuse and segregation of our daughters and mothers all around the world, for religion's sake…aren't *we* the wicked ones? Who will forgive us and wipe away that bad karma we create? Can the church, a priest, a religion or a god forgive us? Sadly, none of the above can. There really is no act or action called forgiveness, when it comes to God forgiving us. We can forgive each other and move on. The God Consciousness does not need to forgive us, which is part of itself; we are part of it. It is just a meaningless word when used in that context of being forgiven by God, just like religiously being "saved" or receiving religious "salvation."

There is no forgiving any bad acts if we continue to do them and allow them. The perpetrator has already done the deed. The other was made the victim. It still happened, when it should not have. That's the important thing. We have to ensure that it does not continue to happen, whatever the bad deed is.

We can't be unwilling to seek the truth, yet expect to find it. *It* is not lost — we are. You just can't see that. Could you see the wind or the currents in the ocean? Yes, you can, if you know how to look for them. It is just as easy to find the truth. Earth is one inhabitant of the universe and everything else inhabits the universe as well. When a religion tells us to not think of the universe, they mislead us. When they tell us this is not our business to think outside the prison of religion, obviously they are misleading us.

We can find the consciousness by simply thinking about it and unlocking it from within. Do you believe all the strange things you read in your scriptures? Written by historic or ancient humans who became psychotic with lead poisoning, or other reasons? You should not. Any era older than 150 years, I consider historic or ancient because they didn't have computers back then, much less cell phones, so religion really does come from the Dark Ages, a bygone age of ignorance.

Step into the light. That's the key now — light. Bring light, wisdom, and common sense into your lives by opening your eyes of understanding, which is what I call your mind. It has been clouded and shut too long. Let the past be buried in the past. Let the old religions stay where they belong, with our ancestors, dead and buried. A new age is upon us, one of light and spirit, in the 21st century, a new beginning for us and our children, in space, colonizing under the oceans and even inside planets and moons. They will provide excellent protection against external forces like meteorites, and also a contained space in a moon or planet will be easier to maintain and provide necessities for, like gravity and air, while mining the planet around you, as ants and viruses do.

Do you think you should dangle the future of your children on those ancient people's imaginative religions? It is time for you to awaken that inner force and discover the truth. It is time to step into the light and embrace scientific education. Scientific education dispels religion and delusion, with reason and common sense. You must strip away the cultural trappings and you will be left with the truth. In the middle of all religions there is the divine consciousness that we all try to connect with. Encircling the consciousness are cultural trappings, like having to reach God through prayer to Jesus, Jehovah, Krishna or anyone else. It makes more sense to progress by your actions of good, all day long, constantly. If God is not a Being sitting on a throne in heaven, how will you reach Him otherwise? How will you convince Him to accept you into heaven? Not by empty words. Prayers are but empty words to the wind unless celebrated and sanctified by the actions of good deeds. People pray every day and still willingly do wrong.

What can you educate God about in your daily prayers? Are you just reciting the same thing over and over? I want, I want, I want. Is He *that* dumb? If you come to God each day and tell Him something He doesn't know, then He will listen, won't He? When you tell Him what you want every time you pray, like a broken record, He becomes your servant, and if you pray for Him to bless you with something you can't do yourself — maybe make you instantly rich — why should He help you? If He is capable of miracles, why should He help the lazy people who don't care to help themselves and others? People pray for good health every day but some still die from illnesses that could be avoided with exercise. I don't see everyone winning the lottery. Prayer is empty. Good deeds are better prayers and they bring better results.

What form does a spirit, soul or demon have? Does light have a form? Does sound have a form? Do you know who or what you are really praying to and sacrificing your children to? Did Abraham? Are you worshiping and praying to the wrong thing? If you don't know what God is, you may not be praying and speaking to God or anything real. How do you know that it is not the Devil or demons, tricking you and answering your prayers? Is that against some rule to trick you, pretend to be God and answer you? Are you dialing God's number and the Devil can't hear you, or the Devil can't answer the call? Your prayers will affect other people and the Devil will like that. He will answer your prayers delightedly.

God does not answer phones, or prayers. Just ask the millions of parents whose kids died of disease. They will attest to that. You must understand, each life brings something back to the God Consciousness, and it is done through your actions, not God's, and not your prayers. Look at how many billions pray to their gods daily. Are these prayers answered? No, or a lot more people would be dead right now, because gods would answer prayers of war and kill the enemies. The Muslim God would kill the Jews, the Jewish God would kill the Muslims, the Hindu Gods would kill the Muslims, the Muslim God would kill the

Hindus, and the Christian God would be in the middle doing the same. Everyone looks for a magical god in the sky but there's nothing there; it never existed. There is not and never was a god up there. It's all a dream that was needed back then in the days of the ancients.

What if you are too unclean spiritually to reach the consciousness you call God? After all, we do fight wars and kill each other. How do you cleanse yourself, cleanse your soul, so as to attain enlightenment? The answer is, by giving up your fears. Don't give up your money, or your courage and confidence in yourself. Just give up your fear, after which, you will begin to do good works, and balance the bad karma or negative vibrations you created. Fear is what rules followers. Leaders conquer or work through their fears. Leaders bow in respect to others, not in fear of others. Leaders do good works in spite of their fears.

The fear of a vengeful religious entity is keeping you imprisoned, by the idea that you need a church or other institution to achieve consciousness of the divine and to save you from demons. You come to pray with problems and fears, and that is why you can't see the light. If I may borrow a phrase from history, you must understand that there is nothing to fear but fear itself.

On Columbus's last voyage he was marooned on the island of Jamaica for a year or so. The year was 1504, and he and his men were starving. The natives were angry with him and were not sharing food with Columbus. Columbus calculated that there would be an eclipse of the moon in February, and he used this knowledge to persuade the natives to believe that his God was angry, and they must feed Columbus and his men or his God would block out the moon. They ignored his warning. When the moon turned red during the eclipse, this convinced the natives that Columbus's God was more powerful than theirs. They fed Columbus and his men until they were rescued. This was just one of many tricks used to fool Native people and inflict fear. This is the same trickery, fear, and slight-of-hand that the church has continued to use against its own people and the new peoples converted by their missions. We are now the ignorant natives being fooled and ruled in fear. Are we any different?

The Amish are some of the most perfect Christians on Earth now, as they follow most of the rules, in my opinion. It is easy to see how they live in the past, and see that this fear of God and their religious beliefs slow their progress. Time stands still for them. When their children reach the age of 16, they are allowed to go out into the world. It is a process called Rumspringa.

The children are sooner or later faced with the decision of going back to their family, to join the community and the Amish church, and become controlled by the church's rules. They have a dilemma of joining the future or living in the past. Some choose the future and never return home. They choose to leave the past where it belongs — behind them.

The Amish will not leave their religious prison and reach the moon on their own accord, nor will they do most other things outside of the church's rules. This is real religious worship. This is the same thinking that has kept mankind's progress at bay for 6,000 years and still does today. The Amish are taught to try to go to heaven and they may live in this modern-day past forever...as all good, well-meaning, real Christians do. To them, heaven is everything, even a dream, as they dream of heaven.

Energy is neither created nor destroyed; it just changes form. If you lost everything, including your family, what would you have left? The answer is everything. Because you and all you thought you lost are still a part of the whole, the consciousness in the universe, and it is still all there, so you have lost nothing. You need not worry about loss because you really have nothing, and only temporarily live an illusionary life of riches. If you lose them, you will be distraught but then you will gain the opportunity to find consciousness, courage, wisdom and peace, as loss is an opportunity in disguise. This in turn teaches you self control of your emotions, and control of self is the ultimate desired destination. Rich people are hard pressed to achieve this, as most are pampered and rooted in a material existence.

Fishes live in an ocean of water. We live in an ocean of air. We live in the ocean of consciousness of the universe. We are the fishes swimming in the consciousness all around us. Can you be peaceful and do well without receiving reward? Yes. The more good deeds you do without reward or payment, the more pride in yourself, truth and peace you will find, which in itself is an unexpected reward. Peace and truth go together. Why are we frantic and stressed each day? It is because we are not pursuing peace and truth. We are pursuing money, fame, power and other vain things. Those of us who do live telling the truth are less stressed than others. We, telling the truth to ourselves and others, unlike the stressed who fool themselves and others, are the way to our destiny of enlightenment.

Can't you be excommunicated, and kicked out of the

churches or temples? Yes. So will any God reject you then, if you are a good person? Religion is a club or a cult that you can join, and be ostracized when it suits them. This is just the games they play. This is not true enlightenment. It is religion and religious slight-of-hand. Can they tell God to reject you? No. They are selling you salvation in return for following them, when they themselves do not know salvation or God. You are trying to reach your real God, your inner self, not build the wallets of the churches. We are at war with greedy churches, and religions who all want to increase their membership and finances. They all tell us theirs is the right one to follow. That's just wrong. Seek the center of truth: your inner self, not the church. You will find that culture has been confused for religion and vice versa; they are fused together like the church and politics, all helping each other to feed like vampires off the people's fears.

When you sit quietly, you can control your breathing, slow down your heartbeat and relax, much like meditation. Soon enough you realize you're feeling much more peaceful and you can get in touch with your peaceful center. You can really think. Some call it finding your chi. The more you practice this, the more in touch with your center you will become. That is the simple truth of enlightenment. When you touch your chi or center, you are touching the center of consciousness within yourself.

Your center, inner spirit, or soul is the same center of the universal consciousness we call God, the same center or God that your religion teaches you about. The trick is that they, the corrupt few in the religions, want you to go through them and drop some money in the collection plate on the way. How can they get you to go through them? They do this by tricking and confusing you to be afraid, follow their psychotic rituals, superstitions and mindless trappings, to look to them as your shepherds, and look down on yourself in shame and disgust as the sinful, following flock of sheep. I say, don't fear God. Fear them!

Look for the truth. People who mislead you are not bringing you to God. They are bringing you to their churches where they can work on you like a surgeon, separate you from your money, courage, peace, and common sense, and replace them with fear of a vengeful god, and the wrath of a vengeful religion and church.

Religion is an institution, a company, a business, and the only profit they can attain is your money, not your salvation. As a servant of theirs, you are being used and do not achieve the inspired enlightenment you seek. Religion is suddenly everywhere because it is a profitable business and is now a product of mass production. This phenomenon started with the advent of the radio, and incorporated television coverage in the '70s and '80s, and really enhanced the distribution to audiences all over the world. Look at the monetary value of the churches, the TV ministries, the Catholic and other religious empires. They are worth billions, rivaled only by the other big businesses and oil interests around the world. Religion was the first multinational company, and all the other companies are learning from and following their lead.

To be realistic, the churches that can get enough money will become strong and be able to expose a lot more people to some brand of God, and to that extent, all the religions are correct in trying to get money — as a business. The only concern is that the good leaders in the religions are unwittingly teaching you the wrong things about God or just not getting you there. It's not their fault; they are trying to find the truth for themselves, so that they can show you the way to enlightenment and end up there themselves. Is there salvation and forgiveness by God? No. We are not cursed by a god. There is no need for it, so it does not exist. Enlightenment is the only thing that can be considered salvation but you are not being saved by a vengeful god, from a vengeful, horn-headed Satan. You are just finding the truth and ascending toward that truth. You, like Jesus said, are right now, "not of this world." Wasn't He trying to get you to follow His path and not the religions? Yes. He knew that the religions were crazy and the ones in the future would be even more mistaken...fast forward 2,000 years and here we are.

All religions that teach us that a spiritual force resides at the center of that religion are correct. What is incorrect are the hoops you have to jump through to get there, or the cyclic misunderstanding of religion that leads you in a circle and no closer to that center — to a realization of your God Consciousness. Clearly, you do not need to switch from one religion to another, as they all should lead to the same place — the source and the truth. What you need to do is strip away the dogma, rituals, fears, cultural trappings and superstition. Find out, to find out; seek information and you will learn.

Your center of consciousness and the consciousness you call God are the same; they are one. You can reach that anytime. You don't have to pay at the pump — collection at the pews — and jump through religious hoops. Just stop allowing yourself to be misled. Think for yourself. Do well and be in touch with your center all day. Instead of trying to pray 10 times a day, be in touch with your center all day.

You are with your god, your light, your inner self, your soul, your chi, your Jesus, Krishna, Buddha, toaster oven and any other names you call it. Those names are all the same and you are a large part of it: the one consciousness — colorless, tasteless and odorless. Kind of sounds like water, right? Try going a week without water. That's what we are doing to ourselves without consciousness. It is the ocean of consciousness we live in, breathe in. It is the light that enters us through our eyes. It is the one source of enlightenment, and it is in you and around you, so don't go to the churches, temples or the evangelist channel on TV to find it anymore. It has been right there all along where Jesus and the others found it — inside you. Take a deep breath of it and wake up.

Jesus and the others were your brothers, not your gods. Do what they did. When we say God's son or God's prophets, you should see that we are the same as they were: flesh and blood. And now we just have to do what they did — break down the walls of ignorance to become enlightened, so as to not be a slave to any religion. Were they? They were not enslaved for too long by any religious sects, rituals, and TV ministries. They walked with the consciousness because they found that it was within them, not something they had to find out there somewhere, like an elusive dream. It's in you too; it is your spirit or soul.

Before Jesus, and apparently after also, there had always been the misunderstanding that there was a god to fear and worship. Jesus came and spoke against that idea, and taught that God was just your force inside you that you can feel and know. This angered the churches and they killed Him for it, and invented the Bible to then ride the wave of unexpected sympathy and anger that was garnered from the crucifixion. They saw that this worked better for them than their old way of control. History has proved them right.

We put these priests and religions so high on a pedestal that we lose sight of what God Consciousness and truth is. We become confused. We exalt the pope and other men, who are just flesh and blood like us, not a learned being put here to guide you. Look at who the churches supported throughout their sordid history: tyrants, murderers, conquerors, psychos….even Hitler. You don't need that brand of misdirection.

We swallow the ideas of the churches' shepherd bringing the sheep, and it becomes the truth that you allow yourself to believe and be led by. You become this sheep willingly. They are not forcing you to be in the church but they are fooling you to stay there. Holy is a word used by the church. Faith is another sword they use to confuse us. Believe is another. You will find within you the truth, and you will know and understand the truth when you look there, and not at the churches.

It is flawed to focus on what or who is out there, like your God, looking in at us, in our religious cage. Rather, our focus should be on what is in here, in our prison, looking out. We, as a world of humans, must try to cleanse and control ourselves gradually of all the feelings and thoughts that resist the good we so desperately need to do. Would your creator want you to be near Him in your evil state? No. Well, it's a little more impersonal than that. You simply have to attain other higher levels of control and consciousness before you can reach His level. On His level, you will meet a "Him," even if it's a "Them" of souls working together. That's irrelevant to us right now but it's nice to know. It's funny how you can understand the levels in government, the levels in the corporate ladder, in your job, in criminal gangs or groups, but yet you did not understand it is the same for the most important things, which are life and our spiritual existence.

Do you think whatever is out there will want us coming there with our selfish and greedy souls, weak minds, unclean spirits, disturbed inner selves, lost chi, and confused selves? The problem is, if we do not cleanse ourselves, by learning to control our senses, what use would we be here or over there? How will we qualify to be there without good deeds? Do you think we will qualify with prayer, donations and political connections? No.

Some say that He is not a loving God to us; if He were, He would not punish us or be vengeful, as we were taught He is. So who's confused? Who's trying to mislead you? Let us say no one is trying to mislead you, so then is it true? No. The people who are charged with the task of leading are not equipped with the right knowledge to do it. They were taught this cyclic tale and they are just bringing it to us, in the most loving way they can.

Our religious leaders were taught these cyclic tales, for centuries, and were asked to teach them with the love and wisdom that they were taught to them. Problem is, it doesn't make much sense, to us or them, but they try to do the right thing anyway because they see the need for, and lack of, enlightenment in our society. They see society receding into extinction and they know something is missing. They see the gangs growing in numbers and escalating their criminal activity. They, like us, also know that they do not have all the answers but use whatever weapons they have, to stem the tide of self destruction that mankind is riding on. Is religion losing the battle to gangs? Yes, gang numbers are growing.

What do they mean by mysterious ways? It means they don't understand it themselves. That's why they claim it's mysterious. They will say the theories of relativity, special relativity and general relativity are all just God's "mysterious ways," and viruses and retroviruses, anti-matter and dark-matter, which have shaped human existence from the earliest life-form to the present, are all religious miracles billions of years in the making. I know better and so do you.

Perception is very important when thinking about religion. We can tell with common sense that all the things we learn about, in all the scriptures, foreign and domestic, are flawed. The authors, who brought those teachings to us, by writing the various religious documents, tried their best to bring us reason and truth as they saw it, as they had been taught. It is a wonderfully courageous attempt and we should all be proud of them. Some are trying to further that teaching now, in a second wave, and bring the knowledge of the existence of enlightenment and science to you in a way that you can understand and accept, and guide your children to their futures among the stars. There won't be wood-burning stoves in a spaceship to cook with, but there will be a microwave oven to warm food on board our spacecrafts. Similarly, old beliefs like religion have no place there; religion's place is in our history books for your great-great-great grandchildren to read about.

Our priests were unintentionally misled, unwittingly led astray, by their peers and leaders throughout history. Misled much like your runaway children in the gangs, who do not want to believe you when you ask them to come home, explaining that life is not as bad as they think it is. They disagree because they saw their friend gunned down mercilessly and senselessly right in front of their eyes, by the rival gang or the police, so to them life isn't fair or *okay*. Hearing this, you still think that they have the wrong perception of what life is. You attempt to impress upon them that life is not that bad and your love is better than their despair. The object of this book is to help you find yourself and get your children back, even before they run away. Millions of parents battle with this issue every day. The growing gang numbers prove this.

Many of the events in religious scriptures are made up of happenings that the author naturally, at that time, mistakenly took to be heaven-sent. The forces of nature batter and overpower us every day, somewhere in the world. Did a god send the Tsunami on Christmas 2004 killing almost 230,000 people? I think not. We know what caused it. Did God cause Mount St. Helen to blow its top off? No, we knew what happened there. Did God cause Pompeii to be destroyed and thousands to perish? No. But to an untrained mind in 79 AD, it would be seen as "an act of God," as Pompeii did have a vibrant sexual culture, much like Sodom and Gomorrah, and many other places of that time. Even the insurance companies use that phrase "act of God" to avoid paying you.

We cannot live in the past, nor can we let the ideas, ideals and misunderstandings of the past prevent us from living in the present or rocketing toward the future. It was impossible for the whole Earth to have been "miraculously" flooded by God in the days of Noah, but it is an amusing story. Other countries were there at the time, functioning with their native populations. You can see that the events were made to fit the storyteller's imagination. Did Noah even exist? The writer would have had enthusiastic ambitions of impressing a highly delirious, ignorant and unimaginative following, who were equally amazed as he was by the idea that such a magical god could actually exist, as they looked forward to the magical God leading them out of their desperate circumstances.

Question: After Noah, who repopulated the Earth and how? Was it more inbreeding, as with Adam and Eve?

History shows us that desperate times call for desperate measures. Desperate measures call for desperate ideas. Desperate ideas call for desperate thinkers. Desperate thinkers call for desperate believers. Desperate believers call for desperate leaders. Desperate leaders call for desperate circumstances. Desperate circumstances call for desperate measures: cyclic. That's the cycle that started religion and continues to fuel religious dogma today.

I grew up reading books from various cultures and religions. My grandmother converted to Catholicism for her last 50 years (she died at 91). My uncle and cousins are Presbyterians. My father was Anglican and my mother is Hindu. My father's cousin was Muslim and so are some of mine. I went to an Anglican school and I sang in the church choir for years, and did all the rituals. I consider myself religiously eclectic. I grew up in a small society where there were multiple cultures living and loving together, sort of like New York where I live now.

There was healthy competition between various races and cultures in this small society. All of the while being taught by life itself to learn from each other, to be tolerant of each other and our differences, and embracing these differences to ultimately become a more patient and balanced community. This made me a better person, husband, son, father, friend, employer, teacher and now, successful author. I think we can do the same here in America and globally, and not let the churches and politicians divide us.

JESUS REVEALED

Religion, without rules and rulers, is more to the point of what is needed to carry mankind forward, but there are people who can't let go or give up their religions, or their fears of the religious leaders and the power they wield. For these people, religion with rules is a start on the road to enlightenment. Then comes religion without rules. Then no religion.

As we learn new things, our thinking must and will change to reflect this. This being true, how will Jesus return to us? If Jesus has to return, does He have to come in the flesh? Can't He come in the teaching presented to you in the Gospel of Thomas? With this gospel, is He not with you in your mind? Doesn't that mean He is there with you; He has returned spiritually and mentally? I think yes. We don't need Him to hold our hand, but just to point our minds in the right direction, as the body is physical and temporary. The Antichrist may be your absence of good deeds and enlightenment, and your belief of the existence of evil. The Christ may be the opposite.

Gnostic Christians were the closest, strongest and only believers of Jesus Christ and his teachings back then, and through his teachings to them, they held the conviction that enlightenment, consciousness and spiritual existence can be accessed and attained by human beings, and the attainment and practice of such knowledge is the highest achievement of mankind while on Earth. This is what Jesus taught to them by His own example, and what He instructed them to do and teach, which they did.

Eventually between the 3rd and 5th century after His death, they were cast aside as heretics and non-orthodox Christians by the Orthodox Church, as they, the Gnostics, were the only ones who ever truly believed in Christ's teachings of becoming enlightened by His example to them. He taught them that all people, women and men, were equal to each other and to Him, and each can and should become enlightened. The church, which capitalized on the ignorance of the masses, chose not to support this teaching and instead taught that Jesus must be followed, through the church's rules and word: the word which was eventually developed and written and rewritten, to be known as the Bible. They also did not support Jesus' teaching that women were equal to men.

It is sad that the church hijacked the very movement of enlightenment that the Gnostics themselves along with their leader Christ built, and stole it and used it to this day, for their own enrichment and the misdirection of the masses under the false banner of Christianity. Christ did not intend nor did He start the Christian religion, as He spoke against the religion of the time, and instead taught enlightenment and consciousness. His teachings were His act of rebellion against religion.

The church with the help of the Gnostic Christians worked on carrying the movement forward after Christ's death. The Gnostics were tricked into thinking the church held the same views as Jesus did. Within three centuries the church took over, overthrew the Gnostics, branded them as heretics, then reclaimed and reinvented the religion we now follow. By the 5th century the Gnostics, as heretics, had to run for their lives as they were hunted down and slaughtered.

Some of the rituals and dogma you encounter in the Christian church were introduced by the Gnostics during the 1st and 2nd century AD, and these were given to them by Jesus, including baptism, anointing with oil and many other rituals. You may ask, if Christ was against rituals and knew they were unnecessary to become enlightened, why did He give the rituals to the Gnostics? Simple answer is, you give your children menial tasks to do all the time. This is to help them take a journey and learn something, which in turn will help them to see and appreciate your point of view or truth as it is then.

Didn't you let your kids put their finger near a flame to feel fire and heat? You are not teaching them to barbecue themselves but to learn just the opposite. So, too, Jesus wanted them to train themselves to control their thoughts and deeds, as they had no control and it is recorded they liked a lot of sex and drink, as did everyone without a TV back then. They were all distracted and carefree like children, and this was the best way to slow them down, and get them to concentrate and pursue enlightenment through personal self control. When you have to venture inward to conquer fear and instability, you must become mentally ready, calm and steady.

Similarly, runners use concentrating and stretching exercises before a marathon to physically and mentally prepare. These exercises become their ritual. Rituals are exactly like trinkets. They are simply used for a purpose. In this case to hold your concentration, put you in the mood, and calm your fidgeting mind. Like trinkets, rituals hold no greater importance. The use of rules and rituals is a practice that all religions have used to keep their flock attentive. Rituals simply keep the mind steady and focused, and are not a requirement by God.

<u>Excerpts Taken from the Gospel of Thomas</u>

1 And he said, "Whoever **discovers** the interpretation of these sayings **will not taste death** (never die)."

3 Jesus said, "If those who lead you say to you, 'See, the kingdom is in the sky,' then the birds of the sky will precede you. If they say to you, 'It is in the sea,' then the fish will precede you. Rather, **the kingdom is inside of you,** and it is outside of you. When you come to know yourselves, then you will become known, and you will realize that **it is you who are the sons** of the living father. But if you will not know yourselves, you dwell in poverty and **it is you who are that poverty.**"

6 His disciples asked him and said to him, "Do you want us to fast? How should we pray? Should we give to charity? What diet should we observe?"

Jesus said, "**Don't lie, and don't do what you hate**, because all things are disclosed before heaven. After all, there is nothing hidden that won't be revealed, and there is nothing covered up that will remain undisclosed.

[Author's Note: Because saying 14 answers the questions asked in saying 6, I have included it right after for continuity.]

14 Jesus said to them, "If you fast, you will bring sin upon yourselves, and if you pray, you will be condemned, and if you give to charity, you will harm your spirits. When you go into any region and walk about in the

countryside, when people take you in, **eat what they serve you and heal the sick among them**. After all, what goes into your mouth won't defile you; what comes out of your mouth will."

[Author's Note: fasting, praying, and observing rules of religious charity are ways of you becoming a follower of religion and its leaders, be they corrupt or not. Jesus tells them that practicing religion is not the way to become enlightened, and thereby qualify to enter "heaven." He also tells them that refusing, and not eating specific foods like pork and shell fish such as shrimp, lobster and the like, is wrong and they should eat whatever they are served, as that is only following religious rules, which have no place in consciousness and his form of truth. When He says, "If you pray you will be condemned," He means that you first have to wrongfully think and accept that you are sinful, cursed and condemned, before you think you need to pray.]

10 Jesus said, "I have cast fire upon the world, and look, I'm guarding it until **it blazes**."

13 Jesus said to his disciples, "Compare me to something and tell me what I am like." Simon Peter said to him, "You are like a just angel."

Matthew said to him, "You are like a wise philosopher."

Thomas said to him, "Teacher, my mouth is utterly unable to say what you are like."

Jesus said, "I am not your teacher. Because you have drunk, you have become intoxicated from the bubbling spring that I have tended."

And he took him, and withdrew, and spoke three sayings to him.

When Thomas came back to his friends, they asked him, "What did Jesus say to you?"

Thomas said to them, "If I tell you one of the sayings he spoke to me, you will pick up rocks and stone me, and fire will come from the rocks and devour you."

[Author's Note: Thomas is saying that if he tells them, they will curse and chastise him (stone him),and will then be burnt (themselves being chastised) by the result of their actions.]

25 Jesus said, "Love your friends (brothers) like your own soul, protect them like the pupil of your eye."

26 Jesus said, "You see the sliver (splinter) in your friend's (brother's) eye, but you don't see the timber (log) in your own eye. When you take the timber (log) out of your own eye, then you will see well enough to remove the sliver (splinter) from your friend's (brother's) eye.

28 Jesus said, "I took my stand in the midst of the world, and in flesh I appeared to them. I found them all drunk, and I did not find any of them thirsty. My soul ached for the children of humanity, because they are blind in their hearts and do not see, **for they came into the world empty, and they also seek to depart from the world empty.** But meanwhile they are drunk. When they shake off their wine, then they will **change their ways.**"

[Author's Note: drunk meaning happy and content in the ways of religion and its bondage, and not thirsty or thirsting for the truth; unwilling to learn the truth and be free. But when they (you) shake off your drunkenness, you will learn the truth about the second part of your journey, which is consciousness through enlightenment. Religious bondage is just the first part of that journey.]

39 Jesus said, "The Pharisees and the scholars have taken the keys of **knowledge** and have hidden them. They have not entered, nor have they allowed those who want to enter to do so. As for you, be as sly as snakes and as simple as doves."

[Author's Note: you can be sly as the snake and learn from them that mislead you, by understanding that the opposite of what they teach you is actually the truth. They do not want to teach you the truth, so simply learn the lies. They teach you to be a follower and slave of religion, and Jesus is teaching you that the opposite, the freedom of enlightenment, is the truth. Being peaceful, like the dove, is the way to live, not following religions and the religions' way, which is war.]

43 His disciples said to him, "Who are you to say these things to us?" (Jesus replies to them) "You don't understand who I am from what I say to you. Rather, you have become like the Judeans, for **they love the tree but hate its fruit, or they love the fruit but hate the tree.**"

[Author's Note: they love Jesus but hate his message of peace.]

61 Jesus said, "Two will recline on a couch; one will die, **one will live.**"

[Author's Note: He means you have a body and a spirit. Your body will die of old age, so strengthen the spirit with enlightenment, as it will live on, to a new existence.]

75 Jesus said, "There are **many standing at the door**, but those who are alone will enter the bridal suite."

[Author's Note: everyone wants to enter the consciousness, the kingdom of heaven, of their god, but to do so you have to leave the company of the crowd, and seek and realize the truth for yourself. Everyone follows the religion, so they will all end up in the same place; outside the kingdom, outside of consciousness, outside the door.]

77 Jesus said, "I am the light that is over all things. I am all: from me all came forth, and to me all attained. **Split a piece of wood; I am there. Lift up the stone, and you will find me there.**"

[Author's Note: Jesus and His realm, which is the consciousness, is everything in this universe, so you do not need a religion or a church to sit in and to worship, or to find truth. Sit by yourself and meditate within, and you will join Him. It's that easy.]

78 Jesus said, "Why have you come out to the countryside? To see a reed shaken by the wind? And to see a person dressed in soft clothes, [like your] rulers and your powerful ones? They are **dressed in soft clothes, and they cannot understand truth.**"

87 Jesus said, "How miserable is the body that depends on a body, and how miserable is the **soul** that depends on these two."

89 Jesus said, "Why do you wash the outside of the cup? Don't you understand that the one who made the **inside** is also the one who made the outside?"

[Author's Note: why do you bathe and dress the outside of your body, and leave the inside spirit, empty and dirty by not making it clean with good acts, and making it shine with the light of enlightenment?]

92 Jesus said, "**Seek and you will find**. In the past, however, I did not tell you the things about which you asked me then. **Now I am willing to tell them**, but you are **not seeking** them."

[Author's Note: in the past Jesus could not tell the truth of enlightenment to an ignorant audience, as they would not have understood. Now it is time to show you the truth but you have to seek it.]

108 Jesus said, "Whoever drinks from my mouth **will become like me**; I myself shall become that person, and the **hidden things will be revealed** to him."

[Author's Note: Jesus' words are the drink that you will consume, after which you will be influenced as he was. You will become enlightened, and know all things.]

112 Jesus said, "Damn the flesh that depends on the soul. **Damn the soul that depends on the flesh.**"

[Author's Note: it is a variation of saying 87. The soul that waits to be enlightened by the body is damned. The body that waits for the soul is also damned because the body is not important or immortal, so it is not sustained by the soul. Use your body, this life, to feed enlightenment to your soul, so when the body dies, your soul will live.]

Was Jesus smart enough to know that religion would fail in the 20th century? Would He have been smart enough to plan a Part 2 of his movement, to the detriment of the Bible and the religion: a continuation of knowledge to be added? I think He was. He may have seen this happen a thousand times before, and knew what was to come. Others tried to enlighten us before. Now I think the Gospel of Thomas can help us to find our way, and I will not question why a complete version of it was found in 1945, as other incomplete parts were discovered years before.

The Gospel of Thomas was discovered among the Dead Sea Scrolls in caves near the Dead Sea, Egypt.

Thomas is widely referred to, and considered in many circles, as the twin brother of Jesus. In the Nag Hammadi library, Jesus is identified as Thomas's other twin. The name Thomas (Aramaic Tau'ma) comes from the Aramaic word for twin — T'oma.

Thomas was sent, possibly by Jesus to India to teach, which is fitting, as India was where Jesus is thought to have special ties and where He learned many things about becoming enlightened. The other disciples went elsewhere to preach. They were present in Jerusalem to witness the death of Mary but Thomas was left to do his work in India. After her death, Thomas was the only one who was allowed and was present in her tomb to witness her assumption.

He is thought to have been the closest person to Jesus, and perhaps this is proven as he was the only witness enlightened enough to see the assumption of "The Virgin Mary," when, it is said, she left with body and spirit intact. This shows the capabilities of the spiritual force at work in the universe, taking her up in a beam or sphere of light, and not some form of ill-conceived magic and miracle. He is said to have been given a girdle by her during the assumption, all of which took place in her closed tomb, to prove the event happened.

That is, if it happened at all, because as many will admit, not all the events in the religious doctrines really occurred. Some were arguably just embellishments by writers to make the religions look good. If some think the events in the religious books did happen, then they are forced by that same reasoning of blind faith to believe the Gospel of Thomas is in fact correct. Likewise, they will not be able to deny its purpose to bring the old books and religions to an end with its information, and begin a new chapter to faith and belief, one with the central understanding that Jesus' teaching meant the pursuit of spiritual enlightenment, not religious slavery.

The Gospel of Thomas, verse 92, says it all. That is the verse we first have to address. In it Jesus says that He did not tell the world the whole truth and that, I think, is obviously because those people were not willing or capable of understanding what enlightenment was. He said that He was now willing to reveal the truth; it could be thought that the knowledge has now been purposely revealed, in 1945, as what was lost and hidden has been found...in the Dead Sea scrolls. The year 1945 is important because that was the year when we used the Atom bomb to annihilate more than 100,000 people in Hiroshima and Nagasaki.

I leave it up to the individual to make any connection between these two events in 1945. It is now time for you to seek the knowledge, because no matter how smart you are, when you close your eyes to the truth or even a lie, you are still blinded, as your eyes are closed. You must seek the truth and the lies, so you may know them and will be able to choose your path, and that of your family.

In another verse, Jesus said that He guarded the fire until it began to blaze. Is it possible that this is what He has done with the knowledge of truth and enlightenment? Is it possible that He meant for this fire of truth to become a blaze at this time? The fire He speaks of is the knowledge contained in verse 77, a verse that I think changes everything we were taught about religion and the church's role in it.

The Gospel of Thomas, verse 77, says briefly: Jesus said, "I am the light, split a piece of wood I am there, look under a stone, you will find me there." This simply means that you do not need the church, the ancient Pharisees and the scholars to find Jesus, who is a drop, in the universal sea of consciousness. This is the fire of knowledge that He is revealing. From this teaching stems everything that we should know about religion, moving past the teachings of the Old and New Testaments, and all other ancient teachings, and possibly bringing about a new era of enlightenment and consciousness, a continuation of the universal plan, a Part 2 of religion.

Jesus was saying that we can find the truth anywhere and do not need a church to become enlightened like Him. You are not tied to the dogmas, rituals or religion itself. He is revealing that we exist inside the living and constantly evolving creation, which we were mistakenly taught to thirst for and seek, through religion. We were part of it all along. That which you were taught is the creation (which is the universe in all its dimensions: physical and non-physical) changes all the time and we simply change with it in various ways. Energy is neither created nor destroyed, but only changes form.

Even death is just a way of changing, as you simply move on to a different reality. Death is just travel: a conversion to a new self in a new and different reality, with the same you, the same spirit, and the same soul. So now we have to change our understanding of what religion really is and what Jesus' lesson of truth and enlightenment is.

In verse 108, He tells us that when you drink of the truth from His mouth and ingest the truth that He speaks, then like Him, you will become enlightened and essentially you will be no different from Him, as we are truly His brethren or petals of the same flower of consciousness — not His followers. Flowers not followers.

Noted people of our time, Tolstoy, Gandhi, Lennon, Jung and many others, recognized this teaching through their own inspiration of peaceful existence (verse 25: protecting the pupil of your eye), through peace as opposed to war and greed. I now try to bring it to you for your enlightenment. It is thought by many scholars that Jesus optimistically taught that we should and could try to repair the Earth as He did, rather than the later writers of the Bible mistakenly teaching us to have an End of Days, or Apocalyptic, point of view. That apocalyptic view was invented by the church centuries after Jesus, to force you to become desperate, and believe in them and their religion to save you from destruction, instead of believing in the good that you can do to change things.

People rush to say they love and follow Jesus, but they still shun His words, His fruit, as verse 43 says. He is the tree that they love but they hate the fruit He brings forth — of an existence without the church and dogma, and without prejudices, hatred and bloodshed.

In verse 39, He shines light on the church, saying they have hidden the truth and their dogma prevents us from entering the door of consciousness, by their cyclic, ritualistic worship. He has brought to light the Pharisees and scholars. Who were they? Weren't they the church — the elites of the society, together with the rulers and politicians, and those who had authority, also those priests who tended the church — that wielded the power of control and enslavement over the masses? Did they not kill Jesus and then His followers after Him?

Verse 78 says that your leaders cannot understand truth. This sadly is what the church and state, the Pharisees and scholars, are guilty of. Jesus met them. They colluded against Him and killed Him. They then wrote the Bible that you and I worshipped with until now. When it was time, the Old Testament was replaced by the New Testament. It is now time to replace the old books again, as verse 92 says — with new information, which He did not want to enlighten you about until now.

Many say the Bible is not to be added to. I agree. This new truth of enlightenment is not a continuation of the old invented religions, and should be a new beginning and a new culture. A culture that does not come from fear and dependence upon the church for some kind of salvation, as this is all false and made up. **Selah.**

That new information is one verse and that is verse 77. That verse marks the new beginning, with a new future to the stars, which has been hidden from you all this time. I can offer one more explanation to the direction we must go in. There are levels of spiritual awareness and enlightenment after you die, but on Earth we are living in level one. In level one we have so far encountered three stages. Stage one was the era of the Old Testament, stage two was the era of the New Testament and stage three is the era of spiritual enlightenment.

To compare them is easy using math for an example, with 100 being the highest achievement of understanding in level one, here on Earth, to become enlightened as Jesus did. Stages one and two use religion and dogma, and that can be thought of as the use of addition, with reward after you die. With the Old Testament, stage one, they would add 1+1+1+1=4, and getting to 100 was a long process with many rituals and hoops. The New Testament, stage two, then taught 2+2+2+2=8. It uses the same principles of addition, but with a simple twist that doubles the progress and shortens the time to reach the goal, which is better than the old way because you may get to 100 a lot faster than the Old Testament. Stage three, spiritual enlightenment, is multiplication, 1x100=100. You use this method to get enlightened as quickly as Jesus did, right here, right now, before physically dying, because the kingdom of "heaven" is here. With the speedy intelligence and impatience of modern man, this simple truth fits quite well.

With all three methods, you reach 100, so all the methods can be used if the dangerous use of rituals and dogma in stages one and two are not followed. They even used sacrifices back then and Christianization was a bloody affair. Stage three is more efficient. I have relied heavily on Jesus and His teachings to bring this message of enlightenment to you, but I would like to remind you that He and His teachings are not the only medium by which the truth has been revealed. It is just the most convenient and acceptable medium for me to use, as history, however skewed, has made Him the most powerful proof of the truth about enlightenment in the last 2,000 years. If Jesus had never walked this Earth, the consciousness would still remain unchanged. The truth would still exist and I may simply have used another medium.

GOVERNMENT MEGALOMANIACS /MORE SHOCK & AWE

The well-being of the family is threatened by corporate interests and their uninhibited, uncompromising and uncontrollable greed. Although the company's job is to make profits, the sad thing is that the Bush government helped them profit at the expense of the citizens. Everyone wants the companies to profit and progress, as we also benefit from this through jobs and investments. When the public is left holding the bag of high prices unnecessarily, then the question turns to one of domestic terrorism on the population, by the willful and intentional use of policies that cause high prices and recessions that have real and lasting consequences for the victims.

I stress that I have no problem with the whole world making profits, but when it is done in a way that leaves the American citizenry broke and on the financial precipice, unable to afford to feed their families, or have proper health care, the tale sours. Bush said, in 50 years, he will be hailed as a hero. I think in 10 years he will be seen as just the opposite: a sellout to corporations and foreign countries, almost causing the collapse of America. At some time in the future, that may even be considered treason.

The country and the world cannot survive another president like Bush. His policies and methods did not make us safer, but only increased the number of new terrorists around the world who hate us, and are planning a thousand times more attacks than they were before Iraq. We may be overwhelmed just by the sheer numbers of attacks.

The rest of the world also has a right to live in peace. They do the same things in other places as we do in America; they play music and games. They have colorful cultures and wonderful families. They are not primitive, and if countries start invading each other willy-nilly, as we did, well, this world simply will not survive. We have already given them our approval by doing it ourselves. Russia followed in 2008. Who's next?

Our leaders teach us with their actions that money is more important than country. Remember the Keating Five, and the savings and loan scandal? We are seeing it happen again. There are troops fighting in Iraq whose homes were being foreclosed on, in America, under Bush's term. The Bush government ignored the predatory lenders who were allowed to trick us and steal from us. They ignored the credit card companies that dishonestly take every penny of our hard-earned money and leave you penniless, by raising their interest rates with no provocation. They removed as much regulation of these companies as they wished, and the problems and debts created will be inherited by our children and grandchildren.

The privatization of the military, in most areas of operations and development, is a great concern as it is a great risk for our top secrets, which are so important to national security, and which are able to be accessed by these companies. Large companies have no patriotism — they are multinational. They will sell our secrets. One of our large airplane and defense companies is already moving some operations to China. What secrets will they trade for contracts?

The U.S. dollar has lost its creditability; pretty soon the world could start using another currency or a combination of currencies, and drop the U.S. dollar as its main currency of trade and investment. The economic policies of the Bush administration had disastrous effects on the dollar, to the extent that some places and businesses around the world have already stopped accepting it.

The trickle down tax cuts for the rich, voodoo economics, were not working. They were not helping the middle class, who are the backbone of the country, as they were just used as a trick to fleece the taxpayers. The middle class is the group of people who exercise their power in voting and protesting policies. They are slowly being extinguished. If this is left unchecked, the middle class will disappear, and the corporations and their owners will have more control over the poorest in the country, further stifling them in their attempt to survive rising costs of living, and preserving good health for themselves and their families.

It is better for the population if government controls or keeps discipline in the marketplace and our economy, in limited ways to keep order instead of having greedy market forces run wild. Controlled, disciplined capitalism within the free market is the steering wheel needed for our country to drive forward in the global marketplace. Our economic vehicle is not swift and agile like a small car, but rather it is like the good ship Titanic — it's large, and takes a while to turn or stop, and it can sink.

Uncontrolled and undisciplined free markets cannot drive by themselves unfettered because of greed, and it takes too long to turn the economy around when something is going wrong. Consequently, the recessionary ripple around the world shows that all economies have to be controlled or one causes the other to crash, because our economies are not traveling in the same direction at the same time; instead, we are constantly maneuvering around each other like bumper cars in a ring.

Our economic crash has caused other countries to also crash. We see them now scrambling to save their economies, as we scramble to do the same. A steering wheel is important after all — disciplined capitalism. I think it has been proven that capitalism can work, but it has to be disciplined and guided like a prized racehorse.

Since the 1980s, amid all the problems America had at that time, the world still had the highest respect for Americans. This translated ultimately into security and safety all over the world for Americans traveling abroad, and assistance and goodwill for American companies, in ways that money couldn't buy. Goodwill was given freely to Americans, just because of the love we had for others and the popularity we garnered in return. After the Bush years, Americans are now frowned upon and it is unsafe to even travel outside the country.

In our haste to keep our country safe, by having strict enforcement of the entry points, we have also placed an invisible prison around ourselves. We need the help of other countries, as we are not self sufficient, so they should be brought on board to enforce their own smuggling laws, and make it safe to trade and travel from their own countries to ours, as smuggling a "dirty bomb" or the like into America at our ports is a great concern.

They can step up their security but there are other things we and they need to consider. While increasing security for travelers at airports around the world, we have had a large decline in professionals, investors, companies and other talent coming to America. One large reason, experts say, is the difficulties faced by these people in acquiring documentation to travel to America.

In some places they are required to have an interview first, which could take as much as two or three months. Some companies cannot wait that long to send their people here to conduct business, so they do business with other countries instead. That represents a large loss of business for us, amounting to billions annually. This necessary interview process must be timely.

Other professionals and investors similarly prefer not to go through the insurmountable hassles to get visas, and they also end up working in other countries. Students who are the best and brightest have always had a role to play in the development of this country, and are opting to go to countries where they are welcomed more enthusiastically. There are so many beautiful and less costly places in Europe, China, India, Japan and elsewhere to study. I think it was an uphill battle to get them to come to the U.S. in the first place. Now that battle is all but lost.

This narrows our gene pool of academic variety, which is a must in developed countries. If all the students come from the same place — here — they will all think the same way, inside the box, and we will drop the ball of being the most innovative country as we have been in the past with their input. You need different people from different backgrounds and understanding to have different ideas; most of our students will just have the same understanding and not as much variety of new ideas.

Can we endanger ourselves by letting foreign interests

invest too heavily in our economy? Yes, it is possible, if not controlled. International trade is the only way to survive in this world today, and it is a large part of our income. We must have foreign trade just so we can keep up with the competition. Throughout Bush's presidency, some policies made it harder for foreign trade to flourish, as people could not come here to represent their foreign companies in meetings and negotiations. Also, they could not attend trade shows in the U.S. in a timely manner. As a result they couldn't meet our U.S. manufacturers to buy from, or set up, contacts with them.

By the time they got visas to come here, the trade show opportunities were gone. Trade shows move around the world and you have to be able to travel at a moment's notice or at least a few weeks' notice. When the smaller foreign companies cannot get visas for their employees in time, they will wait until the trade shows reach their part of the world, but the American manufacturers will not all be there; some are small American businesses and manufacturers, who can only afford to attend the American legs of the shows. We are missing out on key foreign investments in a big way.

It has often been said and seen in the past that defeat comes from within rather than without. That means you can be defeated more quickly from inside your camp, by a traitor or bad planning, than by your outside opponent. We saw this in the Bush years. They forgot that they were elected by us to be leaders, and to protect their constituents and the country, not just to follow their financial contributor's orders. They partially destroyed America from within, and while there, they lost sight of the greatness they were supposed to bring to the offices they held. They became the unpatriotic ones who were bringing about the untimely demise of America.

The Bush team just threw it away. They threw away the *trust* we had in them. They threw away the respect we and the world had for them, and the good things they could have accomplished for the people they were supposed to protect. They threw away all those opportunities. They let us and their party down in the process... Humanity suffers by their hand.

Apparently, no one remembered that what you get in life is simply opportunities to do good things. Sadly, they wasted these opportunities. They did not realize that people all around this little world counted on them to do a good job because doing a bad job weakens America, and by extension weakens the world, and squanders the goodwill that America has created, through the causes it has championed in the past. Defeat from within.

I know when these politicians started their careers years ago, it was not with the intention to cause harm to America, while they enriched themselves. I don't think they had bad intentions. I think that over time, they allowed themselves to become greedy. I have to tell these people, it is never too late to change and make a difference, to start to make things better for the country. Your children will benefit in the end. So go ahead, I humbly implore you to spread goodwill...Please. Cooperate with your adversaries and step away from hate.

Sometimes, what is lost cannot be recovered. Goodwill is weakened and limping badly. Everyone knows that when your opponent is limping you have an advantage. So now we can expect to see other countries rise higher, and acquire stature and control on the world stage. They do this by feeding off the weakness of America's economy and they fill the vacuum we left, as we exited the control room while Bush played hooky.

I don't think they will play the game as nicely as America did and everyone will fall victim to them, including the wealthy. Remember, this is a big game that results in the rise and fall of countries, so who can we expect to lead the world now? China, Russia and India come to mind, although China has the upper hand. That could change at a moment's notice within this economic turbulence.

Americans are complaining about having Spanish radio and TV stations. Well, guess what? While your conservative politicians have been distracting you with petty grievances, they've been losing the world race on economics. They've dropped the ball! I'm not saying that all is lost, but look around; it's quite bleak.

People are being poisoned by mass-produced, chemical-filled food. Others are too vain and uncaring to take care of the needy, or each other. This must not continue. We need to get involved at the local level, in the politics of the state where we live and effect beneficial change. If you don't guide the donkey and the elephant, they will take you to a place you don't want to be. Are you in Shock and Awe? Are you sick of this mess?

HATE

People are ruled by fear and hate. What if Hitler had decided to use a different symbol like a smiley face, a lightning rod or a heart? Would we hate those symbols or pictures instead? People give symbolism too much power, to serve their own purpose. That's not strange or wrong, but it does sometimes create an atmosphere of division in society, if the perpetrator chooses to use it for that purpose.

The noose is sometimes used as a symbol of hate, to create fear and shock to the victim or a specific group: reminding them of what the noose was used for in the past, and obviously a threat of what could be done to them in the future.

Don't give the people who use these symbols and theatrics any power to control you, by giving the slightest importance to symbolism. When people ignore symbolism long enough, the impact is lessened, over and over until it loses its significance. If the perpetrators think people will not be intimidated by the noose, or any other symbol, then over time it will have no impact on the community and will not be effective. Look with pity upon the people who use it for hate, for it just means they are small-minded, spiteful fools. If we make it a problem, only then does it become one to us.

The swastika has been used by many different tribes of people throughout time. For more than 4,000 years now, the Hindus and other people around the world have used this symbol as an important part of their religion and in their daily lives. When Hitler decided to use this symbol, he knew he was using something that was recognized as possibly the oldest religious symbol still used in modern times. Why did he? He could have thought he needed the power that the symbol evokes — showing his cause to be a religious or noble one.

He may have thought he was fulfilling a requirement of his own religion — to bring about the demise of any other religion or religious influence that conflicted with his own teachings of Christianity being the only true religion. I feel sure that he knew it is actually an earlier version of the cross, much like the later Christian cross, and used for religious worship as well. The Hindu people, who have used this cross for thousands of years, have understood the many possible reasons why he used it.

They ignore the use of it as a hate symbol and still use it as a traditional, ancient religious symbol of God and for religious purposes around the world. They don't feel angry or make the issue important, therefore to them it isn't. They know he was a fool and to give him or his tactics any credence, credibility or importance does a disservice to the whole world, so they rise above the issue. Hate is not a harbor they choose to dock in.

Some people follow the mob and believe something is bad not because they themselves think so, but because other people do, even though neither of them wants to find out what the real story or importance of the thing they choose to hate is. They are sometimes too weak to oppose their peers or too spiteful to learn the truth about it. This is one reason why racism is so rampant in America. Some dislike colored people just because the mob says to. It is the same thing with politics. It is amazing how two groups who say they love America cannot live harmoniously and save the country from greed and fanatical religious destruction.

People who commit hate crimes are really defective and should not be charged with a crime, but be committed to the asylum for some time for observation, healing and community service. These people are sick with pain, guilt and hate, and they are usually unstable and prone to suicide, murder, rape, or any other act that fills that need to do something hateful or revengeful. They are full of anger, usually for not being loved as they should have been when they were young. Some were abused and this caused them to change and become what we now see, namely a hate-filled, confused person.

Hate is a bastard child that lives, grows and spreads despair. It always brings unintended results farther down the road. One sad example of this is a hate crime of murder, which happened in Long Island, New York on November 8, 2008. The Suffolk County Executive Steve Levy had long since promoted and supported intolerance to Hispanics in his area of Long Island, in 2007 asking police, and immigration and custom enforcement officers — ICE — to raid homes where illegal immigrants were *believed* to be living.

As it always does, his child creation of hate grew too big for even him to control. One of the many racist mobs that were created, which fed on and shared his contempt for Hispanics, decided to go trolling for a Mexican to mess up on a Saturday night. Instead of a Mexican, they found an Ecuadorian, Marcelo Lucero, and killed him. This event caused Levy to hang his head in shame and guilt, and completely pivot from his former stance.

He now calls for a stop to this senseless and destructive hatred. Sadly, this is just one of many hate crimes against Hispanics on Long Island and around the U.S. Will it stop? Some Hispanics may want revenge, but whether they rise above this senseless hatred and racism remains to be seen. I pray to the gods that they do, as I know they are a loving people and their kindness is not a weakness. Their history proves this.

In some cultures, hitting a person with one's shoe is one of the vilest, vehement curses of disgust that one person gives to another. When a president of a country has shoes thrown at him, as was done to then President Bush in Iraq, it shows the level of disgust that some in the world had for him and his policies of unwarranted war. This is the shame and hatred that America is now faced with after Bush has left office.

He unnecessarily destroyed a whole country, Iraq, and in the process he created more terrorists around the world than anyone could have ever imagined. He takes his place among the world's few who have also inspired such hate, and brought such agony to others on a massive scale. History will record his deeds for all to see, as has been done with the few others in the past who have also caused hundreds of thousands of lives to be lost, by their own hand. Hatred is their legacy. Hatred is man's worst enemy and one that we must strive to quell, with compassion, love and truth.

IMMIGRATION

We have an immigration problem in America, which has been allowed to grow by the same people who now want to wave a magic wand, and make the immigrants disappear or worse. They are in the group that also includes politicians, and conservative TV and talk show hosts, who spit their venom over the public airwaves, contaminating their audiences with their poisonous hatred, causing this unhealthy feeling to fester and multiply. They are best friends with certain politicians who are easily swayed and who want the same thing.

We are constantly reminded that our country is a child of the European apartheid system and the slave trade, and a lot of people are still of that hateful mindset. Luckily, the past slave owners are calling their friends from beyond the grave, so their numbers are dwindling. They ignore the fact that immigrants, in this country, and around the world, are just trying to build a family, and not all of them want to commit crimes. They are abused in so many ways, in order to provide for their families.

Could this group of prejudiced people be secretly supporting racism against the immigrants? Their actions show this, for all to see. We see stories in the news of immigrants having their passports taken, and they are locked in the basement or garage, and not allowed the freedoms of a human being, and worse. They are held captive for years to serve the families they are "owned" by.

The apartheid type system, which we had in the early

days of America's creation, has taught some that to be lords over the immigrants is natural and correct. These good, but mistaken and misguided folks, in private circles, think the immigrants should have no chance to grow in personal pride, privilege and out of poverty in this country — but only in their own.

Just a different form of slavery or technical, not literal, death is all that is offered to these wonderful, downtrodden peoples, from various countries, consisting of white, black, brown and Asian people. Technical death by deporting them is a death sentence because it means the life they have built in this country will be wiped away. They will be sent back to whatever impoverished nation they fled or came from, even if it means death for various medical or financial reasons, when they or their families arrive there. Some are robbed and killed because it is thought that when you come from America, you have money: at least more than the robbers do anyway.

This is just so that the misguided folks can feel powerful in their actions of being able to bully people, deport them, and destroy their lives and anything else that was built. This makes them feel good and superior in a twisted way, over all immigrants. Some of these countries have been torn apart for so many different reasons, including our own slash-and-grab foreign policies, that we are the reason they fled the impoverished nation in the first place.

We, as a human race, should care more about these victims we create, those who in this country we scornfully call illegal immigrants and aliens. You will find that some of the graduating class of "students," from the college of apartheid, do not want legal or illegal immigrants to have a peaceful place in America. Sadly, these "students of ill will" have so far failed in the school of life, failing in subjects like peace, love, compassion and hope. These immigrants are not from another planet as some "students" think. They are humans and that is not yet a crime. I sometimes think the "students" want to take the country back to the days of the American version of apartheid and slavery.

The sad and wretched fact is that many of these "students of hate" claim to be good Christians, serving a God brimming with love, and an outpouring of humanitarian forgiveness and hope for all. That is where they expose themselves to show they are the misguided of this society. Their actions are what give them away. They go to church with their spouses and children, and they pretend to pray in front of their children, their church and the world, while they take advantage of their fellow human, to make a dollar.

They are the most hypocritical people you will ever see, because they are lying in front of their supposedly sacred God, and to their family, while in their most sacred place: their church. Can you find a better example of their mistaken ideology and contempt in their souls than this? Show me where else you see so much deception and hypocrisy blatantly displayed for all to see. They are the descendants of the ancient English *immigrant* worshippers of Christ who settled in America, and they are trying to deport the Hispanic and other *immigrant* worshipers of the same Christ.

Is that Christian love? Christians who are deporting Christians? Listen to them on the radio and TV, and in political engagements, encouraging the authorities to deport Christ's worshipers, their brethren, while they have the front seat in church. Jesus would be so ashamed of them, if He were here right now, but their families are here and their families are ashamed of them too. Their kids hear about their famous parents from friends at school. Their kids also see them and their hater friends on the news, and they see the truth.

These people are truly devious. Although they may act as if they don't hate immigrants, their actions show that they definitely don't like them. They pray and lie deceptively like a "snake in the grass" in a church — a place where they are supposed to be their best: humane, truthful, loving and kind. They hide like serpents beneath the cover of the church...their rock. When their kids find out, they will throw a fit for their parents and in the argument, the apartheid group always resorts to the guilt trip of telling their kids, "I did it all for you." Well kids, take my advice. Leave that blood on their hands. Do not accept this lame excuse because you know that's not true. If you willingly agree, you will be supporting their acts of savagery and you will now take that blood on your hands as well. You will become what you hate most...a racist like your parents.

These poor immigrants are the real deal; they are true Americans like the rest of us and our ancestors who were all immigrants. They answered the call to come to this country and do the menial work they were offered, tricked and even wooed to do: work that the unionized workers did not want to do, as they had higher-paying, secured jobs, with benefits. Now the jobs are being shipped out of the country, just like the immigrants are. Some folks are turning on the poor immigrants, who did nothing wrong but believed in a proud America, and trusted us to secure and protect them, in exchange for their blood, sweat and tears, and being stomped on at the bottom rung in the ladder.

Think if these immigrants were paying taxes. That could be 30 to 50 billion dollars per year. The "students of dislike" often find ways to spin information to say that keeping immigrants here will cost more than the benefits they will give the country in return. I disagree. They are a cheap labor force, the bottom rung, which enable us to all have cheaper food on our table, and they support us who are on the higher rung. It does not matter to these rich "students of disillusion" how much they spend on food but it does to the other 90% of the U.S.

The rich "students who know no love" share the idea that if they keep 90% of us poor, they will be able to be lords over us. These politicians, talk show and TV hosts enjoy driving through the town and snickering at the poorer majority who are trying to hail a cab while they are riding in their private limos. They boast on the airwaves about their cars that cost a half million dollars. They are silently happy that we are poor because they think that someone has to be, and as long as it is not them, they are glad for it to be us, while they tout the wishes of the corporations. They are pure venom, in a devious, hidden way. Some of these haters even dodged the draft; that is how bad they are.

You have to listen to what they say. See their actions and read between the lines. They want us to kick the immigrants out and what do you think that will do to us? We will become the new cheap workforce, by replacing the immigrants on that last rung, to supply the high class people with the luxuries they are accustomed to. The jobs will be freelance or contract as well, so get used to no benefits, as has already started around the country. On our backs they will ride. They even changed the term from high class to upper class, so we won't be offended, but the term lower class stayed the same, didn't it? It means the same thing, people. We are one rung away from the bottom right now and they are trying to remove that bottom rung.

The tricky "students of no compassion" don't care one way or the other about the immigrants, but the immigrants are keeping the rest of us afloat, one rung higher on the ladder, by giving us cheaper products and services which help us provide for our families. The "students of blind faith" realize that if you remove the cheap workforce, the middle class that the immigrants are supporting will collapse.

This will effectively crush us in the middle class and most of us will not be able to maintain our present lifestyles, or even pay our mortgages and buy enough food, gas or diesel. The result is that the middle class will replace the immigrant class as the downtrodden, lower-class workforce. The wealthy "students of ill repute" do not mind this because it does not affect them; it is just a replacement of *their* cheap workforce.

That is exactly what the "high-class elitist students" want. On the radio and TV cable stations, their two-faced shills complain about the war on the middle class, blaming the poor Christian immigrants, because they want to kick the immigrants out. These shills are the ones tricking us and *they* are waging the war on the middle class. If they remove the immigrants, this will destroy the middle class. Some of them now call themselves "independents," so you will forget who they are politically.

Do not be fooled. These cable TV and radio hosts know what they are doing. This is their plan and they are the ones leading the charge to destroy us. They want to trick you to think that they are watching out for you, and protecting you from the bad Christian immigrants who they say are stealing our jobs. Don't believe them; they have all graduated from the "Apartheid School of Liars." They are the A+ students of the class.

If the unthinkable happens and the flawed foreign policies we pursue encourage another terrorist attack, which in turn warrants an immediate large-scale evacuation of the southern part of the country, can we expect the Mexican government to not be selective when allowing Americans to enter their country? Would they not harbor ill will and hurt feelings from our deplorable treatment of their citizens in the past? We may get a taste of that medicine called immigration.

IMMIGRANT ECONOMICS

The current economic plunge is causing America to look for cheaper resources and oil. Both our neighbors are well endowed with those products. Soon, we may want to increase the investment in and importation of their products. The question that comes to mind is, why would the Mexican government share their oil and other natural resources with us, if all we do at every chance is deport them and remove the chances of their citizens to make a better life for themselves and their families, in America? Our hateful actions could very well cause the Mexicans to sell out to the rich developing countries, who are also shopping for resources. What economic shock do you think will befall us when that happens? Notice I did not say IF but WHEN the rich nations go shopping.

These countries' leaders are not naïve and they can outspend us at every opportunity; they even hold our debt. Realizing that we are in a weakened economic state, they may very well take a more forward approach to further stifle our economy, by buying as much oil and other resources as they can from our neighbors, even if they do not need them yet, just to make sure that we don't get them. We may be powerless to stop them. They will follow our lead and start building strategic oil reserves of their own. This means they will increase their purchasing, even if they are not using it.

When you have someone who has a business that's

doing well, the best place for you to start the same kind of business is right next to theirs. More of the same businesses located close by each other encourages more customers to shop with the expectation of getting better deals. That means that when the other developing countries want to take our manufacturing jobs and businesses away, they just have to open up next door, in Mexico and Canada.

Americans will get cheaper products and won't be able to buy the expensive, high-quality American products anyway, as we will already be broke...most of us, anyway. Developing countries will move their companies and factories into Canada and Mexico. This in turn will encourage investment by their companies, into the manufacturing sectors, because a manufacturing industry needs parts, supplies and servicing. This will help the economies of Mexico and Canada to prosper: a win-win situation.

This will strengthen the partnership between our competitors and our neighbors. That means they will get first position in receiving oil and resources from our neighbors, at better prices, effectively shutting us out of the market. We will have to get oil and resources from, and become more dependent, on hostile nations, much as we are doing now, to a certain extent. Who's going to stop our competitors from investing with our neighbors? Not us. We can't plug the hole in our own leaking, sinking economy. Our weakness becomes their strength and will also become an issue of national security, and our competitors are banking on it.

When the foreign governments and investors offer to invest more in Mexico and Canada than they do now, those governments will give us an opportunity to make a better offer, to retain their cooperation and first opportunity at their business, and we will not be able to afford that expense. The policies the Bush government adopted have had a devastating effect in destroying the goodwill that we had created all along the years, which may have helped us in our time of need. The impoverished Mexican nation and the business savvy Canadians will have no choice but to hold on to the hand that feeds them and invests in them. Our hand just slaps and deports their citizens.

It is not a fault or wrongdoing of any developing country to put itself in a better financial position. This is what they have to do for *their* citizenry and their overall safety in a competitive world. Our bad leaders are the ones who have let this country down, by putting *us* in a position of compromise, by allowing our economy to become what it is, and putting us in a position where we can be taken advantage of and exploited by nations that we used to have the upper hand over. Since we became so financially strapped, we have to borrow more. Soon we will reach our credit limit and America will have to pay for everything with cash, and pay higher interest on our loans. The other countries, who can afford to buy more products than we can, will get first choice at our neighbors' best products and America will be priced out of the marketplace. They are going to literally buy our friends and business partners, as we cannot afford to anymore. We will get the low-quality products which are meant for Third World countries. Our competitors will easily replace us as the best customers to our neighbors and as the controlling powers in world economics.

The immigrants, legal and illegal, that we are

complaining about will leave America in droves, as if they are running from a terrorist attack. They will go back to their countries and find better paying jobs, *with* benefits and free health care: a better lifestyle than they had here. We will be left without a cheap labor force. We will manufacture less and we will have to increase cheap imports from other countries. That means that we may now pay five to 10 times more for the same produce and products.

The mangos, for which I pay $5 per pound here, are 10 cents per pound in Mexico and India. What drive the prices up on imports are the transportation costs. How cheap is your gas and diesel right now? How cheap is your airfare? They will rise.

The Spanish-speaking people are not the problem. We need to work together to solve our immigration and economic problem, and not be distracted by petty issues. I would much rather be rich with a married gay couple or Mexican couple living next door than poor and sewing clothes for China, in America, and not even be able to afford to buy the house next door to the gay or Mexican people.

The immigrant haters want to build a wall along the Mexican border to keep the immigrants out, but that wall can also keep us imprisoned and under control, just as the Berlin wall did to the German people. Some suggest there are powerful parties that will try to reunite all of North America, which will be more profitable to commercial interests. We will have to wait and see, because if this country is allowed to become more financially unstable, then it would be easy to merge the countries. Is this someone's plan? Was it all along? I don't know but the future is a footstep away, so we may soon find out. This could be why some do not want President Obama to be successful in his efforts to bring us out of this recession.

MASS MEDIA

MUD — Mindless, useless distractions that are self explanatory are what the media of today gives you. Too many people listen to the radio talk shows and think that it is real news. I remind you, it is a talk show and these are entertainers being paid to do a job. The television news cable shows showed us a story about Anna Nicole's death for days while not revealing anything of importance on the war or other important stories during that time.

There is much misinformation in the various media avenues today. We receive more political slant than news on some cable networks. We have as many entertainers portraying themselves as news anchors, journalists and reporters as we have real professionals, trying to become entertainers, so the lines get blurred. The talk shows are billed as the real news programs with a slight twist politically. The talk show hosts lead their listeners by highlighting the fear of terrorism, and the subliminal division and hatred of different nationalities and races in the society. They also play upon the audience's own ignorance and prejudices, like an intolerance of gay people and immigrants, illegal or not. That's MUD. When they say in a harsh tone that someone is a Muslim, they do not specify legal or not, or someone with a criminal record or not. They are therefore subliminally suggesting that all Muslims are bad people and potential terrorists. We saw that happen with the Japanese during WWII. The government completely degraded a whole race of people to achieve their goals. They put the Japanese living in America in caged off areas, as if they were animals being herded like cattle.

The entertainers say that their job is to bring the truth and real news to the people, which is a blatant lie and misdirection because what the audience does not know is that these shows are just that: shows that do not have to legally disclose the true news. These shows are for entertainment purposes, and are very effective in subconscious and suggestive mind control. Some in the media are experts in convincing the unsuspecting public to follow their ways of ideology. People listen to them religiously and actually believe what they hear, not knowing it is just a show.

Some of these talk show hosts have been around so many years that they have built a multi-million dollar industry out of distracting and misdirecting the public, for political reasons. Propaganda or MUD is ripe in their discourse, like the pied piper leading us off a cliff. When your children see you listening to these snake oil salesmen, they lose respect for you, as everyone knows their games of deception, except maybe you. You can lose your children as a result, for filling your own head with hate. You could end up with a runaway child on your hands and the entertainer tells you to blame gay people for influencing the kids. We should blame them.

Don't believe in anyone or in their prophetic ability to translate the truth, and extract the wisdom from any of the many scriptures. Don't even believe me; seek for yourself. To believe in a person means to give up your own power of choice, thought and belief in yourself, which could ultimately lead to your freedoms or means of survival being reduced or taken away from you. You cannot give up your will to think for yourself. There are always harsh consequences if you do.

Don't settle for someone else's ideas. Just use their ideas to help you further and develop your own understanding. This will serve you well in both religion and politics. Survival 101, believe in you. Not in me or another person; just listen to what we say and let it open your mind. When *you* think, then *you* win. When you enquire, then you learn. Teach your kids that thinking means winning. We can only give you ideas; you and your children have to do the thinking.

I listen to the audience who calls in to these shows, and some of these people are so fractured and out of touch with reality. They try to belong to a group, even if it is with people who divide the population into separate groups for their own interests — Muslims over here, Mexicans over there, gays way over yonder where you can't see them, and pedophiles hidden right behind the alter.

Some in our media today have blood on their hands, by helping to mislead the public into an unjustified war in Iraq. True journalism demands truth in reporting, the lack of which is a powerful tool that can most certainly be used to undermine justice. Most Americans now believe we were lied to and tricked into this war. The absence of truth — lying — is in itself a two-sided sword, for it allows you to cut first and use misdirection, but it cuts you in return when the truth is discovered, as it was with the illegally-invented Iraqi war.

Sex trumps all. It rules the news and sells papers, and

it is always used to hide and replace the real news. That's MUD, and Shock and Awe. It's the old smoke and mirror game. While you are watching the magician's left hand, the right hand is robbing you blind or burying our fallen soldiers without proper recognition to them.

The right and left wing political pundits are as good as we will get for a while because there is always a media war going on, and they are both just espousing the views of their respective parties. They say whatever they are directed to say and they are paid well to say it. It is our job to protect our family by finding out what is really going on. Both sides give you the story from their respective points of view, but at least they are still presenting some part of the story. We cannot be lazy or biased. We must be vigilant to find out the two sides of the story, so we can learn the truth and act on it.

For instance, one political party will blame the other for the sub-prime meltdown and the impending recession, and vice versa. By that, you gather that there is a sub-prime meltdown going on, which may lead to a recession. Do not be distracted by who is to blame, as it has already happened and many had a hand in it. Just start dealing with it and protect your family.

Some speak to you with forked tongues. On one hand, they say that the recession is not the fault of lax regulation but uncontrollable market forces. On the other hand, they say there should be less regulation and we should allow the market forces to correct itself...or not, even if it is too long a wait for your family to survive. So what they are really saying is, we should be left to the mercy of the uncontrollable market forces which caused the problem. If you support that idea, you are blindly going against your own interest and making your family suffer the consequences. They are rich; so they can say anything. The recession does not bother them but we are dying.

Start taking precautions now to secure your family's future in the recession, and the disastrous problems that could result from it; start saving. The media is now an infotainment beast, espousing the views of the highest bidder. They will only give you half-truths and innuendos, and you must piece the information together to arrive at the real situation. Be vigilant. Is this Shock and Awe on us? It most certainly is.

PREDATORY LENDERS AND PERSONAL LOSS

I have heard that the Federal Reserve is *not* a complete governmental body seeking the interests of the public. Instead it operates as a *private entity* with its own priorities, which may not always be in line with the public's priorities. It was set up in the early 20th century by a group of banks, partnering with the government, to always protect *their* interests, not necessarily yours.

The Federal Reserve does not make a profit, as it is governmentally monitored in some ways, but it does seek the interests and profitability of the banks before our interests. This shows why Bear Stearns was bailed out and not us. Banks take care of their own kind but have the government in on the whole deal, so they can legally obtain approval to use our tax dollars to do business and make more money off you. There's the proof that to them, we are the foolish and gullible sheep.

Bush's biggest blunder was to obliterate the middle class. Many in the middle class had their wealth tied to housing. Those with money to invest bought and sold homes, started small businesses, went into construction of homes by themselves or on a larger scale. Some just had their equity in their homes.

These people helped the small businesses in the area — hardware stores, carpet stores, wood floor businesses, plumbers, electrical and HVAC businesses, landscapers, appliance and electronics stores, car dealers and many food stores, supermarkets and others — to stay in business. When the housing market collapsed, all these people were affected severely and that effectively gave the greatest Shock and Awe to the small businesses and to the middle class, wiping them out almost completely in some areas.

There is a group of people I call the Den of Thieves. They look like normal human beings but they are empty inside, devoid of honor, compassion or common sense about life — they only value money. Sometimes I think they have a family just for show and to blend in, because the bad they do also affects their descendants, and they don't seem to care. How many million dollar and billion dollar Ponzi schemes have been uncovered, and how many more are still not yet found out? These greedy and empty people are hard to spot in a crowd of seemingly normal people: in this case, real bankers who dictate good things to their employees and families.

Usually, you have to look at these bankers' work and their deeds to figure them out. We have now seen predatory lending blossom, with the blessing of the past Bush regime, to create havoc in the American and world economy. This is a direct result of the work of this bunch — the Den of Thieves, who are protected by the Federal Reserve. See them by their deeds.

They live in self denial of the damage they do but their work is there in plain sight. How do you tell one child's academic achievements from another? This is done by observing what grades they get, what projects they produce and how much work went into those projects. These predatory lenders worked hard to produce these loans, and they were educated to produce loan products, so I have to congratulate them. They did a good job to achieve this recession — see them by their deeds.

Timing is everything. Predatory lending is a criminal enterprise and those who support them are also predators. Everyone is being warned about predatory lenders now that the closely-held secret is out. If we had been warned in time, 10 or 15 million people may have thought twice before taking a sub-prime mortgage

The banks, credit card companies and the Bush administration's lax regulation monitoring, or total lack thereof, are to blame for the sub-prime mortgage meltdown. The banks have a responsibility to their shareholders to make good loans, which they failed to do. They have many trained and qualified personnel who were not doing their jobs.

Their selfish, main concern was to package these loans to resell to investors as triple "A" rated (AAA) CDO, collateralized debt obligations, thereby setting up the investors, the whole Wall Street system, and the world, with bad loan securities packages that failed. These packages were sold all over the world, hence the ripple of the recession globally. We caused it. We betrayed the world. I'm sure the investors will sue, as they should, and these banks will have to go to court to defend their poor underwriting and their lawyers will drag the case on for years. The rich investors have the money to sue with high-priced lawyers. We don't — we depend on the government to protect us with laws and regulations. The government and the Federal Reserve work together. Woe is me (we).

The Bush administration failed to do its job: to protect us from threats outside and inside the country. That's in the Constitution. That's the law: to protect us. What we saw was the governments past, creating or leaving loopholes, and lax regulation in place, with the knowledge of what could happen if things got out of control, and the responsibility rests on the administration that is there at the time to keep it functioning.

Folks in previous administrations kept an eye out but Bush's administration dropped the ball. They did not keep an eye on the situation, and only admitted the "R" word, recession, one year after it happened on their watch. What we saw was the Bush administration going to the rescue of Bear Stearns and the other failing institutions with bailout deals. By December 2008, they had spent $350 billion on the bailout to banks, with no help to homeowners, which was the Achilles' heel of the recession at the time.

Even now, the predatory lenders, the Den of Thieves, are insisting that "we, the people," were at fault for accepting or signing the faulty loans we weren't educated about, while they were hiding the facts so well, in some confusing language that even their lawyers didn't understand. They did not make it known to us that there were better options available or else we would have taken them. We could not search around the country to find one honest bank in a haystack of dishonest ones, so we were forced to accept what they offered. Look how many banks gave bad loans; that's how far and wide the Den of Thieves has spread throughout the country.

They were doing business with the consent of the governments past, so we trusted them, and they were supposed to maintain standards of safety. We can't walk into the bank and tell them what loan and what rate we want. They are the ones who play the deception game and tell us what, in their "professional opinion," we qualify for, and that is what they will give us, while all the time just setting us up to take the most expensive loan they can force or fool us to take, while giving their friends good loans all the while.

These bank employees and brokers who help the Den are also destructive, as they could have steered us to good loans. They have broken so many laws that even I am ashamed for them. How do they feel at night? How do they explain to their children that they are the set of clowns who caused a worldwide recession and loss of many lives? They should be ashamed, these disingenuous wolves in disguise. I am not hard on them; *they* are hard on the economy and on us.

Some banks purposely did not explain the whole loan and its pitfalls to the borrowers. They have the *legal responsibility* of not trying to fool people into taking the wrong loan product, because of the problems we are facing now with the sub-prime meltdown. When you, the victim, can't afford the faulty trick loan with the highest payment, you and everyone else start defaulting, which leads to banks defaulting to other banks. They will be bailed out, with local and foreign money.

This brings foreign entities into powerful positions in our banking system, which threatens our national security. Is this a cyclic plan we don't know about? It has happened before, many times and in many countries. Is this just a power grab by deep-pocketed banks that know what they are doing and are too big to fail? YES, it is, as they get the opportunities to buy smaller banks when they fail.

The increases in inflation, as a result of the meltdown, strangle your ability to take care of your family. Your family suffers because you buy less with the same money. Your salary won't go up to compensate for the rise in the prices of the goods and services you have to purchase. Some mortgages were more than the property was worth, by the end of 2008, with the foreclosure rate at 10,000 per day in September of 2008.

That caused a lot of "we, the people," to abandon their properties, and those few who continued to stay have slowed their spending in the marketplace, thereby fueling the recession further. Consumer spending accounts for up to 70% of the country's income. The ironic thing is that many of these smaller banks are going bankrupt, and their dishonest employees and brokers who reveled in giving those faulty loans are being laid off or fired as a direct result of their greedy lending practices. If they did not help to cause this recession, they may have been employed right now. Life is a two-edged sword, isn't it?

Now they are on the unemployment line with us. (Hooray?) All the time they treated us like insignificant people when we walked into the banks…treated us just like a source of profits, like sheep and not people. They laughed all the way home every day thinking of the poor fools who they forced or tricked into taking these bad loans, and the commissions they would collect. So who's laughing now?

As a direct result of this recession, many people will lose their livelihoods and as a consequence, their families and their lives in different ways. Suicide and depression will cause their kids to be parentless, cause kids to turn to drugs and gangs, and so on, rippling throughout societies across the world. The loss of lives, that blood, is on the hands of the Den of Thieves — the bankers, employees, brokers and some in the industry who knowingly supported them.

The bankers knew what was going to happen long before, as they were taught how to avoid it. That's why they rewrote the bankruptcy laws. The only ones caught unaware were "we, the people." The bankers have betrayed the country and the world. That's criminal. They, the banking-gangsters — "The Den" — were our first line of defense against this exact thing. Our government regulating the banks was our second line of defense. The Bush team allowed this to happen. They should be charged along with the corrupt bankers, brokers and employees who have done to us what no terrorist outside the country could have done. They turned out to be our internal terrorists. Attack from within.

They tried to distract and confuse us by placing the blame on past administrations, but that will not work because it is always the person driving the vehicle when it crashes who is to blame, not the previous owner. This is their mess, their fault. No one else's, so don't be fooled. Abraham Lincoln did not cause this nor did anyone else in history. It happened while Bush was in charge. They fooled us once by letting the banks give us the bad loans. Don't let them fool you twice by blaming others. They had the helm and the responsibility to steer the ship — they crashed it. The new president and his team are our third line of defense…we wait for them to help us.

The banks brought us to our knees, weakened us so much that we could be easily overcome by any number of enemies, including Bin Laden, his friends with sovereign funds and their foreign banks. That's local terrorism and a security threat. Right now the foreign entities are buying up large amounts of stock, debts and control in the very companies that run this country.

The foreign countries, companies and sovereign funds have now pumped billions of dollars into our economy at a high price: some level of control of our economy, bringing with it a question about our national security and their new role in it. It was a silent coup executed with dazzling stealth, by the Den — the banks, by friends of the banks and by the Bush administration. Undisciplined capitalism at its best.

Osama could not have destroyed the country by himself; they are so greedy, they unintentionally helped him. They too are terrorizing us. Our Constitution says we must defend the country from threats outside and within: from Bin Laden and from them. Bin Laden was laughing while our Christians in the capital turned into capitalist terrorists, and Jesus is hanging His head in shame. They fell into these obvious traps due to their greed. Bin Laden himself could not have thought of a more dangerous plan. He destroyed two buildings. They destroyed the whole country and it is rippling throughout the whole world.

War plus recession equals victory for Osama, but I have a surprise for him...we will overcome this and them, and be better for it in the end. We have to and we will rebuild. We are the *true* Americans, *true* patriots and we are able; our minds and our hands are strong, and our character bold, so chin up, smile and help your neighbor. United we stand! When we cried against the Iraqi Invasion they called us unpatriotic. Now they call for President Obama to fail in various ways. They show by their actions that they are the true obstructionists and really are not patriotic. I say, shame on them.

Sometimes life has a way of helping us when we are too lazy to help ourselves. On the farms, the old folks have a remedy to stop a dog who likes to suck eggs. If you lock your hen house, he goes into your neighbor's hen house. You have all heard you can't teach an old dog new tricks; that's wrong. They take a hot boiled egg and they hold it in his mouth — steaming hot. He learns that lesson the hard way and will never break into any hen house or go near an egg again. This is not cruel because you burn your mouth with hot coffee every day, and we cook and feed hot food to our pets in other countries every day. They love hot food as much as you do, and beg for more, but not too hot!

So too these lenders can be taught a lesson. If they don't fix the problem, some will have no choice but to file bankruptcy, walk away and reward the bankers' greed. If you have a limited amount of income to care for your family, you would not pay it to the banks and watch your kids starve. You may decide to walk away, rent a cheaper apartment and continue to feed your family. That is a phenomenon the banks have been seeing. That is the hot egg in their mouths because people won't trust The Den, the banking gangsters, anymore.

The banks couldn't care less about you. Look at their actions. Do you think that they loved you so much that they gave you bad loans? No. The banks' plan was a free product now, or zero percent down, or cash out, and you pay through the teeth later. They never expected the scheme to collapse. I am saddened by the situation, but I feel avenged that these bad bankers now taste their own bitter medicine.

Some are losing their jobs, their expensive homes and

their fancy cars because of their own greed. When you have a problem in your life, medical or otherwise, which makes you miss a payment, the banks will treat you with contempt. Check the meaning of that word, "contempt," and you will see how important you are to them or what you mean to them.

If you let the loss consume you, you are no help to yourself, your family or your country. Don't blame yourself. Blame the Den of Thieves, the corrupt Bush administration, the corporations, the brokers and the Federal Reserve, for letting this happen. They are the predatory lenders; we are not the predatory borrowers. Don't let them fool you.

This is what happens without proper regulations for greedy companies. They were allowed to self regulate. They can't stop the practice of capitalistic behavior for corporate gain. The law demands it; that's why it must be controlled. The company must try to gain a profit for shareholders but it must be a controlled gain, so it will not go awry. Just imagine, while our soldiers were fighting for their lives and ours in Iraq and Afghanistan, the soldiers' homes were being foreclosed on by our loving, grateful Den of Thieves, the predatory lenders.

This chilling revelation was discovered by one of the last good reporters who engages in the art of "real journalism." His name is Errol Louis and he writes for the *Daily News* in New York. He also mentioned this fact on his radio program on AM 1600 in New York on November 11, 2008. Mr. Louis reported in his newspaper article on October 11, 2007, that an Army Reserve Major, Jahn Foy, was being foreclosed on by her bank while on active duty in the Middle East.[16] Incidentally, Foy had been deployed five times since 9/11. That is just one of many such stories of the foreclosures our soldiers are subjected to.

The family's interests are being overshadowed by corporate interests. Remember: don't give up your family for money. There are thousands of people facing foreclosure. Don't let this loss consume you. After it is all over, you will still have your family and their love. They are more important than the money that you can't take with you when you die, and they will help you in hard times.

Take out life insurance. You may leave more money for them with life insurance than the amount you could have saved and left for them on your own. You have to walk away after the loss and continue living. Look far down the road into the future and see what is important from that point of view. Decide which is more important to you: not losing your family or not losing your temporary riches. Rich people can still be lonely and alone, experiencing stress and unhappiness. A family usually prevents that from happening.

Scale down the amount of waste and spending your family does. Cook at home instead of going out so often. You will end up having more time for each other and some good close family bonding will follow. You can't buy that kind of love and happiness. Would your family prefer that you overwork and die, and leave your riches to them, or live happily with them without riches? I think the answer is

---

[16] "A Lousy Way to Treat a Veteran," NYDailyNews.com, http://www.nydailynews.com/opinions/2007/10/11/2007-10-11_a_lousy_way_to_treat_a_veteran.html, October 11, 2007.

obvious. Riches are not very important. Love and family are.

A change in lifestyle does not mean a step down from respectability and dignity. I also have pressing and important personal concerns just like you, and someone else has more than us. So put yourself in someone else's shoes and walk the fabled mile in them, and you just might realize how lucky you are, and how much happiness you and your family really have together. If your problems are plenty, then breathe, and just seek and tap into the higher truth of enlightenment and consciousness inside you. What you discover there will help you to find peace, and move on to regain your happiness and appreciation for life — the appreciation of the importance of family instead of riches.

PART THREE

FRANKFURT

PRIVATIZATION

Privatization of our infrastructure and the commons are quite a disaster for the American people. It is yet another stab of Shock and Awe to us. When a company is allowed to run any part of our infrastructure, or systems common to all the public, they are going to ensure that they make a profit, which means that the taxpayer is still paying for the product, plus the profit. If we ran the system ourselves, it would cost us less when we cut out the middleman's profit and we would create more jobs in the process.

We have to be careful of privatization because a good thing can turn really bad when the Den of Thieves sneak in to confuse things and snatch profits. We have seen the privatization of parts of the health care industry and the problems it has wreaked on the unsuspecting public. The HMOs operate with limited oversight from the authorities and with as little expense to themselves as possible, which means cutting coverage in most areas, resulting in *us* spending more than we need to in the long run curing people than would have been spent using a preventative-medicine approach, by the companies or us in the absence of the companies.

HMOs do need to make profits, so the best solution is to leave them out of our processes. If we run our own systems without privatization, and hire them as contractors for key jobs within the process, and also limit their authority to turn someone down for pre-existing conditions, we will be better off. The companies will be profitable with the work they do and we will still have control, rather than being subjected to inhumane treatment by these companies when we let them run the whole process. It is strange that insurance companies run our health care system. I think some sort of medical body should be doing that and insurance companies should be insuring cars and homes.

Privatization shows its ugly head in Houston, where the companies are allowed to dump hundreds of times the amount of benzene into the atmosphere, resulting in children developing a 52% higher rate of cancer than is normal. They do not regulate their pollution and they pay their lobbyists to have this overlooked.

Our private food industry is no better and no safer. Modern times call for modern solutions, and ideas to increase productivity, while at the same time increasing efficiency and decreasing pollution, so we can produce more with less materials, and with less waste and toxicity, thereby creating a cleaner world for our children to inherit, and immediately, for us to grow old in.

If we privatize all areas of health care, effectively removing Medicare and Medicaid as some conservatives suggest, the privately run health-care industry would then explode with profits, and we will be subjected to more of the same deplorable care. One ripple effect we will see, after foreclosure and job losses have taken their toll, is poor people being forced by financial needs to enlist in the military to get the health care coverage that they can't afford. We already see a large number of people being forced to declare bankruptcy when afflicted with a medical problem that they cannot afford to pay for. In 2009 more than 60% of the estimated 1.5 million bankruptcies will be due to medical expenses.[17] These will be comprised of mostly well-educated, middle class homeowners. Was that part of the plan all along, to help to get rid of the middle class? Shock and Awe on us.

---

[17] "Medical Bills Prompt More than 60 Percent of U.S. Bankruptcies," CNN.com/health,

http://www.cnn.com/2009/HEALTH/06/05/bankruptcy.medical.bills/, website accessed December 16, 2009.

FOREIGN PROBLEMS, LOCAL IMPACT

There are many unforeseen problems arising from the foreign investments that are also giving us Shock and Awe. The amount of loans that China is granting us can bite us in the end, as our debt to China was already up to $500 billion in 2008.

Firstly, China can exercise a certain amount of power over the American government when it comes to us accepting policy that is not in the best interest of our country but is lobbied by China. They may start dictating to us about assisting countries who have a cold relationship with us. Making us do their bidding to help our enemies, and not our allies, as we want to.

When the Chinese decide to invest heavily in Canada and Mexico, America normally would be able to barter with our neighbors regarding how much trade and investment with foreign countries is too much. This is always a problem that you want to limit, as you do not want the Chinese or other governments and private interests to invest so much that they end up practically owning or controlling the economies of our neighbors.

We had controlled this problem in the past, because it regularly happens, by putting our full weight behind our negotiations, but now that we owe China and others large sums of money, they have some power over how vociferous *we* can be, when it comes to trying to prevent them from over-investing in our neighbor's economy.

Secondly, they can recall the loans and demand payment right now. This is not good, as our economy is weak.

Thirdly, they can sell the loans to our competitors or enemies.

Fourth, they can use the loans as collateral to invest in our enemies' businesses.

Fifth, they can use the loans as leverage to force us to continue buying from them, when we want to do other investments in other countries, which may have cheaper or better products that are not poisonous or lead based.

They can also put pressure on us to not invest in countries or ventures that they do not support, even when we need to, for our own benefit, as with imports of medical supplies. We will become their slaves.

The list can go on and on, as there are so many scenarios which are bad for us.

The developing countries are competing with us for the world's resources all the time. After we received so much bad publicity because of our terrible Bush foreign policy, it put us at a disadvantage by risking that the other competing countries would have better relationships with the countries we are trying to do business with. This translates into them getting the good deals.

When the foreign markets who supply us decide that they don't like our policies, they can make it increasingly difficult for us to get cheaply-priced products. Quite simply, we may have to pay more to them for the same product than another buyer like China is paying because the other buyers can buy more quantity than we can, and can give the seller other resources and benefits that we cannot, like cheap products, computers, cars, technology, toys, small appliances, and large trade and investment projects in the development and infrastructure of the seller's country.

We have to import from so many other countries around the world that we are indebted to the good feelings our business partners have about us. Money can't buy everything we need as a country and we are quickly running out of money. We have to depend on being good friends with other countries to buy cheap products to survive.

Why do you shop at discount stores instead of high-end stores? Same reason as the country; it's what we can afford. Countries can and will raise prices on us because they are disappointed in our past Bush foreign policies which affected them, and we can't afford for them to raise those prices on us right now. If China were to stop trading with us, we would not have cheap products from them and America would collapse because the people cannot afford higher prices at this time of recession.

If America collapsed then China would get all the oil they need as we would not be able to supply ourselves. We use 25% of the world's oil. Countries can start dealing with each other and leave us out. In the past, they loved and respected America, and they would bend backward to be of assistance to us, even by taking some financial losses on our behalf. Now we are losing the respect of the world and we stand to lose more than we could gain in our wars.

The sovereign finance that is lending billions to our banks will surely demand all sorts of tainted requests, which we would be hard pressed to refuse. They can destabilize us by teaming up with our other creditors to call in our debts, for immediate payment. Remember, our money is not backed by any collateral, so we can't pay them. They may offer relief similar to foreclosure and take our country in one way or another, piece by piece, or state by state. The wolves will fight for the food; we are the food. They may have embargoes against us to cripple our already faltering economy.

Was that part of some plan by Bush and his multinational company cohorts: to cripple us? Time will tell. The seed of truth grows out of the dirt of corruption and despair, when wetted by the blood, sweat and tears of the innocents. We, the people, are the innocents. We will find the truth in the end.

We face so many problems when we have lost our honor, and we are not liked and trusted, or do not have power and leverage over our business partners. We are not self sufficient and they can help each other, and watch us drown. Good foreign policy is crucial to our survival, and the multinational companies can help or hurt us in big ways. They are the ones who supply transport and the needed infrastructure for all our imports and exports. I think they can cripple us in less than a week, if they stop shipments. The country will last less than a month with the present amount of products and groceries on the shelves. There will be riots in less than a week, as people will start hording, saving or accumulating goods.

PERSONAL PEACE OF MIND

On a personal level, one always has to mentally rise up to and overcome our challenges to truly enjoy the opportunity of life on this Earth. We are very fortunate to be alive right now and some of us tend to take this life for granted. Put your problems in perspective. Don't make them seem more important to you than you are to yourself, because they are not. Self worth is much better than net worth. (I saw that somewhere.)

Don't consider suicide or murder as Karthik Rajaram did in California in October of 2008. He killed his whole family, his mother-in-law, and then himself. Others have done the same. Some of you think this is the worst time of your life because of the personal problems you are going through, financially and otherwise. The old people have a saying that goes, "When you think you have it bad, your neighbor has it worse," and this is true for the most part.

As bad as you think your life is going, there are people around you who have more problems. These people are handling their problems and they have a bigger smile on their face than you do, and are truly happier to be alive than you are right now. There are times when problems are bad and times when they are even worse. So pause and look around; you may just feel sorry for the next guy more than yourself.

Your problems can be a source to energize you to bloom, so don't sulk: speed to your solutions instead. Keep thinking that these are small problems, and you should pick yourself up and move on. Be strong mentally. If you have bigger problems in the future, this is good practice for you now to make you ready. Be happy that you are not alone. There are more people on Earth, feeling the same as you, and we will all help each other pick up, move on and graduate from this life with honors. I am happy with the few problems that I have, which I can and will solve, and you should realize this in your life too and rise to the challenge — it will make you a stronger person in the end.

Remember, it's all in your mind. It's all mental control, mental stability and mental happiness. There is light in your day, sunshine in your life. You have to control your own thoughts, your own optimism, make your own slice of sunshine. Picture your brain glowing bright like a bulb, full of pure sunshine and energy, which you soak in all day like a battery.

Realize that you are invincible because your problems are not enough to overshadow your bright outlook on life and your existence. There are trillions of souls in the real plane of existence — not this illusion we call Earth — who are all supporting you and waiting for you to succeed in controlling your fears. You should learn about this.

You must allow yourself to be happy internally all the time, even while you work on solving your problems. The light or energy of the universe is shining inside you constantly, keeping you strong and confident and fearless. There is no darkness when there is light, because light dispels the dark and you are light. You don't just *have* light. You *are* the light, just as Jesus said He was the light that would dispel darkness and triumph over negativity.

You can solve your problems one at a time, one step at

a time and one day at a time. There are people, and banks who want you to be weak, so that you will fall to your knees before them begging for their help or mercy. Then they will abuse you and take your money. That's all they ever want, not your life or your well-being, but your money. Pathetic, aren't they?

These banks and others are doing these bad things to you to control you, and harvest your potential to enrich them, but to their surprise and dismay you are stronger than they. You will rise up and control your own destiny. You will overcome all the negativity that they are trying to bring to you. You will believe in yourself.

You are not poor in mind or spirit, so they cannot break you. You will not accept their negativity and greed — you will leave them with the stressful illusions of this world and you will carry on caring for your family. That greed is a burden that they choose to carry. You must choose to carry sunshine and peace in your mind. Leave them with their doom and gloom mentality. Other people opt to carry the darkness with them but not you, as you are light — the light in your life and your family's.

Everything you do will be beneficial to your family, and the children need your guidance and protection against the "Shock and Awe" that they are being subjected to, by the powers that be and the churches. The "Shock and Awe" crowd are ruining your children's future. Polluting their waters, rivers and seas, polluting the air we breathe, polluting the foodstuff we eat.

The possibility of being defeated and ruled by any extremist group of politicians and preachers, bent on bringing about the apocalypse, is not the bright future the children expect or deserve. Reminder, there is no apocalypse in the universe, only in their greedy minds. The patients are running the psych ward and your children are at risk. Protect them from the suicidal or just murderous "Shock and Awe" crowd.

People have gotten lazy. They say, let the politicians save us from terrorism. Let God save us from the politicians. Let the drug companies and mass-producing food companies save us from disease and hunger. Let insurance companies save us from bad health. Let the bankers and credit card companies save the economy. Well, I have bad news. They are all helping themselves to the cookies in the jar and you are left alone with none, to fend for your family.

The only help we can get is from ourselves: safety in numbers. We have to join groups and try to help each other. Together we are a force large enough that they will listen to. We are a large force of voters, a large force of consumers, a large force of parents, and a large force of everything. Become involved, aware and active.

We can take lessons and learn to help ourselves from nature. If you put crabs in a bucket, none get out because they climb over each other and pull each other down. Instead, look at an army of ants; they use themselves to build bridges, so that everyone can get over and across the obstacles. If we cooperate like the ants, we can take care of each other. Follow nature's way.

This is something we do every day, when we take care of our families. This is no different. Our neighbors are our family, too: the American family, the human family, the Earth family. It means the same. It is in helping the sick and poor that you will see how much you have to lose, and will learn to appreciate how much you still have of value in being human. You'll see that all is not lost and you can find the courage to believe in yourselves, not the zigzag politicians, who pander to the banks and corporations.

Have the courage and the patience to overcome your burdens. Patience helps you to think more clearly, and you will make the right decisions to help your families and friends. I have learnt that friends are priceless and they can do for you what you can't do for yourself, so love your friends and stay united with them. United we stand, remember? Jesus said care for your friends, like the pupil of your eye.

RIPPLE EFFECT

Every action has an equal and opposite reaction. One good turn deserves another. Do unto others as you would have them do unto you.

There are a dozen sayings like these, which tell you that all actions have consequences. We have been taught this. Some of us seem to conveniently forget it in our daily lives. Our so-called leaders forget this at every turn but are displeased when we react. When folks marched against racial inequality with Dr. King, they were angry and reacting to a stimulus.

Whatever profits a businessman makes depends on what he does — how much he invests and how he runs the business. Everything can be considered a reaction. The water in your home gets hot because it goes through a boiler. The price of food and supplies rises when the oil prices increase.

The reaction, ripple and consequence of Bush's war are the lost lives, the loss of our good friends and allies around the world, the hatred we have generated, and the loss of restraint that other countries exercised instead of invading each other. Some trade with us now more out of necessity than goodwill.

Our recession is a ripple, or a result caused by greedy, uncaring legislators who let down their guard, and allowed the marketplace to regulate itself. If the leaders from the '70s onward had reacted to the oil problems and realized the crippling effects it had on our economy and security, leaving us vulnerable back then, and foreseen that it could happen again and taken steps to prevent it, we would not be in this mess today.

We are now controlled as a result, by the oil-producing countries, and they can end our way of life anytime they want to. It's not as though they need us or our money anymore. The other developing countries can buy all the oil in the world without a second thought.

Not strongly pursuing alternative sources of energy over the last 35 years has resulted in America being led by other countries' policies now, especially OPEC. Their decisions are never in the favor of the country doing the begging, which is us. America has turned from being a manufacturing, lender nation to a dependent, borrowing nation. A borrower is a beggar and the whole world laughs at us.

Our greed has led us down the path of destruction. Can America regain her place at the top of the food chain? That can only be a result of good leadership and policies, in the country's best interest, with the intention of strengthening our independence against the aggressive oil powers that we humbly bow to at present.

Were the Bush people purposely allowing this lack of independence to happen, for personal gain? Were they trying to perpetuate our weakness against radical nations, so they could profit from our need to secure ourselves? I think so. We see that happening with mercenary companies in Iraq, who I suspect can give secret kickbacks to the leaders in the Bush administration who set it up for them. The action of destabilization has the reaction of needing to increase security, a very profitable business in Iraq and seemingly elsewhere, in the future. That's good company stock for their rich friends to buy.

We cannot fight terrorism only on one front, of violent reaction and war. We have to have an approach on three fronts, all being implemented simultaneously. This is the key, to do them all together. We have to react in whatever fashion we need to, at the time, to alleviate the immediate threat to the type of terror act we face at the moment. This would mean engaging the enemy with force and stealth. At the same time, we have to investigate the cause of the terror action as it may be alleviated that way, thereby restricting the unnecessary loss of our soldier's lives.

Immediately upon starting the other two operations, we must start an education and advertising blitz to stem the support that the enemy can garner against us. If left alone, a foreign population can be turned against us and be used by a handful of terrorists to oppose us, as we have seen in Iraq and Afghanistan. A single action of war as was done by the Bush administration is a failure even before it starts.

Diplomacy with a stick and a book is much more effective to quell opposition against us. We fight them with our stick. We find the cause and use diplomacy to reduce it, and we use media advertising to show the progress that can be realized through peace and education of the population. To that end, helping to invest in schools is an excellent way to turn the population against the terrorists.

When enemies strike against us, it is always a reaction to what our actions were prior to the attack. I say always because they do not ever want to casually go against the strongest and most advanced opponent in the world. They have to be forced to do so. Likewise, when we strike them, it must be for a good reason, not foolhardy and unfounded as with Iraq. When we destabilize a country, it must be for the right reasons. Is that possible? Is that too much to expect?

If you spread hate in your little clique, you may think you're only affecting a small group of people, but remember the ripple effect. If that group of people is a finger, in time when the hate spreads, the hand is affected and cannot feed the mouth. Pretty soon, the whole body suffers from starvation. You think what you do will not affect you, but it does because it affects others around you: your friends, children, parents, spouses.

You have to ask yourself, what kind of world are we creating for our children to inherit? It is not all about making money and walking all over the poorer ones or the weaker ones. Survival of the fittest does not apply anymore because when you beat down the weak, your triumph weakens the pride or human tribe as a whole.

Our lives are now so intertwined that the persons we think are weak in high school or college end up being your children's teachers or your doctors, lawyers and just the guy next door, with a complex of some sort. Weakening the pride usually will make some seek the sanctuary of religion as an external form of security, as a false crutch of support to hide behind and belong to, in compensation for their suffered abuse.

When their jobs are affected, it may have a bad impact that continues to ripple throughout society. As an example, look at the pedophile priests, and the amount of destruction and harm they have caused other people. Some children who were abused by these priests are now adults, and some might have turned to a life of crime to get even with society for what the priests did to them. In fact, the priests may have been victims of a similar pedophile when they were young, and are now continuing the ripple effect to your kids.

All your actions affect other people. We, as a society of highly evolved beings, are held hostage sometimes by a smaller group of agitators who create a large amount of damage. If these people reach a level of power, the results are disastrous; look at the results of the Bush presidency. It turned out to be devastating to the country and the world.

What was the reaction when Bush's father walked away after Desert Storm? He told the people to rise up against Saddam and we would defend them but we didn't, resulting in Saddam killing thousands during that uprising. People still blame and hate us for that. What was the reaction to our support of Saddam against the Iranians during their war? What were the reactions of many in the Middle East after that? We made Saddam a force to be respected and feared in that region when we supported him. We created hatred against ourselves for interfering and even for being a presence in the Middle East then.

Our support caused the entire region to hate us. Is the price of oil so high because the OPEC countries hated our actions and presence there? This may have caused them to hate our friends more, including Israel.

When we took Saddam out, we made Iran the new powerhouse in the region. Iran loves us for that opportunity and they will throw their weight around now, as we are economically weakened. We see that happening in recent years, with their interest in developing nuclear technology, which could in turn be used to create nuclear weapons. Saddam would surely have stymied that.

What will be the reaction to America's recession and the erratic value of the American dollar? Higher prices and less buying power for everything could result. We now see the fall of the ax on the economy. World powers will want to replace our currency as the global currency of trade.

Making money is good but our lives are so intertwined that we are more dependent on each other now than ever before in our lifetime, and bad decisions make more enemies for and of our allies. If a doctor relocates or closes his practice because of the recession, his patients are affected. When a teacher's home is foreclosed, that teacher's school and everyone's kids in the class will surely be impacted by the teacher's problems, financial and emotional.

There is a chain reaction begun by every action we make, sometimes causing us to act in specific ways in the end when the ripple comes back to us. People who don't like their kids' boyfriends or girlfriends sometimes kick the kid out. Later when the kids return with a child, the parents usually blame the kids, when the parent actually carries half the blame. If you had kept the kids at home, you might not have become a grandparent. Even if your child is the one who caused the problem by falling in with the wrong friends, you should not increase the problem, but find common ground to better the situation. You can stop or slow the problem right there, instead of making it worse.

If you check how many juveniles are incarcerated, and how many prisoners are currently locked up or have been in the past, you will get a more accurate picture of the ripple effect of bad parenting and bad religious guidance. These prisoners are a product of a failing system of religious misdirection through misunderstanding. If you compare us to societies abroad who have a more clear understanding of consciousness and spirituality, you will see that the prison count and juvenile count is millions less. The children were failed by the parents, who were failed by the religions; the ripple effect is plainly displayed.

It all takes place in the same society and community that you exist in, starting here and rippling outwards to the larger community, county, state, country and world. Everyone who is murdered changes the world by their demise, even with the act of dying due to no direct fault of their own. The person doing the killing is also causing ripples as well, obviously. When he or she goes to jail, family and friends suffer. Also, in jail they are taking the place of someone else who is worse and should be there, and they are both making new ripples, some good and some bad. The bank robber or cat burglar takes someone's life and leaves a distraught wife and terrified children, also leaving a support group of the victim's family and friends in shambles. The kids sometimes turn to crime as a result.

Of course, life's lessons aren't as short and simpleminded as my little examples; the ripple usually takes a longer time to get back to you. Usually long enough for you to rise higher and sometimes fall farther in the process, if you don't learn to steady yourself. Steady in this context means being at peace, strong and confident. Bad things happen if you don't also help to steady and support those around you.

If you encourage your friend to think he or she has to take drugs, smoke or use alcohol to function better or have a good time, you are encouraging him or her to become unsteady, weak-minded and fractured, accepting the wrong idea that something more than a good attitude is needed.

When friends believe they are weak, they gradually become weak and lose the will to be strong, to fight and to be confident. From there, they can go in any direction, up or down, but usually they go down. Show me your friends and I'll show you who you are. Your friends' weaknesses could pull you down, so strengthen them and they can support you in your time of crisis. Together you can all grow stronger by helping and strengthening the community around you, by sending out good ripples.

When the greedy business people think that their actions will not affect the country's economic health, they do not realize that their children are the ones to suffer. They think their family will have so much money and business income that the recessionary concerns won't be an issue to them. They are wrong.

When an apple is infected by a worm, it is eaten bit by bit from the inside out. People on the outside of the apple don't see the devastation on the inside, and the worm is unaware of the overall weakening health of the apple. From the time the worm starts to eat the apple, decay begins and continues to occur.

When the apple is eaten enough, over time, the result is a rotten apple. If the apple is not removed from the barrel, it destroys the whole barrel. Eventually, the rotting apples being overrun by worms in the barrel will be discarded. You can place yourself anywhere in the story of the apple. It will still affect you in the end, as nothing lasts forever, including financial security and it's all temporary. If the apple is America, every other apple is affected by the decay caused by those greedy corporate worms. We affect the economic barrel of the world.

So, are the other countries going to remove the rotting apple, which is our economy, from the world barrel of economies and start using another currency to trade in? It's easy for them to do that; we are already in a recession and sinking lower, begging for handouts from anyone who will pity our plight. Our communist enemies are now our best friends — why? Didn't we dislike each other at one point?

We have been destroying our goodwill, our honor, through our foreign policies and the invasion of Iraq, and we now have to promise things to our new friends, even to be under their control in certain ways. Soon no one may wish to help us, unless we give up our sovereignty, which many businesses and countries will enjoy.

Our own American businesses seem to be enthusiastically leading the charge, as they are the ones who knowingly or not helped to engineer this recession. I did say engineer — action and reaction — as some economists did warn it could happen. There are those in the regulating authority who knowingly did nothing to stop this recession; their inaction has taken its toll and I dare say their plan was successful.

I would not have this pessimistic reaction if these guys, our elected officials over the past 40-year period, had taken action back then. Forty years is a long enough time to expect someone to do something to save this country from the ravages of oil dependency, which was not done.

The ripple effect of the foreclosures is affecting homeowners by the value of their properties dropping to such a large discount that they have to ease up on their spending. The easing of spending affects the businesses that depend on that consumer spending. They are slowly being starved, and are closing down their businesses or moving. That leaves their employees out of work and encourages more foreclosures, and puts a strain on the people already applying for jobs, as there are now too many applicants competing for the same job. The other people on the market looking to purchase a home are skeptical about buying one, even at discounted prices.

What is the problem with the ripple of falling prices, when you are getting a discounted home? The answer is, homeowners are afraid that the value may drop further after they purchase the home, so that they end up with a higher mortgage than the property will be worth a year or two from the time they bought it. It may be worth 10- to 40% less by then. Even if they are paying their loan properly, the other homes foreclosing in their nearby vicinity drive their property values down. If they have an emergency and have to sell the home, they will not even be able to pay the bank in full.

Was this planned "Shock and Awe" all along, as the bankers and the Fed Chairman knew this could end up happening? They are all graduates of economics who have been taught the various pitfalls to avoid. They are also paid a very handsome price to make sure that this recession would not have come about. Were they enticed by better opportunities, to ensure that it did happen? That is why some experts are saying it was fraudulently allowed to happen. They suggest it was engineered Shock and Awe.

The Republican Party and their minions in the Bush era caused all these problems, yet they seem to think they are the intelligent ones who can solve the problems they created. If they were not intelligent enough to prevent it, how could they all of a sudden become smart enough to solve the problems they created? They haven't gotten any smarter or any less greedy. They are just setting us up for more Shock and Awe.

THE MONEY TREE

There once was a farmer called Mr. Corporation. The farmer planted trees, which he lovingly called The Consumers. Over the years he watered and nurtured them, and in return was rewarded with the fruits from the trees. This kept his family well fed and life was good. His wife, Mrs. CEO, would sometimes pick 30, 40 or sometimes even 50 bushels of fruit per year from each tree. He then met a man called Mr. Greedy Politician, who promised him the world on a silver platter, and more fruits than his family could eat. All he had to do was help Mr. Greedy Politician to squeeze the tree trunks with both their hands, which would make the trees bear more fruit than they normally would, by literally squeezing it out of them.

This sounded like a good idea at the time, so they started squeezing and they have been getting more fruits ever since — hundreds and hundreds of bushels more per year. Things were going so well that Mrs. CEO started buying everything she ever wanted to buy, not just what she needed, with the extra money from fruit sales. She attained so much status amongst her friends that she even changed her name to Mrs. Greedy CEO.

She and her new friends, Mrs. Criminal CFO, Mrs. Dishonest COO and the rest of the members from their exclusive, *executive* country club, were now able to spend as much as they had ever dreamed of, because their sleazy husbands were doing business together, reaping all the fruit the trees could produce. Of course, over a period of years the tree had been producing more fruit than a tree was capable of, and was now 10 times as worn down as it would have normally been. In fact, the other trees on other farms, which had not been subjected to such cruel punishment, had grown taller and stronger and were really flourishing.

Mr. Greedy Politician, and the farmer, Mr. Corporation, and his wife, Mrs. Greedy CEO, realized that the aging tree could not sustain them forever at this pace, and they hungered for more fruits, as there were more new things to buy with the profits. Mr. Corporation always hated paying taxes, so he and his country club friends told Mr. Greedy Politician to do something to pay them back for all their help in getting him elected; therefore, he gave them tax cuts, which kept him in good standing with them, and they allowed him to remain a member of their *executive* country club.

They had seen in the past that other farmers who tried strangling their trees ended up killing those poor, unfortunate, insignificant trees, and they had no intention of easing up on their strangling of their own tree. So, what they did was team up with other farmers, to choke and pillage other trees on other farms around the country and globally as well. Can anyone save the trees? I'm sorry for the trees.

TORTURE

We have lost our honor and have given others around the world our approval to freely torture us — or do worse — by our action of condoning rendition and torture.

Torture was allowed by then President Bush, by being rewritten to permit certain painful and near fatal procedures, for no apparent positive end result. It is well understood by many interrogators that when a person is tortured, he says whatever the interrogators want him to say, in an effort to get them to stop persecuting him.

After they get a statement, they know it will not be admissible in court, so they now send the CIA to question the prisoner a second time, about the same statements, to get one without torture being committed the second time. They obviously threaten him with the possibility of more assaults if he does not repeat the same statement that he gave previously, regardless of the fact that the statement may be false. This second statement is now used in court.

When we use torture, we are giving the world a green light to go ahead and do the same to our people all around the world — military and civilian Americans. This practice makes it unsafe for Americans to be outside the U.S. without some form of protection. Jesus said, "Do unto others as you would have them do unto you," so torture by us is a confirmation of the allowance of the procedure, by any party around the world, with any opposition against us now and in the future.

When you lower your standards to do as the enemy does, you become no different than they are and you lose very important things like honor, reputation and support from others. So when they torture us and we retaliate with the same treatment *that* becomes the new rule, and may be accepted as normal by every terrorist or opposing country. Bush sent people to be interrogated abroad, by different foreign parties, so we will not be connected to the crime, but everything comes to light. Rendition is the term used.

We prosecuted Japanese guards for water-boarding. Are we okay with terrorists water-boarding Americans, and torturing us in other ways, as Bush has done to others as well? When the genie is let out of the bottle, even if we stop the future use of torture, our stopping may not make the enemy stop.

Who is to stop them from cutting off our limbs and leaving us alive to suffer? Beheading us instead, as an alternative seems humane. Before this torture episode, our enemies had been known to release some of their prisoners. Now they are more inclined to execute us instead.

Maher Arar sued for rendition and received almost $10 million in compensation from Canada for their role in passing wrong information to the U.S., who nabbed him as a result.[18] But Arar did not even receive a public apology from Bush, and his lawsuit against the U.S. was dismissed by the 2nd U.S. Circuit Court of Appeals. There have been

---

[18] "Appeals Court Rules Canadian Tortured after Rendition Cannot Sue United States," DemocraticUnderground.com, http://www.democraticunderground.com/discuss/duboard.php?az=view _all&address=102x4129500, website accessed December 19, 2009.

documentary films made of the atrocities we committed in Iraq and elsewhere, and the photos of atrocities at Abu Ghraib are shocking. It is sad to see the proof. We have lost much including our pride and our honor. Humanity becomes the final or ultimate victim and we become a pack of senseless animals; we don't appreciate how much we as humans have been able to elevate ourselves through the ages as a civilization worthy of self praise, and all the good things we promised our children, when we welcomed them into this world. This is Shock and Awe.

WAR

When Saddam Hussein invaded Kuwait, America went to Kuwait's assistance. We consequently had Desert Storm. At that time Dick Cheney was the secretary of defense for Bush's father, the 41st president. At Desert Storm, Dick Cheney was interviewed. He was asked why we didn't go into Baghdad and capture Saddam. His answer was clear and to the point; he indicated that it was not a good idea.

He said first, we did not have the support of the neighboring countries in the vicinity. Second, we did not have a replacement for Saddam, and if we didn't, the country could have fallen apart and crumbled into civil war. He thought that the neighboring countries would also want to invade, lay claim and share parts of Iraq. So the obvious question is, since he knew what not to do initially, why then, when he became vice president, did he go against his own decision and invade Iraq? When did it become a good idea? We were originally told it was an effort to wage a war against terror and terrorists. Insiders in this administration have written books to document that this was a big fat lie.

We were told that Saddam had weapons of mass destruction. That was soon found to be a huge lie. The only reason has to be war profiteering. They knew all the problems we faced were inevitable. They knew, with the ensuing civil war, they would not be able to keep control of the country for any long period of time.

This was just as Cheney had said; civil war erupted

and an insurgency arose. We lost thousands of our soldiers' lives, all for no good reason. Isn't it obvious that it was a plan all along with Dick's predictions all bearing precisely calculated fruit? We have also caused the displacement of millions of Iraqis, not to mention an estimated Iraqi fatality of more than one million, causing countless family members to inch closer to becoming inducted into terror groups, and injuries of grievously wounded Americans in the tens of thousands.

If we are ever invaded by another foreign power, or country, which hangs our president, whether he's good or bad, then I, my friends and my family will immediately become an insurgent force, bent on defeating and ejecting the invading force. We would go into the sewers and set up hives of resistance, just like in the movies and in Vietnam. Why do we think the Iraqis or any other country would be any different?

You've got a few dozen terrorists and millions of angry civilians being manipulated by these terrorists, and engaged and slaughtered by us. It serves the terrorists' purposes to stay there and infiltrate the population, because they can influence the affected and angry civilians, in droves, persuading them to pick up arms against the alleged illegal American invaders. Was that the profitable plan?

To make the terrorists' deception to the people complete, the reason of WMD causing the invasion has been disproved as an unintelligently-constructed fabrication, further but incorrectly convincing the population that we were the lying and evil force occupying their country, as the terrorists claimed. The sad truth is that we have given any and all countries a green light to go ahead and invade any other country, for any reason, as we were the beacon that the other countries used for guidance in the past. They tell us that the terrorists were foolish enough to prefer to fight us there instead of coming here to America. That's not true. The opportunity to control the population against us was simply there. One dozen terrorists can defeat us there using the unlimited resources and lives of the loving Iraqi people, who are fooled into believing the terrorists' lies. Then the more Iraqis we kill simply creates an ever increasing avalanche of new terrorists. There are almost seven billion people alive on this Earth, and it is always easy enough to make any number of them compassionate to a cause if you know how to manipulate them, so the real terrorists can actually recruit people from anywhere in the world.

One question is, do the terrorists know there is a flying machine in the sky called an airplane? How about a floating machine called a ship? Yes, they do. The terrorists can come here anytime if they wanted and they can recruit new sympathizers here. The only reason that they didn't come is that we will go broke fighting them there in Iraq if we stay. It's no secret. The terrorists are happy that Bush was foolhardy and nearsighted enough to fight them there, and break apart our economy here.

General Petraeus indicated some time ago that we should have used 600,000 troops in Iraq. We did not even use 200,000. If the war was so important then why did we not have a draft? It means the war was not important enough and it was a scam. It apparently *was* to enrich the few. While that was being done, the right-wing talk show hosts were distracting people with unimportant topics, like gay marriage.

Will we have any more attacks here in America after we leave Iraq? They can attack us at anytime now here and around the world anyway. We have no real security at our ports, or at our airports, for incoming flights. We do have the needed security though, just on the southern border, so at least we are fighting those bad Mexican terrorists, who want to come here and pick our produce. We have groups of private, patriotic citizens, who cowardly patrol the border instead of enlisting to fight in Iraq. Real patriots enlisted.

The people in the Middle East built the pyramids. We can't build one, even after thousands of years. They are using a smarter war tactic: letting their enemy commit suicide, by falling on its own economic sword. The art of military judo is using your opponent's strength against him; that's what they're doing to us with the Iraq war. After recession comes depression, they may be hoping.

The Bush war was a two-edged sword to our economy. While one side of the sword promised economic gains for a few key companies, by getting some of Iraq's oil profits through oil contracts, reconstruction, food servicing, security and more, the other side of the sword unfortunately, meant the longer we stayed there, the more broke we the people became: monetarily broke, and broke with the dwindling goodwill and assistance of our allies. War is like playing chess, except the casualties are real. The advance of your opponent could turn into his demise, and this is what we saw happen, with us advancing and defeating ourselves financially.

We advanced and could have been successful, if we'd had enough time, larger numbers of troops, better planning and money to stay there, and a good reason to get allies to help us, but staying there alone cost an estimated 10 to 12 billion per month or $4,500 per second, for every second we were there. We had already run out of money and in 2008 were borrowing from anyone who would lend to us, even our communist "friends" and sovereign funds.

The real millionaire terrorists set us up by encouraging the insurgents to fight us, while they fly around the world vacationing. They are rich with oil money and company profits, from many different types of international businesses, including investments here. They are unstoppable because they have unlimited finances. They run the world. We don't anymore. Their game is money and destabilizing America, for any number of reasons, religious or not; that's just part of their strategy.

Lots of terrorists and their supporters do business with each other and with us. We cannot do without the business *they enable* us to do. So, the smarter move to make is to have better diplomatic relations with all individuals and countries involved. We are like David facing Goliath, and David lost his economic sling and stone. He is very thirsty and Goliath owns the well: the oil well.

As in the past, diplomacy may well be our best tool to solve our problems, as war is helping neither our wallet nor theirs, or our thirst while we stay dependent on foreign oil. Even our enemies want peace because it will be more profitable for them.

We invaded Iraq for no reason that warranted it. Our reasons were later believed to possibly range from stealing Iraqi oil; slowing the Iraqi supply line to drive up the price of our own private reserves; pilfering reconstruction money from no-bid contracts, thereby legally plundering

America's wealth from afar; or getting a solid foothold and establishing strategic military installations in Iraq, with the long-term plans to infiltrate more of the region. We screamed WMD so loudly that we could not hear ourselves think clearly, about first needing to have a valid reason to throw the Mideast region into turmoil... on our dime, no less.

Waging that war, as Bush did, was not a very intelligent thing to do. It has backfired on America. It has now become a mess too large for us to control. The planners thought Iraq was far enough away from the homeland (German or American, I'm not sure which.) not to have any disastrous effects here. They overlooked the monetary consequences and its ripple effect around the world. Even our rich enemies lost money but likened to a chess game, their loss of profits was the equivalent of losing a pawn, while the loss of our economic stability was the equivalent of losing our queen.

There are 1.3 billion Muslims worldwide, many of whom were touched by our invasion and occupation of sovereign countries. Some like what we did but some don't. Iraq's neighbors naturally have more interest in the maintenance of a strong and stable region than we do. It is a very thin line between sitting and watching the invasion, and taking up arms against the invading aggressor in their midst. When they are tired of watching the military might of our forces and our influence moves from one country to another, they may be more inclined to become involved, before we reach their country. It is easy to see them realizing that they may be invaded next.

I have heard Middle Eastern people say America has brought anal sex, "BJ's," sexual diseases, orgies, sex toys, porn and openly gay and lesbian lifestyles to the Middle East. We even have an alarmingly high incidence of assault and rape of our own female troops by their male counterparts, and our paid mercenaries. Why would the natives agree with our war, and support it, or our pornographic tendencies as we displayed in Abu Ghraib, if we gave them more problems than they had before? The natives are of the opinion that we are the bringer of bad ways and lifestyles to the Middle Eastern region. It is their region, their house and home that we are visiting.

Some supporters of the war want to stay home, and hug their wives and kids, while someone else dies at war in *their* place, and leaves behind widows and fatherless children. These people are the scum of the Earth, true hypocrites, as they will not enlist. Sadly, some of our leaders have also done this. If you were old enough to be there in Iraq and you vocally supported the war, you should have been there. No chicken excuses. The cowards have fueled the rhetoric and have caused us to be there longer than we had to, wrongly sacrificing more of the country's best. The few that do go, we owe our appreciation, love and respect. I weep in gratitude for you. Thank you.

There's nothing to gain that will suffice to compensate for the massive losses we have endured. Even if everything went according to plan, what does it mean or accomplish? The wasting of our resources there; the bankrupting of our economy as a result here at home; the bringing together of our enemies and our past allies, united against a common enemy, which is now us; the loss of valuable friends and support around the world; the loss of the freedom to travel safely to foreign countries; the loss of our most prized honor and reputation as a world leader, by engaging in torture and rendition; and the worldwide economic demise caused by our hand, further crippling our ability and our allies' ability to protect themselves against future terrorist attacks or threats from a more determined and prepared enemy. An enemy whose numbers we are constantly increasing with our greedy foreign policies.

The realization of a democratic Iraq pales in comparison to all those losses. In fact, a democratic Iraq cannot function in the middle of that region without the continued support and presence of the U.S., which will further infuriate the region's radicals. The good people of the region don't really care why we are there. They are more concerned with the fact that we *are* there, when we shouldn't be. In the middle of a Muslim region, we are using force and firepower to bring our version of democracy and greedy, undisciplined capitalism to all, and trying to make friends in hostile territory. Losing what little friends we have. That is not wise.

It is easier to attack a penniless America and I am sure our enemies are thinking about that, which puts us under great threat of future attacks. In the hand of human-kind, America is just one finger. What if the hand decides to amputate our hostile, invasive finger by enacting sanctions and by reducing trade with us, thereby cutting us off from the world economy which we feed on?

The millions of refugees who have been forced to leave Iraq for their safety and that of their families are not pleased with us, and this is reinforcing the number of fighters in the terrorist organizations around the world. Long ago people would walk up to you and shake your hand. They were proud to know an American. Not many do anymore.

There are many families who say if they had to do it all over again, they would not send their loved ones to die, but keep them at home and just love them. They would have preferred that their loved ones had a fighting chance to defend their families and their foreclosed homes here in America, instead of unnecessarily dying for a lie in Iraq.

I ask you, who is speaking out for the dead, brave American soldiers? Who's speaking on behalf of the one million dead Iraqis? Who is speaking for the two to five million adults and children who have been displaced as collateral damage? Doesn't the term "collateral damage" sound more civil than "Who the hell cares about you?" Our not taking care of these Iraqi families is what the world and the victims see. We are creating destitution in the world instead of reducing it. When we look at ourselves in the mirror, don't we know it too?

That we don't care enough to do the obvious and take care of the Iraqi children is a telling window through which one is allowed to peer, to discover, to confirm what kind of Christians and other loving religious people we really are — contrary to what we believe about ourselves and our God. We grumble when we scrape our cars, yet we are causing the Iraqis to lose their homes, lifestyles, families and even their lives, and we are happy to "support the war." How hypocritical we are! When our bombs kill pregnant women and their unborn children, isn't that supporting abortion? Is that type of warfare abortion okay with Christians? How about the death of existing children as collateral damage? Is that okay? Is that Christian and good?

None of the victims who was lost on September 11th

are being avenged by this war. Has anyone thought of where the victims are now and what they would have wanted done in their name? They are not floating about in different versions of heaven, as per their individual religious beliefs. What is certain is they would not and do not want a war that kills hundreds of thousands of innocent people.

Some 3,000 beautiful people died on 9/11, and still more are sick and dying from the toxic dust at the Ground Zero cleanup site. And so far in our misdirected retaliation, and in their names and memories, we have brought about the death of more than one million lives in Iraq, and thousands of our own troops surpassing the number of deaths on 9/11. Tens of thousands more have been terribly and permanently wounded, and we have caused the condition of PTSD on an estimated 320,000 more.[19]

Do you think our loved ones will feel proud of us? I think not because we could have taken a different approach to achieve an amicable solution to this problem, instead of choosing global war and recession. Make no mistake: many more will be murdered in their names. Sadly, we sully their honorable memory. Had we not been distracted by the purveyors of this war, we may have seen them setting up the dominoes of this economic recession, which caused millions of lost jobs and countless lost lives here and around the world.

Listen to the hateful talk show and TV hosts as they tout support for war. They don't care about the victims or

---

[19] Goldstein, Avram, "Post-War Suicides May Exceed Combat Deaths, U.S. Says (Update1)," Bloomberg.com,
http://www.bloomberg.com/apps/news?sid=a2_71Klo2vig&pid=20601 124, website accessed December 15, 2009.

the survivors, or they would be crying and pleading for an end to this insanity. Their empty battle cries do not show if they care or not. We have to look at their actions. They are not helping to bring about an end, but are certainly and intentionally fueling the fires of war, and as a consequence, hatred toward America. That is being anti-Christian, as Jesus never lobbied for violence of any kind; remember, He asked the sinless to cast the first stone. Was Jesus a liberal teacher? What would He do now? Would He fight or preach tolerance and peace? John Lennon sang, to just "imagine" a world without conflict, or religion, living peacefully, as Jesus also imagined and I'm sure, as do some of us now.

None of the media hosts so far is leading the charge to rescue these displaced Iraqi children, and give them back a life they can be happy about and have some safety in. What are these children going to do when they grow up? The good old guys and gals who planned this war don't care, for they think they will have already died of old age before anyone notices. I think the war will come back to haunt them and us, long before that.

The Iraqi children have already breathed in the scent of spent ammunition and bombs, mixed with the smell of their lost childhood, and with the smell of their parents' burning flesh from lifeless bodies, combined with the smoke of their burning hopes and homes. That smell, that disgust, that despair does not fade away in one's mind nor does it go very far away. That's PTSD, on a child, no less.

You have to understand PTSD. It's like when you cut the lawn; there is nothing that smells the same, as good and fresh as that. Our brains remember that smell, all smells.

With PTSD, there are so many scents that will remind them of their tragic trauma and loss — even smelling barbeque or the sulfur in a lit match. The children are mentally scarred for life. Many will want to exact revenge and they will try for as long as they live, however short a time it takes them to become a suicide bomber. They won't care about life anymore.

Their impression of life is to live and then die. There's no life in between for them, but in their minds, there is a yearning for sweet revenge and justice for their parents. Some of these children are shells, dead inside, walking zombies, planning and waiting to get revenge. They are live grenades waiting to go off. They are easy targets for the terrorists to convert into suicide bombers…by the thousands.

That's all they live for now, revenge. They can only smile with their mouths but not their inner selves. They have no emotions of love and comfort, only hate and fear, anger and sorrow. Parents cannot be replaced or brought back to life. Maybe someone can help them to deal with their loss and come out of it without a vengeful ambition. Maybe we…

Have you ever heard of "Operation Baghdad Pups?" I heard of this organization while listening to Ron Kuby on his syndicated talk show on Air America radio in the fall of 2008. He was doing an interview with someone from this agency about what they do. They rescue dogs in Baghdad. After listening to the interview, I had a brilliant idea! Could someone please help to get "Operation Baghdad Kids" going? Kids are being shot, wounded and killed every single day. I am, as others are I'm sure, willing to start this operation with your help, so tell your friends, please… let's save some kids to give to those dogs. It will also result in fewer terrorists for us to face later.

The people who supported the war in Iraq bear responsibility for those Iraqi children. They all carry that blame and blood on their hands. To them I say, when you look at your children's happy, smiling faces, you should always remember this crime you have helped to commit against the Iraqi children.

I think you can understand the part you played as an accomplice in this crime, so you may feel guilt around your own children and grandchildren when you smile with them, because inside you will be crying; your insides will be drowning in the tears of guilt and grief from the sadness you caused these Iraqi children.

When you learn the truth, of this unnecessary war, you will cry. History has put you on the opposite side of reason and justice, as these children did you no wrong. Please try to help us make amends. This is as much for your kids as it is for the Iraqis'. You are still a compassionate human being, no matter how disgusted you may feel about the war and its consequences. Help us to help them.

Trying to be in the political crowd has caused folks to make bad decisions about invading someone else's country, and destroying it and their lives. So, is our own economic, suicidal destruction a form of payback for our invasion? Maybe there is a god punishing us. Nah, it is just our bad ripples, our bad foreign policies of the past. How can you hold them, your children, in your loving arms and not feel sorry for the Iraqi families we have destroyed? You know you will carry this burden of guilt and shame for the rest of your life. We all will. Please try to fix our mistake, by starting to help the Iraqi refugees.

Maybe, together we can mend a few broken lives, and in some way, make amends for our part in this travesty because there are not many people who care for the lost Iraqi families or surviving children, and that is anti-American and anti-Christian isn't it? Americans are more compassionate than that. Please help them. Help to start Operation Baghdad Kids. You'll sleep better.

Look inside yourself; do you feel as hurt when someone does a bad thing to you and your family? How do you feel now about your support for the war, which is doing bad things to the innocent Iraqi families and children? Someone hurting you is a bad thing. You hurting someone else, the wrong people, for revenge, is even worse. When you support the fight — not a real war — which destroys the Iraqi family, you are an accomplice doing harm to them.

It has morphed from fighting a small group of insurgents to destroying the majority of the families in the country in many ways. Do you feel worse being the destroyer or the victim? Which is the bigger sin? The Iraqi family is the victim and we are destroying them. We did the wrong thing to *them*. We invaded them, killed them and destroyed their country, while they were trying to fight off an invader. Were there other solutions? Are there now? Yes.

Would a real, loving Christian do these things? No, because war is evil. Nothing comes after the phrase "thou shall not kill," certainly not the word "except." There is no God or Jesus in war — only evil. Seek good, not evil and death. How can we believe these lies we are fed each day by the hateful media? Warmongers are not real Christians.

You won't be forgiven by Jesus or anyone else for this, if indeed you believe in Jesus as you say. Look at him. He was a liberal. Look at His record of peace and love, not war, hate and death. Do not think you can support war and be a child of God. That does not make sense, supporting evil war and thinking that it makes you a good Christian. Some in the media fool people into thinking that. To be a great American, we first have to be a good person and not support evil wars.

I understand how easy it was for them to crucify Him, as we are doing the same to Iraqis right now. We are crucifying the Iraqi children, mentally. We need to do something to help them. The suffering we caused them will never go away, even when we leave Baghdad. Operation Baghdad Kids could help to make some things right. Crucifying someone is not the answer. You know that. So let's put an end to the mental crucifixion of these innocent kids. If you believe in Jesus Christ and His way of peace, don't crucify Him, over and over again, through these kids and these wars we wage.

This Iraq war is our burden to bear. We are responsible. That's why the hateful talk radio hosts can't help you forget what we've done. Their lies won't make you feel any better, and when you listen to them, you will feel disgusted that you let them fool you in the first place. What lie can a man tell you to validate your support of mass murder, and make you give up your honor or lose your soul? Your answer should be none.

The old people have a saying, "Your friends will lead you there, but won't bring you back." The hateful TV and radio hosts, who like pied pipers have led you down this evil path of war, can't lead you back. Don't they all claim to be real Christians? Their actions do not. They do have that blood on their hands. I sleep peacefully at night. I can love and embrace myself, my wife and my kids without guilt. They can't.

I know the anger and sorrow you felt then and still feel about 9/11. I was there too. I drove to the school to get my kids. There was hysteria, panic and a sense of urgency everywhere. I carried my kids home where I sat, holding my children, and we watched the television. We saw the victims and we were sorry for them, and crying for them, and wishing them safe passage, as we watched them desperately jump through the windows of the Twin Towers to their deaths, to escape the approaching fires that were burning them alive. I let my children watch that event with me, and I explained everything to them so they would know the truth and not forget how evil man can be to each other. They were eight and nine at the time; my son turned ten the next week. They understood and they've not forgotten. My daughter now goes to high school blocks away from Ground Zero. I don't think we are bad people for wanting revenge but it is a mistake to take it.

After the buildings fell, I drove to the Brooklyn Bridge to pick up my brother-in-law who literally ran across the bridge to escape the cloud of flying debris. He was covered in the dust, as was almost everyone else. This was as close as anyone came to the trauma without dying that day. Both he and I worked blocks away from Ground Zero. I was lucky to be home and not in the city that day.

Our soldiers suffer a wide range of Military Mental Trauma. It is the shock, regret and grief our brave veterans experience there and also after they return home, having had real blood on their hands, on their faces, having seen their friends die around them in unfriendly circumstances and having taken lives themselves. Post Traumatic Stress Disorder is the term used for their anguish and for those Iraqi families living there still…and the kids.

The veterans who come home are all torn in various ways. Some have flashbacks when they light a match and smell the sulfur. Some have flashbacks while they are simply driving a vehicle. Some can't ride elevators. They cry themselves to sleep or dose themselves with sleeping pills. Their attempted suicide rate back home is well above 150 per month sometimes, but this fact usually goes under-reported.[20]

They suffer from severe anxiety attacks, and sometimes panic from seemingly normal situations like seeing a speeding, blaring fire truck.

Some have such heightened senses of smell and sound that they have become unique, and will be awakened at the slightest whisper in the bedroom. Some sleep alone because they may wake up in the middle of the night and choke their spouses, thinking they are still in combat and under attack. And of course, some sleep with their weapons all the time. There are thousands of broken soldiers trying to re-enter or be assimilated into society, and become productive members of the community once again and many are not being helped to do this.

---

[20] "Concern Mounts over Rising Troop Suicides," CNN.com, http://edition.cnn.com/2008/US/02/01/military.suicides/index.html, February 3, 2008.

Timothy McVeigh was a startling reality of what we can expect in the future, from our overstressed and overworked soldiers, if we don't give them the proper care they need. Rachel Maddow, on Air America radio, interviewed someone who provided the statistic that 69% of our soldiers have killed a woman or a child. Some of these women were pregnant. It is not easy to live with that knowledge. They can't sleep at night. They develop hatred for themselves and for the leaders, who made them do this instead of finding other solutions and alternatives to unnecessary war.

We have learned over time how difficult it is for returning war veterans to re-enter society, as we have had many Vietnam veterans, who were in need of treatment, return and not get it. Insufficient treatment resulted in the disastrously high incidence of homelessness among them.

CBSNEWS.com found in their investigations that in 2005 there were at least 6,256 suicides among those who had served in our armed forces. Shockingly, that means approximately 120 troops per week, throughout the year of 2005, committed suicide.[21] This number roughly coincides with the VA's higher estimate of 6,500 annually, as cited in a *Chicago Tribune* story.[22] On 9/11, 3,000

---

[21] Keteyian, Armen, "Suicide Epidemic among Veterans," CBSNews.com,
http://www.cbsnews.com/stories/2007/11/13/cbsnews_investigates/main3496471.shtml?tag=contentMain;contentBody, website accessed December 17, 2009.

[22] "Military Suicide Rate," ChicagoTribune.com,
http://www.chicagotribune.com/news/nationworld/chi-military-suicide-rate-http://www.chicagotribune.com/news/nationworld/chi-military-suicide-rate-080529-ht,0,6105432.story, website accessed December 17, 2009.

people died, so Bush started two wars, but this information means we have been having approximately two 9/11 events taking place every year, with over 6,000 suicides, and Bush and his followers did nothing significant to stop this atrocity. This is Bush's true shameful legacy of Shock and Awe.

The CBS article showed that veterans were twice as likely to commit suicide as civilians, veterans having a suicide rate of 18.7 to 20.8 per 100,000 compared to civilians, which was 8.9 per 100,000. The article also pointed to a really shocking fact among troops aged 20 to 24 years old. Their suicide rate is *two to four times higher* than civilians of the same age; civilians that age have suicide rates of about 8.3 per 100,000, while vets that age were found to commit suicide between 22.9 and 31.9 times per 100,000. It is expected that the number of those who attempted suicide and were saved is much higher than the suicides recorded. A Bloomberg.com article reported that about 1.6 million troops have fought in the two wars since 2001, and an estimated 20% or 320,000 suffer from PTSD or depression.[23] This echoes a Rand Corporation study that was published in April 2008. I am truly Shocked and in Awe that Bush and his people did nothing significant to stop this...their actions prove they don't support the troops...so don't trust or follow anyone or their radio and

---

[23] Goldstein, Avram, "Post-War Suicides May Exceed Combat Deaths, U.S. Says (Update1)," Bloomberg.com, http://www.bloomberg.com/apps/news?sid=a2_71Klo2vig&pid=20601 124, website accessed December 17, 2009.

TV mouthpieces who still says they do.

Whatever number it is, it's too much.

Look at the Walter Reed Hospital and the pitiful treatment our soldiers were given. Lots of people are vociferous about being patriotic and supporting the war, and labeling those who speak out against the war and the past Bush administration as unpatriotic. But I have yet to see any one of these talk radio and TV hosts speak in any public forum about the deplorable treatment we give to the bravest of our soil, or even offer assistance themselves. I think they will come out against President Obama now that he has to clean up their mess and try to pin the blame on him.

They hide from the truth, as if they are ashamed. I am ashamed…of them. When the Bush folks fought to not raise the pay of our soldiers, and refused them care for PTSD, saying it was a pre-existing condition, the conservative media supported this, by remaining silent.

Any psychiatrist will tell you that the soldiers are in need of rehabilitation to better their chances of a smooth assimilation into society. It is hard for them without proper support but that is the reality of the situation. Services for our veterans are sorely lacking. The Walter Reed Hospital was scandalously discovered to have so many ill-fated problems under the very noses of the commanders overseeing the facility. This is a quote from one story in *The Washington Post*. "Behind the door of Army Spec. Jeremy Duncan's room, part of the wall is torn and hangs in the air, weighted down with black mold. When the wounded combat engineer stands in his shower and looks up, he can see the bathtub on the floor above through a rotted hole. The entire building, constructed between the world wars, often smells like greasy carry-out. Signs of neglect are everywhere: mouse droppings, belly-up cockroaches, stained carpets, cheap mattresses."[24]

Some of the soldiers were living in conditions that were so reprehensible that it brought shame and ridicule to the Bush administration for allowing this to happen because some knew about it; they would visit the hospital for their photo-ops. The commander and others were fired over the scandal but little was done after that…shame on them.

Was it an accident? No. It was negligence of the highest order because it was a place frequented by top officials of the military and the Bush administration. It is worth your while to observe how little was and still is done for the veterans, as well as what was not done for them. If the problems in the hospital were few and far apart, one might draw the conclusion that the overwhelming conditions were a mistake or a simple oversight, but unfortunately, this cannot be deduced from the evidence. This suggests a lack of basic concern and compassion for our most courageous and loyal brethren.

---

[24] Priest, Dana and Hull, Anne, "Soldiers Face Neglect, Frustration at Army's Top Medical Facility," WashingtonPost.com,

http://www.washingtonpost.com/wp-dyn/content/article/2007/02/17/AR2007021701172.html, February 18th, 2007.

WAR PROFITEERING

War profiteering has a negative impact on our ailing economy. Profiteers are parasites draining the life from America. While the economic outlook seems uncertain, these individuals and companies are making huge profits from contracts that can't even be traced to the real contractors who are hired in Iraq. The contractors give the jobs to subcontractors and also run the contracts through numerous shell companies, so we cannot trace where the money has gone. Everyone knows the money ends up in secret accounts in the Cayman Islands and Switzerland, but we don't know whose accounts; that's the trick. This is something I refer to as the Den of Thieves' syndrome, and it's an infected sore on the backside of our economy.

There had been discoveries during Bush's term in 2008, of information that the Pentagon had been dealing with an arms dealer who sold arms to terrorists around the world. He has been supporting terrorism for years. The UN blacklisted him so that it was illegal to do business with him in any capacity. The Bush Pentagon had been using his facilities around the world to varying degrees, instead of using our own resources.

He was arrested and is now awaiting prosecution. It will be interesting to see what secrets of Pentagon arms-dealing and possible torture at his facilities he will divulge. Watch the movie *Lord of War*, to learn who he is, as the movie was made about him and his arms-dealing empire.

The end of that movie shows the Pentagon releasing him, so that could happen in real life as well...we will see.

The main companies who are profiteering are contracting the jobs to shell companies registered in foreign countries, so as not to be traceable or to have the responsibility to pay Social Security, and other taxes and benefits for their employees, some of whom are disguised as subcontractors. The jobs get done, albeit with substandard quality to save cost. One example of bad workmanship is the multiple incidences of our soldiers being electrocuted to death while taking showers, on their bases in Iraq. Many of the showers have faulty wiring and grounding on the electrical water pumps and the pipes. This causes soldiers to be electrocuted when they are taking a shower.[25]

The economy has been wounded and the profiteering wolves' insatiable thirst for blood is in full view. We've seen it happen before with other corrupt governments and companies working together around the world. They are unstoppable, getting larger and stronger, becoming multinational companies. Where, oh where is Superman when we need him? I wish President Obama well. I hope he came with a big shovel, because some of the bad ripples from Bush's and Cheney's policies will cause problems for the next five years, in my estimation, and the past Republican leaders and their shills will ultimately try to blame President Obama for it, alluding that it happened by

---

[25] Boudreau, Abbie and Bronstein, Scott, CNN.com, "Green Beret Electrocuted in Shower on Iraq Base,"
http://www.cnn.com/2008/US/05/28/soldier.electrocutions/index.html, May 28, 2008.

his hand, while not confessing that he is just trying to clean up the mess created by the Republicans' bad policies.

The profiteers have grown into multinational companies who bring in more multinational wolves from around the globe to help them bring their victim to its knees, and suck the life blood until it's done: until America's once proud, respected reputation as the leader of the free world is dead or dependent on them for its very survival, as a new and emerging Third World type country — a banana republic.

Here's what I suspect happened under our noses: the real Shock and Awe to America. Step number one, the Bush and Cheney clique were looking for large, untraceable sums of money, as all bandits do, so they established a deep well, into which they were literally sending all of America's wealth to disappear, namely the Iraqi war. The money was paid to their cohorts' companies, who in turn funneled the money to shell companies in the Cayman Islands and other untraceable accounts around the world — they divvied up the lot, some money for the cohorts and some for the clique. That was only part one of the plan. Next, as we ran out of money, America was still useful to them because they could continue to get credit from other countries, in America's name, so they did.

So that's their step number two — borrow any amount of money from any source or country, communist or not, sovereign or not. That money was sent straight to the vacuum cleaner Iraqi war, to get sucked up and disappear into foreign accounts again.

Step number three, destabilize or slow the oil delivery and refinery network in Iraq. This was done in various ways, the end result being the same. That is, the price of oil and company stocks they controlled, and the price for their oil products, rose tremendously, resulting in more money in their pockets. While oil storage has increased, gas prices still went up. Read *The Tyranny of Oil* by Antonia Juhasz, for more proof and insight. Oil companies saw record profits in 2008, even with the drop in oil prices that we have seen in 2009.

Fourth part of the plan, leave office squeaky clean and do not have any liability for this massive debt. The citizens will have to pay it back, which means we will have to work cheaply for their companies in the end because of their engineered recession. The result of part four is cheap labor for their companies.

Step five, because steps one through four did ensure a recession, they will now be able to bring in their multinational companies from here and around the world to reinvest in and rebuild America on their terms, thereby creating more profits for their companies than normally would occur. It will be done with many unpublicized strings attached, so they will have a guaranteed prosperous future at our expense.

We have paid mercenaries working for profiteers in Iraq. There are more of them there than our own troops. They kept on starting trouble over and over while there, to perpetuate their presence, which is precisely what it seems was done. They shot into crowds of innocent people just to fuel the fire of insurgents. Were they simply ensuring the need to keep them there and it was just business as usual? When the FBI was sent there to investigate them, they were the same company out of many who were assigned to guard and protect the FBI during their investigation. Is that a bad joke or what? It is planned Shock and Awe.

WATER — THE NEW OIL AND POISON

Can water be used as a source of Shock and Awe? Yes.

Water is already one of the most expensive and widely-used liquids necessary for life, and soon it may become the sought after commodity on Earth needed for human's survival. It is already the most sought after commodity in space, as we need it to support us in many ways, for breathable air production, and for fuels just to name a few uses.

As we in the developed world pollute our water sources, we will have an increased need to find new sources. Unfortunately, there are only a finite number of sources available on this planet. We are already seeing a preparation for a global water war by the strategic purchasing of land that supplies water to key areas in foreign countries.

To this end, an almost 100,000 acre parcel of land in Paraguay, South America, with allegedly one of the largest water resources on the planet, has been purchased by the Bush family.[26]

It is one of the largest known underground water reserves in South America, running beneath Argentina,

---

[26] Faal, Sorcha of "whatdoesitmean.com", Indymedia.com, "Bush Makes Massive Land Purchase in Paraguay ahead of Expected War Crimes Charges,"
http://arizona.indymedia.org/news/2006/10/51221.php, October 19, 2006.

Brazil, Paraguay and Uruguay. It is expected that while living there he will be protected from prosecution for his political crimes during his presidency, and at the same time he will become a world power himself, with the control of this vast water empire.

Obviously, there will be other wealthy families doing the same in the future, in different areas around the world, in order to control the global water markets, just as we now have a few oil companies controlling the oil and petroleum industry globally, and a few large grocery and retail chains controlling the retail markets in America.

When we decide to donate more of our funding and efforts to invent cheaper, organic fuels like ethanol and other crop-grown fuels, we will need a larger supply of the most precious commodity itself, water, so we can grow the corn and other products that will give us ethanol or other fuels for our cars. This is apparently what the thinkers are betting on to be the future, most sought after product, just like oil is now.

We have already found vast reserves of oil and natural gas in the Gulf of Mexico and off the coast of Florida, causing China to make agreements with Cuba to start slant drilling off the Cuban coast and tap into the US reserves there. This find among others has all but put to rest the argument that we have reached the peak of oil production.[27] [28]

---

[27] Live Science Staff, "Big Oil Deposit Found beneath Gulf of Mexico," Live Science.com,
http://www.livescience.com/technology/etc/090902-big-oil-deposit-found-beneath-gulf-mexico.html, September 02, 2009.

[28] Blair, Mike, "China Starts Oil Drilling off Florida," AmericanFreePress.net,

We have also discovered large oil shale reserves in North Dakota and Montana, so we are already starting to explore ways to extract the oil from within the deposits. It could be the largest US reserves outside of Alaska, if estimates prove correct.[29]

Within a few short years from now it is expected that people will lessen their use of oil products like gasoline and heating oil, much more than we have already started to do with the increased use of hybrid vehicles, using natural gas for heating homes and the expected use of all-electrical vehicles.

It is anticipated that due to less domestic demand and increased efficiency in retrieving oil from the various deposits, oil will become cheaper and more readily available in the near future, and this will spur expansion in lots of varying industries. These new industries will demand increased water supplies, for the growing and manufacturing of products including food and energy. The next question obviously is, where are those new industrial areas going to be? The answer is: where the abundant sources of water remain on the globe, coupled with a cheap labor force. As we can see, decision makers are already leaving America in droves, to develop these new industries in foreign countries, as that is where the remaining unpolluted water supplies are.

Cheap labor, relaxed laws, corrupt Third World

---

http://www.americanfreepress.net/html/china_starts_oil_drilling.html, May 29, 2006.

[29] Corsi, Jerome R., "Billions of Gallons of Oil in North Dakota, Montana," WorldNetDaily.com,
http://www.wnd.com/index.php?pageId=61488, April 13, 2008.

governments and clean, abundant water in South America and other poor countries around the world will help these places to become the new powerhouses in economic growth globally. North America will become the giant of the past, unless we give in to the big companies who want to merge the whole of North America into one big country. We may still have immigration restrictions, but big business and trade will ensure workers' travel not be restricted within North America.

In terms of alternative sources of energy, sun, wind and wave are the best and safest forms that we should be researching, as nuclear, organic, oil and coal cause big problems in one way or another. The others are neither dangerous nor require large amounts of precious water...so far. We have already had a largely unknown water shortage of worldwide proportions for decades and it is getting worse with increased demand each year.

Right now we import foreign brands of water and we pay $1.50 for a 12- or 15 ounce bottle in the supermarket. For local water we pay $1.00 per bottle. If you check the retail cost, there are 10 bottles in a gallon of water and a barrel is 50 gallons. We actually pay an average of $500 for a barrel of water on the retail market. That's five to ten times what we pay for a barrel of oil!

The water industry is more profitable than the oil business because you just bottle the water and sell it. You will have a source of demand that will always grow as the population increases. Soon we may have only hybrid cars and other sources of power, so we will not need oil in large amounts, but we'll always need water, even if we slow the use of plastic bottles and continue to depend on glass bottles to bottle the water products.

George Bush has already bought that water shed land in South America, where he may bottle and sell us water from there, which is a better business than oil, as you don't have to spend billions in drilling, exploration, transporting and pipelines, refining and all the other processes they pay for, to produce and transport oil products. The Bush family will be swimming in water and money for a long time, and will be free to start gouging and feeding off a new market — South America, just as was done with North America.

We have seen a startling rise in the pollution levels of our water supplies in most of our developed cities, and it is a problem that is becoming more pronounced as we go about our daily lives, clueless to the facts. There is a rise in the chemicals that we flush into the sewers and that water comes back to us as drinking water.

Cities do not extract the chemicals from the water they supply to the public, as the Federal Government does not demand it, and they are not currently equipped to do so. That could create a whole new set of side effects from the consumption of this polluted water. We have estrogen, antidepressants and other chemicals that could be harmful to infants, when consumed. There are up to 15 chemicals in the water I get in New York. You should find out how many chemicals are in your water supply.

Is the dirty water a carefully unfolding plan of not preventing pollution? Unknown to us, lobbyists are sent to key officials with the expressed intention to lobby for relaxed regulations, many of which will affect our lives adversely. We see this done in other industries such as finance, oil, food, chemicals and many more that we are not even aware of.

That's how smart people make money, by creating conditions or allowing those conditions to naturally come about, for the secret purpose that they can profit from it in some way down the line (for example, buying the water supply in South America while letting the water supplies in North America become undrinkable. Then selling clean water back to us at $500 per barrel or more, five or 10 years from now.). Wow!

Our country has become obsessed with drug use, for medical purposes. For every minor complaint we are afflicted with, we run to the store to buy over-the-counter drugs, commonly called OTCs. These OTCs, when combined with other medications which are also flushed into the sewers, form concoctions that can be quite deadly to infants in large or regular doses.

Clearly, the small doses found in the water supply could, over time, slowly poison our families. Pre-teen adolescence could become a normal occurrence in the near future because of the drugged-up water our children are drinking. Children becoming afflicted for no obvious reason can become the norm. Well, it is obvious; it is in the water we give them.

Remember, our babies are the most vulnerable to these drugs. While we need a large enough dose to affect us, babies may need a thousand times less to harm them. Their little growing bodies cannot deal with these drug poisoning problems as well as we can. The water may not be harmful to us adults right now in the short term, but the babies may be high off this stuff all day, and their little kidneys could shut down, or worse, as their bodies may be in Shock (and Awe) from these drugs all the time, each time you feed them their formula.

These chemicals are known to cause suicidal tendencies, cancers and a plethora of other diseases or disorders to the human body. Different people with varying degrees of health will see many unexplained medical complaints, so much so that the drug industry will explode with profits. Which begs the question, will the drug industry lobby the policy makers to turn a blind eye to the water problem?

Again, it will be what is *not done* that will be the problem. The policy makers could be "encouraged" by lobbyists to simply turn their attention to other matters, as they usually do, and not address our water woes. Please help them to not do this, by getting involved in groups that will keep our elected officials accountable. Keep calling and writing them. Our kids are being poisoned daily!

There are many organizations worldwide that try to make a difference and help with the world's water problems. One of them is the International Water Management Institute, and a search for them on the Internet will open your eyes to our growing, worldwide water problems.

9/11

This is hard for me to write but necessary.

SEPTEMBER 11, 2001 IS A DATE THAT IS BURNED INTO OUR MEMORIES. WE WILL NOT FORGET. The first question is, why did this happen? Was it "blowback" or payback? How do we move on? I saw people on the streets at Times Square who said that we should bomb everyone in the Middle East and kill everyone. No. That is not the way to deal with this — by ourselves becoming murderers. Let me say this: whoever was involved in this crime should be punished to the full extent of international law. This event crossed borders and no country is safe.

This tragedy did not have to take place there and then. 9/11 did not start on 9/11. Not for others around the world, only for us. It ended at our doorstep *on* that day, and started a new action by us at that time. That new action was the wars we started. We have to look at cause and effect to prevent it from happening again. The perpetrators put plans in place for the event to unfold as it did when it did, but what we saw was only the *end* result. We became aware at the end of the whole tragic mess. We woke up then but it started elsewhere.

Timing is everything. While the terrorists were planning their attack on us, what was happening at that time? The Republicans were impeaching a sitting President Clinton…for sex! If you think like a criminal would, then you will see that the impeachment…for sex...was the trigger to tell the terrorists that the timing was right for an attack. Why? Simple: united we stand, divided we fall...for sex! Imagine that. At that time we were the most divided and vulnerable nation that we had ever been...for sex! There was no way that Bush's bumbling administration could have kept a watchful eye on security. America's security comes first. America's economic survival is second. Sex is way down, like 20th on the list, but that is always what his group is obsessed with: issues relating to sex. How simpleminded is that?

The terrorist sharks smelled blood in the water, as they already had people in the country training to fly airplanes for just this type of attack. They had been circling their prey, us, for years, like hungry sharks just waiting for the right opportunity. The terrorists were our friends once and were trained by us in wartime strategies when the Russians invaded Afghanistan.

We taught them well on how to spot an opening. When it came, make no mistake — they were ready, when we were not, because we trained them to be ready. We taught them that a divided enemy is a weak enemy. They saw that the best opportunity would come with the election of Bush and the most opportune time would be in his first year when he was green, before he learned what his job description was, so they waited and hoped.

The Bush administration was warned by our intelligence people that this 9/11 scenario could unfold, but they ignored this information of impending disaster. We have been divided again, even more now for a multitude of reasons: race and gender politics during and after the election year, our first African American president, and

Bush's recession coupled with loss of jobs all keep us distracted and vulnerable. Our enemies see this and we are bleeding in the waters of time. So they circle us…again, waiting and plotting, always.

Many beautiful people died in that tragedy on that day, in and around those towers. Now years after, more good people are still dying from that day's event. Firstly, from the illnesses they got after the clean-up at the site at Ground Zero. There are so many people who have different medical problems from breathing in the toxic dust. Secondly, people lost their businesses and others lost their jobs, and they can't recover physically, mentally or financially, to deal with their medical costs...so they die, a slow agonizing death. Thirdly, we went to war and more of us are dying there.

I now work with a company in New York City, which had a permanent communication station on the roof of one of the towers, in The World Trade Center. This was always manned by someone. That wonderful person died there that day as well. They were all wonderful…those who died. Those who helped are also wonderful…and suffering terribly from health issues.

We must always remember and honor them…with life, not death. They are loved and their lives weren't wasted. Yes, they were taken from us but their heartfelt sacrifice on that dreadful day will go a long way to shaping this developing world, and ultimately, will save countless more lives. 9/11 is part of a longer history that is still being written. The loss of loved ones was, is and will continue to be in the future, a necessary part of the human experience, and part of our ever-evolving existence on this Earth and beyond — to be grabbed by the ear and shook back into reality, to be reeducated, reorganized and reenergized.

Reeducated because until 9/11, we had forgotten how much destruction man is capable of creating on himself and others. We also were reminded of how close we are to tragedy, even though we tend to ignore the signs when they are in another country. These signs include civil wars, revolutions, assassinations and genocide, and we do not usually think about how they can affect us, especially when we supply the weaponry and finances to carry on such activities.

Even passively starving a nation by putting sanctions on them instead of finding solutions will generate ill will toward us. Remember, Pearl Harbor was a direct result of this. When we are in a position to help others and we selfishly don't, we create all sorts of negative feelings, directed toward us by those we let down and inflict sanctions upon even if we are right. When we destabilize nations or desecrate things or places that are sacred to others, we create reasons for them to retaliate against us. One or all of those reasons put together was the trigger that caused 9/11. September 11th was a wake-up call for us.

The Bush administration's elite may have thought that they would retire to a nice place in another part of this little globe, after they'd concluded their mischief. Little did they realize that the ill will would be everywhere, so like us, they and their loved ones will now have to live in constant fear of what the new terrorists they continually create, possibly some of these Iraqi children, will do to us.

They will have to survive life — not truly live a free life — but one under guarded surveillance with security, much like celebrities live, except celebrities don't have the threat of terrorists wanting to kill them. Now that they have tortured freely in our name, they've made the rest of us unsafe as well.

Reorganized, because people now realize that their loved ones can be vulnerable, to the actions and reactions of others and also from our own actions. This game of tit for tat is okay when the results are far away in another country, but when the results come home it isn't amusing anymore. You are forced to realize that money and power are not so important after all, at least not more important than your family's well being.

You tend to appreciate and cherish each moment that you spend with your family and loved ones. People realized that they had to be more protective of loved ones, more vigilant and intelligent. We also must learn to be more tolerant of other cultures. Everyone shares the world stage and any country can become a rogue nation, if forced, no matter how small they are.

Right now we are being lumped into that list of radical rogue nations, since we invaded Iraq. These include Cuba, Iran and North Korea, who are perceived to be small threats, but they have big brothers in the ring, so our journey forward should be one of a cautious, tactful and certainly diplomatic nature, before being militarily heavy-handed.

Reenergized to learn from what happened — learn what caused it and how to prevent it in the future. We, as citizens, cannot let our government or any external power destroy our children's future and that of our country. We must not be lazy. We must be patiently willing to voice our opinion strongly to our elected leaders over and over again, beyond our cyclic elections, until they listen and do our bidding. That is why we elected them — to represent "we, the people."

We must all exercise our right to vote, and call and write our leaders and elected officials constantly. We must time and again let them know what we want them to do for the community. We have to demand accountability from them. We have to become groups of intelligent minds working together with our elected officials, helping them to stand up against the terrorists and any opposition to our well being, physically and economically, as well as ensuring that their actions and foreign policies do not encourage or perpetuate terrorist reactions to our country.

Even if they fail to deliver, but give it a good attempt, we will know that they are trying and we will hail them as heroes, as anything is better than Bush's disastrous presidency. We are tired of the corruption and party politics, where the only people who get something are the lobbyists, politicians and party hacks. We need to make the politicians do the right things, so our children can inherit a world that is better and healthier than ours.

Be energized to keep calling and writing them, and don't let them off the hook. If they receive 500 calls per day, 100 letters and 400 e-mails, they will not miss a day's work because the next day they know they will have twice as many calls and mail to answer. We must show them that we will not let up and let them rest. When they run for office it is to do the people's work, not waste or steal the people's money or time, and live the high life on our dime.

When an election comes around we must double our efforts to point them in the right direction. That is the only way that we will get some respect or help. Right now they don't respect us. We are just mindless, lazy sheep. If you need proof, just listen to the talk shows. If you don't police your politicians they will stay as lazy as they are and do nothing. Who suffers? Your kids suffer. Remember a donkey and an elephant both need a stick on their backs to do work. We are the sticks. They are the lazy animals and even lazier politicians. Isn't it amazing how they used those symbols for their political parties? The truth always comes to light.

The people who died on 9/11 shouldn't have, and neither should the hundreds of thousands who have died as a consequence already, and those who are still dying right now, every day in our wars. We can stop it with our voices. Use the pen instead of the sword. The sword has not been working well in Iraq or Afghanistan.

People are unnecessarily dying in our wars, showing us the truth — that man's greed fuels his self destruction. Man's diabolical need to keep increasing his profits will lead to his eventual detriment. Greed makes him pollute and poison the same air he breathes. Mankind's greed is insatiable. That's why women have 50 pairs of shoes and two dozen handbags. They don't need that many. The marketplace has to find new and cheaper ways to supply and make profits, which unfortunately results in excessive waste and landfills.

The blame for 9/11 is large enough to spread around to be truthful, and on behalf of those we lost that day, we should be truthful. The terrorists who did it are to blame for reacting to whatever they were reacting to, in that violent way. But as a parent you don't look at one side of an argument between your two kids. On the other side of the disaster is the awful, flawed foreign policy that caused it. It was started by the past administrations going back so many years ago, long before the Bush administration came into power.

It's tragic and unbelievable that something like this could ever have happened. We have been poking these countries in their eyes with our bad policies for years. There are now other countries that we have been hostile to, in the past, who are positioning themselves to do worse things to us now. The developing countries, who are buying up all our debt, are soon going to be able to strangle us economically.

We cannot fight terrorism only on one front, of violent reaction and war. We have to have an approach on three fronts, all being implemented simultaneously. This is the key, to do them all together. Firstly, we have to react immediately in whatever fashion we need to at the time, to alleviate the threat to the type of terror act we face. This could mean engaging the enemy with force and stealth. At the same time we have to investigate the cause of the terror action as it may be alleviated diplomatically, thereby restricting the unnecessary loss of our soldier's lives.

We've had more than eight years of war in Iraq, when the proper diplomatic approach may have solved the issue in one, two or even three years, and saved thousands of American lives, and tens of thousands of others. These investigative actions are supported by the CIA, FBI and other covert operations, and unlike with Bush, it would serve us well to listen to them and heed their warnings this time around.

Immediately upon starting the other two operations, we must start an education and advertising blitz to the target, to stem the support that the enemy can garner against us. If left alone, a foreign population can be turned against us and be used by a handful of terrorists, to oppose us, as we have seen in Iraq and Afghanistan. Even after eight years there, advertising and educating the populace will help us tremendously.

Sometimes when we advertise and educate the population directly, about who we are and what we represent (freedom, peace and global prosperity), this will put us on a stronger footing with the support we will create. When it comes time to approach and negotiate through diplomatic channels, we will have a large part of the locals on our side.

Using a stick, a pen and a book are much more effective to quell opposition against us. We fight them with our stick, we find the cause and use diplomacy to reduce it, and we use media advertising to show the progress that can be realized through peace and education of the population. To that end, helping to invest in schools is an excellent way to turn the population against the terrorists, as increasing education directly reduces potential terror inductees. The common wisdom is that when you educate a woman, you educate the whole community.

We have used this three-pronged approach for the 50 years of the Cold War, and it has been tried and proven over and again throughout this time. Our meager attempts to advertise, educate and win the hearts and minds of the populations in the Iraq and Afghanistan wars are mirrored by the opposition and casualties we have sustained, which could have been much less had a sustained and vibrant attempt been made during the first eight years. Our soldiers largely have done and still do this on their own, and it has had a lasting and helpful positive effect.

When enemies strike against us, it is always a reaction to what our actions were prior to the attack. I say always because they do not ever want to casually go against the strongest and most advanced opponent in the world; they have to be forced to do so. Likewise, when we strike them, it must be for a good reason, not unfounded as with Iraq. When we destabilize a country it must be for the right reasons. Is that possible? Is that too much to expect?

Why would someone try to attack us? Why would they try to destabilize us? What was the reaction to the Iran Contra affair? What caused Japan to attack Pearl Harbor? What was the action that caused 9/11? Can't we react or counter without war, or are we that unimaginative? Our presence in the Middle East is creating more new terrorists there and around the world. We lose more than we gain being there and they will react. The few of us who make billions on foreign oil are not enough of a reason to lose so many American lives, and cause so much destruction as we have in Iraq.

If our leaders had guided us to become independent of oil 30 or 40 years ago, we would not be in the Middle East causing trouble right now. We would not have been attacked. This attack is a direct ripple effect of our leaders' unwillingness to become oil independent since then.

Let me make this clear. I think like a parent who needs to protect my children and yours, and not send them into war to become cannon fodder. As a concerned parent, you look more at the cause for the bruise on your child than the bruise itself. As a father-in-law you look for the cause of your daughter's black eye because she may need a divorce. As a doctor or policeman, you look for the cause of the child's broken jaw, or swollen brain, as it may be an abusive situation. Remember, seven-year-old Nix Marie Brown in NY. She was beaten to death, sadly, by her parents, no less. The cause of the problem is sometimes as important as the crime committed. Be a parent and look; you will find the truth about all prior attacks on us, including 9/11. It is the pursuit of oil. It is in plain sight.

If you ask Republicans, conservatives, neo cons, and whatever else they call themselves now, about the Carter, Clinton and previous Democratic administrations, they will all tell you that bad Democratic governance and bad foreign policies caused the global community to be angry with the United States.

On the other hand, if you ask the Democrats and Independents about Reagan, Nixon, big and little Bush, and some of the other Republican administrations, they will tell you that the former Republicans' rules, foreign policies and interventions are what angered people and created the global hatred for America.

So if our most patriotic and intelligent people and parties are saying this, I think it is true. I accept their opinions. 9/11 did not start on that day. My theory is supported by the whole country: Republicans, Democrats, Independents, and even the little green men on Mars. The blame is laid, so now let's move on and solve the problem, with the pen, not only the sword.

The tapes from Air Traffic Control of that day were mysteriously missing or destroyed. Ask the Republicans. They will confirm this. Ask the Democrats. They will also. Ask the media. They also reported on it. There appears to be a cover-up.

What happened with Pearl Harbor? When was it? What was it? Why was it? Where was it? I'm sure everyone knows the story but not the whole story. The Japanese attacked the military installation at Pearl Harbor but why? Did they go mad that day? No. They wanted to advance into Malaya and the Dutch East Indies to steal their oil and other resources.

They mostly wanted oil, as they were heavily dependent upon oil from the U.S. The U.S. stopped oil exports to Japan in the summer of 1941. The Japanese attacked in December of 1941. Why did the U.S. stop their oil exports? That's anybody's guess. Politics, I'm sure. It could even have been the same people who dreamed up the Gulf of Tonkin scheme. Who knows? They've come back in government, and in control again and again over the decades.

Pearl Harbor was as much an attack of retaliation against us for crippling them with sanctions, as it was a preemptive strike for the purpose of preventative removal of our forces in their quest to go to war with Britain, the Netherlands and the U.S. We knew that they were wrong. We were right to stand up against them, and defend Malaya and the Dutch East Indies, just as we knew Bush's preemptive strike in Iraq was also wrong.

They retaliated against us for doing the right thing in our opinion. What was the trigger though? What gave them the reason to take this desperate course of action? We could have worked out a better plan, instead of sanctions. Oil was the trigger, with sanctions and a slap in the face instead of diplomacy and solutions. When you are in a position of power, as America usually is, you have to solve problems not create new ones with sanctions, as we did. There is more than one right way to solve a problem. If you alleviate one problem by causing another, then you have not solved it but just changed it to another.

It is sad that we have followed imperial Japan, and invaded Iraq for oil and resources — for 9/11, for WMDs, for oil contracts, for reconstruction and no bid contracts, to rescue the Iraqis, to spread democracy, for this and that, and some other reason — since reasons for the Iraq war keep changing with the seasons. They give us MUD, mindless useless distractions, to keep us from finding the real reason for the invasion, but time will tell, as oil usually floats to the surface.

We have now done what Japan was going to do before we stopped them. Were Bush's reasons any better now than the Japanese's were then? Don't we remember how horrible Pearl Harbor was? Don't we remember how terrified we were? Don't we realize that this is what we did to Iraq and its people? Did we forget the horror of people jumping to their deaths on 9/11?

Did we forget the useless loss of lives? Or did it just teach some of us that war is profitable, and an opportunity for no-bid contracts? Sadly, we did not learn the real lesson. This loss of lives and traumatic upheaval of the global community for riches are not worth it. So we inflicted on Iraq what Japan inflicted on us. Japan was wrong then and so was Bush.

When you wake up in the morning, do you just start beating your wife or girlfriend like a madman? Maybe you may have a reason to take that course of action, if she took your last hit of heroin or crystal meth, but you will not normally engage in that crazy behavior without reason. So too, 9/11 was not just a knee-jerk reaction or a spur of the moment event; it was started long before and was a long time in planning.

What caused 9/11? Can we prevent a recurrence? We saw the results of *not* having the foresight to prevent it or ignoring the intelligence agencies' findings — 9/11 happened. Could we have prevented it? Yes — because people who had the foresight to predict this, and to connect the dots, continue to work in our agencies and on our foreign policies constantly. It is up to the administration in office at the time to act on the advice they receive from their foreign policy strategists and agents in the field. That's why we put them there: to observe and report.

Some ask, why should we run unprofitably to the aid of countries in turmoil and civil unrest, like Rwanda, Somalia and Darfur? Yet that is the same reason they gave us for invading Iraq. They say they were feeling heroic, like Superman with the red cape and everything. They wanted to bring democracy to the country and the people, and bravely save them from our longtime puppet creation, Saddam. How noble they want to appear. How stupid do they think "we, the people" are to believe those lies? They think so slowly and unimaginatively, and think we do also — but we don't.

The impact of 9/11 was dreadful on our citizens, economy, country, reputation and our now non-existent honor. It was another Pearl Harbor, just what the PNAC Doctor ordered. How can we prevent it a third time, after Pearl Harbor and 9/11? What does a vaccination do to a disease? It cures or prevents it. Diplomacy is our vaccine. The pen should be used, not the sword. Can we use that approach to avoid a third attack? Maybe we can use more than one vaccination at the same time to subdue the disease of terror and retaliation. Have a three pronged approach; have a stick, use covert advertising and education for the population, and thirdly, diplomacy, coupled with more than one country negotiating along with us.

Multiple pens are mightier than one, lone-wolf American sword. Diplomacy works if we do it right. A gun to your enemy's head is also diplomacy if you don't pull the trigger, so I do not mean we should stoop to them. We should use diplomacy and if we keep disrespecting our neighbors around the world, we won't survive, as there's more of them than there are of us.

We have learned that you do not need to be a large country to attack us. Any motivated handful of radicals will do, and when they mislead and use the population to do their dirty-work and suicide bombing, it is a hundred times worse. People retaliate when they think you have done wrong to them. We learned that lesson on 9/11. That's a worrisome thing, as we are still not correcting our old mistakes, as fast as we are making new ones. The Iraq war was a mistake larger than any previous ones in the Middle East, and they will remember us for it. Their orphaned children will be converted by them, to take revenge.

I see over 4,000 soldiers dead so far, thousands wounded and tens of thousands suffering from PTSD. I see a million Iraqis dead, and their relatives are mourning and swearing revenge. Some of our soldiers and their relatives also want revenge. Where will it end? How many more attacks will we have to endure because of our greedy foreign policies and politicians?

Instead of us having an 80-20 or 70-30 divide of the oil

profits, we could give them 50-50. Then they would be happy and we would be safe. Then it would be in their best interest to not fight. Doesn't greed for money cause and solve most problems? Yes. If they have problems, throw more money or economic opportunities at them. This can solve the problem. Don't try to steal from them. That is what causes wars and we don't want wars, but the warmongers want to fight because it is profitable to them. The Military Industrial Complex is always hard at work planning how to sell their weapons, and their lobbyists pay our politicians handsomely.

Other countries have to stand up for and defend themselves, and when their citizens think we are interfering with them, they retaliate. To some around the world, retaliation is not something they want to do, but something they may be *forced* to do — they may want to stop the bad things we do, stop *us* from desecrating sacred ground, gun-running, drug smuggling, overthrowing leaders, installing and supporting bad rulers like Saddam, and encouraging destabilization in their countries. We can solve this before someone else swears revenge on us. The count of dead Iraqis and their mourning families swearing revenge rises daily.

The answer does not lie in violence with the world at large; we have fought many wars before. War does not always create peace, as broken eggs do not hatch chickens. We have broken the egg of peace in the Middle East. All King Bush's horses and all King Cheney's men couldn't put Humpty Dumpty together again, and after eight years, even under a new administration, we bravely fight on. We can still unite as men from different countries and backgrounds, cooperating to build a better world for our children to inherit. This I trust President Obama will try to do.

Right now there is an island — the size is estimated to be as much as twice the size of the continental USA — made up of plastic and other waste, floating in the middle of the Pacific Ocean, in a region called the North Pacific Gyre.[30]

There is also a hole in the ozone layer that can sometimes average the size of the USA, which lets in the sun's dangerous radiation.[31]

The suppliers have continued to use child labor and sweat shops to keep up with demand for their products. The world is going through the trauma of global warming. The seas are rising. The North Pole is melting. AIDS, the common flu, the bird flu, the swine flu and other diseases are still wiping us out. Religious psychosis rules the day. We need to develop alternative sources of power. These are the real threats we face in this world and everyone can make unlimited, tons of money solving them. We don't have to fight and steal oil and oil profits from each other. For mankind to move in any meaningful direction, people must change the course of the country and the world, and stop the hatred and the wars. Can't we be and do better? Don't children deserve better?

When you look anywhere in history, you'll see that by

---

[30] "Great Pacific Garbage Patch," Wikipedia.com, http://en.wikipedia.org/wiki/Great_Pacific_Garbage_Patch, website accessed December 17, 2009.

[31] "Ozone Depletion," Wikipedia.com, http://en.wikipedia.org/wiki/Ozone_hole, website accessed December 17, 2009.

our own hands — by wars and the spread of disease, plagues, the flu, AIDS — or by Mother Nature's hand — typhoons, volcanoes, earthquakes, droughts and hurricanes — or by fate — car accidents, work accidents, and so on — people die. We must keep learning about the causes and deaths from each accident and occurrence, so we can be better protected in our own lives and protect our one planet, Earth.

The 9/11 event was a certainty resulting from bad policy. Now that could mean that we could change certainty and bad policy. We don't have to end the story with another predictable 9/11, as our leaders and warmongers want us to believe is inevitable. Even that guy who lost the election kept saying, "There will be more wars, my friends" because they have a one-track policy, a one-trick pony and agenda, of "take what we want" and annihilate anyone who gets in our way, with our big bombs. They even made up a song to bomb Iran based on the Beach Boy's song, Barbara Ann — subliminal conditioning for sheep.

It did not have to be the World Trade Center on September 11th. It could have been the Epcot Center on 9/11 or the Russian nuclear site closest to a large population on 9/11, but regardless of location, it was certain to occur with bad politics worldwide. A 9/11 type event happening somewhere is fate because of greed. It just did not have to happen in the U.S.

Because the world is so close-knit, dependent on each other, and sometimes offensive to each other, a 9/11 type event happens over and over. The true size and scope are sometimes hidden from the public, and often ignored by the industrialized countries. We must be vigilant to avoid a next event anywhere we have a presence in the world, as they may not attack us at home, but at one of our bases, embassies or ships outside of the U.S.

The Christians and Muslims have been at war since the Crusades. Since that time the groups have had a tumultuous relationship, which goes from hot to cold. This last episode came about when the U.S. decided to keep troops on Saudi Arabia's sacred grounds. The religious Muslims did not approve and started the wheels turning that resulted in 9/11. To better prepare the radicals, the U.S. had trained them years before as freedom fighters while the Soviets were invading Afghanistan.

WOMEN

It's very important what women think — they are our guides in this world (to us men).

Our women are taught at an early age that they are ugly and need to cover their faces with makeup to hide their features and their true beauty. They are taught if they can't look like a 16-year-old in a bikini, they are overweight. Their various skin textures and blemishes are taught to be to their detriment if seen. They grow up seeing this stupid and unfounded idea of ugliness in skin and body, accepted in society as the norm and the right way of thinking: that by covering up their uniqueness they will be accepted by others and fit into the human family.

They know they are living a lie, and deceiving others and themselves when they hide behind makeup. This makes them depressed, and over a period of years they come to believe the lies that they are ugly and defective. Consequently, they become truly mentally fractured, and lose confidence in themselves and their abilities. They know that by lying to everyone they are daily falling into a deeper hole of denial and deception, but society demands it. This is why cosmetic surgery is so popular.

They are drowning in their fears and silently screaming for help, and they are looking to every new skin care product for salvation. They are taught to look at their faces in the morning with disgust, and they race to wash their faces, and rub off and disguise that ugly face they see in the mirror. Who are they seeing? They are seeing themselves, so they wrongly think that the person in the mirror is not whole and beautiful, and they feel so badly that the world in turn loses its beauty. They see beauty as a fleeting, temporary condition that can be changed with a little outside influence, namely cosmetics. It's a subtle effect but over the years it becomes easy to convince themselves that they are ugly, inside and out. They pass that insecurity on to their kids and the cycle continues. They see themselves as too fat, even though they may be anorexic. The truth is they are beautiful as they are.

Our female soldiers who survive our wars are coming home with mental injuries. Our women are particularly vulnerable to combat pressures because war makes demands on women quite differently than men. Added to the normal stresses that all soldiers face, our female soldiers are raped and abused, mentally, verbally and physically. This happens so often that it is actually identified by the military. These women come home with the scars of wars and abuses which are internal, and separate from the external scars of wars we all see. They are terrorized by their own comrades. They suffer from Military Mental Trauma.

They live in temperatures above 100 degrees in Iraq, and they try *not* to drink water at night, so they will not have to go to the bathroom in the middle of the night, as they are routinely harassed, beaten and raped when they do, by our own male soldiers. The commanding officers insist they go to the bathroom with a weapon for the war and a knife to kill their fellow soldier who is raping them. They also tell them to go with an armed buddy to watch their back while they are in the bathroom.³² ³³Does that sicken you? It should.

The past Bush authorities did not even think this was an important enough issue to address, hence the reason no one knows about this. Ask the female soldiers; they'll tell you. It's all over the Internet as well, but the media and talk show cowards will not cover it. That's why I learned about it on the Rachel Maddow radio show in 2008, and nowhere on conservative radio. She's got courage and she cares. Bush's people swept these abhorrent reports under the rug. They really did not care for these soldiers. They are unpatriotic. They did not support our troops, your children, who are bravely going through hell in the wars…for us. That's Shock and Awe.

---

[32] "Sexual Assault in Military 'Jawdropping,' Lawmaker Says," CNN.com, http://www.cnn.com/2008/US/07/31/military.sexabuse/index.html, July 31, 2008.
[33] Benedict, Helen, "The Private War of Women Soldiers," Salon.com, http://www.salon.com/news/feature/2007/03/07/women_in_military/, March 7, 2007.

YOU AND THEM

Religion is a modern-day fad but is the oldest, ongoing fashionable trend among a circle of folks who do not have a clue as to what they worship, or why they worship it. Christians must seek to learn about the institution called Christianity, and the abhorrent terror this organization that they support has wreaked on man since its conception. In my estimate it has wreaked a global trail of terror, carnage and bloodshed, more than all the plagues and natural disasters combined that mankind has been made to endure, but like all inventions, its influence now wanes.

The evidence of its waning is the fact that the Catholic Church, in 2009, like any good business, has gone the corporate route and offered to incorporate the Anglican sect into its organization. This will bolster its failing numbers and faltering pockets. Remember, they took a huge financial hit when they had to pay the former victims of child abuse by their roving pedophile clan. This in turn took a large bite out of their attending flock of faithful worshippers, who finally woke up. Fewer followers meant less income for the company, so this merging of religious factions, Catholic and Anglican, is the next natural move.

There is no good or God in carnage, terror and bloodshed. Unknown to many worshippers, and as history shows with Christianization (the Crusades and the Inquisition), they are not supporters of God's house while they support the church, but in fact are supporting an organization that has done just the opposite of what they think. Throughout history religious causes have spilt more blood globally than any other single cause, and that process is ongoing to this very day.

Why do atheists, non-Christians and non-believers get the inspiration to invent things that improve the lives of mankind, from gadgets, to medicine, to spacecraft and everything in between? If God were the source of inspiration, then He would surely inspire His own flock of "righteous and deserving believers," and not the enemy. Of course some small numbers of inventors are believers in the act of worshiping thin air, and I'm sure that God has inspired the Amish, the only stringent group of Christian worshippers, to invent a better way to churn butter, but that's not what I'm talking about. Neither God nor butter brought us out of the Dark Ages, and made your lives so wonderful today. Science did.

I don't think that in this modern time, God has been inspiring many worshippers to have life-changing inventions, equations or scientific theories, be they mathematical, chemical, medical or other theories. Many in the medical and pharmaceutical industry refuse to even dispense condoms, and other forms of birth control, or even further some forms of stem cell research, due to their religious beliefs about stem cells, a subject that was never outlined in the Bible. Obviously, these people should be selling insurance instead of being in the medical field.

For all the Christians who are not afraid to be real Christians, the only true path without having a dependence on atheistic inventions is to join the Amish. Anything else is just a watered-down version of Christianity and is really disguised hypocrisy. They should give up TV, cell phones, cars, medicine, electrical appliances, airplane flight, space exploration, and all other forms of modern technologies that Christians have become dependent upon to live comfortably and grow a family, as these have all been tainted by atheists' hands and the minds of non-believers, from invention to production.

Religion retards progress, and has for thousands of years, and it is hypocritical to use atheist man's inventions and then praise the gods for them. Throughout history great thinkers and inventors like Darwin, Freud, Newton, Bell, Pythagoras, Einstein, Galileo and others of that ilk had to be very mindful about what they said about their religious beliefs lest they be ostracized and even killed by the delusionary faithful among them, but it is clear that many inventors were and are atheists. The wheel and fire were discovered when man observed nature, and saw a round rock and saw lightning strike a tree. I'm sure God did not inspire these inventions — nature did — and God did not put the clouds there that caused the lightning, as common sense dictates.

After thousands of years of flying chariots, miracles going off left and right like fireworks, plagues descending like gifts from heaven given by a fire-breathing, vengeful God, within the last century, the deafening din of religion has quieted to a low hum with no sight of the mysterious entity we call God. He is in hiding, scared away by reasoning, common sense and science...or maybe He just got cable TV.

The silence is now deafening, as our worthless prayers for miracles go unanswered. Wars are still being fought outside the bases of our female soldiers in Iraq, who are being raped inside the bases at the same time, and disease is still affecting us because He has abandoned us. We have been reduced to thinking that catching a bus to work and getting there on time is an act of divine intervention, and the taste of cheesecake is a miracle. In the boxing-ring of reality, the "miracles" of science by modern man have put God on the ropes, as He battles to rear His once proud head...but alas, He is down for the count. God has grown tired of Himself and His minions traveling by fiery chariot and has not been seen for centuries, and this invisibility proves His nonexistence without a doubt.

This obviously shows the delirium experienced by the writers and inventors of religion in the first place, to think that there was a God. Too much lead poisoned wine, I imagine. Stories of once magnificent gods and miracles have been predictably, pathetically, and hysterically been revealed to be just that... stories for the minds of children, now followed by those adults who never grew up.

Hysterical because it is really mind-boggling to see billions of people around the world believing the world's biggest fabrication: a magical genie, called God, who is unfortunate enough to be ruled by ancient man's unimaginative rules, of being frighteningly shortsighted, childishly vengeful and not ruling with love and peace, opting instead to rule with fear, killing millions with plagues and killing innocents, such as in one instance, killing all the first born, an act that heralded the occasion of Passover.

Gods do not answer our prayers for life anymore and they never did, as proven by millions who have died in just the last century, and even more in all the wars of centuries past, for thousands of years, all pleading, praying, begging for life, while they were brutally hanged, chopped to death, shot to death or blown to bits.

This was proven here in the U.S. by the "Black Blizzard" in the "Dust Bowl," in the Great Plains, during the 1930 to 1940 drought and resulting dust storms. It was so severe that the dust went from the middle of the country all the way to the east coast states, and out into the Atlantic Ocean. People prayed to God for years, while they lost everything: towns, crops, livestock and many lives, all this while "God" was blessing us with the Great Depression, or at least refusing to bring a swift end to it. Their prayers were never answered. Remember the past and the God that never was.

People still suffer from denial and religious delirium to this very day. When calamities befall them, and gods leave them to suffer and do not answer their prayers for relief, they simply stay silent as they did in the "Black Blizzard," and when the going is good, they proclaim that God is good, forgetting the unaided calamities they went through. They make up little stories to explain away God's absence when needed, like the "Footsteps in the Sand" poem. This is hypocrisy, or at least insanity with a hint of denial and pinch of delusion.

God did not give us the "Black Blizzard." Man did by poor farming habits and trying to bend nature to his will. Earth and nature revolted, and man humbly learned to respect nature, and live and grow crops in a way that was in harmony with his surroundings, his little patch of earth. Other people in other countries are still learning that lesson, the hard way, as severe dust storms are occurring there right now, killing many. God did not give us the "Great Depression." Man's greed did.

Religion is just snake oil and hypocrisy, as religion has morphed into something that is far different now, to what was first invented. The truth of the imaginary God is plain to see and proven, in every drop of blood that is shed and every life lost. I see that man was not created by God's imagination, in His image. Instead God was created by man's imagination, in man's image. God is indeed man's invention.

Some people did not look at who they were voting for, in the 2000 and 2004 elections. They looked at the party they were voting for, and did not think of the country or its well being. They put the interests of company and self before country, of ideology before country and of social intolerance against others, before country. They are their own worst enemy.

Had they taken the time to see the history of George Bush while he was governor, or in his other jobs, they may have thought twice before electing him. Today their kids and ours are dying in foreign wars to enrich someone's pocket. Today their homes and ours are being foreclosed on. Today the credit card companies are making it hell for them, and us, with new bankruptcy laws and raising their interest rates.

Today they have regrets, because they helped to cause the country to inherit leaders that have destroyed America as we knew it, from within. People were tricked and bullied into thinking gay people living next to them or getting married, paying taxes, or some foolish point about stem cell research and abortions were much more important than anything else, including their families' well being or the state of the country.

Now they will gladly accept everything, if they could go back to the way it was before Bush. They would have their homes, their jobs, and a living, unbroken soldier who was their child. They were blindsided and fooled by the real intentions of the party they voted into power, when conservatives and Republicans in the party showed their true colors, and were indistinguishable. They always are because to me they are two sides of the same coin; they are one in the same.

Now folks think having their sacrificed soldier back in their arms would make up for the gays next door, or abortion and stem cell issues…if they had a choice. Having not had their home foreclosed on would more than make up for paying taxes. Not being in a recession and headed for a depression, or even just having a job would have definitely made up for not caring for and about women, or for not helping to resolve abortion issues, salary issues, rape issues, medical coverage issues, domestic violence issues and many more during Bush's misuse of power. It was literally torture for women.

Thousands or millions around the world will die as a result of this recession, a result of unwary Republican votes, but even more, as a result of those who didn't vote. To those who voted for George Bush, I say it's okay. It's good. You did what you wanted to do, albeit without much thought for the well being of the country or its women, and that is democracy. You did not know what he and Dick and Don would do. They were part of PNAC, the Project for the New American Century, and we all are just victims of their policies. Thank goodness Bush fumbled the ball. It could have been much worse.

The people who really let the country down were the

ones who didn't vote. They are the ones who could have changed the outcome of the elections...legally. In my estimate only a maximum of one third of the country is made up of conservatives (closet Republicans). The other two thirds of the country are Democrats and Independents, and I think if the majority of them had voted, we would never have had George Bush in office. Well, we have to let the past stay there. Remember it always and look toward the future with the foresight we need from the experience of that past, to guide our country in a new direction, with a better outcome.

We have to realize that our actions are the axis upon which the survival of the world's economy, and ours, depends. We need the world's economy to be healthy for our comparably smaller American economy to maintain good health. Our spending only amounts to 25% of the world's GDP, but it is key for the overall health of the world economy, as we see with our recession spreading throughout the world and rippling back to affect us even more.

The world community is suffering such drastic consequences from the recession that will result in millions of deaths worldwide. Before the recession, there had been children dying every day, in the poorer countries, from starvation, disease, drought and other problems. What will happen now that we are in a recession? Is this a multiplying death sentence for them in the millions? Yes, it is.

Who's responsible? Did we have a hand in this recession, and by extension, those deaths? Yes, we put the administration in place that caused the recession. Our elections were the trigger in the gun of recession. The bad policies the Bush team (the PNAC boys) and their party had were the bullets. Greed was the finger that pulled the trigger.

A new America is going to emerge from our present recession, hopefully a better one that can give us and the world back some of what we have lost. What we see happening here in this part of our journey on Earth is an upheaval of the old ways and a blossoming of the new; if we use the past to guide us to make good decisions, ones not based on greed.

It is always difficult for us to accept change in our lives as we get comfortable, but that is how nature and evolution work. A volcano can destroy but also create a new land in its wake. One that is more fertile than the last. This Earth is crying out for love and peace above war and hate, and it is going to renew itself, by the processes of nature and evolution. America is just a small part of that change.

The Earth we live on is changing now and we are along for the ride. It is widely thought in some circles that the Earth could be a spiritually living being, a spiritual entity — unlike anything most of us have had the honor and delight of experiencing, just as the billions of bacteria that live and feed on us daily do not even know that we exist or that we are a living entity.

This entity, the Earth, is one part of the whole living spiritual entity, which is the universe. This entity, the universe, demands constant evolution by all species of living things, to keep pace with each other. If one species creates an advantage over another, the other species grows a toxin, a camouflage or an antidote, to protect against the advantage, thereby avoiding extinction. There are spiritual forces at work helping to bring about this change of the Earth, and that is a topic we can explore in more detail in the future. Suffice it to say we are but a wart on the backside of the Godless universe. Put yourself in your children's shoes. They are more threatened by privatized health care than from any terrorist group. Terrorists can kill dozens, hundreds, or even a couple of thousand at a time. Do you realize how many people die each year due to lack of proper, preventative health care in America? One estimate is 36,000 deaths associated with flu and pneumonia alone. The other preventable and treatable illnesses are too numerous to count...per year.

It makes you think you are living in a Third World country. The health care industry milks the economy by harvesting us, letting the more risky or sick among us just die like cattle, as a new crop is coming up. Diseases are maintained instead of being cured, for a steady stream of profits. Call your elected officials. Make them do the jobs we elected them for.

Domestic terrorism is a definite threat to you and your family. Bush's warrant-less surveillance program was not only illegal but also useless. The terrorists don't need to use the phones; only we do. Why is it useless, you ask? Here are a few reasons: (1) worldwide delivery companies, (2) e-mail, (3) U.S. mail, (4) coded words in any mail, regular or e-mail, (5) prepaid cell phones to call each other, and the list goes on. In the wars we have fought, WWII and others, we used Morse code, and other coded messages and actions to elude the enemy. Watch the movie *Wind Talkers*. It worked for us; it can work for anyone and all countries do it. Espionage is an old game with many ways of communication.

The enemy can use codes anytime and they are just as intelligent as us. They can use one-time, prepaid cell phones to each other, which are discarded after each use. This I think is their main way. They have the use of technology globally and are spread out around the world just as we are. I understand the need to have certain wiretaps and I know that the government does not need a warrant to start one.

After starting one, they can simply waltz in, nonchalantly, hero like, toothpick in the mouth like a cowboy, and get a warrant from the Foreign Intelligence Surveillance Act (FISA) court. There is a procedure that is simple and effective, and there is no good reason to not follow it.

The only reason the Bush team did not follow the procedure of getting a warrant is to exercise domestic terrorism against you and your family. Just who collected that information and what diabolical scheme they will use it for now and in the future, we don't know…maybe another PNAC type plan. PNAC has apparently been succeeded by a new project, called the Foreign Policy Initiative, headed by the same group as PNAC: same leopard, different spots.

Bush and his lackeys shrank your Constitutional rights of privacy and free speech. You obviously will not speak freely on the phone if you think someone is listening or recording you. Because they would have had to show cause for each warrant, they could not spy and gather info on the other 99.9% of the population without this surveillance program, hence we were inflicted with it.

I shake my head in shame when I hear people on TV and radio lying to you, and fooling you into thinking there is a problem: that there is a war. There is no war, only a business being run. A time-tested, profitable business. If we left Iraq and Afghanistan in the morning, we would be no worse off.

It has always been profitable to manufacture weapons, sell them, and have customers use them against each other in conflicts and buy more from you. In this way, the politicians, the military and the weapon manufacturers all work as a team to make it happen. They each get what they want from the equation. It has always been lucrative to destabilize countries and groups; it provides the best opportunity to sell to them the weapons which we manufacture, to gain power in other countries militarily by having a base there, and to secure lucrative contracts for the companies who control the politicians. The monetary gains for companies are staggering; oil, precious metals and other natural resources bring in tremendous profits in the billions, making it easy to throw crumbs — a couple of million to the politicians.

Why must they stop there, at destabilizing *foreign* countries? To some, America is just another country to plunder. Doesn't a cancer eat the flesh of the same body it lives in and off? Doesn't that eventually kill off the host body? Cancers kill. America is the body. The warmongering politicians, weapon manufacturers, banks and multinational companies are the cancers, feeding on our country's flesh. If they successfully stymie President Obama's efforts and America dies, they move on, some to Dubai and South America, apparently. We will then see a new America, one that stretches from Mexico to Canada.

Weapons come from private manufacturing

companies and go to all the fighting groups in Iraq and elsewhere around the world. Who's paying for the war in Iraq, and buying the weapons to send to our troops and the warring groups who pretend to help us, but then shoot us in our backs? We are. Nice profitable business all around. Remember Nicaragua and the Iran Contra affair? We did that there as well.

Only one thing was missing...your soldiers as the plastic game pieces — plastic GI Joes. Just like the ones the good old boys at the top grew up playing with. This is all a game to them. Plastic armies and playing war games are what they understand. They are rich kids who are disconnected from the world. Disconnected from real feelings, real sorrow, and are shielded and sheltered from reality by their money and stature. You may well discover these are usually the draft dodgers of the past.

To them it's still a game, in contrast to real people who wage war as a necessity to their times, as WWII was. They never felt consequences because their rich parents would bail them out of jail, or shield them from being there at all. The parents created carefree monsters. Now the monsters are parents. Observe George, Dick, Don and their PNAC friends. Funny thing in nature though, sometimes the kids turn out opposite to their parents, so some of their kids may be just fine, as they see firsthand what *not* to become. Ron Reagan, President Reagan's son, gallantly comes to mind in that respect, as he resists becoming a Republican or a religious zealot, for all the right reasons.

There is a movement of media people who were trying to fool you to take away your rights when Bush was our dictator. They are shameful liars and they should be avoided. To them I recommend verse 14 of the Gospel of

Thomas: "What comes out of your mouth will defile you." Listen to them tout the need for more war and you will know them.

Their message of hate subliminally suggests to their audience that war is the right thing for you to follow. In fact, it isn't very subliminal anymore. They blatantly try to convince you that Bush's war in Iraq was justified. They are a cancer. They are fake Christians, as real Christians don't support violence, war, torture and murder. Killing is anti-Christian and even some Mega Churches support the wars, so you need to know them by their actions.

Supporting your troops does not mean supporting any wars. That's a different subject altogether. Supporting the troops means keeping them out of harm's way when possible, and not deploying them unnecessarily, and without a good plan or reason. It is a cloudy subject and one that you have to be well informed of to make decisions.

I ask you, if we leave Iraq and Afghanistan immediately, will we be at a greater risk? That answer is no. We will be able to save billions of dollars per month, and reinvest it into our military and better protect ourselves. We will also have fewer soldiers in harm's way and thereby not have the medical expense or the casualties: your children. We will save the troops from the combat-related mental stress that they — your children — are exposed to, as the numbers of those with PTSD reveal. We will stop the incidence of creating new terrorists with our presence, and can then concentrate on improving our image and the monetary profits that will bring around the region and globally. These positives certainly outweigh the status quo of staying there.

We do not know the classified information the White House knows, and we can't depend on these *entertainers* on TV and radio, who mislead us about the decisions the White House makes. They are just entertainers giving *opinions* on a show. They are not real and true news reporters. If we trust our men in the field, as Bush should have done before 9/11, then we are sure that the White House will always make the good but hard decisions. Sometimes they have to take the lesser of two or four evils, and us trusting their decisions is key, because we all know that they have America's best interest at heart. The entertainers try to breed mistrust into us, so don't listen to them.

Instead of listening to these shysters who encourage you to believe in Gods and magic, I would invite you to listen to Professor Michio Kaku on his radio and TV shows, or learn about science from him on his website. He will open up a whole new world to you, one that is based in the wonderful world of fact and science, not fictional religion.

If you do not wish to become a real Christian zealot and join the only true Christians, the Amish, then it is well worth your time to learn about this world and universe that we live on and in, and Professor Kaku's website is the perfect place to start. I guarantee that you will not see religion, the world, the universe or the future in such a limited way again. Religion does not grow if you think, learn, experiment, and experience life and science working together. Religion only survives within the walls of ignorance, blindness and laziness to think for oneself.

The past actions of Bush's team cause you and yours today to be unsafe anywhere in the world, due to the threat of attack from the millions of real terrorists they have since created. Their foreign policies caused that. America can live in peace and prosperity with the entire world, but our politicians chose to be greedy, and cause trouble and wars.

Naturally, the citizens of these other countries don't like this. They are forced to try to defend themselves and stop the perceived threats to their countries. Apart from stealing countries' profits with bad oil and other contracts, using dictators who we put there and support, we are also gunrunners. This threatens those people and their families in various ways, for their very survival.

Look at our history of gunrunning. (1) America's Iran Contra affair; supplying the Contras in Nicaragua with support and arms, with proceeds made from the sale of arms going indirectly to Iran via Israel. Israel supplied Iran with weapons and then bought new weapons from America;[34] (2) America supplied Saddam Hussein with weapons to fight Iran;[35] (3) America supplied and trained Afghan Mujahideen rebels and Muslim volunteer foreign fighters, including Bin Laden, to fight the Soviets in Afghanistan in the American sponsored jihad, named Operation Cyclone; and there are so many more instances. Sometimes we help the good guys, sometimes the bad guys, and sometimes, as with Bin Laden and his group, there are no good guys.[36]

---

[34] "Iran-Contra Affair," Wikipedia.com, http://en.wikipedia.org/wiki/Iran%E2%80%93Contra_affair, website accessed December 17, 2009.
[35] "Iran-Iraq War," Wikipedia.com, http://en.wikipedia.org/wiki/Iran%E2%80%93Iraq_War, website accessed December 17, 2009.
[36] "Operation Cyclone," Wikipedia.com,

Just look at how many Iraqi families have been torn apart by Bush's war: millions. We in New York face a similar threat. While we control our local weaponry, out-of-state weaponry is brought in to be used in crimes. Gunrunning is not good.

We sell arms to rogue elements, to governments and independent groups in many countries and they cause chaos there. Do we carry out terrorist actions by gunrunning in other countries? Yes! How can we achieve freedom in Iraq and elsewhere, by crooked ways and democracy at the end of a gun? Can we really expect that to work?

Big countries have the opportunities to sell war. Some do and some don't. The warmongers rely on the fact that people on both sides of the conflict can make more children, which will be a never-ending supply of soldiers (plastic GI Joes, as the warmongers consider them), and new terrorists (the "enemies'" children). Demand and supply…just a good, up-and-running, time-tested, successful business plan.

We need wars and unrest to use the weapons that we produce, so we can make more to sell and also to update our own stock with better, more high-tech weaponry. When we develop new weapons, we sell the old ones to other parties to recoup our money. The whole world knows it because they are the marketplace. We don't bring peace; we bring war. We bring despair and destruction — not democracy — to our customers. Just death. That's our curse, one that we can change in the future.

Ever since we wiped out an entire civilization of

---

http://en.wikipedia.org/wiki/Operation_Cyclone, website accessed December 17, 2009.

Native Americans, I think we've been cursed. They numbered in the millions and they were in touch with the spirits — a good energy. Jesus in tribal form, as God, Universe and Consciousness, are all one force entwined, not a rigid religion. They were peaceful. They were loved. Unlike our warmongers, they cared about life.

That untimely release of millions of spirits — the murdered Natives — had a rippling and changing effect on the Earth and America. That may be why we flounder in the sands of time, still killing and causing wars. I think religion was the main spark and the drive behind the greed to steal their land and convert them to Christianity, which is why we annihilated them. So, you can see for yourself how devastating religion really is.

We care about money, vanity and temporary power over others. It's going now — that fickle and intangible power, disappearing as Bush's recession tightens its grip on the global economy. All we are left with is regret and maybe the curse on the dying breaths of the natives past. If you believe in God and the Devil, then you will believe they cursed us and we cursed ourselves while we were murdering, raping and burning them alive in their huts, whole families, by the millions. It was even done again to at least one family we know of, in America's name, in Iraq during Bush's war.[37]

Doing good can be a way to fix that, in the universe.

Church and state were meant to be separate, so that the

---

[37] Alsup, Dave, "Iraqi Family Survivors: We Wish U.S. Soldiers Had Also Killed Us," CNN.com,
http://www.cnn.com/2009/CRIME/05/12/kentucky.iraq.murder/index.html, May 12, 2009.

church would protect you from the evils of the state, which gets drunk with power. They now sleep together, so you are not protected. Show me your friends. The Mega Church's friends are the politicians. We are doomed. Neither can lead you to God. Neither is friends with God or knows God. Why do they both carry death with them, wherever they go? Is that a gift from God? Why do they support each other in wars? They know not God. Don't follow them. Their path is death. Save yourself, so you can save your family.

You have to be strong right now. Believe in no one but yourself: no one else, nothing else, but goodness and light. Those who do good deeds are your true friends. Search for the good people in the churches by their actions. They are there. Not the churches themselves, just some of the people. There is nothing to fear from God, the church, the politicians, the terrorists or death. That is how they first tricked us. Fear: fear of God, and the Devil, then fear of terrorists, fear of death and fear of gay people, to name a few.

Are they scared? No, they think there is no judgment to fear. They're correct but that's not all. There are consequences. They will have no wealth of enlightenment and consciousness for the next journey, and that's the important part. Don't be scared. Have courage and faith…in yourself and your ability to do good and to overcome your fears. We need to save the future, the children, your children, our children…even their children. They are all in danger from man's mischief. Keep it simple. Drop religion and just do good deeds.

In the past, to obtain money, education and health care, some of us were forced by economic pressures, inflicted by warmongering politicians, to join the wars as soldiers. This still happens. We lose our children to their wars in many ways: some when the children fight in wars, some when we parents fight in wars. Warmongers need us to hate. Hate everything and everyone, so we will fight. Fight their wars for them.

They will disguise it to look like good economic opportunity and patriotism. You getting a salary and a college education while fighting the enemy, the terrorists they create over and over. They will not fight. They only fight for their intangible power. They will send you to fight and watch you die. That's what they do. They are voyeurs. They watch in amusement. They watch you fight. They watch you die. They are the rich masters. They don't fight. They smile and say you were a patriot…at your funeral, after they shamelessly sneak you back into the country in a body bag in the dead of night. What does that mean to them…your service? It means another hand to till the soil for death. It is another hand to draw blood for their coffers. It is another hand to spill innocent blood. That's who they work for… death.

Everyone wants to be idolized…as a patriot…a good citizen…another pair of hands is what you become…Patriotic hands?…Sure, why not?…Sounds nice…You…Your children…Patriots...Hands… Soldiers… fodder…reserves…troops…lambs-to-the-slaughter … dead … silence…then...to…where? Heaven?… Please?… No, you can't…The children soldiers…can't…sacred blood… innocent blood…It's on their hands too….The hate in them…It won't go away…It's with them always…the door is shut…They are unclean…They are lost…Shattered souls...In limbo...For how long?... I cry.

You don't need their lies. Their Devil is only in their Bible and in your mind. Be good and you will never see their Devil, or any version of Hell. They are the real devils — they spread war, and they will run away when they are exposed, when the light of truth brings them out of the darkness. These are dark times indeed with war and recession on our minds. These devils will go away when they can't feed on you like parasites anymore, when they see that you know the truth about them, and about religion and consciousness. So learn.

It will be all right. Keep saying that, and thinking that, and believing that. Think of helping the children, before a pied piper on the radio or TV takes them away to war. The child soldiers you send to war never really come back. They change with PTSD. A different person comes back, not the innocent, loving child you sent, but a shell of a person, an empty, tormented person who can't sleep but dreams of death all day long.

Think that it's never too late. Tell the kids that. Hug them and tell them it will be okay. Tell them their future will be better. Tell them the jobs will return. Help them to have hope and get a good education to help themselves. Tell them the war and recession will pass. They need to hear it and it does comfort them. They can believe it from you.

You can believe it too. Let your courage be your God. Don't give it up to hate and despair. Let self love be your God. Let unselfishness be your God. Let love be your God. Let life, not war be your God. Let happiness and family be your God. Let friendly peace be your God. Let freedom from religion become your guide. Freedom in your mind, and in your soul, is your destiny; slavery to a God is not.

It is worthy to note that as the recession wears on, church attendance is up, because people are still looking for hope, or a magical miracle to solve their problems instead of exercising the freedom to help themselves and their families. Look at how many run to get an ashen cross on Ash Wednesday. They too still believe in rituals, like communion, just like the native tribes they hypocritically dismiss as primitive. They are still giving away their power of self control to the church, instead of empowering themselves. They enslave themselves mentally, by blaming God for their adversities, as everything is "By the grace of God."

You can be free and still be in a prison, a religious cage of rules and rituals. You can be in a prison and your mind is free: free to feel good, to grow, to love, to think, to hope, to succeed and to become enlightened. Anyone who teaches love, and does not support wars and death, is someone who can change the world.

You don't need someone in a Mega Church to tell you what to do. If the church supports war and a philosophy of destruction instead of love, that's no church, but something dark that you should stay away from. Thou shall not kill. When you do good things, you are closer to being part of the god and consciousness that you seek. You are the strong. Your young children are the weak. The strong care for and teach the weak.

Christianization has always been enforced with violence and death. That's dark. It's not walking in the light of Jesus' teachings. The churches will come after the weak link, the children. We can lead the weak to become strong themselves. Depend on and help each other, selflessly. We will shine with the light of goodness within us; we will not be from the dark side, as Cheney says.

It is important not to lose sight of the ball — the children. Their inheritance was taken away by foreclosure and job loss. When we die, we may have nothing to pass on to them to help them have an upper hand in the race. They may be penniless, facing "tough economic times," as the bigwigs like to phrase it. We have let the politicians, their business partners and the misguided leaders of the Mega Churches have free reign, and this is the obvious result.

If the politicians worked alone, this would not have happened, but the few greedy church leaders, and radio and TV hosts who together control a large audience, sold us down the river for backroom deals of war. We can recover without them.

These pied pipers convinced the masses to follow the warmongers. They all swim in money, millions, but drown in darkness. They are still high and dry, still have million-dollar jobs while we are starving and dying. Our children are shooting up schools, joining gangs, and committing suicide or worse by going to war while they get richer. That's their way — undisciplined capitalism. What's worse than dying? That answer is killing.

Society is decaying and America is under attack from the greedy within. The politicians are still distracting you with party politics for the purpose of robbing you blind. Gays, immigration, pro-choice, and all these other foolish follies, or tools for amusement that they give us to play with like an unaware child, are meant to distract the gullible, and trustingly simple-minded among us. It's MUD: mindless, useless distractions. It is working. Look around. Lots of people are more concerned with gay marriage and immigration than treasonous acts from within the highest office in the land by the former Bush regime.

Everyone is suffering. The past Bush administration's incompetence is tightening the economic noose around our necks even now. They watched us drown in debt while they bailed out the banks. That reminds me of Katrina all over again. They watched people drowning there too. Remember, the financial system was invented by the bankers, is run by the banks, for the bankers, and almost every player is a puppet of that philosophy. The Fed Reserve is not even ours; it's theirs.

This engineered recession is a most effective way to eliminate the middle class, and deepen the divide between rich and poor. Getting rid of the immigrant population will help a great deal in achieving this plan. The radio and TV hosts want to send away the millions of illegal immigrants who work here. If they succeed, what will be the result? We are seeing it already; they will make us into that lower-class, impoverished worker, as the saying goes, by hook or by crook. They are really crooks and their hook is MUD — mindless, useless distractions.

Their trick is to remove the last block, the illegal immigrants, from the bottom of the economic pillar. That moves you down one block. Bad news, the pillar is only six financial blocks or steps on the economic ladder. The top block is companies — foreign, domestic and multinational, worth billions. Second are the super rich, who own the majority in those companies, and are worth at least a quarter billion dollars. Third is the rich or high class: the millionaires. Fourth is the middle class. Fifth is the lower class on food stamps, and sixth is the lowest step, the people who live in the shadows, the illegal immigrants.

When they remove the immigrants, who will replace them? We will, both Republicans and Democrats and all those in between. Everyone in the two rungs above them will drop down one step because the companies and the elite are engineering it so we will be broke and have to do those jobs, just to eat, just to survive. The fourth and fifth levels will be merged to become one. Another thing to remember, 12 or 15 million immigrants to be deported includes an average of five million kids in my estimate, which shows how heartless and un-Christian these people really are.

Do you want to do the immigrants' jobs? Picking lettuce and oranges? Gutting animals in the slaughterhouses? No, I know you are ambitious; you want to go higher, to the next block up. If the elite can instill hatred in you and fool you with that idea, to remove the illegal immigrants, and you fall for it, then you do your family and the country a disservice. If you deport all the illegal apple pickers, averagely 70% of them by some estimates, then you may end up paying $10 for one apple, and it will happen in all other areas.

How much money will you then save, for your kids to inherit, when you let them trick you? Nothing, I'm sure. Remember that prices will increase as a result and you will have a pay cut. You don't want that. As it is now, you already can't supply most of the things you want to provide for your kids. Why do you work? To try to move up to the next block or step. These elite people want to push you down.

Do you know how hard these immigrants work? As

hard, and even harder, than you and I do because they do not have the security of legality, so they are trodden on all the time. When you are legal, it is easier to work — any job is easier to do...mentally — and they are working with an ax of deportation over their heads and a knife of illegality at their throats, all in the name of progress for their own family.

Please don't be a part of that hatred and racism to do ill to these innocent immigrants. It will do you well to remember we are all a product of immigrants who came to America to find hope...and we killed the real citizens, the Native Americans. Don't take their hope away. I don't think that was Jesus' way. Do you? Jesus discouraged hatred in its many forms. He loved the prostitute, the tax collector (today's Democrats?), and everyone else, so why should you hate immigrants when you love Jesus?

Most of them work seven days a week, with not many days off for illness, and no pay for sick days. Also, they have no vacation, no medical and no benefits. We *can* work that hard under those conditions but I don't want to work that hard for little reward. If you do, that's fine with me. I want my kids to work as hard as they want, not to be forced to work hard just to eat. That's slavery, with poverty and desperation as the master, the driving force.

If you let the government privatize health care and give insurance companies more control, you won't be able to buy good coverage for yourself and your families. As a matter of fact, you can't do that right now, and they deny you for phony "preexisting conditions," but it will be worse when they remove the immigrants and you plummet one step farther. It's a long, hard drop to the bottom and it feels like you are falling on cement. The immigrants support those of us on the higher economic block. Don't sink to the lower level of heartlessness by letting the elite remove your lower block, the legs that support you.

There are many of us who did not vote, and that allowed the minority among us to put a group of greedy, self-serving people in power. Do people who vote against their own family's interests deserve to get what they voted for? Yes, but unfortunately we are all in that same boiling pot. So, because of the large numbers of people who didn't vote against the grain, the weaker minority amongst us were fooled and permitted George to get elected.

This is the non-voters' folly and one that must not happen in the future. The result was suicide. You are slowly suffering economically right now, aren't you? We are all suffering by you not voting, unfortunately. You let the foxes into the hen house. The foxes will destroy your eggs, which are your kids. They will suck the life out of the children, like the greedy parasites they are. The kids are already born into debt. We are the collateral damage of the rich capitalists, who convince us that government is bad and feeding your young to the war machine is good. They believe in that system of greed and undisciplined capitalism. Instead of undisciplined capitalism, a good government will enable you to earn twice as much as you do already, so paying taxes will not bother you, and the taxes will keep the country's affairs running smoothly, so let's hope the Obama administration can achieve this, with our help of course, not our resistance.

The children are already being sent into wars that are unnecessary and they die. They all, every last one of them who survive, come back mentally scared and scarred for life. They are the new replacements for the illegal immigrant population. They will do the jobs of the immigrants, as their willpower has been broken, by parents who sold them to war for issues of gay marriage and MUD, and a Bush government that didn't care. They come back broken in so many ways. Many were let down by their parents and their parent's prejudices, and inability to see the deceptions that the warmongers perpetrated: the MUD. We were all deceived by Bush.

We did not ask what we could do for the country. Some Americans voted while not looking at the better Republicans to vote for. There were Republicans who would have done a better job of protecting the country instead of Bush. But after Bush messed up, the party can't seem to run fast enough in the other direction. Even the talk show pied pipers are jumping from the sinking ship, trying to distance themselves from the folks they were once proud to put into office.

They have coined many names, to hide from and fool you — but you know it's the same bunch. A leopard can't change its spots, so they hide in the tall reeds of deception, calling themselves Independents. The results are obvious, if you let things go too far and give anyone from any party absolute power without accountability. Don't you feel the destructive results right now? Think of what your children will feel in a few years, with misdirection and unaccountability from those in power. They may become slaves to another developing country, while living in their own. Slavery all over again. Physically or mentally, it's the same thing. The trick is this, Republicans abuse the powers of government when they are elected and then say government is bad. That is not true. Government, and almost everything else, has a good purpose, if controlled and used with intelligence, not greed.

Capitalism is good if used with discipline. The so-called free markets are good if controlled like a thoroughbred race horse; you don't hold it back, but you do ride and guide it. Food is good if you don't eat too much. Exercise is good, provided you eat food at some time in your life or you'll become anorexic. Control is the most important exercise of all, in all areas of life, so don't be fooled into thinking government is bad or government is the problem, because it is not; uncontrolled and undisciplined greed is. For a country like America, government is a tool, like a knife, which is detrimental in the hands of a serial killer, but useful in the hands of a chef, and necessary in the hands of a surgeon. When a person tells you that government is the problem, they mislead you, and they do not really understand the true importance of why we invented the knife and the government.

This book is a desperate plea on behalf of a dying giant in the struggle of world economics. This giant is America, and it's dying, being torn apart violently, by wolves in sheep's clothing. Treasonous people in multinational corporate clothing with no patriotism and no laws to retard them, only greed in their souls, consuming them, sadly, to our demise, helped by the politicians their lobbyists pay.

The greedy politicians and corporations realized the Christian evangelists and other religious Christian sects were the key, the way to achieve the winning edge in the elections of 2000 and 2004, so they fooled them and the rest is history. Their relatives are dying in the Iraqi occupation, and from the poisoned air, food and water we consume. Their homes are being taken away by their own Christian capitalist brethren, who are foreclosing on them and moving jobs out of the country. That has now become the new way. Eat your own kind. Have they forgotten Jesus? This was never His way and everyone knows He would never have approved of this mischief of man against man.

There are a few bad parents who don't take care of their children. Parents who let kids hang out on the corner while Mommy or Daddy heads to the bar or wherever they go, for their own enjoyment or criminal activities. Even at home they leave the kids without a parental system. They will be at home locked in their rooms doing anything because the *parents* are watching TV. When disaster strikes they look up from the TV and all they can tell the police is who won this reality contest or that.

They know nothing about their own little survivor locked in the bedroom, crying out silently for a parent. They do not realize that they were the great American Idols that their kids once looked up to and tried to emulate. There are the rest of us good parents who have to work long hours and don't have enough family time to rear our young adults properly. The gangs are there to take advantage of these opportunities and get new recruits. There are obviously many other reasons why kids grow up badly but those are smaller in number, though equally as significant. No TV or video games during the school week is a good rule to use, until they become teens. You will spend more time together and they will get much better grades.

Regardless of your like or dislike for the government

we now have, we must rally together as a country and assist the new administration to rebuild America. We should not resist and further pull ourselves down the path of economic starvation that puts America at the mercy of other developing countries who can stomp us into the ground. The Republican agenda right now is to resist any good advances made by the present administration, under the guise of keeping them honest, and it is a quaint but childish game that can be played at another time, when the wolves of hard times and recession are not growling and scratching at the door of this once powerful country. It's simply a case of the pot calling the kettle black. America needs you, and when Uncle Sam points at you, he is not pointing at a particular political persuasion, be it Republican, Democrat or Independent, neither legal immigrant or not. He is pointing at each and everyone who stands on this parcel of land that is the gateway of freedom and democracy, and we must all stand up, and stand together and answer this call…America needs you…us…now.

YOU AND YOUR CHILDREN

Parenting is not the easiest thing in modern society but it is the most important. As we have seen, your children are bombarded from all sides by things and people who are not the best influences. Education is so expensive that some families cannot afford to educate their young ones to the standard that they know the children are capable of achieving. The kids are scared of the war and the crashing economy. The country's treasury was legally emptied.

The children are inheriting huge debts, and are not encouraged to be the best individual persons they can be, but instead to become zombie religious sheep or gang members: not very good choices. The children are afraid. If you think parenting is not that important, to teach your kids about truth and honor, then look around and see the results.

The children are not zombie sheep and they know it. So, they fight back and are misunderstood, and thought to be rebellious and anti-everything. You try to restrain them with harsh punishments, and cause them to run away and put themselves in more dire circumstances than if they had stayed at home under your helpful and watchful eye.

I know that you want to do well for them, but you must take time to think about it, about them, and find subtle ways to reinforce the fact that you love them. I would start right there, by telling them you love them, all the time. Many kids are not told that. Spend time with them and around them. When they see you are there, it makes a difference. They feel comforted, even if you don't speak much and are reading the newspaper. Just spend time together.

The bad parents wrongly say that it is the children's fault when they get in trouble or pregnant. This is after they have allowed their kids to get hurt or worse, by not caring to help if the kids take drugs, or are in gangs and out at 2 a.m., when they should be in bed early to get up to go to school the next day. Those parents are the ones who are wrong. It is our duty to guide and protect the children properly, to save them when they can still be trained.

Your children do not start out being anti-anything; they are not anti-good children. They are really good children. Corruption kills them: kills their chances for a good life. They are the victims, and they see it and don't like it. They are not getting enough support from the most important people in their lives... you. They become despondent, ashamed and angry...and rightly so. They need an injection of hope, an injection of encouragement and inspiration. They need to see *you* get involved in the fight for *their* future. A fight with a pen, not a sword — a fight with your vote against corrupt officials, not your unwavering support for injustice, and corruption of our elected leaders and support for pedophile-filled religions. That's another thing. God will not have pedophiles in His ranks, so think about that.

They are so smart, your teenagers. They think they know everything. They can show you the right thing to do. Ask them. Your way is not working in this changing world anymore, is it? You are losing the battle, getting poorer while the rich are getting richer. Ask your teens for advice. That way you will get to know *them*, see where their head is at.

You will be surprised to learn that they know and understand more than you think. Why is that? They have brilliant young minds going to waste — they have ideas, they can invent things, they are innovative and their potential is not being tapped. They are being trained to fight and kill, being sent to war to kill and die. I am sure they are scared of a draft (so am I, because my kids are teens).

We adults are bogged down with the futile ways of the past, the religions of the past, the teachings of the past, the prejudices of the past, the fears of the past, traditions and rituals of the past and the lack of understanding of the future. Some are still of the opinion that whites should only marry whites, blacks should only marry blacks, and the children of polygamists should not have abortions when impregnated by their own fathers. If you believe in these flawed things, then what kind of gamble are you taking with your children's lives and futures? Soon, it may not matter, as you may be able to do and get away with just about anything in the Third World country of America.

Many people fool themselves and look away from the truth. You may want to continue with your present gamble in life: that you can keep your child out of trouble and depression using the old ways, but the prisons and the gangs are full of millions of people who took that bet and lost. They followed the politicians, Mega Churches and Jim Jones type cult leaders and polygamists. They all lost their families, and in the cases of Jim Jones and David Koresh, they also lost their lives.

How many gang members, drug pushers, drug addicts,

criminals, prisoners and runaway kids are there in the world or even just in this country? Millions, and each represents a broken family, a bet lost, and each is a testament to the impact of the absence of the real truth of consciousness, and of the misguidance and misdirection in religious beliefs. If salvation were as simple as following religious rules, then we would all be saved, but it is not that simple; you cannot be greedy or wicked and be saved by religion. You have to cleanse your mind of negativity and then you will be living a good life.

Don't shoot the messengers; find the answer to the message. Challenge my words, find the answers and save your lost children. The many messengers are not the problem. Your lost and runaway children are; your gang member children are; your drug-pushing children are; your drug-taking children are; your incarcerated children are; your confused children are; your children, following misguided religions with pedophile priests are; your children following fanatic suicidal cults, bent on Columbine type violence and death are; their lost futures are; their lost hopes are; their lost dreams are; and sadly, their lost and mistaken parents are. I am not the one making you poor. Find the answers. Please prove me wrong or listen to what I'm saying. Save your children.

A large number of parents have lost their kids, alienated them because the children are smart enough to see that their parents are not standing up to the government, the corporations or the church. The parents appear to be weak and the children are outraged, so some become shooters and gang members. They see through the church's ploy of trying to fleece their followers and not even try to help them in their struggle against the banks and bad governments.

They see their parents as sheep, leading them to the slaughter, to become sheep as well. I didn't hear or see the church running to your rescue against the banks. Why? Because the recession has driven people to the church in droves, so they like the results of the recession. It is Christianization all over again, with the sword of recession at your backs.

In life, we are all interconnected gears or cogs, intertwined, living and working with each other in a beautiful and harmonious relationship in this engine or network of existence. We are connected on all sides: on the top, the bottom, left side, right side, front, back and many more angles and connections, like the inside of a watch or a massive computer worldwide network. Each relationship or meeting with friends and family, or even complete strangers, is another cog or connection in our life's journey, our life's engine, Earth's engine, humanity's engine. It is the ripple effect in motion.

Some people, including some close to me, ask how and why it is necessary or even rewarding to help others out of goodness and kindness, for nothing in return. My answer is, life is like a square with a human on each of the four corners, which we call corners ABCD.

Mr. A gives to Mr. B, who in turn gives to Mr. C, who in turn gives to Mr. D, who in turn gives back to Mr. A. This is life in the simplest example. Mr. A can only see what he gives to Mr. B, and see what he receives from Mr. D.

Mr. A does not see Mr. C, and does not realize that Mr. C is there and is the one who is enabling Mr. D to give back to him, Mr. A. If Mr. A does not start the giving, he will not receive in return from Mr. D, because Mr. D will get nothing from Mr. C and will have nothing to give back to Mr. A. So in a real sense, when we do good and kind things for others, we are not paying anyone back but as the saying goes, we are paying it forward, so we will be rewarded for and from it in the end. In real life the square shape is really a shape with not four sides and corners, but a larger shape with multiple sides and corners — a human network with countless sides and corners. All paying forward.

The human network is like a living computer network, similar in ways to computers sharing files and other functions. When everything works together, like the computers, we have a human network which can multitask, and when the networks work together we have the World Wide Web, the Internet.

Whatever we do affects everyone, now or later on. Sometimes we have some kind of alleged or perceived problem, and we allow the problem to interrupt the harmony of our interaction with others, by reacting to the problem in the wrong way. This human network of interaction, or the engine, our journey, is interrupted and impacted in a negative way.

The *new* problems we unnecessarily cause, as a result of reacting wrongly to the old problem, are what make changes to the smooth operation of the engine which we exist in. When we do that, life does go on around us but the outcome of everyone's lives now becomes changed, by your wrong actions or reactions. I say alleged problems because you can sometimes find a way to simplify the situation and ignore, bypass or go around the things you cannot change, and deal with what is left. The problems more often than not will tend to disappear, or decrease to a smaller problem with a lower level of difficulty, one which you are better able to solve, ignore or deal with and not cause a bigger problem.

One example of the wrong reaction is a parent putting out their promiscuous daughter or their gay or gang member child. You cause these kids to do more wrong things in their lives, and you end up either with a grandchild, a distant and loveless relationship with your gay child, or a dead or convicted gang member. It is a chain reaction that does not stop or have a happy ending for you, them or their victims. If you react to the problem differently, with more thought and understanding, and a lot of patience, you can actually save their victims and sometimes save them in the process, from the mistakes they are about to make. You may keep them at home and stop the spiral of unfortunate circumstances they may have gone on to create.

If your family is fractured, you can reunite your family, regain the respect of your children, and you can all find your way in this life's journey, if you seek the real selfless love of goodness, of enlightenment. I am not telling you what to think or believe. I am asking you to look for and find the truth, rather than blindly believing in politicians and religions.

Look around at all the lost children and broken families. You can avoid this for your family. For those whose families are already broken, you will be able to do good and turn the tables. When you do good for others with no reward, you will start to change and understand true love. Your family will see this change in you and they will want you back in their lives again. They will see that they can accept you and you can become a whole family again.

When you let your children go astray, you must understand that you are as much kicked out of their lives as they are kicked out from yours. So don't think it is a simple matter of you accepting them and allowing them back into your lives because it works the same way for them too. They have to *allow* you back into their lives and any authoritarian style approach from you will not work. You have to seek their acceptance of you, to let you back into their lives.

Even if you are of the opinion that the kids were the ones who made the mistakes, your forgiveness or acceptance of them is not going to magically bring them back to your side of the fence. It is a two-way street and they have to accept you. You have to be the one to give up more than they do, for their sakes. If you are not willing to give up the old problems, pride, and prejudices and start over, then don't even bother because you may just cause more damage than was already done. Remember, it is not important who was right or who was to blame. It is only important to now rebuild the relationship with them, so you can save them from themselves and from the problems that *you know* are coming with this bad economy: problems that they do not realize are ahead. You are their hero, but you have to act like it and build the relationship. Throw aside the politics of who is right. That is not important. Rebuild.

I am just showing you how much you, your family and our country are under attack. You can use the information in this book to turn back the tide, or you can ignore it and look for some other solution to fix your problems…maybe find a religion. I have seen that truth and love for others can be reciprocal, and help you in the long run. Right now you are doing good deeds to find favor with your God. You are doing good for a reward of heaven. You cower to and play tricks on your God with empty prayers, for Him to save you from your own self, your own deeds, your own addictions and your own misunderstandings. How gullible do you think your God is that you can trick Him? You are selling your God short. If you had a real God, who is as vengeful as the Bible says, you would not be that foolish to trick Him because His magic would make you disappear immediately. You know the truth. You know that doesn't happen to people except when the Bush government made them disappear.

The truth is that there is no vengeful God. Everyone says, "Thank God" because it is only slang, a saying to be in the crowd. Humans keep saying, "Oh God," over and over, while they are doing all sorts of things, good or bad — when they are working, when they are happy and playing, when they are angry and fighting, when they are giving birth, when they are having sex, when they are filming porn, when they are scared and even when they are killing. It is only a slang expression.

Your actions suggest you don't believe there is a god or you would have been a better person. You would not need alcohol, drugs, cigarettes, power, fame, or to steal or lie. You would not be greedy, envious, jealous or vengeful and depressed. You would not have a fractured or broken family. That is your proof. You, you are your proof. You just don't want to admit it to yourself. Look around and you will see that most people are in some addictive or negative practice. They lack the strength of truth, so they are weak and empty. Find the truth inside you, about consciousness, and find yourself, your family and your destiny.

Religion is a thing from the past, for the past. Move your family toward the future with enlightenment and consciousness. Many people are tired of religion and superstitions they suspect, think or know are bogus, but they do not have anything else to do or believe in. Listen to my message. Enlightenment is something better to believe in, and easier. Drop all the rules and rituals, and just think good and do good. Pay it forward. No churches to attend, no rules, no rituals, just simplicity and love.

YOUR GRADUATION

Man is a being with a spirit inside; we are not empty vessels. We are spiritual beings, who are trying to be religious, to follow religion instead of following light, and living in a state of spirituality. Being in touch with your spirit or soul, your inner being, is the only way to truly live and not just be a functioning shell, which is what we are convinced by others, and by religion, to be: an empty, functioning shell for religion, to be saved in the end. Religion is a psychosis of the inventors, sprinkled through the world, and allowed to permeate our cultures for thousands of years.

Our use of religion has had the unintended result of restricting the achievements of this evolving being called man. Religion has stymied our progress. It is plain to see that sweets like candy, sugar and so on can be good for some uses, but if you use too much, for too long, problems develop, and cavities and medical problems are common. Religion is having that effect on us now. It was useful and fulfilling in the primitive past. The promise of heaven's sweetness, real or not, causes us to become religious fanatics and self defeatists — convinced that we are sinners, convinced that we need religion's help and guidance to function on Earth. What about after death? Do we still need religion's help? In the afterlife, is there a customer care representative? Religion says no, but they really do not know as they are not allowed to pursue such knowledge.

Is there life after death? Yes. How? Simple answer; your body dies, your spirit or soul does not. All religions teach that there is life in heaven after death. This much they knew. I ask, life in heaven with your physical body? No. They all teach that it is a heavenly body. But then, what about the Earthly pleasures promised? What about the virgins, revenge, wings and all that? Too bad.

We are taught to be short-sighted and superstitious, just like children are taught to be bad, spoiled rotten or taught religion. Children are not born bad but why are children born good-natured? This is really who they are, who we are. We are then taught all these negative things and negative ways on Earth.

Wisdom is not allowing yourself to believe that you are a negative entity, who is ashamed, sinful and seeking something positive to follow or hold on to, like a religion of a god. To accept a god means that you have defeated yourself into thinking you need one, when in fact you are already part of the whole. You are taught to defeat yourself, so as to need and follow religion. You cannot follow religion if you are not ashamed of yourself…your perceived negative, sinful self. You have to defeat yourself to look for God. How strange is that? You incorrectly try to go back to your source when you die, being broken and defeated, kneeling in fear of your maker, your source, your light, loving God, or whatever term or name you call it. Why not return strong, whole and enlightened, feeling good about the unselfishly good works you have done to help mankind on its way to the future?

If you want to follow a religion, then go inside the religions as Jesus said; don't stand at the door. Find the teaching of peace at the core and lose the dogma. The one and only rule you will find at the core in any good religion is to practice good and peace. No good religion teaches war or violence or death to others. Everything else is misdirection and dogma. Peace encompasses everything you need to know and do regarding any religion of the world. This is the only way you can connect with your inner self: the treasure, the jewel, of religious worship. When you are enlightened you will not only do peaceful things but rather you will *be* at peace. Being and doing merges to become one. Don't only do peace but be the peace. It is as much a sense of doing as well as a sense of being.

We are taught that you, the self, are sinful when you are really not. The sinful thoughts come from your mind, which has been taught by man and religion to be that way. You were not born with any ideas, except peace. There is no path to greatness, to become good or enlightened. We were born that way already and all you have to do is live it. You only need a path to get to something that you are away from; that you are not, but you are already that, so you do not need a path to you. Just do. Just live, with good, with yourself, your inner self, your higher self, from this moment on. You do not have to qualify, through some test or ritual, to be enlightened. There is only one step…do, for you already are. You always were.

We are taught by the prejudices we encounter on this Earth. If you are a child of God, then why can't you visit His other worlds, homes and creations? Why are you a prisoner suffering in this one? Your mind's eye can make you see many things you were not aware of. You have not been taught the ways of any God, but the ways of superstitious man who tells you that you are suffering and need saving. The ways and prejudices of man are controlling and limiting your thoughts, instead of it being the other way around, which would be you in control of your own thoughts, without limits.

We have to change this world, change the ways of man, back to the purity of birth. Are vanity and greed something we are born with? No. Those are ways of man that we are taught. Truth be told, it is actually a way of descending into the abyss of selfishness, and contrary to popular belief, that is not a good thing. Why contrary? Look around at this little world called Earth. Selfishness is a way of life around here, and I remind you, on a sinking ship the more gold you grab, the less your ability to swim, so take things that will not drown you.

The ways of God and spirit are the same, and they involve much more than just empty words and worship to a force you do not know. We look at that blind worship in other native cultures and tribes, and we say they are praying to the sun, to the Earth, to the water, to nature and other things, and they are indigenous tribes who do not know better. They were primitive, the Incas, Mayas, and Egyptians and so on, but are we not doing the same? If everyone pays lip service to his religion — prays without good actions — and says their religion is the right one, then we are doing the same as the natives did, and theirs made as much sense to them as ours do to us. Some of the natives still live in peace, while most of us don't, so maybe they are more in touch than we naysayers.

You stand outside and see the fallacy in their concept of God. You should look from the outside of yours as well. You may be surprised to discover the same fallacy. We should observe what the natives saw about their way of worship and we may see ourselves. They and we worship something outward, outside of ourselves, while God, or the good force, is within us. Where did each religion come from, and what was there before we replaced it with the notion of sin and worship? Religion comes from man's mind. There has always been peace and light and truth in us from birth, not religion, and we don't have to worship it.

Does difficulty or defeat really bring greatness? Yes, it can, if you rise to it and overcome it. That is a real part of the greatness of the human being. The greatness of overcoming adversity is something that shows the true character of the human existence. Others throughout the universe, like here on Earth, live, win and lose the battle against adversity; humans have thus far shown that we can prevail and excel in our endeavors, to persevere and reach the stars, although an impending WW III is a concern. Our place among the stars awaits us and we simply need to grow, and reach the realization that we are greater than any one issue. We are greater than any one idea or religion. We are greater than any one party or country. We each are humanity's hope, humanity's fear and above all, humanity's future, as Michael Jackson said…start change with the man in the mirror.

When we discover the old tribes and see their ways of worship, we quickly come to the conclusion that they — compared to us — were primitive tribes with primitive ideas about gods and our place in the universe. We have the same ideas they did. Whatever you believe about creationism, you have to admit that we were not created alone and have not evolved alone in this universe. If you think God created us, you will have to admit that He is powerful enough and smart enough to create others on other worlds, or you will be saying that He is not powerful enough or smart enough to do so.

If you think mankind evolved, you will also have to admit that there have been before, there are now, and there will be others evolving in the millions, billions and trillions of planets out in the vast universe. Whatever you think, whatever is your informed opinion, what do you think will happen when we are discovered by other intelligent life-forms? We will become the primitive, superstitious Earth tribe, thinking of and haunted by devils, demons and gods, just as we now think about the tribes alive now and those who have existed before. We are no different from them. We live in the past. We cower before magical gods and we are holding back mankind, from faster progress and from taking our rightful place in this universe.

Some say that creationism is wrong and also evolution is wrong. Neither is complete and there is a third answer as to how we got here and why we are here. They say that you will find that third answer when you think about it, when you seek it, and you will find the answer while you are searching for it, not after the search. This will also mean that as you grow during your search, you will learn more. You will understand more and as you increase your knowledge, you will find answers. It is a simple truth, that when we go from grade two to grade three, we learn more and therefore we understand more. When we are in grade ten, we can work out problems, understand more and find more answers than the third grader can. This is simply what is happening with your understanding of religion and the universe. You may believe in a fourth grade version of

God, or a tenth grade version of God, but you can still go farther, on to the college of life and find out more about truth, and the force of light, and you can then go on to the university of life to get your degree and learn more about enlightenment. Then you can continue to get your doctorate, and learn more about consciousness and eventually you will learn all there is to know.

So, you can liken your religious understanding to a schooling process, where you keep learning about your religion and use it to move you from one level to the next. This is a natural learning process that humans go through. Do not be confused or scared. Learning and going to a higher grade can be intimidating, but one thing you do know is that this is the natural human process of schooling, and there are many students who graduated before you in this school of life. Some became teachers and are going to be waiting there to teach you, so don't be afraid. Graduate. It's natural.

Give your children the future they deserve. Don't bog them down in the beliefs of the past. The future awaits us and them. You can empower them to step up to their destinies, but first you have to empower yourself; if you do not exercise power and control of yourself, how will you know it to pass it on to your children? Graduate, empower yourself, empower your kids and feel the power of being a hero to your children and their future. Learn, about learning life's lessons.

Religion is only your first step in the journey to find the truth. You can go inside your religion and inside yourself to graduate to the next step. When you find the truth — the goodness at the core of your religion and yourself — then you share that. You project that outward to others, your fellow men, your children, who need the help, kindness and guidance — much as I am doing with you right now... Pass it on. There is no full bucket of riches, rewards or nirvana at the end of your journey, as promised by the religions: only an empty bucket. Through life you pick up the small trinkets of divinity and at the rainbow's end you will deposit those trinkets into the empty bucket. Voila, there's your savings, your reward, your nirvana. You fill the bucket with *your* treasure. It's what you pick up along the way, so it's a journey you have to travel for yourself. It is not a reward from God that you will get in the end. That's a misconceived notion.

The proverbial straw that breaks the back of the church is truth. Long ago, in the absence of truth, the church shone its own ignorant light of reason and religion. The challenge in changing this unscientific approach is that just under 50% of Americans still believe that the Earth is a Biblical 10,000 years old. They do not believe anything existed before this time...yet they believe in UFOs. If they can see UFOs, then they have to believe there is more out there than the religions are teaching, unless....God makes UFOs.

Now, we have the Hubble Telescope, black holes, matter, dark matter, the Hubble Deep Field, dark energy, The Schumacher Levy 9 Comet fragments, and retroviruses which define our humble beginnings and disprove the religious theory of Adam and Eve's creation, and a 10,000-year-old planet. Even though a Solar Storm from the sun can send as much as 10 billion tons of matter in a single burst hurtling toward the Earth, we still cannot see it with the naked eye, but we face them time and again, and can now predict when one will reach Earth, as they do cause blackouts to our power grids. Religion has no clue that these things even exist, and if they did, they would surely say God sends them each time.

Some say that modern man is trying to replace religion with science. I think we can leave the word "science" on the side, and just deal with facts and knowledge. Leave personal beliefs and fears on the side and think of proof, and what it reveals to us. When you can't see something, or can't understand scientific ideas and theories, that is not proof that they are not real and do not exist. Because the Bible does not describe space or the galaxies does not mean they do not exist. Science is helping us discover and realize the true history of human evolution on Earth, and helping us to write a new chapter about our future in this universe.

During biblical times, the stars were just lights in the sky, created by and supporting the notion of the existence of God. Now that we can see them in detail, they represent something totally new, different and powerful. They are the new faces of truth and reality. Science and technology have pulled back the dark, secretive and ignorant drapes of religion and delusion, and revealed a new light: one of planets, suns, black holes and evolving life that may not be exactly what the church wants you to see and know.

They see the light of this new era, and are threatened by it shining into the dark corners of ignorance, where religion was conceived and once lived. Celestial bodies are revealed to not be religious in nature or origin anymore, but something else, physical not magical, which they have yet to concede: the truth that cannot be concealed or ignored, the truth that proves that religion may be more fiction than fact.

The Vatican and the churches are also coming to realize that the tide of ignorance and delusion is changing, and they are admitting as much. They have conceded to there being a whole undiscovered universe out there. Finally, a first step. They admit that there could be life and activity outside of the Earth. Wow, a second step. Back in the days of the Bible, primitive man would see flaming asteroids and comets, and think he saw angels and gods flying by on flaming chariots.

We now know the truth about these celestial bodies and we can even predict what they will do. The Schumacher Levy 9 comet fragments are a testament to our science. This same science predicted that these comet fragments were to crash into Jupiter, and we then photographed the event, showing that the truth is no more frightening or mysterious. Long ago it was mysterious, but now it is just predictable and factual. Science has been moving mankind forward for centuries, and we all are thankful to our inventors for making their discoveries, especially medicine which has saved billions of lives. I know everyone likes the point to where science has gotten us today: cell phones, TV, airplanes and air conditioning, and I do not see anyone pounding down the Amish's doors to join up. Even the priests love their new shiny cars and computers, so let's continue moving forward with science and not backward with superstition and religion.

Religion was good back then, in the past, in the absence of logic and civility. The population was always forced to kneel, live in slavery and be subservient to some ruler of the time. They needed a larger or better ruler to follow, so they would not have to totally relinquish their power, their independence and sanity, to the brutal rulers.

They invented and used these ideas, collectively called religion, to rebel against the rulers and they understood that if the ruler's enemy was an entity, a god in thin air that they could not touch, and some belief in the slaves' minds, where the rulers' soldiers could not locate and kill or destroy it, then the rulers could not fight it, and it, the religious system would still be there to help, when the next ruler came around. This is how they survived.

Now the religious ideas of the past are just a hindrance to our progress. Over the years, some of the different leaders have tried to update the religious system, to make it more connected to modern man, and even politicizing it to some degree, as we see in American politics. But without a brutal ruler, slavery, chariots and the lack of knowledge, the religious systems have outlived their usefulness, except of course, as a history lesson.

If the religious system can be used to teach peace, civility and goodness, without the existence of a vengeful, demanding, photocopied God, then maybe it can still be of some use. Why photocopied? Because every religious system around the world has a god in thin air, some more vengeful than others, all copied from the original invention. We can no longer hold our children's progress at bay, to the misconceptions of the past, to appease the followers of ambitious, inventive men and primitive religious systems. Your children's well-being comes first. So, on your life's journey, buckle up. It's a fast and bumpy ride.

Most people wonder why our loved ones die early, before they have a chance to really reach the prime of their lives. Briefly, I can offer a simplified explanation that only applies to some. When we come to Earth, we come here of our own planning and free will. We place ourselves where we think we will accomplish the tasks we hope to experience. We are born in a specific country to a specific family for this very purpose of achieving our desired goals in life. At this stage, we do not know if we will successfully achieve our predetermined tasks, so we go on adventurously hopeful.

After we are born, we make choices as we grow, which take us in many different directions. Some may be perceived as bad but we have no way of knowing if these paths are useful to achieve our tasks. Some of us are learning our true paths while reading books like this one in prison. Some of us find religion in prison and take a different path. If we continue filling ourselves along the way with the particular range of gifts, of the kinds of knowledge and experiences that we came to Earth for, then we continue on our path. If we do not get what we came here for, then we remain empty, regardless of who we are, where we are, how old we are, who we've helped or how much success and money we have accumulated. At some time, we reach the point of no return and we depart this life as an empty vessel, devoid of the required gifts. At that point it does not matter how you depart…or die, as it is only a transportation point in your spiritual journey. To be blunt, if you take the bus, the train, the heart attack, the burning building, the bullet or the knife, you still depart, and the funerals and fanfare are only for the benefit of the living.

You may ask, why depart? Because you can still learn what you need to, later in life. That answer is simple. While on Earth, you are also here to work in tandem with others whom you are here to assist while they assist you in your tasks. When these people move on, or when you move on to a different path, there is no more need for you to stay on Earth, as you are both not in a position to assist each other. There is simply no more need for you to stay as they are not within your reach; staying here will be just wasting your precious and invaluable time, and you can be more useful to yourself and others elsewhere. So you go back to headquarters, to plan your next adventure. Of course if you continue along your path even without their assistance, then you will stay for as long as you need. Remember the spirit is the real you, and it is the more important thing that you need to enrich, not your limited physical existence alone, or your wallets. Your physical life here is just a pathway of the soul. Ponder this, for a moment.

YOUR POWER OVER ADDICTION

People say, "I need a drink." They say, "I need a smoke." They say, "I need a hit." Mind control is everything. They say they *need* when truly it started out being I *want* — not I need — a smoke or drink. Years upon years of mischaracterization caused them to be repeating, "I need, I need, I need," until they convinced themselves that they really needed that drink or smoke instead of just wanting it. They persuaded themselves that they were addicted and in need of this thing, be it smoke, drink or whatever they were taking at the time. They slowly, over a period of years, gave up their power of control and chose to need instead of want. It was not a physical need at the start but a mental one, which turned physical as the years went on.

It's all in your mind. Your mind controls your body and you have the power of decision in your mind. You live inside your body…temporarily. You are not your body but rather a being, inhabiting your body —your shell — and you have control over it, not the other way around. When you smoke or drink you do it for your enjoyment, and you should…until you decide that you will do something else instead, or even stop and do nothing at all. You decide to not be addicted to anything. You simply have to see the issue from the correct angle, which is that you *want* to do it for one reason or another, not *need* to do it. Your body says want, not your inner self. See how easy it is to let go of one substance and replace it with another, without withdrawal symptoms. This means you can replace something harmful with something that is not. That is because you are satisfying your mind, like a child with a new toy.

Go ahead and enjoy doing what you are doing, all the while constantly seeing and understanding that this is an action that you are *willingly* doing right now — and each time — because you *want* to do it. You are enjoying the action, while you are taking control of yourself by your own willing decision to do it. Each time you decide to smoke or drink, you will yourself to do it; you are taking and exercising *control*. Before each drag you take, on whatever you are smoking, say in your mind, or at least recognize, "I decide" or "I want to take a drag," because you already did subconsciously anyway, which then enabled you to carry out the action. Before each sip or chug you take of whatever you are drinking, consciously decide to take that sip or gulp. Why? What you are doing is training yourself. Don't worry. If and when you decide to slow down...you will...later...much later. What if you eventually slowed down so much, it looks as if you have stopped?

Repetition this way, of *deciding* each time to smoke, drink or whatever else you are doing, is a way of retraining yourself to make conscious decisions. You are controlling your body to do the actions you want. You are regaining control of yourself mentally, by having your inner self control your outer body. Your body is a dumb animal — a mindless animal — and it will do anything you tell it to. Mine works out in the gym all the time. You are and you have the mind that controls the animal. The animal will not bite you back, as you have conscious control and most people don't bite themselves. When you are comfortable being a leader and being in control of your body, maybe months or years from now, you will decide to stop when you are good and ready. Remember, you may slow down so much that it looks as if you have stopped, or it doesn't continue to be a problem anymore.

By deciding to do whatever you do, you are distancing yourself from your body. You are separating management from the employee. You are going back inside your mind, taking the helm, the reigns and exercising control of your animal again. You are not your body — your animal. It was all a mind-control game that you did not understand, so you thought you were your body when in reality you were not. You were incorrectly taught this. Money pleased you, food pleased you, and revenge pleased you, when they were all illusions and not real satisfaction. Proof: a person can be molested, abused, beaten, tortured or raped and not be destroyed. That is because people can learn that they are not their body, and they cope with their situation in that way. When it is over, and afterwards, over time, they can help themselves to heal, and move forward, as their mind is in control of the body. Time is obviously important as each individual takes a longer time to separate himself from his body, and to regain and retain control of his mind.

Same with addiction. Take all the time you need to enjoy your smoke or drink. That is the thing — enjoyment — that made you start using it, and that made you feel satisfied after. Over time, self control will make you feel and realize that you have had enough, and you will begin to feel happy and relieved now to slow down, eventually to move on, and you will stop smoking or drinking. You realize over time that you do not need it; you just wanted it and decided to take it. It was a conscious decision you made to take it and now to give it up, after slowing down gradually.

I saw a movie a long time ago where the family was beaten by a gang of thieves. The father was held down and made to watch his daughter being raped. He told his daughter to take herself to a happy place and she did. This control of the mind that she exercised enabled her to survive the ordeal and move on with life afterwards. Yes, it was a movie but when you find out how often a woman is raped, you will be surprised and disgusted. I believe it's every 18 seconds. Some of these women exercise this mind control while they are being raped, even our female soldiers in Iraq. It saves them in the end and they carry on. The numbers are shocking.

We all do this, in our daily lives — separate our minds from our bodily shell. Handicapped persons do it all day long, bypassing their limitations to get something done. This shows you that you are independent of your body, which is only a machine, a vessel for you to use while you are here on Earth. There will be other vessels for you when you leave this Earth. There is no Devil with a trident waiting to poke you when you die. That is laughable and really psychotic…honestly, so don't believe these fairy tales. These stories are just distractions to the real you and to your real life.

The problem is that we live for our bodies, not our minds, when it should be the other way around. We think we are controlled by our bodies instead of recognizing that we control our bodies. That's the reason that religion is mistaken. We, as our bodies, are thinking that we want to ascend to become spiritual bodies in heaven, not realizing we are already spiritual bodies right here, right now. We do not need religion to become a spirit like God; we already are. We do not need religion to save us. Save us from what? We are spiritual energy, and energy is neither created nor destroyed. It's all in your mind control. How do you think you can train yourself to smoke that toxic thing or drink that toxic substance in the first place? (Both excessively, in my case). You are practicing mind control. So just practice good control and then conscious abstinence...over time, lots of time, patiently, and in no hurry.

It is said that time heals wounds. Well, it doesn't. Time simply puts some distance between you and the event, and this is good because you now have some space to maneuver — to relax, to not feel so much stress or closeness to it. Some space to breathe. You still need to remember the bitter taste of losing something or someone, and the hurt feelings of the event. This space helps you to remember without becoming overwhelmed and powerless to help yourself. The worst thing that can happen to you in any circumstance is to be powerless. If you think clearly, patiently, you can let the bad event take place if you cannot stop it, but with the thought that you are not powerless, and that you will pick up the pieces and move on after the bad event. This thought of still having power during the event will help you get through the trauma much better, stronger and easier. You will not be as terrorized by the situation, as you have confidence that you have the power to overcome it and move on after.

Empowerment is a big part of life. When you have the power to think for yourself, you can decide to stop doing any bad thing to yourself and others. You can stop smoking, drinking, grieving, being greedy, needing the church, needing false salvation, thinking you are a bad person or a sinner, being weak in the face of danger or despair, and so many other things that self empowerment, and the confidence it brings, can help you do.

When you accept the church's fairy tales — of your sins, failure and defeat — and you then follow the churches' rules for religion, you empower the church. You give up your power to think for yourself and control yourself. You undermine yourself, you sabotage yourself, and you weaken yourself. You and your kids are already spiritual beings and the church can't change that. You all are not failing any God, as you are already part of that great system some call God.

When we think we are the body, we behave with animal instincts and behavior. We will train ourselves to act and become animals in varying degrees. We will train ourselves to eat raw flesh, smoke poisonous things, drink poisonous things and do bad things, while all the time being okay with them, convincing ourselves that we like them, that it is normal. Look at yourself. My guess is that you are already there. You like sushi and alcohol, don't you? It took years to get there doing whatever things you do, and it may take some time to empower yourselves and change yourselves...that's okay. As long as you can start the process, in your mind, it will become easier as you go along. Each hurdle you conquer will spur you on to confidently face the next. You will clean yourself up as you go along because it's a process and not a pill from a bottle. Almost everyone is fractured in some way and looking for an instant remedy, like a magic pill, but this is *you* we are fixing, not a car or a toaster, so time will be our medicine: one of our tools to get some breathing room. That is something we have plenty of, as it only takes an instant to decide to turn over a new, healthy leaf in your life...in your mind, to decide to start the process of recovery. After you do this, life continues...anew. It's like when people think they are saved and born again, they willingly start to change their lives without the help of any gods.

Remember, you don't have to please any church or any god; you just have to please yourself that you are taking back your power of control over yourself and you will be on your way — thinking for yourself and doing what you should be doing. What is it that you should be doing? That answer, and each answer, is a succession of bridges you will cross when you meet them one by one. It may be taking one less drink per day or one less cigarette, but it's patient progress. Each step will be easier because you will meet each successive one with more thought and confidence, gained from the previous achievement. Go ahead bravely, my friends. I will meet you on the way.

As you go along, you will realize that it is not important how far you reach along the path but what you do while on it. Forget about dying and salvation, or pleasing the churches or gods, as these things are not of concern for intelligent and powerful spiritual beings, as you are. These things are just illusions that change all the time. The only constant is you...so have no fear about these things. They were just meant to scare you and to rule you with that fear, but you are smarter than that. Abraham and Moses may have been ignorant, delusional and scared, but you and your family are not, so embrace your power and not the fear religion peddles.

The great civilizations of the world conclude that the world will change in the year 2012. Fanatics think it will just end, as they have predicted numerous times in history. The simple truth is that we do not have to be pessimistic and accept fanatical "end of the world" delirium. We can rise up and change the world to one that will stand the test of time and space.

Luke 17:20-21 (King James Version)

[20]And when he was demanded of the Pharisees, when the kingdom of God should come, he answered them and said, The kingdom of God cometh not with observation:

[21]Neither shall they say, Lo here! or, lo there! for, behold, the kingdom of God is within you.

Obviously, there is still much to discuss, but that is left for another day... Be well.
Teeluck

RECOMMENDED READING

God Is Not Great: How Religion Poisons Everything by Christopher Hitchens

The Awakening: The Life and Work of Eve Kerwin, White Buffalo Woman by Eve Kerwin

The Celestine Prophecy by James Redfield

The Shock Doctrine by Naomi Klein

The Third Jesus by Deepak Chopra

The Tyranny of Oil by Antonia Juhasz

Threshold: The Crisis of Western Culture by Thom Hartmann

Physics of the Impossible by Michio Kaku

AND *The Gospel of Thomas,* as well as anything written by Lobsang Rampa

REFERENCES

"A Lousy Way to Treat a Veteran," NYDailyNews.com, [http://www.nydailynews.com/opinions/2007/10/11/20 07-10-11_a_lousy_way_to_treat_a_veteran.html], October 11, 2007.

Alsup, Dave, "Iraqi Family Survivors: We Wish U.S. Soldiers Had Also Killed Us," CNN.com, [http://www.cnn.com/2009/CRIME/05/12/kentucky.iraq.murder/index.html], May 12, 2009.

"Appeals Court Rules Canadian Tortured after Rendition Cannot Sue United States," Democratic Underground.com, [http://www.democraticunderground.com/discuss/duboard.php?az=view_all&address=102x4129500], website accessed December 19, 2009.

"Aspartame / NutraSweet - Report - WTVJ (NBC) - Part 1 of 2," YouTube.com, [http://www.youtube.com/watch?v=zf5Rfbjcx5I&NR=1], website accessed December 18, 2009.

"Aspartame - Part 1 of 2 -- 60 Minutes Segment -- 12/29/1996," YouTube.com, [http://www.youtube.com/watch?v=dDqUpuZu8mY], website accessed December 18, 2009.

"Bayer Exposed (HIV Contaminated Vaccine),"
YouTube.com,
[http://www.youtube.com/watch?v=wg-52mHIjhs],
website accessed November 17, 2009.

Benedict, Helen, "The Private War of Women Soldiers," Salon.com,
[http://www.salon.com/news/feature/2007/03/07/wome n_in_military/], March 7, 2007.

Blair, Mike, "China Starts Oil Drilling off Florida," AmericanFreePress.net,
[http://www.americanfreepress.net/html/china_starts_o il_drilling.html], May 29, 2006.

Boudreau, Abbie and Bronstein, Scott, "Green Beret Electrocuted in Shower on Iraq Base," CNN.com,
[http://www.cnn.com/2008/US/05/28/soldier.electrocut ions/index.html], May 28, 2008.

"Concern Mounts over Rising Troop Suicides," CNN.com,
[http://edition.cnn.com/2008/US/02/01/military.suicide s/index.html], February 3, 2008.

Corsi, Jerome R., "Billions of Gallons of Oil in North Dakota, Montana," WorldNetDaily.com,
[http://www.wnd.com/index.php?pageId=61488], April 13, 2008.

Faal, Sorcha of "whatdoesitmean.com", Indymedia.com, "Bush Makes Massive Land Purchase in Paraguay Ahead of Expected War Crimes Charges," [http://arizona.indymedia.org/news/2006/10/51221.php], October 19, 2006.

Fahrenthold, David A, "Male Bass in Potomac Producing Eggs," WashingtonPost.com, [http://www.washingtonpost.com/wp-dyn/articles/A33850-2004Oct14.html], October 15, 2004.

"Feds Fight Broad Testing for Mad Cow Disease: False Positives Could Harm Meat Industry, USDA Argues," *Associated Press*, [http://www.msnbc.msn.com/id/18924801/], May 29, 2007.

"Fox NutraSweet Equal Aspartame," YouTube.com, [http://www.youtube.com/watch?v=ELgW4KBY-o4], website accessed December 18, 2009.

Goldstein, Avram, "Post-War Suicides May Exceed Combat Deaths, U.S. Says (Update1)," Bloomberg.com, [http://www.bloomberg.com/apps/news?sid=a2_71Klo2vig&pid=20601124], website accessed December 15, 2009.

Gordon-Conwell Theological Seminary, "Status of Global Mission 2009," [http://ockenga.gordonconwell.edu/], website accessed November 17, 2009.

"Great Pacific Garbage Patch," Wikipedia.com, [http://en.wikipedia.org/wiki/Great_Pacific_Garbage_Patch], website accessed December 17, 2009.

"Homeowner Equity Below 50% for First Time since 1945," CNBC.com, [http://www.cnbc.com/id/23503784], March 6, 2008.

"Iran-Contra Affair," Wikipedia.com, [http://en.wikipedia.org/wiki/Iran%E2%80%93Contra_affair], website accessed December 17, 2009.

"Iran-Iraq War," Wikipedia.com, [http://en.wikipedia.org/wiki/Iran%E2%80%93Iraq_War], website accessed December 17, 2009.

Iraq Casualty Coalition, "Operation Iraqi Freedom," [http://www.icasualties.org], website accessed November 17, 2009.

Keteyian, Armen, "Suicide Epidemic among Veterans," CBSNews.com, [http://www.cbsnews.com/stories/2007/11/13/cbsnews_investigates/main3496471.shtml?tag=contentMain;contentBody], website accessed December 17, 2009.

Live Science Staff, "Big Oil Deposit Found beneath Gulf of Mexico," Live Science.com, [http://www.livescience.com/technology/etc/090902-

big-oil-deposit-found-beneath-gulf-mexico.html], posted September 02, 2009.

"Medical Bills Prompt More than 60 Percent of U.S. Bankruptcies," CNN.com/health, [http://www.cnn.com/2009/HEALTH/06/05/bankruptcy.medical.bills/], website accessed December 16, 2009.

"Military Suicide Rate," ChicagoTribune.com, [http://www.chicagotribune.com/news/nationworld/chi-military-suicide-rate-080529-ht,0,6105432.story], website accessed December 17, 2009.

Moss, Michael, "E. Coli Path Shows Flaws in Beef Inspection," NYTimes.com, [http://www.nytimes.com/2009/10/04/health/04meat.html?_r=1], October 3, 2009.

The NutraSweet Company, [http://www.nutrasweet.com/], website accessed December 18, 2009. NWV Staff Writer, "Donald Rumsfeld and Aspartame," NewsWithViews.com, [http://www.newswithviews.com/NWVexclusive/exclusive15.htm], May 9, 2004.

"Operation Cyclone," Wikipedia.com, [http://en.wikipedia.org/wiki/Operation_Cyclone], website accessed December 17, 2009.

"Ozone Depletion," Wikipedia.com, [http://en.wikipedia.org/wiki/Ozone_hole], website accessed December 17, 2009.

Priest, Dana and Hull, Anne, "Soldiers Face Neglect, Frustration at Army's Top Medical Facility," Washington Post.com, [http://www.washingtonpost.com/wp-dyn/content/article/2007/02/17/AR2007021701172.html], February 18th, 2007.

"PTSD Combat: Winning the War within," PTSD Combat Blog, [http://ptsdcombat.blogspot.com/2006/04/ptsd-statistics-wwii-to-iraq.html], website accessed November 17, 2009.

"Sexual Assault in Military 'Jawdropping,' Lawmaker Says," CNN.com, [http://www.cnn.com/2008/US/07/31/military.sexabuse/index.html], July 31, 2008.

Shenn, Jody, "'Underwater' Mortgages to Hit 48%, Deutsche Bank Says (Update1)", Bloomberg.com, [http://www.bloomberg.com/apps/news?pid=20603037&sid=adBYDzUMt68k], website accessed November 17, 2009.

Singh, Jyotsna, "Dollars No Good for the Taj Mahal," BBC.com (BBC News, Delhi), [http://news.bbc.co.uk/2/hi/7098370.stm.], November 16, 2007.

ABOUT THE AUTHOR

Throughout history, messengers encouraged mankind to reflect inward, to see the person we each have become, and the person we each need to become. These messengers showed a path that can have a great impact on those who are lost to the way of enlightenment through spiritual consciousness; history has had many of these messengers.

Teeluck Sooknarine is such a person. Born into a family that had many differing religious views, he was able to interact and learn about the inner sanctuary of each religion and come away with a central view of what each wanted to teach to the worshipper. Having experienced these religious and other ways of life since his teenage years, and having that knowledge mature through his life's journey, he is now in a position of clarity and understanding, and is ready to impart this knowledge through the misunderstood eyes of the loved Nazarene, Jesus.

Index

9/11, 268, 398, 404, 422–40
administration, 21–26
ambition, 27–29
Amish, 289, 445, 458, 494
Bear Stearns, 346, 349
beginning, 129–32
Bin Laden, Osama, 33, 53, 54, 62, 85, 352, 353, 459
BPA (Bisphenol A), 80
broken examples, 30–32
Bush, George Sr., 35
Bush, George W., 21, 25, 50, 93, 261, 387, 419, 449
Christianity, 86, 122, 129, 135, 156, 184, 194, 208–20, 230, 302, 326, 444, 461
Christianization, 144–96
Columbine, 38–49, 478
conspiracy theories, 23, 54
Constitution, 21, 35–37, 348, 353
credit card companies, 31, 36, 48, 318, 348, 371, 449
cult, 130, 131, 275
   Jim Jones, 153, 165, 279
   religious, 291
Dead Sea scrolls, 311
deception, 50–56
developing countries, 64, 336, 365, 374, 429, 474
diabetes, 59, 94, 95, 98
DNA, 78, 226, 275
dogma, 131, 153, 154, 155, 187–94, 199, 204, 230, 229–37, 247, 263, 265, 266, 278, 313, 315
drug companies, 57, 59, 61, 57–61, 97, 184, 254, 371
E. Coli bacteria, 92
economics, 62–65
economy
   american economy, 23, 62
   economic demise, 34
   economic recovery, 22
   Third World economy, 26
education, 31, 66–72, 283
   and terrorism, 430
   cost, 475
   heightened level of, 121
   scientific, 286
enlightenment, 178, 209, 215, 235, 242, 247, 315, 484
evolution, 73–79, 80, 452, 490
   animals, 78
   or extinction, 80–84
   religion, 166, 493
executive bonuses, 23
FDA, 99, 100, 163
fear, 85–87
financial hostage, 88–91
food, 92–102
foreign
   investments, 23, 321, 337, 364
   policy, 330, 335, 365, 381, 396, 401, 427, 428, 432, 435, 436, 459
Foreign Intelligence Surveillance Act, 454
Foreign Policy Initiative, 454

foreign problems, 364–67
gangs, 103–8, 121, 124, 180, 197, 296, 298, 351
   children, 466, 473, 476, 478, 481
   Tookie Williams, 224
global warming, 33, 438
God, 113–28, 177, 178, 195, 202, 215
   consciousness and awareness, 221–76
   protect your family, don't wait for God, 197–207
   religious illusion, 277–300
   who or what is, 133–43
government megalomaniacs, 317–24
government policies, 21
Great Depression, 448
greed, 109, 110, 109–10
hate, 325–28
health care, 317, 339, 462
   benefits, 65
   industry, 361
   privatize, 362, 453, 469
Hitler, 127, 224, 295, 325, 326
HMO, 361
homosexuality, 73, 74, 76, 84, 86, 179, 185, 239, 339, 395, 481
   gay rights, 205
hurricane Katrina, 33, 50, 202
Hussein, Saddam, 25, 52, 54, 377, 389, 435, 437, 459
immigration, 329–35
   immigrant economics, 336–40
Iran, 25, 148, 377, 426, 431, 439, 456, 459, 514

Iraq, 25, 29
   Iraq Casualty Coalition, 28, 51, 52, 514
   Iraq war, 37
   Iraqi occupation, 24, 472
Jesus, 301–16
Kennedy, Bobby, 60
King James, 166, 209, 214, 217
lead poisoning, 158
Mad Cow disease, 92
Madoff, Bernie, 103
Magna Carta, 36
mass media, 341–45
McVeigh, Timothy, 34, 269, 406
Mega Church, 462
Mega Churches, 141, 153
money tree, 384–85
multinational companies, 24
Nazi invasions, 65
Obama, Barack, 411
Papantonio, Mike, 60
Patriot Act, 35, 36
Pearl Harbor, 425, 431, 433, 434, 435
personal peace of mind, 368–72
Ponzi scheme, 26, 30, 88
predatory lenders, 3, 31, 318, 349, 346–57
prison system, 106
privatization, 318, 361–63
profiteering, 411
PTSD (post traumatic stress disorder), 51, 398, 405, 408, 436, 457, 464
Reagan, Ronald, 99, 101
recession, 26, 30, 55

ripple effect, 373–83
Roman Catholic Church, 147
Roman Catholics, 203
Rumsfeld, Donald, 98, 100
salvation, 136
Stockholm Syndrome, 36, 227
sub-prime mortgage, 35
suicide, 31, 188, 327, 368, 392, 400, 405, 406, 407, 436, 466, 470, 515
tax break, 32, 35
terrorists, 33–34
The Roman Empire, 157, 161
torture, 386–88

Troubled Asset Relief Program (TARP), 23, 63
Vietnam War, 53
Virginia Tech, 38
Wall Street, 89
war, 389–409
   profiteering, 410–14
water, 415–21
women, 441–43
you and them, 444–74
you and your children, 474–84
your graduation, 485–97
your power over addiction, 498–505

www.ingramcontent.com/pod-product-compliance
Lightning Source LLC
Chambersburg PA
CBHW071055230426
43666CB00009B/1722